To my son, Joseph Emmanuel

Acknowledgments

My procrastination in writing a substantially revised and expanded new edition of this book could not resist the initiative of Ruth Yaron of the Israel National Defense College, who deprived me of my last excuse by providing a scanned text of the original version. Marco Moretti, then a graduate student in the School of Foreign Service of Georgetown University, Washington, D.C., was my invaluable assistant. I am grateful to the many reviewers of the first edition and its foreign-language versions for their critical advice, even more than for their generous praise, although regretfully I cannot name them all. But I can recall Walter Z. Laqueur, who offered his steady wisdom and encyclopedic knowledge in a continuing dialogue that has spanned the years and both editions; David M. Abshire, who received me into his Center for Strategic and International Studies when I first arrived in Washington; Max King Morris, Amos A. Jordan, the late Christa D. K. Dantzler, A. Lawrence Chickering, W. Seth Carus, and Stephen P. Glick, all of whom helped in substantial ways in the writing of the first edition, as did Robert A. Mosbacher, Jr., of Houston, Texas, who alleviated a most unusual obstacle that official bodies should have confronted. Michael A. Aronson of Harvard University Press in a collaboration that started in 1975 nurtured both editions. With this book I join the authors who have had the benefit of Elizabeth Hurwit's remarkable editorial talent and Donna Bouvier's impeccable standards as senior production editor.

Contents

Preface

Perhaps it is because I was born in the disputed borderland of Transylvania, during the greatest and most sinister of wars, that strategy has always been my occupation, and also my passion. That is a strong word for a subject both ill-defined and suspect as an encouragement to strife. But to define the inner meaning of strategy is the very purpose of this book, and any excuses become unnecessary once it is recognized that the logic of strategy pervades the upkeep of peace as much as the making of war.

No strategies are here suggested for the United States or any other country. My purpose, rather, is to uncover the universal logic that conditions all forms of war as well as the adversarial dealings of nations even in peace. Whatever humans can do, however absurd or self-destructive, magnificent or sordid, has been done in both war and statecraft, and no logic at all can be detected in the deeds themselves. But the logic of strategy is manifest in the outcome of what is done or not done, and it is by examining those often unintended consequences that the nature and workings of the logic can best be understood.

By now the critical reader will have had reason to pause before the inordinate ambition of this quest. Knowing that the events of war and peace are too irregular to be explained by science in its only proper meaning, namely by theories that can actually predict, one might suspect that only platitudes lie ahead or, worse, the pointless elaborations of pseudo-science. I can only plead that the verdict be deferred till the reading is done—but a word of explanation may be in order.

What became a long journey to a compelling destination began with no such ambitious purpose. In reading the literature of military history, in studying more particularly the Roman and Byzantine empires, in my professional work both as a deskbound military analyst and also in the field in varied conflict settings, I like others before me concluded that each experience of war is unique, the product of an unrepeatable convergence of political aims, transient emotions, technical limits, tactical moves, operational schemes, and geographical factors. And yet, over the years, tantalizing continuities began to emerge, forming patterns more and more definite, some clarified by the literature of strategy-as-study, chiefly the *On War* of Carl von Clausewitz, while others had seemingly remained undetected. What made the investigation compelling was that these patterns did not conform to commonsense expectations: they were not ordered by any familiar, straightforwardly causal logic.

As a vision of strategy emerged out of the shadows of words read, problems investigated, and warlike events actually experienced, I found that its content was not the prosaic stuff of platitudes, but instead paradox, irony, and contradiction. Moreover, the logic of strategy seemed to unfold in two dimensions: the "horizontal" contentions of adversaries who seek to oppose, deflect, and reverse each other's moves—and that is what makes strategy paradoxical; and the "vertical" interplay of the different levels of conflict, technical, tactical, operational, and higher—among which there is no natural harmony.

What follows, then, is the route map of an exploration. The quest begins in a series of encounters with the dynamic forces of the horizontal dimension; it continues as an ascent, level by level, through the vertical dimension of strategy; and it ends when the confluence of both dimensions is reached, at the level of grand strategy, the level of final results.

Once the original edition was consigned to the printers, I did not cease to study strategy and war, nor did I stop working professionally, in practical ways in the field and as an adviser. Whether from theory or practice, the original idea continued to evolve, yielding the results incorporated in this new edition. They include the novelty of "postheroic" war—the striving to fight without casualties, and its unexpected implications—an analysis of the consequences of interrupting wars by outside intervention, and, in a radically different vein, a reevaluation of the potential and limitations of air bombardment since the advent of routine precision. Thus, although the structure of the book is unchanged, large parts of the text are entirely new, while the rest has been extensively revised and updated. The end of the Cold War has not changed the logic of strategy, but it does call for a somewhat different array of examples.

PART I

THE LOGIC OF STRATEGY

Si vis pacem, para bellum. If you want peace, prepare war, goes the Roman proverb, still much quoted by speakers preaching the virtues of strong armament. We are told that readiness to fight dissuades attacks that weakness could invite, thus keeping the peace. It is just as true that readiness to fight can ensure peace in quite another way, by persuading the weak to yield to the strong without a fight. Worn down by overuse, the Roman admonition has lost the power to arouse our thoughts, but it is precisely its banality that is revealing: the phrase is of course paradoxical in presenting a blatant contradiction as if it were a straightforwardly logical proposition—and that is scarcely what we would expect in a mere banality.

Why is the contradictory argument accepted so unresistingly, indeed dismissed as obvious? To be sure, there are some who disagree, and the entire academic venture of "peace studies" is dedicated to the proposition that peace should be studied as a phenomenon in itself and actively worked for in real life: *si vis pacem, para pacem,* its advocates might say. But even those who reject the paradoxical advice do not denounce it as a self-evidently foolish contradiction that common sense should sweep away. On the contrary, they see it as a piece of wrongheaded *conventional* wisdom, to which they oppose ideas they themselves would describe as novel and unconventional.

And so the question remains: why is the blatant contradiction so easily accepted? Consider the absurdity of equivalent advice in any sphere of life but the strategic: if you want A, strive for B, its opposite, as in "if you want to lose weight, eat more" or "if you want to become rich, earn less"—surely we would reject

1

all such. It is only in the realm of strategy, which encompasses *the conduct and consequences of human relations in the context of actual or possible armed conflict,** that we have learned to accept paradoxical propositions as valid. The most obvious example is the entire notion of nuclear "deterrence," so thoroughly absorbed during the Cold War years that to many it seems prosaic. To defend, we must stand ready to attack at all times. To derive their benefit, we must never use the nuclear weapons acquired and maintained at great cost. To be ready to attack—in retaliation—is evidence of peaceful intent, but to prepare antinuclear defenses is aggressive, or at least "provocative"—such are the conventional views on the subject. Controversy over the safety of nuclear deterrence was periodically rekindled during the Cold War, and there was certainly much debate on every detailed aspect of nuclear-weapons policy. But the obvious paradoxes that form the very substance of nuclear deterrence were deemed unremarkable.

The large claim I advance here is that strategy does not merely entail this or that paradoxical proposition, blatantly contradictory and yet thought valid, but rather that *the entire realm of strategy is pervaded by a paradoxical logic* very different from the ordinary "linear" logic by which we live in all other spheres of life. When conflict is absent or merely incidental to purposes of production and consumption, of commerce and culture, of social or familial relations and consensual government,† whenever that is, strife and competition are more or less bound by law and custom, a noncontradictory linear logic rules, whose essence is mere common sense. Within the sphere of strategy, however, where human relations are conditioned by armed conflict actual or possible, another and quite different logic is at work and routinely violates ordinary linear logic by *inducing the coming together and reversal of opposites.* Therefore it tends to reward paradoxical conduct while defeating straightforwardly logical action, yielding results that are ironical or even lethally damaging.

---

* Lacking a good definition, *strategy* has many meanings. The word is used variously for strategy as a fixed *doctrine* or merely a plan, to describe actual *practice* or a body of theories. See Appendix A for some standard definitions.

† The politics of repression, by contrast, are warlike, even if bloodless. All its manifestations resemble military operations, with their own versions of attack and defense, of the ambush and the raid. As in war, secrecy and deception are essential: the police seek to infiltrate dissident circles by deception, while for the dissidents secrecy is survival, and surprise is indispensable for any action.

1

The Conscious Use of Paradox in War

Consider an ordinary tactical choice, of the sort frequently made in war. To move toward its objective, an advancing force can choose between two roads, one good and one bad, the first broad, direct, and well paved, the second narrow, circuitous, and unpaved. Only in the paradoxical realm of strategy would the choice arise at all, because it is only in war that a bad road can be good *precisely because it is bad* and may therefore be less strongly defended or even left unguarded by the enemy. Equally, the good road can be bad precisely because it is the much better road, whose use by the advancing force is more likely to be anticipated and opposed. In this case, the paradoxical logic of strategy reaches the extreme of a full reversal: instead of *A* moving toward its opposite *B*, as war preparation is supposed to preserve peace, *A* actually becomes *B*, and *B* becomes *A*.

Nor is this example contrived. On the contrary, a paradoxical preference for *inefficient* methods of action, for preparations left visibly incomplete, for approaches seemingly too dangerous, for combat at night or in bad weather, is a common expression of tactical ingenuity—and for a reason that derives from the essential nature of war. Although each separate element in its conduct can be quite simple for a well-trained force, a matter of moving from one place to another, of using weapons in ways drilled a hundred times before, of issuing and understanding clear-cut orders, the *totality* of those simple things can become enormously complicated when there is a live enemy opposite, who is reacting to undo everything being attempted, with his own mind and his own strength.

First there are the merely mechanical complications that arise when action is opposed by the enemy's reaction, as in the naval battles of the age of sail in which each side tried to present broadside guns to impotent prow or hull; as in the classic gun combat of fighter aircraft, when each pilot seeks to position himself behind the enemy; and as in land combat perpetually, whenever there are strong fronts, weak flanks, and weaker rears that induce reciprocal attempts to outflank and penetrate fronts. To think faster than the enemy, to be more clever in shaping the action *may* count for much (although good tactics may be bad, as we shall see) but cannot in themselves overcome the elemental difficulty created by the enemy's use of his own force, of his own deadly weapons, of his own mind and will. In the imminence of possible death, the simplest action that increases exposure to danger will remain undone unless all sorts of complex intangibles—of individual morale, of group cohesion, and of leadership—can overcome the individual instinct for survival. And once the central importance of these intangibles is duly recognized in what happens and fails to happen, no simplicity remains even in the most elementary of tactical actions conducted against a living, reacting enemy.

To obtain the advantage of an enemy who cannot react because he is surprised and unready, or at least of an enemy who cannot react promptly and in full force, all sorts of paradoxical choices may be justified. Violating commonsense criteria of what is best and most efficient—as the shorter route is preferable to the longer, as daylight is preferable to the confusions of the night, as completed preparations are preferable to hurried improvisations—the bad option may deliberately be chosen in the hope that the unfolding action will be not be expected by the enemy, thus diminishing his ability to react. Surprise in war can now be recognized for what it is: not merely one advantage among many, such as material superiority or a better initial position, *but rather the suspension, if only brief, if only partial, of the entire predicament of strategy.* Against a nonreacting enemy or, more realistically, within the limits of time and space of the surprise actually achieved, the conduct of war becomes mere administration, as simple in its total reality as each one of its elements seems to be simple in theory.

Although a widely influential thesis for the conduct of war has been erected on this one proposition,* advising paradoxical choices whenever possible in order to shape military action according to the "line of least expectation," the advice is routinely ignored, and with good reason.

---

* This is Basil Liddell Hart's "indirect approach"; his ideas on the subject are scattered in biographies and diverse books and articles. For a coherent exposition, see Brian Bond, *Liddell Hart* (1977), pp. 37–61.

The Costs of Surprise

Each paradoxical choice made for the sake of surprise must be paid for, it must cause some loss of strength. In ground combat, the longer or more difficult route will tire men, wear out vehicles, and consume more supplies, and if the approach to combat is at all difficult or simply long, it will increase the proportion of stragglers who do not reach the fight when they are needed. Even with the best night-vision devices, forces cannot be deployed and moved so well, nor weapons used as effectively, at night as in clear daylight, and some, much, or even most of the strength in hand may therefore be less effective or even inactive during the fight. Similarly, to act more rapidly than an enemy might expect, on the basis of his own calculations of how long preparations should take, normally requires shortcuts and improvisations that prevent the full use of the men and machines that might otherwise be available for combat. More generally, all forms of *maneuver*— paradoxical action that seeks to circumvent the greater strengths of the enemy and to exploit his weaknesses—will have their costs, regardless of the medium and nature of combat. (The word "maneuver" is often misused to describe mere movement. Actually there may be no movement at all; but the action must be paradoxical because the enemy's strengths will presumably be arrayed against the expected forms of action.)

As for secrecy and deception, the two agencies of surprise that often set the stage for maneuver, they too exact some costs of their own. The strictest secrecy is often recommended to those who practice war as if it were costless, but an enemy can rarely be denied all knowledge of an impeding action without sacrificing valuable preparations. Stringent security measures will usually interfere with the early alert and thorough organization of the forces involved in the fight; they may limit the collection of intelligence and restrict the scope of the planning effort, excluding expertise that might be useful; they will constrain the scope and realism of exercises that can greatly improve performance in many forms of combat and that are especially necessary if the action to come is inherently complicated, as in amphibious landings or elaborate commando operations. And of course every limitation imposed on the assembly and preliminary approach of the combat forces for the sake of surprise will leave them less well positioned than they might have been. One reason for the April 25, 1980, failure of the Desert One raid that was meant to rescue U.S. diplomats then captive in Iran, was that very strict security measures (later judged excessive) prevented joint rehearsals by the army, air force, and marine units involved, which came together only on the scene itself in a remote wasteland of southeast Iran, with deadly consequences: diverse procedures had not been harmonized, the chain of command was unclear, and orders were misunderstood or even ignored. On a far wider scale, offensives such as the German Barbarossa invasion of the Soviet Union in June 1941 and Japan's Pearl Harbor air raid of December 7, 1941, successfully achieved surprise only by sacrificing valuable preparations that might have made the intent too obvious.* Nothing can be had for nothing in war. With secrecy rarely absolute, the leakage of the truth can be countered only by deception, in the hope that the "signals" generated by all that is done to prepare for action will be submerged by the contrived "noise" of misleading, outdated, or just irrelevant information.†

Deception can sometimes be achieved without any loss of strength by well-planted lies alone. But more often it will require substantive diversionary actions that misdirect the observant enemy because they do not contribute much or anything to the intended purpose, thereby detracting strength from it. Bombers sent to attack secondary targets to divert attention from aircraft headed toward the major objective will still inflict some damage if only at a less critical point; but ships sent out as a feint, whose only duty is to turn back as soon as the enemy has set course in their direction, may not contribute anything at all to the fight. More commonly, the use of (passive) dummies and (active) decoys of any kind, from fake tanks and guns or complete units, to flying or navigating decoys that simulate specific aircraft or submarines, are much cheaper than the real thing but still absorb resources that would otherwise increase the strength on hand. That was certainly true of the most successful deception campaign in modern military history, the masking of the June 1944 D-day landings in Normandy. The "turning" of German spies to have them report that the Allies would land their main forces far to the north in the Pas de Calais was almost costless, as well as enduringly effective: even after D-day, the Germans were persuaded that the Normandy landings were only a feint and still expected the major attack in the Pas de Calais—the shortest crossing of the English Channel after all. But great quantities of dummies were produced at considerable cost to ensure that German air reconnaissance would also report that vast armies were waiting to cross the Channel (in

---

* Some German units were kept back; the Japanese did without overflights that would have revealed the absence of aircraft carriers on the crucial day.

† These communications engineering terms were imported into strategic discourse by Roberta Wohlstetter in her seminal study of surprise: *Pearl Harbor* (1962).

the event that effort was wasted, for the Luftwaffe was no longer capable of penetrating Allied air defenses with its slow reconnaissance aircraft).

All that is done by way of paradoxical action as well as secrecy and deception must weaken the overall effort and perhaps greatly, but surprise yields its advantage whenever the enemy's reaction is weakened to an even greater extent. At the limit, surprise could in theory best be achieved by acting in a manner so completely paradoxical as to be utterly self-defeating: if almost the entire force available is used to mislead, leaving only a faction of it for the real fight, the enemy should certainly be surprised, but the venture will most likely be easily defeated even by an enemy completely unprepared. Obviously the paradoxical path of "least expectation" must stop short of self-defeating extremes, but beyond that it is a matter of probabilistic calculations neither safe nor precise.

Risk

When embarking on deliberately paradoxical action, the loss of some strength is certain but success in actually achieving surprise can only be hoped for. And while the costs of paradoxical action can be tightly calculated, the likelihood and extent of the benefit must remain uncertain until the deed is done. In theory at least, risks too can be calculated, and indeed there is an entire discipline—and profession—of "risk analysis." But failures to achieve surprise are damaging and possibly catastrophic not only because of the strength deliberately sacrificed that is absent from the fight (the starting point of risk-management calculations) but also because of the psychological impact of the collision between optimistic expectations and harsh reality. Whoever plans a surprise attack is speculating on the outcome, much as does a stock market operator who knowingly invests in high-risk paper. Both can fail, but no stock market investor is summoned to fight in deadly combat immediately after seeing his hopes of easy success cruelly disappointed. The bloodiest defeats of the First World War, and most famously the ruinous collapse of the 1917 Nivelle offensive that wrecked the French army, ensued from failed attempts to achieve surprise. Inflexible battle plans that fed more and more units into the fight—with railways and land-line telephony no greater flexibility was possible—resulted in massacres when enough enemy strength survived the preliminary bombardment of massed artillery (the intended instrument of surprise) to cut down the advancing infantry with machine-gun and mortar fire.

The failure of surprise was also a key reason for the German defeat in the July 1943 battle of Kursk, arguably the turning point of the Second World War in Europe. The strongest armored forces of the German army (including all three Waffen SS Panzer divisions) with a total of two thousand tanks were sent to penetrate and cut off from both sides a two-hundred-mile bulge in front of and on both sides of Kursk. On the map, that vast protrusion looked very vulnerable. But instead of a fast advance and an easy victory, the Germans were trapped in multiple layers of elaborate antitank defenses shielded by dense minefields. Behind them, massed Soviet tank units were waiting to counterattack. In the ensuing fight, the Soviet army for the first time defeated the Germans in their own specialty of mobile armored warfare; the exhausted Germans had lost not only many men, tanks, and self-propelled guns to mines and antitank guns before the armor-against-armor combat had even began, but also their confidence: it was all too evident that the third and final German summer offensive of the war had utterly failed to achieve any sort of surprise. Well served by its spies, scouts, and air reconnaissance and by the fruits of Anglo-American communications intelligence (by then much German radio traffic was routinely decrypted), Soviet Intelligence had uncovered the German plan. Overcoming doubts and suspicions, Stalin with his high command had taken the risk of trusting the intelligence assessment (it had been catastrophically wrong in the past), weakening all other parts of the thousand-mile front to defend the Kursk sector most strongly. The German army never recovered from its defeat; after the summer of 1943, it could only resist the relentless Soviet advance with local counterattacks, lacking the strength for any major offensive that offered any hope of victory.

Friction

The entire purpose of striving to achieve surprise is to diminish the risk of exposure to the enemy's strength—the *combat* risk, that is. But there is also another kind of risk, perhaps not deadly in itself to any one unit in the fight but potentially even more dangerous to the entire force.

That second kind of risk, which tends to increase with any deviation from the simplicities of the direct approach and the frontal attack, is the *organizational* risk of failure in implementing whatever is intended—that is, failure caused not by the enemy's reaction but rather by ordinary errors, misunderstandings, delays, and mechanical breakdowns in the deployment, supply, planning, command, and operation of military forces. When the attempt is made to reduce anticipated combat risks by any form of paradoxical action, including maneuver, secrecy, and deception, the overall action will tend to become more complicated and more extended, thereby increasing organizational risks.

In between episodes of actual combat that might be quite brief, it is the organizational aspect of warfare that looms largest for those charged with its conduct. Again, every single thing that must be done to supply, maintain, command, and operate the armed forces may be simple. Yet in their totality those simple things become so complicated that the natural state of military forces of any size is a paralyzed immobility, from which only strong leadership and discipline can generate any purposeful action.

Imagine a group of friends setting out for a trip to the beach, in several automobiles, carrying as many families. They were to meet at the best-placed house at 9:00 A.M. and immediately drive out so as to reach their destination by 11:00 A.M. One of the families was already in its car, all set to drive out to the rendezvous, when a child announced urgent need; the locked house was unlocked, the child went and came back, the car was restarted, and the rendezvous was reached with only brief delay by 9:15. A second family, which had a longer drive to the rendezvous, was somewhat more seriously delayed: an essential picnic box had been forgotten. Its absence was discovered almost within sight of the rendezvous, and by the time the long drive back was done, the box found, and the meeting finally joined, it was nearer 10:00 than 9:00.

A third family caused even greater delay: with everything loaded and everyone aboard, the car would not start—the battery was depleted. After familiar remedies were tried as time passed, there was a longer wait for a towtruck with its stronger batteries. Once the engine finally started, the driving was impatiently fast, but by the time the third family arrived at the rendezvous it was well after 10:00. Still the journey could not begin. Some children had been waiting for more than an hour, and now it was their turn to ask for a brief delay. By the time everyone was ready, the road to the beach was no longer uncrowded, and instead of the planned two hours the journey lasted for over three—including unscheduled stops for one car's refueling and for another family's cold drinks. In the end the beach was reached, but by then the planned arrival time of 11:00 had long passed.

At no point was our imaginary group impeded by the active will of an enemy; everything that happened was the consequence of unintended delays and petty accidents, akin to the *friction* that impedes the workings of all moving machinery. The term is of course from Clausewitz's *On War*, whose tonalities will have been recognized by now: "Everything in war is very simple, but the simplest thing is difficult. The difficulties accumulate and end by producing a kind of friction that is inconceivable unless one has experienced war."[1] Friction is the very medium in which any kind of strategic action must unfold, and war's most constant companion.

In our mundane example, the initial delay at the journey's start was more than one hour, and the cumulative delay much longer. It is easy to imagine how the delay might grow with more families included. Eventually, if enough of them are added to the group, the point can be reached where the journey could not start at all, so long as all must wait for the last arrival. How many families must be included in the outing to prolong immobility till the day is done, one cannot say, but a few dozen should do the trick. Yet even that unwieldy assembly would not begin to compete in size with quite small military units, the several hundred men of a single army battalion, a modest warship crew, or the manpower of an air squadron or two.

A military force includes no children to delay it and can repress lesser whims by discipline, but in all else it is likely to be far worse off than our ill-fated families aiming for the beach. For one thing, supply needs will have quite other dimensions, and any needs insufficiently anticipated cannot be made good by brief roadside pauses; a fleet at sea may be thoroughly supplied, but whatever is missing will have to wait until the next replenishment; and for any air or ground unit away from well-stocked bases, the country around them might as well be a desert, now that food and hay no longer suffice to sustain war.

There was only one mechanical breakdown in my example, but there will be many more in military forces whose major weapons and vehicles, radars and radios, and all other things electronic and mechanical will only rarely be as reliable as most automobiles now are. Military equipment is generally produced in far smaller numbers, used much less often, and is often far more complicated than any family automobile. Battle tanks, so strongly protected against the enemy's fire, are nevertheless surprisingly delicate in their inner machinery (especially transmissions, notoriously), while each one of the thousands of electronic devices contained in a single combat aircraft is just as likely to malfunction as the ignition of a family car.

No operating errors intervened to delay the beach party, in which all drivers performed without flaw. But in spite of the best of training, severe tests, and frequent exercises, no military force can hope for such perfection from all who must operate its varied equipment. Much unconscious skill is actually required to drive a car in traffic, but far more is needed to work a great many of the machines of war, and instead of the many years of daily practice that even youngish car drivers can have, a good many military operators will have only a few months of infrequent experience, because they themselves or their equipment are new to the task.

In our example, the plan was simple, with one starting point, a single route, and a fixed destination; it was also perfect, except for the failure to anticipate that a 9:00 A.M. starting time did not allow enough leeway to avoid the rush hour on the highway to the beach. Military plans soundly crafted will strive for such simplicity but rarely attain it, because the several elements of any given force must be coordinated, often to carry out several different actions in a fixed sequence. Although competent planners will attempt to the best of their ability to allow for all other kinds of friction, their own errors will add one more.

Finally there is the friction that afflicts the command of the action, or more fully the ongoing intelligence monitoring and assessment, the decision making itself, the intercommunication, and the supervision ("control") that make up the command function as a whole. In our example, there was a plan of action but no command, intelligence, intercommunication, or supervision; had there been, the rest of the group might have rapidly discovered the third family's plight and stepped in to provide a replacement car. Military command structures with their Intelligence and communications adjuncts exist precisely to detect and overcome frictions large and small by timely interventions, as well as to exploit the fleeting opportunities of combat and to contend with its sudden dangers. But their own workings offer many hostages to friction: wrong, outdated, or misleading intelligence induces errors of decision; communications networks may be highly advanced, reliable, and secure in every way, but messages may still be garbled or sent astray or not sent at all; the only task of the U.S. Navy intelligence ship *Liberty,* attacked in error by the Israelis in June 1967, was to intercept communications, but it did not receive its own orders to leave the war zone until after the attack. Since then, every sort of technical progress has been made, yet grievous telecommunications errors persist—chiefly because of overloading. Any spare capacity is immediately filled up: whenever new communications systems or techniques add capacity, as they frequently do, the traffic increases in turn, as messages previously relegated to paper and mailbags are upgraded (there is much to be said for silence when it comes to telecommunications that are free for the communicators). As for errors of "control" in military command-and-control structures, they are virtually inevitable given the delicate balance between the need to supervise subordinate combat units and the opposite need to allow some room for initiative to each one.

Once all sources of friction are taken into account, once it is recognized that their totality is usually more than their sum, as some frictions interact with others to worsen the outcome, the full significance of organizational risk becomes clear. Just as our imaginary group of families could miss its day at the beach altogether if it becomes large enough, any military action can fail *internally* even without encountering the enemy's deliberate counteraction.* Breakdowns, errors, and delays, each perhaps almost insignificant in itself, can accumulate into an insurmountable obstacle to any purposeful action. Nothing is more frequently encountered in war than unscheduled postponements, lasting hours or perhaps critical days or even weeks. They fill the record of military history, accounting for many defeats. It is in this context—the impeding medium of friction—that any striving to obtain surprise must be seen: each paradoxical choice introduced for the sake of surprise, with its own deviation from the easiest and simplest course of action, will further increase friction and therefore the risk of organizational failure.

When combat risk materializes, it takes the bloody form of injury and death. When organizational risk materializes, the action fails in a manner that might be bloodless. It might therefore seem that organizational risk can be balanced against combat risk when deciding how much complication is accepted for the sake of surprise. But this is only true of a single act of war, as in the case of a commando action carried out in peacetime. Otherwise, one risk compounds the other. Of course the warship that misses the battle by being misdirected through command friction, the tank battalion that runs out of fuel on its way to the front because of supply friction, and the fighter aircraft that cannot accomplish the intercept because maintenance friction prevents its takeoff will all remain quite safe at the time. The direct approach and frontal attack are therefore easily condemned by advocates of paradoxical circumvention who focus on the single engagement, seeing very clearly the resulting lessening of combat

---

* But a clever enemy will strive to compound inherent frictions, attacking supply lines if supplies are already short; communications, if they are already overburdened; command centers, if enemy officers are lacking in initiative; and so on. These are instances of the most ambitious kind of military operation: *relational maneuver*, the application of strength against specifically identified enemy weaknesses—a form of warfare, discussed later, which is itself highly vulnerable to friction.

risk, while being only dimly aware of the resulting increase in organizational risk.

But once we examine not the single engagement of the single unit but the fight as a whole, it becomes clear that organizational risk is quite likely to compound combat risk. The fleet is weakened in battle by the absence of the misdirected ship, leaving its remaining warships more exposed to combat risk; it is the same for the battalions that advance without the one stopped by the lack of fuel, and for the other fighters of the squadron that do take off. On the next occasion, those who missed the earlier fight will probably have to fight alongside forces weaker than they might have been, because of the added losses caused by their absence during the previous round—and this will increase their own combat risk as well.

The Prevalence of Paradoxical Action

The advantages of surprise that paradoxical schemes offer are thus offset not only by the lost combat potential deliberately sacrificed but also by added organizational risk. Yet straightforward military actions, entirely shaped by linear logic to make the fullest use of all available resources by the most direct methods, are not that common in the record of war, and still more rarely do they escape criticism in the aftermath. At least some paradoxical elements will be present in the preparation and conduct of most competent military actions.

To be sure, military leaders whose forces are altogether superior may be quite justified in spurning surprise, for the sake of ample preparations to use their full strength with the simplest methods, to minimize organizational risk. That was the case, for example, in the first stages of colonial warfare in any one place; until the local warriors learned to disperse when faced by well-drilled European troops armed with rapid-fire weapons, frontal attacks were very effective. And it was also true during the last months of the Second World War in Europe, when American, British, and Soviet armies with overwhelming firepower favored overtly prepared frontal offensives against a German army in decline, just as the respective air forces abandoned all artifice to launch massed daylight bombing raids virtually unresisted by German and Japanese air defenses. That was still warfare, *but the logic of strategy no longer applied,* because the enemy's reaction—indeed his very existence as a conscious, living entity—could simply be disregarded. If the enemy is so weak that his forces can be treated as passive targets that might as well be inanimate, the normal linear logic of industrial production, with all its usual criteria of productive efficiency, is fully valid, and the paradoxical logic of strategy is irrelevant. (Clausewitz: "The essential difference is that war is not an exercise of the will directed at inanimate matter, as is the case with the mechanical arts . . . In war, the will is directed at an animate object that reacts. It must be obvious that the intellectual codification used in the arts and sciences is inappropriate to such an activity.")[2]

Although strategy comprehends both the avoidance of war and its conduct at all levels from tactics to grand strategy, it can tell us nothing about the purely *administrative* aspect of warfare, in which the reacting will of the enemy has no role. Just as there is nothing to be gained by deliberately choosing boots three sizes too small or willfully misusing weapons, because neither boots nor weapons will respond advantageously to such paradoxical action, so too there is no need to circumvent and surprise an enemy so weak that his entire reaction can be safely disregarded. Such fortunate conditions, however, are necessarily rare: few enemies will deliberately choose to fight a vastly more powerful force.

Somewhat more common is the phenomenon of armed forces that overestimate their own strength and therefore follow linear logic to optimize the administration of their own resources, without even trying to surprise the enemy by suitably paradoxical moves. Actually the role given to the paradoxical in the conduct of war should reflect the perceived balance of strength, and it often does.

In a manner itself paradoxical, it is those who are materially weaker, and therefore have good reason to fear a straightforward clash of strength against strength, who can most benefit by self-weakening paradoxical conduct—if it obtains the advantage of surprise, which may yet offer victory.

If the unfavorable balance is not merely an accident of time and place in the context of a single engagement, battle, or campaign, but rather reflects the permanent circumstances of a given state among other states, then the pursuit of the "line of least expectation" by paradoxical action may become the defining characteristic of its *national style of warfare*. Israel is an interesting contemporary example of this phenomenon. Originally, its armed forces systematically tried to avoid any direct clash of strength against strength, seeking instead paradoxical alternatives because they expected their enemies to be materially stronger, in their combined numbers, or in equipment, or both. As the overall balance of strength shifted in Israel's favor over the decades, occasions in which Israeli forces were actually outnumbered or outgunned were reduced to such cases as commando raids, when small forces were deliberately introduced deep into enemy territory. Increasingly, the Israelis could count on material superiority, in addition to their advantage in training, cohesion, and leadership. There was some adjustment to new circumstances—less night fighting by choice, for example. Yet they still avoided direct force-on-force engagements in most cases, partly by habit but mostly because they hoped to minimize casualties. In war after war, and in many isolated acts of combat in between, the Israelis chose to accept both self-weakening and added organizational risks for the sake of surprise. Israeli forces much weaker materially than they need have been (because of the constraints of secrecy and deception, because of hurried improvisation, or because of overextension), and operating with so much self-imposed friction that their condition bordered on the chaotic, regularly defeated enemies caught by surprise, whose strength was not concentrated on the scene or whose forces were materially or morally unready for combat.

The Israelis' routine preference for counterconventional, paradoxical action could not persist without eventually undoing its purpose. Over time, their antagonists began to revise their expectations. They learned from experience to mistrust estimates of Israeli moves that were based on commonsense calculations of the "best" course of action open to them. Finally, in the Lebanon war of June 1982, the Syrians were not at all surprised by the Israeli attempt to send an entire armored division into their rear through a single, one-lane road winding its way across the Chouf mountains, and they acted in good time to block the narrow passage.[3] It was the next Israeli move that the Syrians completely failed to predict, and then watched with disbelief, scarcely reacting as the hours passed: a perfectly straightforward frontal offensive by massed armored divisions into the Vale of Lebanon.[4] With a greatly favorable balance of forces, and with no time to lose because of the imminence of a cease-fire, the Israelis chose to sacrifice any hope of surprise by attacking frontally and in broad daylight—only to be pleasantly surprised by Syrian unpreparedness. Obviously by 1982, with their paradoxical style of war so fully exposed in countless previous engagements, for the Israelis the line of least expectation could only be the most direct, frontal approach.

2

The Logic in Action

That surprise cannot repeatedly be achieved by the same methods is obvious. But it is also an example, if by no means very important in itself, of the workings of the paradoxical logic of strategy in its full, two-sided, dynamic form. So far that logic has mostly been considered from the viewpoint of only one participant, specifically, a participant who understood the logic and consciously tried to exploit it. Moreover, I have mostly examined single situations and single decisions, and therefore the logic of strategy has been viewed in a series of static glimpses. But there are of course at least two conscious, opposed wills in any strategical encounter of war or peace, and the action is only rarely accomplished instantaneously, as in a pistol duel; usually there is a sequence of actions on both sides that evolve reciprocally over time.

Once we focus instead on the paradoxical logic of strategy as an objective phenomenon, which determines outcomes whether or not the participants try to exploit it or are even conscious of its workings; and once time is duly introduced to make the process dynamic, we can recognize the logic in its totality as the *coming together, even the reversal, of opposites*. And this is a process manifest not merely in the fate of counterconventional actions intended to achieve surprise, which eventually become quite predictable, but rather in all that is strategical, in all that is characterized by the struggle of adversary wills. In other words, when the paradoxical logic of strategy assumes a dynamic form, it *becomes* the coming together, even the reversal, of opposites.

In the entire realm of strategy, therefore, a course of action cannot persist indefinitely. It will instead tend to evolve into its opposite, unless the entire logic of strategy is outweighed by some externally induced change in the circumstances of the participants. Without such change, the logic will induce a self-negating evolution, which may reach the extreme of a full reversal, undoing war and peace, victory and defeat, and all they include.

Consider what happens to an army advancing victoriously in a large theater of war. More than one battle many have been fought, but without any alternation of fortunes. One army is forcing the other to retreat. Perhaps the defeated are scattering in panic or are about to be trapped and destroyed; the war may therefore be coming to an end by negotiation or surrender. In that case there is still a possibility of a reversal of opposites as we shall see, but not within the span of this war. But if the defeated army is still fighting, even in retreat, a pattern of reversal will begin to emerge.

The victorious army is advancing away from its homeland, whose training camps, industry, supply depots, and workshops sustained its recent successes. It must obtain all that it needs from supply lines that are becoming longer and longer. Whether it is horse-drawn wagons, railways, trucks, or the latest transport aircraft that are delivering fuel, ordnance, spare parts, and all else, distance diminishes their capacity. Longer transits also increase breakdowns and maintenance pauses, of importance if total capacity is not in excess all along. The defeated army by contrast is presumably falling back toward its own bases, so that its own supply lines are becoming shorter. Reinforcements must travel further to reach the advancing army; the retreating army may have no source of reinforcements; if it does, their journey to the front is becoming shorter.

The victorious army must therefore increase its effort merely to sustain itself. It may have to withdraw people and equipment from frontline combat to strengthen its supply units or divert reinforcements for that purpose. The defeated army by contrast can reduce its own transport effort; its commanders may be able to skim combat-worthy manpower and equipment from supply units to strengthen frontline forces.

The victorious army is entering territory until then in its enemy's keeping, which may contain an unfriendly population, armed partisans perhaps, or even regular units deliberately left behind to fight as guerrillas. At best, the military government of the newly occupied population will require some manpower and resources, perhaps offset by what can be requisitioned locally. At worst, if there is armed resistance, with attacks and sabotage against rail lines, road convoys, supply dumps, service units, and rear headquarters, the victorious army will have to call back combat units from frontline duties to provide guards, security patrols, and quick-reaction forces in rear areas judged unsafe.

Even if the victorious army is liberating friendly civilians who will offer no resistance themselves, nor any help to enemy troops staying behind, its advance will still cause another kind of relative disadvantage: for in that case, it is the defeated army that was the occupier, so it can now return guards, patrol units, and reaction forces to frontline combat duties.

The victorious army has momentum, and the freedom of the initiative in setting the pace and directions of the advance, so that its forward echelons may be able to outpace and cut off the retreat of the defeated. But otherwise the army in retreat, unless harried without cease, can have the powerful advantage of the tactical defensive. Its rear-guard units can choose favorable terrain for each fighting pause, so as to fire on the moving, exposed enemy from behind cover; perhaps they can successfully ambush enemy forces advancing too eagerly.

The effects of victory and defeat upon morale, cohesion, and leadership are much less predictable. Combat morale defines not happiness but rather the willingness to fight. Victory may increase the former but reduce the latter: having just fought and won, the troops may both be happy and also feel that they have done enough. (Clausewitz described this phenomenon as "the relaxation of effort.") Such things are not easily proved, but military historians agree that the veterans of the British Eighth Army of the Second World War, who had long fought and finally won against the Germans and Italians in North Africa, were done with risky fighting by 1943; yet they had two more years of campaigning left, both in Italy and in northwest Europe after D-day. They did not desert individually, their units did not run away from battle, but British field commanders just had to accept that there would be no dash, daring, or determination on the attack from veteran formations, only a steady caution that left the role of cutting edge to others: elite units, new units, allied units.

Conversely, defeat is demoralizing. It may induce passivity—not much of which is needed to nullify an army—or even desertion if circumstances allow.* But it can also sting men to fight harder in the next battle, especially if they feel that their previous efforts could have been greater. That too happened to the British Eighth Army during its earlier North African campaign: having yielded too easily to Erwin Rommel's dashing advance of 1942 across Libya, most of its units were determined to fight harder by the time the Germans crossed into Egypt to reach El Alamein. In the first battle, of July 1–10, 1942, the British held their positions instead of retreating once again; in the second, starting on October 23, they counterattacked in force.

---

* The 1991 Gulf war ended with mass desertions by Iraqi troops who expected good treatment from their enemies; but such benevolence is rare in transcultural wars.

Leadership too can be greatly enhanced by victory, or just as easily undone. With success already achieved once or several times, the impulse to drive men into the dangers of combat may be spent. In the defeated army in retreat, leaders may have lost all authority; but if that is not the case, bitter memories of recent failure may drive them to demand more from their men and give them the energy to do so. But when it comes to the skills and procedures of war, the balance of possibilities is not even: victory misleads, defeat educates.

With victory, all of the army's habits, procedures, structures, tactics, and methods will indiscriminately be confirmed as valid or even brilliant— including those that could benefit from improvement or even drastic reform. That is what happened to the Israeli army after its spectacular victory of 1967. Having swiftly defeated the numerous Egyptians, the well-entrenched Syrians, and the disciplined Jordanians with the same combination of unsupported tank assaults and air interdiction,* the leaders of the Israeli army ignored evidence that both were highly vulnerable to the mass deployment of weapons that the Soviet Union could provide and the Arabs could use: antitank and antiaircraft missiles. Wonderful victory on three fronts in six days had obscured the implications of the few episodes in which Israeli forces had suffered short-lived tactical defeats or unexpected losses. Therefore the Israeli Army made no great efforts to strengthen its tank units with self-propelled artillery and high-grade infantry equipped with modern armored carriers. Its funds were instead spent mostly to buy more and better tanks, with little left for the artillery, while the infantry—mostly lower-grade reservists—remained with its ancient, open-topped, half-tracked carriers dating back to the Second World War. When war came again in 1973, unsupported tank forces did quite well defensively but suffered many losses on the attack to Egyptian antitank weapons, having neither enough artillery to suppress them nor accompanying infantry to defeat them directly. The Israeli air force likewise had easily evaded the air-defense missiles of the Arabs in 1967, and preferred to acquire more combat aircraft rather than electronic-warfare equipment. In 1973, it was nevertheless ready to deal with the vast number of newer Soviet antiaircraft missiles in Arab hands, but only if it could

---

* "Air interdiction" refers to air attacks against force concentrations and supply lines, as opposed to "close air support" aimed at frontal forces to directly assist the ground forces.

start the war by attacking them systematically in ultralow altitudes strikes to evade their radars. When the Israeli air force was instead required to engage advancing Arab ground forces with no preliminary suppression campaign at all, it suffered many losses to antiaircraft missiles and guns.

Defeat is by far the better teacher. Not only are critical faculties sharpened by failure: if remedies are offered, they are much less likely to be resisted because defeat weakens the resistance to change of the defenders of the status quo. That is what happened to the Arabs after their crushing defeat of 1967. They learned to accept their limitations and no longer tried to compete directly with the Israelis. Instead of trying to match mobile armored warfare with their own too-slow armor maneuver, they relied on static but dense antitank defenses; instead of air combat in which they were outmatched, they relied on dense antiaircraft defenses. In the end they lost the 1973 war as well, but much less disastrously than in 1967; Egypt actually conquered and held some territory in the Sinai, though it lost more in Egypt proper.

It was just the same for the Israelis. All the lessons that could have been learned by careful examination of what actually happened in 1967 were finally learned in 1973. By the time the Israelis fought their next war in 1982 both the armored and air forces suffered little from missile defenses.

If industry and population are still being mobilized, and the victorious army is receiving powerful reinforcements, its rising strength is ensured even as it continues to advance. In other words, "exogenous" change can nullify the logic that would weaken the offense. But if that is not so, if there is no great flow of reinforcements to the victorious army, its very advance will tend to weaken it, while failure and retreat will tend to strengthen the army previously defeated.

Culmination and Reversal

In the dynamic setting of a continuing war, the coming together of victory and defeat may extend beyond a new equilibrium, to reach the extreme of a full reversal. If a victorious army can achieve total conquest or impose surrender, its subtle weakening will not matter, any more than the tendencies that tend to strengthen the defeated. But if the depth of territory or just their tenacity prolong the fighting, the defeated will be able to benefit from the dynamic paradox, perhaps to the extent of becoming victorious in turn. If the army till then successful simply persists in its advance and is not reinforced sufficiently, it will ruin itself by overshooting the culminating point of victory, beyond which it is increasingly weakened.

That was the fate of the German forces that invaded the Soviet Union in June 1941. They were hugely successful at the outset, easily defeating both the Soviet forces thinly spread out along the front and the larger formations not far behind them. Easy success launched the Germans on fast offensives deep into Russia toward both Leningrad (St. Petersburg) and Moscow, winning huge victories along the way. Soviet losses were enormous. But as they continued to advance over distances of hundreds of miles, the German invasion columns were not reinforced sufficiently to overcome the extension of supply lines, the psychological "relaxation of effort," and the accumulating tactical errors of victory—while by contrast the Soviet forces were strengthened by drastically shortened supply lines, the moral pressure of shameful failure, and the many practical lessons taught by defeat. By December 1941, the Germans had overshot the culminating point of victory, while the Soviet forces were strong enough to launch their first counteroffensive, aided by the winter freeze. Although their victories were only tactical (because the German front did not collapse), the Russians had proved to be better students of Clausewitz than the Germans. Yet more remarkably, the sequence of a victorious summer offensive overextended beyond the culminating point, followed by the winter counteroffensive of the recently defeated was repeated in 1942—except that the German front at Stalingrad did collapse, with huge losses. In July 1943, it was a much weaker German army that launched its third and last summer offensive against the Kursk sector; the Soviet army did not have to await the winter to counterattack in great strength. But from July 1943, it was the Germans who benefited in many ways from the paradoxical logic that weakens the advancing strong and strengthens the retreating weak. That is why the Soviet army did not enter Berlin until the end of April 1945.

None of this means that victory must inevitably lead to defeat if war continues. But unless it benefits from overpowering reinforcements derived from its ultimate sources of military strength (that is, from factors exogenous to the logic), the victorious army will have to pause and recuperate from its own successful advance to overcome the unfavorable tendencies at work. By restoring its energies of morale and leadership through rest and troop replacements; by bringing forward its entire supply organization; by providing for the security of rear areas if threatened; and by revising those procedures, tactics, and methods that the enemy is learning to anticipate and defeat, the victorious army can restore its capacity for further success, in effect pushing outward and into the future its culminating point of victory.

The continental warfare of the Second World War incorporated every variant of the coming together and reversal of victory and defeat. Because armored warfare and air power brought back deep maneuver on a Napoleonic scale, overcoming the defensive primacy of the static trenchlines of the First World War, the fighting unfolded in a series of dramatic moves.

The German invasion of the Netherlands, Belgium, and France, which began on May 10, 1940, and ended on June 17 with the French request for an armistice, was achieved (but only just) within the span of a single all-out effort.[1] By June 17, the ten Panzer divisions that spearheaded the German advance had suffered so many breakdowns among tanks, half-tracked carriers, and trucks that their strength was more show and noise than substance; they had to resort to expedients such as the mounting of machine-gun crews on captured French trucks. In the infantry divisions that formed the great bulk of the advancing German armies, the troops had been marching on foot from the start, and most were utterly exhausted. As for the German supply organization, which had to rely on the circulation of horse-drawn carts from the nearest functioning railhead to the combat units, it was so overextended that only the abundance of food and fodder in the prosperous lands just conquered prevented crippling shortages in the conquering army. Ammunition resupply was not as serious a problem in a campaign of rapid maneuver and brief offensive thrusts, in which most combat encounters were little more than skirmishes. Mostly marching on foot, mostly supplied by horse-drawn carts, the German army did not need much fuel—yet it too was insufficient; the dashing Panzer divisions kept going only because they could confiscate civilian gasoline as they advanced.[2] But before the Germans decisively overshot their culminating point of victory, all their accumulating weaknesses were nullified by the armistice: their one-bound range of penetration had proved greater than the geographic and moral depth of France.

When Hitler's armies attacked the Soviet Union almost exactly one year later, on June 22, 1941, their one-bound reach had only marginally increased with the addition of captured French trucks as well as a slight expansion in the mechanized forces. Among the 142 German divisions of the three army groups arrayed on the eve of invasion across the vast front from the Baltic to the Black Sea, only 23 were Panzer, part-armored Light, or Motorized divisions. In the entire German army everywhere, a total of 88 divisions were by then equipped with French vehicles. Even so, 75 of the infantry divisions deployed on the eastern front had to be stripped of their trucks altogether to equip army-group supply columns, receiving instead 200 peasant carts.[3] Such was the reality behind the facade of mechanized modernity that played such a large part in the psychological impact of Hitler's blitzkrieg.

But the Soviet Union is a country far deeper than France; its rail lines were much less readily usable because of a different track width and also a great deal of sabotage; its few roads were unpaved so that motor vehicles were rapidly worn out; and the tenacity of its resistance did not seem to diminish with successive, catastrophic defeats. Thus in mid-October 1941, when the German forces reached what in retrospect can be recognized as their culminating point of victory, Moscow was still some sixty miles beyond their most forward columns of advance.[4] But with Hitler in command, there could be no pause for recuperation. The German forces on the central sector of the front, now with Moscow as their target, continued to advance through the month of November in twin thrusts from both north and south, to achieve one more great encirclement that would finish off the Soviet army, and the war. With this advance, the German army decisively overshot its culminating point of success and was forced onto the downslope of the curve. Growing shortages of ammunition at the front lines were silencing the artillery and leaving even the infantry short, because distances from railheads to front were too great for the circulating horsecart columns and the few trucks available. The railways were in any case unable to keep up with the supply needs because of an acute shortage of Russian-gauge rolling stock. In the process, ominously, winter clothing and cold-weather lubricants were left behind at remote marshaling yards, as immediate essentials of food, fuel, and ammunition received highest priority.

In the mechanized forces, the number of functioning tanks, half-tracked carriers, and artillery tractors continued to decline, as wear and tear accumulated and field repair fell behind. By then, commandeered Russian peasant carts had become essential transport even for the Panzer divisions. An active resistance of partisans and bypassed regulars had already begun in the rear, adding policeman's work to the duties of genocidal massacre and confiscation that already occupied Germans who could have been on the front. As it was, the flow of replacement manpower was steadily falling behind the rising number of casualties. Above all, German frontline soldiers were increasingly afflicted by the cold, physically exhausted, and demoralized by their very success. They had continued to advance mile after mile ever since June 22, capturing some three million

Soviet troops by November and killing them by the tens of thousands in one engagement after another, but it seemed that just as many unconquered miles remained ahead and just as many Soviet troops still stood to resist them, with no end in sight. But Hitler and his generals would not stop with Moscow so tantalizingly near. One more great effort was made, and the final offensive of 1941, launched on December 1 at a time when the most advanced German troops stood a mere twenty miles from the Kremlin, was carried out in subzero temperatures by forces whose last strength was rapidly ebbing.[5] Four days later, in the early morning of Friday, December 5, the Red Army launched its first large offensive of the war. Soviet troops in winter whites pushed the Germans back over a distance twice as great as the depth of their last, ruinously successful, advance. After this Soviet offensive finally checked the unbroken progress of German arms, three more years of alternating war followed in which, as wave and counterwave, further spectacular German summer offensives only led to greater retreats before Soviet attacks in growing strength.

After losing hugely by their own overextension, when epic victory against the Stalingrad salient was followed by excessive advance, setting the stage for the German counterstroke of March 1943,[6] Stalin and his high command learned to alternate each successful advance with a deliberate pause, to keep their armies safely short of the culminating point of victory. As the Soviet Union fully mobilized its population and industry, and obtained much American and British help (including no fewer than 409,526 jeeps and trucks),[7] it fielded increasingly superior forces, which were employed with growing skill by a new breed of war-taught officers. With the increasing imbalance in the ultimate sources of military strength, the alternation of German and Soviet offensives of 1942 and 1943 gave way to an unbroken sequence of Soviet victories, until the final thrust into Berlin. But to the very end, even as German forces in the east were reduced to an assemblage of worn-out veterans, raw recruits, abruptly reassigned sailors and airmen never trained for infantry combat, young boys, old men, and the partially disabled, each victorious Soviet offensive was carefully measured out to stop short of excess; any signs of "adventurism" evoked Stalin's dangerous displeasure.[8]

The eleven-month war of the western front, from the Normandy landings of June 6, 1944, to the German surrender, did not lack its episodes of victory overshot on both sides, though only one side could truly recover from overextension. And the war in North Africa, fought back and forth across the twelve hundred miles of desert between Tripoli and the Nile delta, was nothing but an entire series of such episodes. By the time the crushing material superiority of the British forces finally powered a slow but irreversible advance from the El Alamein lines on October 23, 1942, two years of warfare in the romantic-adventurist style by the British first, and then by Rommel's Germans and Italians, had given the fullest demonstration of the principle. Victorious advances were so grossly overshot that offensive arrows sweeping across the map might amount to a mere handful of tanks running out of fuel—all set to be overrun by the formerly defeated on the rebound, on their way to victories just as fragile.[9]

That was the pattern of the Korean war also, in which each side pursued its offensives to self-defeating extremes. The swift advance of the North Koreans that began on June 25, 1950, had conquered almost the entire peninsula by August except for the Taegu-Pusan enclave in its southern tip. By then, however, the North Koreans had advanced on foot across track distances of three hundred miles or more, overshooting their culminating point of success. When General Douglas MacArthur launched his counteroffensive on September 15 with the daring stroke of the Inchon landings deep behind the overextended North Koreans, their hurried retreat turned into a miserable debacle. Splendid victory gained by a high-risk surprise attack was almost immediately overshot by an incautiously rapid advance. By October 26, 1950, a thin final thrust of the American-South Korean advance had cut through the whole of North Korea to reach the Yalu River and the Chinese border.

Mounting warnings that the Chinese would react by entering the war only induced a slight tactical withdrawal from the Yalu River itself. In November 1950 MacArthur's "front," which stretched across the broad base of North Korea from sea to sea, existed mostly on the paper of his maps. Instead of a solid chain of units deployed shoulder to shoulder and reinforced by strength in depth, there were large gaps between the forward elements of the American-South Korean columns: they had advanced in several valleys widely separated by mountain terrain that was not even patrolled, let alone controlled. Had the Chinese been road-bound as the U.S. Army was, depending on trucks to move troops as well as supplies, the obvious geographic vulnerability of MacArthur's separate thrusts would have been purely theoretical, because the mountains were impassable to motorized vehicles. As it was, the Chinese advanced on foot across the mountains with all their supplies on the backs of porters, inserting themselves between the American-South Korean columns. Moving at night, hiding during the day, they remained undetected. Except for the U.S. Marines on the eastern side of the peninsula, MacArthur's forces were also though less obviously vulnerable because his units were disorganized by their hurried advance and most newly arrived U.S. Army troops were badly undertrained (the South Koreans were simply untrained). As important, both Americans and South Koreans were morally exhausted by the widespread belief that the war had already been fought and won.

With undefended mountain passages open to them, the Chinese had the advantage of being able to advance deeply by infiltration before having to attack at all. When the overt Chinese offensive was launched on November 26 with mortar bombings and infantry assaults against the flanks of U.S. Army and South Korean columns strung out along narrow valley roads, the columns could neither counterattack up the steep slopes nor hold their ground. The ensuing retreat was disastrous: increasingly disorganized and demoralized troops could not just go back the way they came riding on trucks, they had to *fight* through successive ambushes and roadblocks to evade capture. Nothing is more demanding than an orderly retreat under attack; the U.S. Marines did it so well in their own sector on the eastern side of the peninsula that their withdrawal amounted to an offensive in reverse; but many U.S. Army units and almost all South Korean units disintegrated into a mass of fleeing individuals.

By the end of January 1951 the Chinese had inflicted a vast defeat on MacArthur's forces. With that they advanced right through North Korea and into the South, reaching some forty miles beyond Seoul—much too far and much too fast as it turned out. To march on foot through the mountains was an excellent way of evading detection, but supplies carried on the backs of porters could not sustain a large army far from its bases. Thus the Chinese defeat by overextension was well prepared when the U.S. counteroffensive of February, March, and April 1951 liberated Seoul for the second time in six months, along with most of South Korea.

Many more such examples can be found in the record of warfare. But to elaborate further would merely obscure the universal applicability of the paradoxical logic of strategy, whose dynamic form is the coming together and even the reversal of opposites. For its manifestation in large-scale ground warfare is only the most obvious example of a much broader phenomenon. The purely mechanical aspects of overextension are important when the theater of combat is large enough and war leaders lack prudence, *but the same interaction between success and failure occurs in all forms of warfare.* That is true even if the factor of overextension is entirely absent. Whenever the action lasts long enough to allow move and countermove, the same dynamic paradox will be manifest.

That was true for example in the six-year struggle between British bomber forces and German air defenses during the Second World War. It too was marked by drastic reversals of fortune, even though there were no abruptly extended distances to exceed transport capacities, no wearing out of unrepaired trucks and unrested horses, no exhausting infantry marches, and no other such physical processes at work. The cycles of success and failure in the air war over Germany were instead brought about by the (delayed) reaction of each side to the successes of the other.

Convinced at the start of the war that the German fighter force, though trained for battlefield use,[10] could also assure Germany's air defense along with the antiaircraft guns of each locality, and indeed prevent any bombs at all from falling on German cities, the chiefs of the Luftwaffe discovered that they were wrong as early as the summer of 1940. That is when the British Bomber Command started to bomb at night, with insignificant results at first but in virtual immunity: Luftwaffe fighters had no effective way of finding and attacking aircraft in the dark even if they were detected and tracked by long-range radars on the ground.[11] Only the small bomb loads and inaccuracy of British bomber raids prevented serious damage to German cities.

By the summer of 1942, the leaders of Bomber Command had therefore convinced themselves that it would require only the training of sufficient aircrew and the production of enough bombers to inflict irreparable damage on the German war effort, ensuring victory without any need of armies or navies. But instead of more easy penetrations of German air space, by the end of 1942 Bomber Command was faced with the delayed reaction to its own earlier successes. Greatly improved German air defenses, with more and better warning and tracking radars, new searchlight barriers, the first night fighters with radar, and more abundant antiaircraft guns, inflicted losses that Bomber Command could not sustain.[12]

Content with the growing success of its radar-based air defenses, and unwilling to take away any more men, aircraft, and guns from the war fronts, the Germans were unprepared for the British reaction: the introduction of effective electronic countermeasures against both ground-based and airborne radar. The result was a sharp rise in the effectiveness of night bombing during the spring and summer of 1943.[13] Increasingly outmatched, with their night fighters often reduced to visual detection, the Germans were shocked when Bomber Command totally blinded German warning radars with its "Window" countermeasure, strips of reflecting foil that are released in bundles into the airstream to simulate entire formations of aircraft.[14] Used for the first time on a large scale to maximize the surprise effect, Window opened the way for the combined

British-U.S. raids on Hamburg of July 24–August 3, 1943, which utterly devastated that great city in mankind's first experience of the firestorm effect.[15]

By then quite certain of the steady increase in its strength, as more and better bombers were flying out on each successive raid, in November 1943 Bomber Command set out to destroy Berlin as Hamburg had been destroyed. Instead of another great victory, the British bombing offensive against Berlin collided with the German reaction to Britain's earlier victory, in the form of effective Luftwaffe counter-countermeasures: higher-frequency radars for the night fighters, which were largely immune to jamming; new tactics with day fighters, whose pilots exploited the ambient light of the flames below; better warning and tracking radars; and a greatly improved "running-commentary" method of interceptor control from the ground.

German air defenses had become so effective that only the diversion of Allied bombing to immobilize the French railways in preparation for D-day masked the British defeat in the so-called Battle of Berlin, even though it was by then the spring of 1944 and Germany was plainly losing the war. The damage inflicted was unimpressive, while British bomber losses exceeded the flow of replacements.[16] As important, the morale of Bomber Command aircrew was breaking: more bomber crews turned back after takeoff, reporting mysterious technical problems; others dropped their bombs before reaching Berlin; still others dropped half their bomb loads into the sea to gain height and speed before having to cope with German fighters.

In the British-German air war of the Second World War, the effects of the paradoxical logic of strategy in its dynamic form were encountered both at the technical level and at the level of grand strategy—dominated as always by political choices and political concerns.

Measures and Countermeasures

The "action-reaction" sequence in the development of new war equipment and newer countermeasures, which induce in turn the development of counter-countermeasures and still newer equipment, is deceptively familiar. That the technical devices of war will be opposed whenever possible by other devices designed specifically against them is obvious enough.

Slightly less obvious is the relationship between the very success of new devices and the likelihood of their eventual failure: any sensible enemy will focus his most urgent efforts to develop countermeasures against the opposing equipment that seems most dangerous at the time. Thus, paradoxically, *less* successful devices may retain their modest utility even when those originally most successful have already been countered and perhaps made entirely useless.[17] Eventually, of course, the less successful device is also likely to be countered, but in the meantime it may offer some span of utility—and that is all any equipment can offer in technological areas that happen to be evolving rapidly.

That was so in the aerial electronic warfare of the Second World War, whose turbulent progress was propelled by dramatic scientific breakthroughs, by the furious pace of work in laboratories and factories, and by the intensity of intelligence efforts to uncover enemy devices and techniques. In the ebb and flow of reciprocal development, the same device could be highly effective when originally introduced, then totally useless, and finally positively dangerous, and all within a matter of months. That was the case with the rearward-looking radars fitted on British bombers to warn that fighters were approaching them, which were lifesavers at first, then were jammed, and soon became a deadly danger to those who used them: a new receiver allowed German fighters to detect their beams to find the bombers at night.[18]

The useful life span of new technical innovations determines the utility of their performance—a most confusing thought for scientists and engineers for whom, normally, utility and performance are one and the same. But that is true only when performance acts on inanimate (or cooperative) objects. Then utility and performance are indeed identical, and a device that performs better cannot possibly be less useful than one that performs less well. In the paradoxical realm of war, however, the impossible becomes possible. For example, a variety of electronic methods were invented to guide aircraft during the Second World War; at each stage both British and Germans, and later Americans, naturally chose the most accurate and longest-range method, devoting scarce production resources to obtain the navigation equipment in optimal form—only to see it countered while other methods only slightly inferior, and other equipment only marginally less optimal, could still be used effectively. It was eventually realized on all sides that the introduction of new methods and innovative equipment had to be managed deliberately, and that superior options were best kept in reserve for campaigns of unusual importance.

Without such management, the life cycle of each new navigation device would begin with an experimental phase in which few were available and the crews were still unskilled in their use, and be followed by a phase of rising success to a culminating level (which coincided with the preparation of enemy countermeasures), which was followed in turn by an abrupt decline when enemy countermeasures were also widely employed. Having acquired by bitter experience an insight into this manifestation of the logic of strategy, the leaders on all sides intervened to control the progression of technology, to make its span of success coincide more closely with their operational priorities.

The prescriptive implication for nations at war is clear: when scarce development resources must be allocated between competing scientific concepts and engineering configurations, it is unwise to rely on the judgment of scientists and engineers. As such (although they can be wise strategists too), scientists and engineers are unlikely to see merit in the diversion of resources to develop second-best equipment alongside the best.

But that is precisely what prudence demands. It will no doubt be argued that resistance to countermeasures is also an aspect of performance, one that would be given the highest priority if appropriate, eliminating any distinction between utility in conflict and performance in general. The argument is plausible, but it slights the full meaning of the predicament of war. It assumes that the scientists and engineers who have the technological expertise to develop new equipment will also correctly predict the countermeasures to come, against which resistance is to be designed in from the start, as part of overall performance.

This may be true in some cases, especially for minor innovations that will not disturb adversaries very much, and are therefore likely to evoke an equally minor response within established lines of technical development. But it is much less likely when the new equipment is a major innovation or a notable success with a strong impact on the perceived balance of military strength.

In the competitive production of weapons that may occur in peacetime (much of it is one-sided, not competitive at all), and much more so in war, the greater the success of any one technological innovation, and the more drastic the reaction evoked, the more likely it is that a wide variety of scientific principles will be explored in attempting to design countermeasures. That reduces the likelihood that countermeasures will be successfully anticipated.

Moreover, once the creativity of the adversary is unleashed, countermeasures may take the form of new tactics, operational methods, military structures, or even strategies—whose successful prediction is not at all a matter of scientific or engineering expertise.

That was the case in the aerial electronic warfare of the Second World

War when the German response to the substantial British innovations that blinded German air defenses in the summer of 1943 was an entirely new combination of signaling with searchlights and ground control by "running commentary." That amounted to a new *method* of air operations, in which fighters were no longer directed to intercept individual bombers but instead were sent to pursue the hundreds of aircraft of entire bomber "streams." So effective was this method, which was highly resilient to radar jamming, that the Germans were able to add greatly to their fighter strength by employing radarless day fighters for night interception as well. Concurrently, the Germans explored all kinds of new techniques to overcome British radar countermeasures, including infrared detection, quite outside the radar field of expertise. The British experts who had been so talented in designing both radars and countermeasures based on radar principles, and who were very successful in predicting German *radar* countermeasures, naturally failed to anticipate the major German response to their own great success of the summer of 1943, which did not rely on radar principles at all.

In this instance, as so often, utility in conflict and performance were not the same, since the latter only covers resistance to *known and predictable* countermeasures. It cannot possibly anticipate the full range of reactions that a major innovation can evoke in an observant and creative enemy. The sphere of strategy is defined precisely by the presence of a reacting enemy, and that is what prohibits the pursuit of optimality. To design a bridge to cross a river, much is involved: soils must be tested to ascertain load-bearing properties, the dynamic forces the bridge will have to withstand must be calculated, and the standard mechanical theorems must then be applied. Once all the calculations are done, the bridge can be built in safety. It is true that rivers sometimes flood their banks, or even abandon their accustomed channels to cut new ones, but no river of nature will deliberately set out to erode the structures of a bridge, nor will it deliberately flood beyond its span. The targets of military technology are much less cooperative. As soon as a significant innovation appears on the scene, efforts will be made to circumvent it—hence the virtue of suboptimal but more rapid solutions that give less warning of the intent and of suboptimal but more resilient solutions. This is why the scientist's natural pursuit of elegant solutions and the engineer's quest for optimality often fail in the paradoxical realm of strategy.

3

Efficiency and the Culminating Point of Success

Having noted the obvious likelihood of a counterreaction to any technical innovation, and the slightly less obvious relationship between the success of an innovation and the probability of its neutralization, we can approach the much less obvious connection between the technical efficiency of new weapons and their vulnerability to countermeasures of all kinds.

In its familiar definition as the ratio of output to input, technical efficiency is the great virtue in all material endeavors. Although it is invoked in loose language to comment on the worth of entire institutions that may have no measurable output at all, the criterion of efficiency can only be applied with mathematical precision to machines, including the machines of war, by adding up the initial costs of acquisition and current operating costs, to then compare the sum of both with the ultimate output.

Technical efficiency is not of course the only criterion to be applied in evaluating machines, for the ratio of current output to current input tells us nothing about the likely duration of their performance (reliability) and the costs of the upkeep that will be necessary over time. Subject to these factors, however, technical efficiency is the valid criterion whether in selecting between different types of trucks or choosing machine tools, rifles, or tanks.

Some increases in technical efficiency can be obtained by the use of better materials or better design within established forms, or even by minor adjustments in the inner workings of machines. It is by such processes that today's trucks can carry more tonnage than their predecessors of twenty years ago, of equal initial cost and greater fuel consumption, and that well-tuned truck engines can yield more horsepower than their poorly calibrated counterparts.

More dramatic efficiency increases, however, will usually require the introduction of new design configurations. Sometimes this is made possible by exploiting different scientific principles, as with today's computer-based word processors, which are much more efficient than electric typewriters, just as they in turn were more efficient than their mechanical forerunners. But otherwise, dramatic increases in efficiency can be obtained only by replacing generic equipment built to do many things at varying levels of efficiency with much more *specialized* equipment built to produce one output altogether more efficiently, just as can openers open cans with much less effort than more versatile knives, and forklift trucks position crates more efficiently than far more costly, more versatile, mobile cranes.

The pursuit of high efficiency through narrow specialization has played a large role in the modern evolution of military technology. Each time around, new, highly specialized weapons have offered the attractive prospect of defeating far more elaborate and costly weapons, versatile in many ways but nevertheless vulnerable to the only "output" of specialized weapons. From the 1870s, for example, the combination of the newly invented self-propelled torpedo[1] with fast steamboats to provide its launching platform seemed to offer the possibility of defeating efficiently the altogether more expensive battleships on which naval power then rested. Battleships, built as they were to fight other large warships, were armed with long-barreled guns of large caliber. Those guns could not be depressed low enough to defeat torpedo boats approaching under the cover of the night and revealed only at close range. In addition, even oceangoing torpedo boats would present only a small and unstable target, very difficult to hit. Moreover, the heavy armor of the battleship, which made it so costly and formidable, was then mainly applied to decks and superstructures, in order to resist the descending armor-piercing shells of other big-gun ships; therefore the explosion of torpedo charges against the unprotected sides below the waterline could be devastatingly effective.

The conclusion to be reached seemed quite obvious: with the advent of the torpedo boat, the costly battleship had become fatally vulnerable, and if inert conservatism could be overcome, naval power could be acquired on a new and far more economical basis. That was the reasoning of the "young school" of naval officers, the Jeune Ecole that influenced French naval policy from the 1880s,[2] which found supporters even in the Royal Navy, as well as in lesser navies that had far more reason to welcome the demise of the battleship.

The design of mobile cranes has not evolved to nullify the virtues of forklift trucks, any more than knives have been modified to dispute the primacy of can openers in their one and only function. But neither inhabits the realm of strategy, where each action is apt to evoke a conscious and creative outmaneuvering reaction, which induces the paradoxical coming together of success and failure in a manner all the more dynamic if the initial action is of strong effect. And that applies as much to major technical innovations as to success and failure in the broader endeavors of war and peace.

Because of the extreme efficiency of their narrow specialization, which allowed small and cheap torpedo boats (the input) to destroy large and costly battleships (the output), the new weapon greatly disturbed the equilibrium of naval power. The reaction was correspondingly powerful. First, however, on the rising curve of success, torpedoes were steadily improved to offer longer ranges, higher speeds, and greater accuracy, while a new kind of very small yet oceangoing warship with the fastest propulsion available was built to launch them: the torpedo boat. On this rising curve of success, the new concept was rapidly implemented on a large scale. The French attempted to nullify their perpetual inferiority to the Royal Navy's battleships by building no fewer than 370 *torpilleurs* from 1877 to 1903; and even the British built 117 "1st class Torpedo Boats" by 1904.[3] The emerging German imperial navy did not neglect the innovation, and neither did the navy of modernizing Japan, which actually used its oceangoing torpedo boats with great success in the surprise attack against the Russian fleet at Port Arthur in February 1904.

Thus the vision of ultraefficient naval power, which the naval reformers of the 1870s had so vigorously promoted against the conservatism of "old school" admirals, was fully realized long before the First World War.

Yet torpedo boats did not play an important role in the naval warfare of 1914–1918 except as a threat to be guarded against. Far from having made all larger and more costly warships obsolete, it was the torpedo boat itself that became obsolescent, surviving only as a minor weapon of marginal value. For by then the innovation had long passed its culminating point of success and was already largely neutralized *because* of its efficiency, which had both evoked a strong reaction and prevented any remedial response. Platforms or weapon systems that are highly efficient because they are narrowly specialized cannot accommodate *broad* counter-countermeasures.

By 1914 all modern battleships and battle cruisers, indeed all large modern warships, were prepared to neutralize the torpedo boat. Although the long-barreled guns of their main batteries still could not be depressed to fire at short ranges, the searchlights by then universally employed made it much more difficult for torpedo boats to approach closely undetected, even at night. And, just in case, quick-firing guns of small caliber had been added to attack them at close range. Though armor protection was still at its thickest on decks and superstructures, new and highly effective protection was also provided below the waterline, not only by armor plate but by sealed bulges that could absorb the impact of torpedo detonations. At anchor, wire nets suspended alongside could shield warships by detonating torpedo charges at a safe distance from the hull.

The ability of larger warships to carry extra armor, provide ample electrical power for searchlights, and accommodate quick-firing guns and heavy steel nets derived of course from the same characteristics that had made them appear so inefficient in the visualized duel with the torpedo boat. Their size and power had merely seemed to increase their value as targets, while being irrelevant to the duel—until all that costly versatility was exploited to defeat the new threat. Thus the broad prevails over the narrow to cut short its span of success.

Far from inaugurating a new era of naval power, the great victory of the Japanese torpedo boats at Port Arthur was already an anachronism—a reflection of Russian naval backwardness. Against more modern navies, the new weapon's culminating point of success had already passed, although its sharp decline was not evident before 1914. That the torpedo itself remained a useful naval weapon, and remains so still, is not in question. It found its proper place as one more specialized weapon for surface warships and especially for the new kind of warship originally built to hunt torpedo boats, the torpedo-boat destroyer, or destroyer for short. The torpedo also became significant in aerial use and far more important as the key weapon of the submarine, with which it formed a much *less* efficient (more input for the same output) but far more effective combination in two world wars. And of course even the original torpedo-boat combination did have an important effect upon the naval balance, by forcing the large-ship navies to divert resources to provide the defenses that eventually neutralized the new threat.

As we shall see, such *reciprocal force-development effects* can sometimes be of greater value to one side or another in asymmetrical contests than the original combat ability offered by narrowly specialized new weapons. However, if any nation had embraced reformist innovation wholeheartedly, entrusting its naval strength to the originally ultraefficient torpedo boat, it would soon have found its strength inadequate.

The relationship between the initial efficiency of narrowly specialized weapons and their vulnerability to technical, tactical, or operational countermeasures is not accidental. It is a typical expression of the paradoxical logic of strategy in its dynamic form. The same phenomenon is evident whenever the attempt is made to defeat broad capabilities with narrowly specialized ones that achieve efficiencies all the more ephemeral the larger they are at the beginning of the action-reaction cycle. And yet the sequence keeps repeating itself, propelled by the irresistible attraction of defeating costly weapons with cheap ones.

Thus, for example, when antitank missiles were used to great effect by Egyptian infantry against Israeli battle tanks during the first few days of the surprise attack that inaugurated the 1973 October war, much was said about their "revolutionary" impact on land warfare. Loud voices proclaimed the obsolescence of the expensive battle tank, and there were demands for reform to overcome the conservatism of the "tank generals" and thereby save a great deal of money. How could multimillion dollar tanks justify their cost, it was asked, when they could so easily be destroyed by antitank missiles that cost mere thousands? (And, incidentally, why was there so much anxiety over the strength of the Soviet army, which was largely dependent on its tank formations?) Very quickly a new Jeune Ecole emerged, which offered the attractive vision of a new kind of high-technology infantry, cheaply armed with antitank missiles to offer military strength not only highly efficient but also virtuously defensive.

Actually the fundamental innovation that made the antitank missile possible was not new at all: the hollow-charge chemical warhead first used during the Second World War. Instead of depending on kinetic energy to penetrate armor by brute force, hollow-charge warheads project a high-speed stream of vaporized metal that can burn through the thickest armor without need of costly long-barreled guns with their recoil mechanisms and elevating assemblies, which only large and costly vehicles can carry into battle. Any means at all of conveying the charge to the target will do the job, whether by rockets light enough to be hand-launched as in the original U.S. bazooka and German Panzerschrek, the ubiquitous Soviet-designed RPG, or cheap low-velocity recoilless guns, or even by hand in the form of satchel charges simply thrown at tanks.

When the bazooka and its equivalents first appeared, some thought that the day of the tank was done. Any infantryman could now carry a weapon that could destroy tanks. If every squad of the two hundred or more of each infantry division were to contain just two or three, the infantry would be able to block armored forces, so much more costly to equip and train, so much harder to supply in the field, and altogether more difficult to transport across great distances. Had it been a time of peace, the delusion might have prospered. But since a world war was underway to swiftly punish fallacy, the bazooka and the rest of the hollow-charge rockets introduced by 1945 were almost immediately recognized for what they were: excellent morale boosters for the infantry, until then apt to be shocked into flight by the mere approach of enemy tanks; weapons fairly effective in forests and jungle—scarcely tank country—but also in cities, unless the tanks sacrificed speed and momentum to proceed at a walking pace with escorting infantry alongside; and then of course as weapons highly suitable for the aspiring hero, who would stand his ground amid the artillery explosions that commonly prepare the way for attacking armor and who would aim his one ready shot at a tank whose machine guns had been firing at him long before the hundred-yard rocket could be launched. Of course, such duels were great rarities on the battlefield, for tanks fight in groups that protect one another as they advance. As we shall see, moreover, there are levels other than the tactical in the encounter, which favor the mobile armored force even more.

The introduction of man-portable missiles to launch hollow charges decisively remedied the most obvious defect of their predecessors. Guided to the target, missiles can be propelled with great accuracy over long ranges, so they need not be launched within machine-gun reach of their targets. But otherwise this narrowly specialized weapon is in no better position to make the tank obsolete than the bazooka was during the Second World War. In the fighting of the first few days of the October 1973 war, Egyptian infantry encountered Israeli tanks in small numbers, with no infantry escort and without significant supporting artillery fire (both being mostly reserve forces, they were still unmobilized when the Egyptians launched their surprise attack).[4] Israeli tank crews, moreover, had received no particular training to prepare them for a fight with determined missile infantry that would stand its ground; and the tanks themselves were armed only for combat with other tanks. As a result, it was not only antitank missiles that destroyed Israeli tanks but old-style unguided rockets as well, and in fact in greater numbers.

With its extreme efficiency against unprepared tanks, the antitank missile evoked a strong reaction, triggering the dynamic paradox that would turn success into failure; and because of its narrow capabilities—the reason for its efficiency—the reaction was effective almost immediately and would become even more so over time. The same Israeli tank battalions that the antitank missile had seemingly made obsolete, or at least incapable of offensive action, by October 9, 1973, were penetrating the Egyptian front one week later, and they advanced to encircle entire divisions just one week after that. Obviously there had been no time for the development of any sort of technical countermeasure. The response that turned success into failure was largely tactical.

With initial surprise overcome, and the reserve mechanized infantry and artillery forces mobilized to the front, Israeli tank battalions no longer had to fight on their own, violating their established operational doctrine. Instead, they could advance behind a rolling barrage of artillery fire, not heavy enough to do much harm to Egyptian armor or entrenched infantry but very effective against antitank missiles, whose operators could not keep a target in their sights long enough amid the explosions, even if they braved the dangers of exposing themselves. The mechanized infantry, advancing alongside the tanks in their troop carriers, added to the suppressive effect with its own mortars and machine guns, which swept the ground ahead to force antitank missile crews to keep their heads down.[5] Even more effective were mortar smoke bombs, which could keep curtains of smoke just ahead of the tanks, thus preventing missile operators from seeing their moving targets for long enough to guide their weapons to intercept. Finally, the tanks also had some means to protect themselves once the new threat was recognized: some of the armor-piercing rounds carried on board could be replaced with high-explosive shells or fléchette rounds, both effective against infantry, and tanks had their own machine guns as well as launchers for smoke grenades.

Thus the armored force, so costly because of its broad and versatile abilities, could outmaneuver the narrow efficiency of the antitank missile— even before there was time to develop, produce, and distribute specific countermeasures. Some of the latter were already in use during the 1982 Lebanon war, when Israeli tanks went into action with "active armor"— detonating plates meant to destroy hollow-charge warheads before they could explode to project their superheated stream, as well as with more machine guns and better launchers for smoke grenades.

By then far more effective antitank missiles had appeared on the scene, but they had little effect on the fighting except when launched from helicopters, to yield a combination no longer cheap at all, much less efficient therefore, but altogether more effective.[6]

Strategy versus Economics

The ever present adversary reaction that is the essence of the strategic predicament will not only disappoint most hopes of drastic efficiencies achieved by narrow specialization, but can also deny the more modest ambition of pursuing (linear-logical) economic practices in military matters. For example, although the armed forces are usually the largest of all social institutions, they cannot freely pursue economies of scale in acquiring their equipment. The uninspiring uniformity that is the curse of modern industrial society is also the key to its blessings: displacing the individual artifacts of the traditional craftsman, with their multitude of designs, a few standardized products are manufactured in far greater numbers at much smaller cost by efficient, specialized machines, tools, and jigs combined in labor-saving production lines. It is the *homogeneity* of the products and their components that allows economical mass production, and the greater the homogeneity in all that is produced, the greater the economies. (It is only recently that the introduction of computer-controlled machinery is beginning to break that pattern, by allowing the production of different models on the same assembly line.) For products that are themselves machines—including those too unusual to be mass-produced—homogeneity is still the key to economies of scale, in maintenance and operation if not production. The greater the homogeneity of a stock of machines, the smaller the number of different replacement parts and supplies that must be kept in inventory, achieving savings not merely in administration but also in substantive capital: the size of the replacement inventories required for uninterrupted operation can be more finely calculated when there is much use of fewer machines, rather than small use of many different ones. Similarly, the more homogeneous the machines, the more economical the training of their repairmen and operators, and the greater the likelihood that they will learn enough to do their work properly.

In different ways, homogeneity is therefore the essential quality that allows economies of scale in acquisition, maintenance, and operation. As we have seen, not all that is involved in war belongs to the realm of strategy. Nothing prevents armed forces from pursuing economies of scale by homogeneity in all that is purely *administrative*, where adversary wills have no role.[7] There is no obstacle to the efficient mass purchasing of boots or helmets, trucks or ammunition. But for military equipment that must function in direct interaction with the enemy—within the strategic realm, that is—homogeneity can easily become a potential vulnerability. If, for example, antiaircraft missiles are standardized on a single homogeneous type, in order to obtain economies of scale in production, maintenance, and training, the resulting savings could be very large as compared to an array of several different missile types. But in war a competent enemy will identify the weapon's equally homogeneous performance boundaries and then proceed to evade interception by transcending those boundaries. Any given type of missile will have minimum and maximum altitude limits, and enemy aircraft can therefore underfly or overfly those limits. The missile can still exact a price because aircraft flying very low or very high cannot be fully effective, but such "virtual attrition" may not suffice to achieve the purposes of an antiaircraft defense (aircraft can still attack targets by ultralow penetration or by high-altitude bombing even if less effectively than at some optimal medium altitude).

The single homogeneous missile, moreover, will be vulnerable to a single, homogeneous set of countermeasures. Perhaps the economies of scale of standardizing on a single type can be so great that the one missile and its battery complex can be made highly resistant to countermeasures, for example by combining different forms of guidance that can automatically replace one another. But the single target presented to the enemy's countermeasure effort will still allow him to focus all his efforts, increasing the likelihood that a weak point in the missile system will be found.

What is true of antiaircraft missiles is just as true of any other machine of war that must function in direct interaction with a reacting enemy—that is, the vast majority of weapons. In each case, the application of linear-logical economic principles would result in standardization on a single type to obtain large savings in production, maintenance, and training, just as with the trucks of a well-run commercial fleet or the machine tools of a competent engineering enterprise. Both trucks and machine tools exist in a competitive environment, and both the truck fleet and the engineering company face the danger that their rivals will be able to undercut their prices by obtaining more efficient trucks or machine tools. But there are legal boundaries to what can be done in economic competition: competitors will not undermine the bridges that the trucks must cross so that their standardized weight will exceed the bridge load limits, nor will they conspire with suppliers to deny raw materials compatible with the specific tolerance limits of the standardized machine tools. In war, however, where there are no such legal boundaries, standardization must result in vulnerability for any weapon or device that interacts with the enemy, from fighter aircraft to missile submarines, from warning radars to field radios.

In the realm of strategy, therefore, economic principles collide with the demands of war-effectiveness. Although there is an obvious cost barrier to unlimited variety, there is also a vulnerability barrier to the unlimited pursuit of economies of scale by homogeneity. A criterion of "equal marginal risk" could be calculated to determine just how much uneconomical diversity should be accepted in purchasing weapons, but perhaps it is enough to recognize that commonsense economic thinking does not apply when it comes to strategy.[8] True, armed forces are notoriously fragmented bureaucratically, and that alone may safeguard them against dangerous extremes of homogeneity. Even without benefit of any strategical insight, armies, navies, air forces, coast guards, armed police, and others are forever trying to emphasize their distinct identity by choosing their own distinctive weapons, as well as uniforms and insignia.

But there is no such protection against the pursuit of economies of scale in the sizing of complex weapons, notably warships. The large warship offers exactly the same economies of acquisition and operation over smaller ships that have led to the concentration of a large part of the world's shipping capacity in less than a thousand huge tankers, bulk carriers, and container ships. As size increases, crews do not increase in proportion: a colossal 500,000-ton tanker may have no more sailors than a 3,000-ton freighter. Neither do the dimensions and costs of machinery from bilge pumps to main engines increase in proportion, especially when it comes to communications and control equipment. Large ships are also more stable in rough seas and have an important hydrodynamic advantage when moving at speed.

All these advantages, however, are obtained at the price of a proportionate concentration of value against which an enemy can focus his efforts. Should the world experience another campaign against commercial shipping in the style of the two world wars, it may turn out that the advent of the supertanker confers a greater advantage on the attacker than even the transformation of the submarine from the diesel-electric boats of the two world wars that could only submerge for slow and short transits into today's nuclear-powered underwater battleships, which can remain underwater for weeks, even months. For commercial fleets that must survive in the peacetime setting of competitive freight markets, the unlimited pursuit of economies of scale is essential. But when we encounter a similar concentration of value in combat ships and auxiliaries several times larger than their predecessors of the Second World War, in major airbases and repair depots in places quite close to enemy territory,[9] we can see that military logic has been displaced by economic priorities that are valid only in peacetime.

Descending the Curve: From Success to Failure

Except for passing mention of "reciprocal" effects in the development of weapons and of "virtual attrition," the fate of the other side in the dynamic interaction—the *reacting* side—has been overlooked. But of course the coming together of opposites that leads from success to failure, and from failure to success, affects both sides in exactly the same way, whether in the largest actions of war and peace or in the technical encounter between weapons and countermeasures.

The side that is reacting successfully to some new threat is itself on an upward path to a culminating point, perhaps distant or perhaps near, but which in any case marks the start of its own decline.

On the one hand, once the initial surprise is overcome, the reaction to the new threat becomes increasingly effective as creativity and resources are increasingly applied to the task. On the other hand, those resources and creative energies are being diverted from some other action already under way—often a deliberate offensive action. Eventually, if the culminating point of success is overshot, the resources expended to counter the new threat will be greater than the result is worth. In other words, more can be lost through the weakening of one's own positive action than is gained by reducing damage from the new threat. Ballistic missiles for example are dramatic weapons, but if they do not have nuclear warheads, they are simply expensive vehicles for modest quantities of ordinary high explosives, or unreliable chemicals, or even less reliable biological agents. It is therefore easy to overshoot the culminating point of effectiveness in developing countermeasures to nonnuclear ballistic missiles—in fact the best defense against an ineffectual threat is no defense at all, for drama does not count in war, only results.

In the meantime, while the countering reaction is under way, the other side, which first introduced the new threat, will have started to react in turn, to resist the increasing success of the countermeasures, with fewer possibilities if the threat was narrowly efficient and with more if it was not, but either way starting another cycle in the dynamic, paradoxical process of strategy.

Enthusiasts persuaded of the power of some marvelous new weapon will invariably be surprised by the variety of adversary reactions that will deny the success that seemed so certain. Likewise, however, those who are reacting successfully against the new weapon may easily overlook the danger of overshooting the culminating point of success by sacrificing too much offensive strength. This has yet to happen in the response to the antitank missile, but the costs of success have been high, adding to those already imposed by the hollow-charge threat in its unguided form, now present in a variety of hand-held rocket and recoilless weapons distinctly superior to their predecessors of the Second World War. Until then threatened only by other tanks, and by high velocity antitank guns themselves rather costly and scarce, tank crews had learned by 1943 to fear all places where soldiers equipped with hollow-charge rockets or recoilless weapons might await their coming. By the end of the Second World War, with those weapons in widespread use, any passage through woods or narrow streets had become a dangerous experience for tanks, if the enemy was highly motivated.

Soon after the first of the new weapons appeared, it was discovered that their threat could be reduced or even eliminated by a close escort of infantry moving alongside, whose many eyes could probe the surroundings and whose small arms could suppress and react in detail. But the cost of that effective precaution was high because tank units in need of a foot escort could no longer surge ahead on their own even for tactical movements, and thus lost much of the dash and momentum that is the true strength of attacking armor.

The advent of the antitank missile greatly compounds the effect. Artillery fires once reserved for definite and concentrated targets must now be diverted to suppress missile crews by firing on whatever covered ground may hold them, where in fact there may be only a few or none at all. And if mechanized infantry units are to advance alongside the tanks to protect them, they need combat vehicles much more elaborate and costly than the simple troop carriers that sufficed when the infantry's task was chiefly to mop up behind the advancing tanks. Finally, in the tank units themselves there must be a diversion of effort from offensive action to self-protection, by way of both material changes—"reactive" armor, extra machine guns and ammunition, even mortars—and more cautious tactics. Armored forces earn their keep by offensive strength, and everything done to protect them from the hollow-charge threat diminishes their positive value, even if the culminating point—where more is lost than gained in the process—is not yet reached. For example, the U.S. Navy had lost substantial positive value in the final phases of the Cold

War, when its aircraft-carrier groups were increasingly focused on self-protection against Soviet submarines and naval bombers, at the expense of their offensive strength.

Protecting the Fleet: Overdoing Success

When several British warships were sunk by the fighter bombers of Argentina during the 1982 Falklands war, the world learned that brave and skillful pilots could overcome all manner of material inadequacies, from the absence of in-flight refueling that forced them to operate at extreme range with no reserve, to the lack of suitable weapons (they only had five effective antiship missiles in all), to the incompetence of ordnance technicians who sent them off with bombs wrongly fuzed to attack ship targets. Another lesson of the episode was that complex antiaircraft missiles should not be relied upon unless they can be frequently tested—a difficult requirement because each is so expensive. But in the United States, the losses of the Royal Navy provoked a much broader debate, which echoed the torpedo-boat controversy of a hundred years before. Once again the cheap weapon of narrow effect—the air-launched antiship missile this time—was promoted as decisively lethal to warships a thousand times more costly; once again demands were heard for a drastic change of naval policy to stop the waste of public money on elaborate warships, on aircraft carriers especially, now supposedly made obsolete by their new vulnerability to missiles.

This time, however, there was no need to await the development of countermeasures. In another echo from the past, the effectiveness of the antiship missiles of 1982 was due to the peculiar unpreparedness of the Royal Navy, whose lag in adopting widely used countermeasures was as severe as that of the tsar's navy of 1905 in opposing the torpedo. Actually by 1982 the antiship missile had already passed its culminating point of success, owing to the strong reaction evoked by its earlier appearances, first in the middle years of the Second World War and then in the 1950s, when the Soviet navy gave antiship missiles a large role in arming surface ships, submarines, patrol aircraft, and even land vehicles for coastal defense.[10]

The chiefs of the U.S. Navy therefore won the debate quite easily. They explained that aircraft carriers would operate with a panoply of escorting destroyers and cruisers, devoted almost entirely to their protection from antiship missiles as well as submarines. Radar-confusing chaff and infrared flares projected by rockets from their decks as well as electronic jamming would divert antiship missiles aimed at the aircraft carriers, while the antiaircraft missiles and guns of the escorting ships would shoot down the remaining missiles—and also any aircraft that ventured too close in order to launch them. And that, the Navy chiefs pointed out, was only the middle layer of the defense. Twenty-four long-range fighter interceptors on each carrier, with four early-warning radar aircraft and four jamming aircraft to aid them, would assure the outer layer of the defense, while four tanker aircraft could keep them refueled at their distant stations. Finally, there was the inner layer of the defense, the radars, countermeasures, antiaircraft missiles and guns of each ship, including special automatic guns reserved for that one purpose.

So devastating was this answer to the missile enthusiasts of 1982 that the other side of the coin scarcely attracted notice. When all that was required to react (successfully) to the antiship missile is calculated, it becomes clear that in addition to exceptionally costly escort warships, much of the aircraft carrier's own capacity is also absorbed by the need for self-protection against missile attack, with thirty-six aircraft out of ninety or so on each carrier being thus employed.[11]

As it happens, no Argentinian submarine was successful in sinking a British warship during the Falklands war. Had that been the case, provoking debate on the vulnerability of American warships to modern submarines as well, the U.S. Navy chiefs would no doubt have described the abundance of antisubmarine forces that also protected the aircraft carrier. These included an attack submarine as an underwater escort, sixteen aircraft fitted out with detection gear and depth charges, and the weapons and sensors of escorting destroyers and cruisers. Once this further self-protection was added, it turned out that an entire carrier group, with its several destroyers and one cruiser, its escort submarine and several supply ships, with almost ten thousand crew members in all, could provide only thirty-four aircraft for offensive action, along with a dozen guns of middling caliber and sundry cruise missiles.

Isolated in clear contrast between sea and sky, unable to hide in the terrain as ground forces can, unable to move as rapidly as aircraft, surface warships were increasingly endangered by the scientific advances that permit long-range observation and attack in many forms. To contend against adverse trends propelled by the entire progress of science, increasing expense and ingenuity as well as ship capacity were consumed for self-protection. The *net* vulnerability of the U.S. Navy increased only slightly as the Soviet navy's offensive power grew from the 1960s till its demise in the 1990s, but less and less U.S. naval strength could serve the national interest, as more and more was consumed by self-protection.

In historical retrospect, the sequence of the dynamic paradox starts with the supremacy of the American aircraft-carrier task forces originally built to fight the Japanese navy but after 1945 left to face a Soviet Union that was strong only on land. To preserve the institution, the postwar chiefs of the U.S. Navy emphasized the offensive potential of carrier aviation against land targets, with nuclear weapons too. Great efforts were made to quickly acquire jet bombers small enough to take off from carrier decks yet capable of long-range strikes. Once the reaction began, Soviet coastal-defense, air, submarine and surface forces all grew in size and capacity year by year, and it was the Soviet Union that developed the first really effective antiship missiles. The results were increasingly impressive, and the Soviet navy would have reached a culminating point of defensive supremacy if its efforts had not been resisted. But of course the U.S. Navy did react, by equipping its warships with increasingly effective antiair and antisubmarine weapons, by greatly advancing both radar and sonar detection techniques and placing chains of sonars on the ocean floor, by converting more and more of its on-board aircraft capacity to defensive use, and by learning to stay away from dangerous seas close to Soviet bases. With a reaction so vigorous, the Soviet counterthreat to the U.S. Navy's aircraft carriers began to slide down the curve toward failure, so that by the time the Falklands war reminded the world of naval combat, American carrier task forces were exceedingly well protected—but only at vast expense and with a great loss of offensive power.

Far more precise calculation than this text allows would have been needed to determine the culminating point of defensive success in protecting the U.S. Navy's surface fleets, beyond which oceanic strength could have been better assured against the Soviet navy at its peak by underwater and aerial forces.[12] Certainly no judgment can be made in mere prose, any more than the U.S. Navy, deeply devoted to navigation on the surface as it is, could have been expected to repudiate tradition in obedience to strategic logic. But such a culminating point did exist, and to exceed it meant failure even in apparent success, with aircraft carriers defended all too well to be worth keeping.

Now that the Russian Federation has inherited much-diminished and far less active naval forces, the U.S. Navy finds itself once again without a serious enemy at sea—with its carriers secure from enemy attack but not from domestic critics who note the great cost of carrier aviation, as compared to its land-based counterparts (twenty stealthy intercontinental bombers can be bought for the price of a carrier task force, and their bombing capacity is at least ten times as great). Once again, the U.S. Navy has reacted by off-loading defensive aircraft from the carriers and replacing them with fighter bombers; once again it emphasizes its ability to attack land targets from the open sea. But back in 1945, land-based bombers had a far more limited reach, while now carrier aviation must compete with aircraft capable of attacking worldwide.

The Failure of Success

Far more common is the overdoing of a successful defense in territorial warfare. The outpost, fortified zone, or garrisoned city that is deliberately left in front of the main defense lines, or that remains cut off in the course of a retreat, may serve the defense well by providing warning, blocking approach routes, and absorbing disproportionate enemy attention. The attacker may find himself weakened in the theater of war as a whole when he fights at great cost to conquer places that might have been bypassed, had their resistance been correctly anticipated from the start.

It is usually the defense, however, that suffers the consequences of an oversuccessful resistance. If the forces cut off are quickly defeated, they may still have obtained an advantage for the defense. But if their resistance persists in prolonged, heroic endurance, attracting public notice, the locality that was perhaps once quite obscure or just another name on the map can be transformed into a weighty symbol, into which the reputation of military or political leaders may become inflexibly invested. If no help can be sent to the beleaguered, the defense will continue to obtain an advantage, moral as well as material, as long as resistance persists. But if there are ways of sending reinforcements by perilous routes under attack, by yet more precarious infiltration, or by air transport, then the continued success of the defense can become ruinous in a larger perspective.

So it was most famously at Verdun in the First World War, where the failure of a German surprise attack in February 1916 gave the French a greatly needed defensive success—and also impaled their army on that victory, bleeding it white in ten months of battle (arguably the longest in history) to defend the Verdun forts. To keep up the resistance, day after day a great stream of men was sent forward under steady bombardment, with a great many falling before they ever reached the forts. By official figures notoriously understated, the French army suffered 162,308 killed and missing, with another 214,932 wounded. The Germans gained a definite advantage from the *French* success in defending the forts, because their artillery could strike at French approach roads better than the French artillery could reciprocate against the German rear. Their casualty lists, also understated, included only some 100,000 dead and missing. More reliable modern calculations arrive at an estimate of 420,000 dead, two-thirds of them French—far too many to be given decent burial in the very small area in which the battle was concentrated.[13] That number may be compared to the 344,959 Americans who died in battle during *both* world wars, on all fronts worldwide and in all services. The massacre was still in its early stages when it became clear that the Verdun forts could more advantageously be abandoned than defended: as an exposed salient wedged into German-held territory they weakened rather than strengthened the French front as a whole. But it was already too late for any such calculation: the forts had become a symbol beyond any strategical reckoning, and the more Frenchmen were lost in their defense—thus further proving their military disutility—the more impossible it was to confess the futility of all previous losses by an advantageous withdrawal. In such cases the successful defense persists at a cost that may emerge in future failure. And indeed after Verdun the French army was so badly weakened that the next major offensive in 1917 provoked widespread mutinies. The lingering effect of Verdun was still being felt two decades later in the fatal shrinkage of the French army that faced Hitler.

So it was again at Stalingrad, where the Germans consumed the strength of the Luftwaffe in the futile attempt to supply the encircled Sixth Army of Von Paulus during its eight weeks of resistance under siege that ended on February 2, 1943. Had there been no air supply at all, had the resistance failed at an early stage, the Luftwaffe might have been saved for more useful duties, and many German troops might have broken through the siege lines (quite thin at first) to fight another day. Such encirclements and breakouts were almost a routine of the entire campaign, but the name of Stalingrad affixed to those square miles of ruins had become a symbol that Hitler would not surrender, until the decision was taken out of his hands by the capitulation of the generals on the scene.

Even the postwar years included a dramatic case of a defense that exceeded the culminating point of success: of the French at Dien Bien Phu in Indochina. Dropped by air in November 1953 into contested territory in northwest Vietnam, elite French troops withstood the initial Vietminh attacks so well that the exotic name of Dien Bien Phu instantly acquired a heroic resonance—a unique distinction in a confused, confusing, and most unpopular war. As the Vietminh gathered round in ever greater strength, the garrison held out for 112 days until May 7, 1954, claiming steady reinforcements by the best troops of the French army, brought in by aircraft that had to fly straight into the fire of antiaircraft guns. Originally meant as a limited, strictly practical operation, whose modest aim was to oppose Vietminh infiltration into Laos, the defense of Dien Bien Phu instead absorbed a ruinously disproportionate effort, which could not be interrupted because the place had acquired so much symbolic value in the eyes of the French public. When the besieged garrison was at last overrun, the entire French enterprise of Vietnam was repudiated by public and politicians alike; Vietnam might not have been abandoned so soon or so precipitously, if the paratroopers who first landed on November 20–21, 1953, had not succeeded so well in their combat of the first few days.[14]

In strategy's dynamic paradox, a defense as much as an offensive can be too successful. It can evolve into a wider failure, whether in defending outposts, in protecting fleets that technical advances are making insecure, or in preserving any other military instrument that emotions and institutional interests transform from servant to master.

4

The Coming Together of Opposites

We have encountered the workings of the dynamic paradox and the ensuing reversals at the technical and tactical levels; we have yet to consider the middle levels of strategy, but it is enlightening at this point to ascend briefly to the level of grand strategy, where each particular matter interacts with the entire predicament of conflict.

The warlike dealings of national leaders and governments with one another are subject to exactly the same logic of strategy as the interactions of their fighting forces. But it is far more difficult for national leaders to understand that logic beneath all the complications of the multiple levels of an entire war. Besides, national leaders can rarely apply whatever strategical insight they may have. To preserve their power and authority within their own societies, democratic leaders must obey the linear logic of consensual politics. That means, for example, that they cannot act paradoxically to surprise external enemies, because they must inform and prepare their public before acting. Nor can they deviate from the conventions of the time and place without a loss of authority. In any case, a conscious understanding of the phenomena of strategy is a great rarity among political leaders, whose talent is precisely to understand and guide public opinion, itself wedded to a commonsense logic that is very different from the paradoxical logic of strategy. They can still win wars of course, but only by mobilizing superior resources, being condemned to failure whenever they lack material superiority. There are exceptions however. Winston Churchill is the most notable modern example—a rather marginal politician in peacetime significantly enough, but a premier strategist in wartime—quite aside from his role as an inspiring leader. His specifically strategical talents, moreover, can be precisely documented.

In the earlier discussion of the contest between the British Bomber Command and German air defenses, we examined only its technical and tactical aspects. But both were of course encompassed by the predicament of each side at the level of grand strategy. The British bombardment of Germany, at first only against carefully selected military and industrial targets remote from cities, was precipitated by the initial successes of the German forces in May 1940—their swift invasions of Holland and Belgium. Thus among the paradoxical first fruits of an advance that had not yet reached the culminating point of success, Germany experienced its first air attacks. When the Werhmacht most unexpectedly rapidly defeated France as well, driving the British army from the continent in June 1940, it deprived the British government of any means of waging war except by air. And because German air defenses inflicted disastrous losses on aircraft attempting to bomb specific military and industrial targets in daylight, Bomber Command had to fly at night, when its aircraft could hit no target smaller than a fairly large city. Thus the paradoxical reward that the Germans obtained for the victory of their army, and the effectiveness of their fighters and antiaircraft artillery in daylight interception, was the beginning of the destruction of German cities.

The rising curve of British success in that longest of all the campaigns of the Second World War started off from the lowest point of national failure. In August 1940, the Royal Navy was cowering in distant Scapa Flow in fear of German air strikes, the British army was hoping only to defend England's beaches, and the Royal Air Force was so badly damaged by the Luftwaffe's bombing of its airfields that it actually welcomed the first (accidental) German bombing of London on August 24, 1940.[1]

On the following night, Bomber Command carried out its first raid on Berlin, even though it was not until July 1941 that the expedient of night bombing—which necessarily meant city bombing—became deliberate policy. As Britain's industrial and military mobilization was steadily accelerating, yielding more bombers and trained aircrew ready at the takeoff line for each successive raid; and as the curve of success was rising with little effective German reaction, acceptable loss rates, and no culminating point in sight, Charles Portal, marshal of the Royal Air Force and chief of the Air Staff, offered a plan for a straightforward progression toward victory by bombardment alone: forty-three selected German cities and towns, containing a combined population of some fifteen million people and the largest part of German war industry, were to be bombed heavily in six successive strikes each, to leave them "beyond all hope of recovery."

In submitting his plan to Prime Minister Winston Churchill on September 25, 1941, Portal suggested that with four thousand first-line aircraft, Bomber Command could "break" Germany in six months.[2] Characteristically, the plan was based on detailed calculations, in the style of an engineer designing a bridge over an unresisting river, with no calculation whatever of the enemy's likely reactions. For example, the amount of destruction required in the forty-three cities was not set arbitrarily but rather carefully calculated on the basis of an "index of activity," itself based on statistics collected in the wake of the German bombing of British industrial towns. After each bombing raid, factory production would suffer because of interruptions in the gas, water, and electricity supply; workers would absent themselves from fear, fatigue, or lack of food, breakdowns in public transport, and the general disruption of urban life. A given tonnage of bombs per unit of population would reduce the index of activity to a given residual percentage: in the case of Coventry, for example, the index fell to 63 percent on the day after the massed German bombing of November 14, 1940, in which one ton of bombs was dropped per every eight hundred people. Then a gradual recovery would begin, but if further attacks were made, the index would each time start increasing from a lower and lower base. Eventually, after the fourth, fifth, or sixth bombing raid, the index would be reduced to zero, and war production would completely cease.

The plan, moreover, was admirably conservative in all its assumptions. No fewer than six attacks, delivering one ton of bombs per eight hundred inhabitants would be made on each of the forty-three cities and towns. So generous was the allowance made for navigational errors, technical aborts, and intercepts that a mere 25 percent of the aircraft were expected to reach their targets; and each sixteen-aircraft squadron was assumed to fly only one hundred sorties per month in all (substantially less than actual rates), while the unit bomb load was modestly set at three tons per aircraft. Two hundred and fifty squadrons would therefore be needed on line during the six months of the campaign, for a grand total of four thousand bombers.

In a classic case of linear-logical thinking, the plan implicitly assumed that the Germans would neither dramatically increase their modest air-defense effort, nor disperse their war industries, even as they were systematically destroyed. Portal and his subordinates were not fools, and no doubt if individually summoned to reflect on the matter, they would have repudiated any conception of war that ignored the enemy's entire creative energy and will of self-protection. But consider the circumstances and emotional urgencies of the time: in September 1941, when the plan was submitted to Churchill, the Germans were sweeping all before them in Russia, smashing defense lines and entire armies week by week, rounding up prisoners by the hundreds of thousands. Only memories of Napoleon's fate stood against the hard facts that suggested an imminent Soviet collapse. Nor was there any sign of significant armed resistance to the German occupiers anywhere in Europe. In the United States, a modest rearmament was under way, but public opinion was largely opposed to intervention in the war—as it would continue to be until the Japanese decided otherwise by attacking Pearl Harbor.

As for Britain, it was entirely unrealistic to hope that the British army would ever be able to land on the continent of Europe with forces large enough to avoid prompt defeat—while Rommel's fighting in North Africa showed that only a vast material superiority could prevail over the German army's high morale, superior skills, and talented officers. If Hitler won his Russian war, as he had won his wars of Poland, Denmark, Norway, Belgium, the Netherlands, France, Yugoslavia, and Greece, only the Royal Air Force would stand in his path when he would turn back from the east to finish off Britain—after first strengthening the Luftwaffe with the vast resources that his conquests and the army's demobilization could provide. The year before, the Royal Air Force had won a defensive victory in the skies of Britain but only by a thin margin—and that too against German fighters and bombers that had just fought against France and were quite unprepared for the totally different conditions of the Battle of Britain. No such luck could be expected in a second battle of Britain, for which the Germans would prepare properly, after defeating Russia. Once the Luftwaffe was organized for the task, the Royal Air Force would be gradually destroyed in a futile struggle to prevent British cities from being bombed into ruins, before the inevitable invasion that would bring the new order of the Gestapo, SS, and concentration camp in its wake. Even if the Soviet Union somehow survived, which then seemed most improbable, and a protracted war ensued, saving Britain from invasion, only the Royal Air Force would be left to serve as a valid military instrument to bring the war to some acceptable conclusion. Hence Sir Charles Portal and his colleagues of the Royal Air Force—until recently distinctly the junior service—found themselves in a position of unexpected importance, inspiring perhaps but of such enormous responsibility as to be viewed with awe, if not terror. In that vortex of emotions, of pride, hope, and the deepest anxiety, it was natural to seek a way through the dark woods by following a systematic plan, in whose mechanics they could absorb themselves and whose precise arithmetic offered relief from the dreadful uncertainties of the hour.

Winston Churchill inhabited exactly the same circumstances, and as a man of strong and uninhibited feelings he must have been subject to that same emotional vortex, compounded by his far greater personal responsibility. It was his refusal to accept Hitler's peace proposals of June 1940 that had caused 93,000 British civilian men, women, and children to die in the ensuing bombings. It was his policy that left Britain in sinister isolation, facing the almost certain prospect of invasion as soon as Germany completed the defeat of Russia. A parliamentary rejection of his leadership, his replacement by more reasonable men who could better parley with Hitler, a negotiated British admission into Europe's New Order, his exile to die in obscurity or perhaps under arrest are all black fantasies today, but they were sober possibilities in September 1941, as the contemporary evidence shows.[3]

For Churchill, too, a successful campaign by Bomber Command was the only possible instrument of salvation—national, political, even personal. And yet, in a triumph of strategic insight that overcame all the emotional turbulence and cut across all technical complexities, Winston Churchill's reply to Portal (1) decisively refuted the proposition that war could be won by bombardment alone ("all that we have learned since the war began, shows that its effects, both physical and moral, are greatly exaggerated"); (2) anticipated the coming German defensive reaction to the modest amount of bombing already under way, *specifically* forecasting the introduction of effective night fighters to counter night bombing; (3) therefore expected that the current campaign would fail as Germany reacted ("it seems very likely that the ground defenses and night fighters will *overtake* the Air attack,") as indeed they did after mid-1942; (4) predicted that if British area bombing *were* to become successful, the Germans would disperse and decentralize the war industries, rather than passively accept their cumulative destruction ("all things are always on the move simultaneously [the source of the dynamic paradox], and it is quite possible that the Nazi war-making power in 1943 will be so widely spread throughout Europe as to be to a large extent independent of the actual buildings in the homeland"); and (5) warned against the treachery of precise numbers in calculations that could not possibly include the great unknown variable of the enemy's reaction ("I deprecate . . . expressing that confidence [in the plan] in terms of arithmetic").

Churchill concluded with these words: "One has to do the best one can, but he is an unwise man who thinks that there is any *certain* method of winning this war, or any other war, between equals in strength. The only plan is to persevere."[4]

Bomber Command was Britain's sole offensive instrument, and it did receive high priority for scarce high-quality manpower and industrial production. But it never attained a strength of 4,000 bombers on line—at its peak, in April 1945, it had 1,609 first-line bombers[5]—because Portal's suggestion that the army and navy be reduced for its sake was firmly rejected. It is interesting to note that, after the entry of the United States into the war and the arrival of its Eighth Air Force on the scene, a plan of systematic bombardment was actually implemented in 1943. That plan, moreover, not only violated the logic of strategy by ignoring the enemy's defensive reaction, but also aspired to high efficiency by focusing the bombing effort on just one industrial sector, thus ignoring the enemy's industrial response as well.

Because their B-17 bombers were heavily armed with eleven machine guns apiece, the leaders of the Eighth Air Force were convinced that they could protect themselves against German fighters by forming mutually protective formations, without need of fighter escorts or the cover of the night. They decided to bomb in daylight in order to be able to hit specific industrial targets, as opposed to the random city bombing of Bomber Command. Their raids, moreover, would obtain a high output for the bombing input by attacking specific "bottlenecks" in Germany's war industry as a whole. The British Ministry of Economic Warfare had long advocated just such an approach, and it had identified an ideal target in the Schweinfurt factories that reportedly produced two-thirds of all German ball bearings. Because each tank and truck, every engine for aircraft, ships, or submarines, indeed virtually all machinery of any kind that had moving parts, required ball bearings, the ministry had long claimed that the destruction of the Schweinfurt factories would cause a colossal decline in German war capacity across the board.[6] Air Marshal Arthur Harris, chief of Bomber Command, ridiculed such schemes; scathingly referring to "panacea" targets, he declared that the target experts "went completely mad" over the ball bearings.[7] One wag who agreed with Harris suggested that perhaps it was shoelace factories that should be destroyed, forcing the Germans to surrender once they could no longer keep boots on their feet. The Eighth Air Force, however, was rigidly committed to precision daylight bombing; and because its strength could not grow quickly enough to make much of an impact by industry-wide bombing, the narrowly focused bottleneck approach was attractive to its leaders.

In the event, the Eighth Air Force first bombed the Schweinfurt ball-bearing factories on August 17, 1943, and then again on October 14. Its concept of unescorted, self-defending, bomber formations flying in broad daylight met its test, failing decisively. In spite of their eleven machine guns apiece, the bombers did so poorly against German fighters that their losses exceeded any sustainable level: 60 out of 376 American bombers were shot down in the first raid, and 77 out of 291 in the second.[8]

As for the damage inflicted, it was not insignificant—but the impact on Germany's war capacity certainly was. Ball bearings already in stock and some imports from Sweden and Switzerland supplied immediate needs; full production was soon restarted, and slide bearings were substituted in many uses, circumventing the potential bottleneck.[9] Thus the narrowly specialized attack on Schweinfurt stimulated a broad organizational reaction that defeated its purpose, just as the large warships of the past had neutralized the highly specialized torpedo boat, and modern armored forces have evolved to cope with the antitank missile.

While the specific response to precision bombing was decentralization and substitution, the wider German reaction to the intensification of bombing in general was to restructure the entire economy in order to maximize war production—a "total-war economy" in Nazi language. That was a response that the Americans and British could not possibly have anticipated in 1942, because of the universal belief that the German economy was already fully mobilized for war and had been even before the outbreak of war in 1939. With compulsory universal labor enforced in Britain since 1940, and with all nonessential trades and services eliminated or severely restricted, it was never imagined that until mid-1943 most German women were still at home, that there were more than a million domestic servants, and that such nonessential trades as bookbinding were still thriving. Having quite deliberately started the war, Hitler could not demand extreme sacrifices from the German people—and the state of the German war economy reflected that fundamental political reality. It was only from February 1943 that a full mobilization began, in the wake of the Stalingrad defeat with its catastrophic losses. Once German energies were more fully harnessed, the output of military equipment and supplies rose sharply and kept increasing, so that the rising tonnage of bombs dropped on Germany during 1944 coincided with a steady increase in the volume of war production.

But it was not only coincidence: in some ways, the bombing itself contributed to war production by destroying the social framework of the leisurely days of peace. With restaurants bombed out, much more efficient canteens became the only alternative. With houses destroyed and their residents evacuated, house servants were forced into war production, as were shopkeepers, craftsmen, and clerical employees. This shift too allowed the broad German war economy to outmaneuver the narrow phenomenon of bombing.

The story is well known and has been recounted many times.[10] It is a classic case of seemingly definitive and systematically cumulative "linear" action not only impeded but also in part made self-defeating by the very nature of the strategic predicament. Churchill was of course exceptional in his intuitive understanding of the paradoxical logic of strategy, with its perversion of every logical action and its recurring reversals of opposites. (The title of the concluding volume of his war memoirs is *Triumph and Tragedy;* it could have been "victory and defeat.") But there is no need of Churchills to cause grand strategy to exist. Just as the laws of physics governed the universe long before there were physicists to study them, so those who command nations in war are subject to the logic of strategy even if they know nothing of strategy. Whether their decisions are made in wisdom or folly, in criminal ambition or sincere benevolence, whether they are praised or condemned in the aftermath, the *consequences* of what they do or fail to do are determined by the paradoxical logic, disappointing all expectations of continuity, all hopes of linear progression.

From War to Peace, from Peace to War

War may be the great evil, but it does have a great virtue. By consuming and destroying the material and moral resources needed to keep fighting, war prevents its own continuation. Instead, as with any other action within the paradoxical realm of strategy, war must eventually turn into its opposite after passing a culminating point. That opposite may be only a becalmed passivity, an unrecognized state of nonwar rather than a negotiated peace, an armistice, or even a temporary cease-fire. And whatever nonwar it is, that result may not be reached for a very long time, because the speed with which war destroys itself obviously depends on its intensity and scale. In civil wars, the intensity of the fighting is often low, the scale small, with violence localized within a wider environment that the fighting might affect only marginally if at all. In Sri Lanka, civil war has continued for decades in the north, while foreign tourists continue to frequent tranquil beaches in the south. In Sudan, the fighting has been limited to the south, and there too it has mostly been seasonal. Civil wars can therefore last for decades. No intense, large-scale war can last for many years, let alone decades, and some have burned themselves out in weeks or even days.

War can become the origin of peace by the total victory of one side or another, by the sheer exhaustion of both, or—more often—because the conflict of aims that originally caused the war is resolved by the transformations that war itself brings about. As the fighting continues, the worth of whatever was to be gained or defended is reconsidered against its costs in blood, treasure, and agony, eventually diminishing or nullifying the ambitions that motivated war in the first place.

That is not, however, a straightforward process, because the political commitment to go to war is self-strengthening. Having started the fight hoping to gain something of value at acceptable cost, the attacker who collides with unexpectedly strong resistance might persist even as the full gain he hoped for cannot compensate for what he has lost in blood, treasure, tranquillity, and prestige. Having started to fight by another's choice, the defender will also have framed some initial purpose for his resistance—a purpose deemed worthy of sacrifice, before the full extent of that sacrifice could be known. Even when the original hopes of attack or defense are disappointed, as so often happens, success may yet seem tantalizingly near, perhaps to be won with just one more fight, a few more casualties, a little more wealth expended after so many casualties suffered and after so much wealth consumed (the asymmetrical position of those who face the loss of everything in defeat obviously strengthens their resistance). It may have been the prospect of gaining much for little that originally made war attractive. But if the costs of war are unexpectedly large, their very magnitude will be an incentive to persist during an intermediate stage: the greater the sacrifices already made, the greater the need to justify them by finally achieving the aim. During that stage, the behavior of belligerents is conditioned by the political stance of the original war party or war leader, whose fortunes will depend on how past responsibility for having started the war is viewed—which in turn depends on the present view of the future outcome. The incentive to sustain the hope of victory is then very strong.

But as the war continues, perspectives eventually shift. The results originally hoped for are increasingly compared not to the sacrifices already made, but rather to the further sacrifices that seem likely if the fighting does not end. Even if the original war party or war leader remains in power, their ambitions can be diminished or even extinguished, to the point where they may give up all hope of gain, being content to moderate their loss. As that process unfolds, hostilities can eventually come to an end, as the aims of each side become congruent instead of being mutually exclusive. Even the Pacific war, a most peculiar struggle between Japanese aggressors with large but not unlimited aims and their erstwhile American victims at Pearl Harbor and the Philippines who demanded unconditional surrender, only came to an end when the Americans tacitly accepted the minimal Japanese demand for the continuity of the imperial institution and the less minimal demand of Emperor Hirohito for impunity.

War fully achieved, with forces fought out and every promising expedient tried, with much destruction suffered and inflicted, with hopes of greater success finally spent, may lead to a peace that *can* be stable. But if war is interrupted before its self-destruction is achieved, no peace need ensue at all. So it was in Europe's past when wars were still fought intermittently during spring and summer campaigning seasons, each time coming to an end with the arrival of winter—only to resume afresh in the spring. And so it has been again ever since the establishment of the United Nations (UN) and the formalization of Great Power politics in its Security Council.

Since 1945, wars among lesser powers have rarely been allowed to follow their natural course. Instead, they have typically been interrupted long before they could burn out the energies of war to establish the preconditions of peace. It has become the fixed routine of the permanent members of the UN Security Council to abruptly stop the combat of lesser powers by ordering cease-fires. Unless further diplomatic interventions directly ensue to impose peace negotiations as well, cease-fires merely relieve war-induced exhaustion, favoring the reconstitution and rearming of the belligerents, thus intensifying and prolonging the fighting once the cease-fire comes to an end. That was true of the Arab-Israeli war of 1948–49, which might have ended in a matter of weeks by sheer exhaustion, if two successive cease-fires ordained by the UN Security Council had not allowed the belligerents to recuperate till they were ready to resume fighting. It was so again after the disintegration of Yugoslavia in 1991. Dozens of imposed UN cease-fires interrupted the fighting between Serbs and Croats in the Krajina borderlands, between the forces of the Serb-Montenegrin federation and the Croat army, and among the Serbs, Croats, and Muslims of Bosnia. Each time, the belligerents exploited the pause to recruit, train, and equip additional forces for further combat. Indeed, it was under the protection of successive cease-fires that both the Croats and the Bosnian Muslims were able to build up their own armed forces to confront the well-armed Serbs. That is an outcome that many may have found desirable, but the overall effect was to greatly prolong the war and widen the scope of its killings, atrocities, and destructions.

It has also become routine to interrupt wars in more lasting fashion by imposing armistices. Again, unless directly followed by successful peace negotiations, armistices perpetuate the state of war indefinitely because they shield the weaker side from the consequences of refusing the concessions needed for peace. Fearing no further defeats or territorial losses behind the indirect protection of the great powers that guarantee the armistice, the losing side can deny peace to the winning side, and even attack its lands in deniable ways by infiltrating raiders and guerillas. Armistices in themselves are not way stations to peace but rather frozen wars. They are therefore the strongest possible incentive to endlessly prolonged competitive arms races, as in the case of India and Pakistan and the two Koreas to this day.

Nevertheless, as long as the Cold War persisted, cease-fires and armistices imposed by the United States and the Soviet Union acting in concert had a compelling justification. At a time when both countries were greatly inclined to intervene in the wars of lesser powers to avert the defeat of their respective clients, U.S. and Soviet leaders prudently preferred to act jointly stop the fighting in many cases. That made competitive interventions unnecessary, avoiding the eventual danger of a direct clash between American and Soviet forces that could escalate to the nuclear level. While the imposed cease-fires of the Cold War years ultimately increased the sum total of warfare among the lesser powers themselves, and armistices did perpetuate the state of war among them, both were clearly the lesser evil from a global point of view, as compared to the possibility of a globally catastrophic Soviet-American war caused by reciprocal interventions.

After the Cold War by contrast, neither Americans nor Russians had any inclination to intervene *competitively* in the wars of lesser powers. The United States acted with many allies to reverse Iraq's conquest of Kuwait of August 1990. The Russian Federation for its part has sent combat forces as well as weapons in support of one side or the other in Caucasian and Central Asian wars and insurgencies. Neither, however, has acted specifically to thwart the other, and neither now seems ready to contemplate armed interventions against the other. And the same is true of such other Great Powers as can still be said to exist. It follows that the evil consequences of interrupting war still persist in full, while no greater danger is being averted.

In the absence of anything resembling a classic Great Power competition, cease-fires and armistices are now generally imposed on lesser powers multilaterally, for essentially disinterested motives—often, indeed, for no better reason than the revulsion of television audiences exposed to harrowing scenes of war. Of course the result is to ensure that there will be many more such scenes.

It is well known that disinterested behavior, not guided by self-interested calculations, randomizes outcomes. What is now happening, however, is typically much worse than a scattering of random outcomes, because cease-fires and armistices imposed on warring lesser powers *systematically* prevent the transformation of war into peace. The Dayton accords of November 1995 are typical of the kind: they condemn Bosnia to remain divided into three rival armed camps, with combat suspended between the Croats, Muslims, and Serbs, but with the state of war indefinitely prolonged. Because no side is threatened by defeat and loss, no side has a sufficient incentive to negotiate peace; because no path to peace is even visible, the dominant priority is to prepare for another war rather than to reconstruct devastated economies and ravaged societies. The outcome of uninterrupted war would certainly have been unjust from one perspective or another but would eventually have imposed some sort of peace, allowing people to rebuild their lives and communities.

At this writing, in addition to the United Nations a series of multilateral organizations make it their business to intervene in other peoples' wars. Their common, inherent, characteristic is that they insert themselves in war situations while refusing to engage in combat. That greatly adds to the damage.

The dominant priority of UN "peace-keeping" contingents is to avoid casualties to themselves. Their unit commanders therefore habitually appease the *locally* stronger belligerent, accepting its dictates, tolerating its abuses. If the totality of UN peace-keeping forces in a given context would appease the stronger side, for example the Bosnian Serbs in the early stages of the Bosnia fighting, the result could be conducive to peace. For in that case, the UN presence would actually enhance the peace-making potential of war, by helping the strong to defeat the weak that much faster and more decisively. Unfortunately, the appeasement that is inevitable when forces that do not want to fight are thrust into war situations, is neither homogeneous nor strategically purposeful. Instead, it merely reflects the determination of each UN contingent to avoid confrontations and casualties to itself. As each unit appeases the locally stronger side, the overall result is to prevent the emergence of any coherent *im*balance of strength capable of ending the fighting.

Nor can UN contingents determined to avoid combat protect civilians caught up in the fighting or deliberately attacked. At best, UN peace-keeping forces remain the passive spectators of violence and outright massacres, as in Bosnia and Rwanda. At worst, they collaborate in massacre, as Dutch UN troops did in the Srebenica enclave in July 1995, by helping the Bosnian Serbs to separate the men of military age (broadly defined) from women and children; all were killed.

At the same time, the very presence of UN forces inhibits the normal remedy of endangered civilians, which is to escape from the combat zone. Deluded into thinking that they will be protected, civilians in danger remain in place until it is too late to flee. Moreover, prospective host countries deny war-refugee status to civilians coming from areas where UN troops are supposedly keeping the peace—even though they are entirely failing to shield civilians under attack. In the specific case of the siege of Sarajevo in 1992–1994, appeasement interacted with the pretense of protection in an especially perverse way: UN personnel strictly inspected outgoing flights to prevent the escape of Sarajevo civilians in obedience to a cease-fire agreement negotiated with the locally dominant Bosnian Serbs—who for their part habitually violated that cease-fire.

Institutions such as the former Western European Union and the Organization of Security and Cooperation in Europe lack even the UN's rudimentary command structure and have no assigned, let alone organic, military forces of their own. Yet they too seek to intervene in warlike situations, with predictable consequences. Bereft of forces even theoretically capable of combat, they satisfy interventionist urges mandated by member states, or even motivated by their own institutional ambitions, by sending lightly armed or unarmed policemen, gendarmes, or simply "observers." All of the latter must necessarily act as UN peace-keeping troops habitually do, only more so, by accommodating the wishes of the locally stronger side. And of course they cannot even try to protect endangered civilians, while their presence again inhibits the private remedy of flight.

Warlike organizations such as the North Atlantic Treaty Organization (NATO) and the Economic Community of West African States Cease-Fire Monitoring Group (ECOMOG), which presided over the chaos of Liberia and Sierra Leone, are potentially capable of stopping warfare. Their interventions also have destructive consequences by prolonging the state of war but should at least protect civilians from the consequences of the wars they are prolonging. Even that fails to happen, however. Multinational military commands engaged in disinterested interventions that do not justify casualties to their own forces avoid risks at all costs. That is true of Third World forces, whose assignment to the UN is largely a matter of gaining generous monetary compensation for poorly armed, poorly trained, and poorly paid soldiers (who often recoup themselves by looting or black-market trafficking). But it is also true of the best-trained and best-paid forces of the most ambitious armies. When U.S. troops arrived in Bosnia in the wake of the 1995 Dayton accords, they were under strict orders to avoid armed clashes, and it was under those orders that in subsequent years they failed to arrest known war criminals passing through their checkpoints. More broadly, because no differences in troop performance can be admitted, multinational commands are institutionally incapable of exercising quality control over the troops offered by member states, and neither can they impose uniform standards of tactical or ethical conduct. Deliberately risk-minimizing policies aside, the conjoined deployment of potentially combat-capable and hopelessly ineffectual troops tends to reduce the performance of all troops involved to the lowest common denominator. That was even true of otherwise fine British troops in Bosnia before 1995 and of otherwise vigorous Nigerian marines in Sierra Leone. Soon even quasi-elite troops adopt passive, self-protective tactics that prevent them from actually keeping the peace or protecting civilians.

The phenomenon of "multinationally induced troop degradation" can rarely be documented as such, though its consequences have been abundantly visible in the litter of the dead, mutilated, raped, and tortured that attends UN interventions. But sometimes the true state of affairs is powerfully illuminated by the rare exception, such as when the vigorous Danish tank unit in Bosnia promptly replied to each episode of firing against it in 1993–94, quickly stopping all attacks. If the pattern of degradation into ineffectual passivity were not so normal, such a case of combat troops acting as combat troops would not have attracted attention. The record of the ECOMOG troops in Sierra Leone has by contrast included over the years frequent routs at the hands of small bands of rebel child soldiers, many episodes of organized looting directed by unit commanders themselves, countless rapes, and some summary executions, but no protection of civilians under attack.

The most disinterested of all interventions in other people's wars are humanitarian relief activities. They are also the most destructive.

The largest and most protracted, and still continuing, humanitarian intervention in all of human history is the United Nations Relief and Works Agency (UNRWA). On the model of its predecessor, the United Nations Relief and Rehabilitation Agency (UNRRA), which was then still op-

erating displaced persons' camps in Europe, UNRWA was originally established during the 1948–49 Arab-Israeli war. Its mission was to feed, shelter, educate, and provide health services to Arab refugees who had fled
from Israeli zones in the former territory of Palestine to other parts of
Palestine under Egyptian or Jordanian control (the Gaza strip and the
West Bank) or to Lebanon, Syria, and Trans-Jordan, as it then was.

By keeping refugees alive in Spartan conditions that encouraged their
rapid emigration or local resettlement, UNRRA's camps in Europe served
to absorb postwar resentments. By policy, nationalities were mixed, to
prevent the emergence of groups bent on revenge under wartime leaders,
many of them inevitably ex-collaborators with the Germans. Not truly
because of any Arab state policies let alone any ideological patriotism, but
simply because UNRWA camps provided a higher standard of living than
most Arab villagers had previously enjoyed, with an assured and more
varied diet, organized schooling, infinitely superior medical care, and no
backbreaking labor in stony fields, they instantly became desirable homes
rather than eagerly abandoned transit camps. They thus turned escaping
civilians into lifelong refugees, who gave birth to refugee children, who
grew up in turn to have refugee children of their own.

During more than a half-century of operation to date, UNRWA thus
perpetuated a Palestinian refugee nation, perfectly preserving its resentments in as fresh a condition as they were in 1948, keeping the first bloom
of vengeful emotions intact. The young were not allowed to find their
own way to new lives; instead they were kept under the control of their
defeated elders, to be taught their duties of revenge and reconquest in
UNRWA-financed schools from the earliest childhood. By its very existence,
UNRWA dissuades integration into local societies and inhibits emigration,
but in addition the mere concentration of Palestinians in the camps has
always facilitated the voluntary or forced enlistment of refugee youths by
armed organizations that have fought both Israel and each other. In these
different ways, UNWRA has greatly contributed to half a century of Arab-
Israeli violence, and still now powerfully retards the advent of peace.

Had each European war been attended by its own postwar UNWRA,
equipped to provide a higher standard of living than the ambient, today's
Europe would be filled with giant camps for tens of millions of descendants of uprooted Gallo-Romans, abandoned Vandals, defeated Burgun-
dians, and misplaced Visigoths—not to speak of more recent refugee nations such as post-1945 Sudeten Germans. Europe would have remained
a purely geographic expression, a mosaic of warring tribes undigested and
unreconciled in their separate feeding camps. And the number of unre-

solved conflicts would roughly correspond to the total number of wars ever fought.

UNWRA is not unique, having had various counterparts elsewhere, such as the Cambodian refugee camps along the Thai border, which incidentally provided safe bases for the mass-murdering Khmer Rouge. But because UN activities are mercifully limited by ungenerous national contributions to its treasury, their sabotage of peace is at least localized. That is not true of the proliferation of feverishly competitive Non-Government Organizations (NGOs) that nowadays seek war refugees to help. The absolute, existential priority of NGOs is to keep attracting charitable contributions. Their principal means of doing so is to promote their activities in high-visibility situations. Only the most dramatic natural disasters attract any significant mass-media attention, and even then only briefly. After an earthquake or flood, the cameras soon depart to record the next disaster. War refugees by contrast can attract sustained mass-media attention if kept conveniently concentrated in reasonably accessible camps. Because regular forms of warfare among well-organized belligerents in more developed areas offer few opportunities for NGOs, they naturally focus their efforts elsewhere, aiding war refugees in the poorest parts of the world, especially in Africa. There, the feeding, shelter, and health care offered, while perhaps abysmal by global standards, are sufficient to keep refugees in place perpetually. The consequences are entirely predictable. Among many lesser examples, the huge refugee camps established along the Congo-Zaire border with Rwanda in the wake of the 1994 genocide of Tutsis by the Hutu, which was followed by the Tutsi conquest of Rwanda, stand out as a particularly egregious case. NGOs that answered to no authority sustained a Hutu nation in exile that would otherwise have dispersed to find a myriad of private destinies in the vastness of Zaire. The presence of a million or so Hutus still under their genocidal leaders made the consolidation of Rwanda impossible. Armed Hutu activists, fed by NGOs along with everyone else, kept the other refugees under oppressive control, enlisting, training, and arming their young to raid across the Rwanda border to kill more Tutsis.

To keep refugee nations in existence forever, to fuel unending conflict by artificially preserved resentments, is bad enough. But to insert material aid into combat situations is even worse. Many NGOs that operate in an odor of sanctity routinely supply the logistics of war. Themselves defenseless, they cannot exclude active warriors from their feeding stations, clinics, and such shelter as they provide. Refugees are presumptively on the losing side, the warriors among them in retreat. By intervening to help them, NGOs systematically impede the progress of their enemies toward a decisive victory that can bring war to an end. Impartial to a fault, NGOs sometimes help both sides, thus also sabotaging the transformation of war into peace by mutual exhaustion.

When especially threatened, moreover, as in Somalia through the 1990s but less visibly in other places too, NGOs purchase security from local war bands, often the very same bands that threaten them. No recondite strategic calculation is needed to uncover the result: unless the totality of their payments are insignificantly small—which was definitely not true of Somalia—NGOs themselves prolong the warfare whose consequences they seek to mitigate.

Almost all wars nowadays become endemic conflicts that never end, because the transformative effects of both decisive victories and exhaustion are blocked by outside interventions of one kind or another. Thus the evils of war persist, but without the compensation of eventually compelling peace.

Even when fought with spears or clubs, war could always be totally destructive for the participants, to the point of causing the extinction of entire human communities. But until the advent of nuclear weapons, it was possible to be optimistic about the destructions that an intended war might cause. The gains promised by war might be seen in sharp, idealized relief against the dull background of its potential losses, which could easily be expected to be tolerable, almost insignificant. By the normal workings of the paradoxical logic of strategy, nuclear weapons have remained unused ever since they evolved from the extreme destructive power of the very first fission devices (whose energy was equivalent to ten or twenty thousand tons of conventional explosive), to the altogether greater destructive power of thermonuclear weapons, whose energy output is equivalent to millions of tons of conventional explosive—without reckoning the destructive power of radiation. No more than anything else in strategy, the utility of explosives could not increase in linear continuity. The ten-ton loads of American and British bombers in 1944–45 were certainly more useful than the two-ton loads of 1940 German bombers, and hundred-ton or even thousand-ton bomb loads could have been more useful still had they been feasible. But the destructive power of thermonuclear weapons overshoots by far the culminating point of military utility. In the right circumstances, they can therefore achieve the peace-inducing effects of war without need of actual combat.

It is true that in comparing envisaged gains and possible sacrifices when deciding to start a war, the scope of the possible damage that could be suffered may still be clouded by uncertainty. Even powers amply supplied with nuclear weapons can plan to fight without them. But it is not possible to minimize the destructive consequences of any nuclear war in the way that the consequences of cavalry incursions, sieges, or even conventional bombing raids could be minimized in the past. Animal optimism, and the perceptual asymmetry between war gains vividly imagined and war losses dimly feared, both require hopeful uncertainty. It is the definitive, measurable, character of nuclear destruction rather than its possible magnitude that inhibits nuclear war. This quality of scientific predictability has altered the millennial terms of comparison between the worth of victory and its cost. In the presence of nuclear weapons, the perceptual balance that was once achieved only *during* war, once its costs were experienced in the flesh, is now present before it begins, preventing any nuclear war, so far at least.

Peace can be the origin of war in different ways, even though peace is only a negative abstraction that cannot contain any self-destructive phenomenon, as war contains the destruction that eventually destroys war itself. Nevertheless, the condition of peace, that is the absence of war, can create the precondition of war, for example by dissuading the peaceful from maintaining persuasive defenses, encouraging potential aggressors to plan war. Often in history, peace led to war because its conditions allowed demographic, cultural, economic, and social changes that upset the balance of strength that had previously assured peace. Having no substance of its own, the state of peace cannot disturb anything, but it does indifferently favor the diverging evolution of human capacities and mentalities, without regard to the factors that inhibited war. It was thus that the famously pacific Germans came to regard themselves as a warrior nation by 1870, in unfortunate symmetry with the French, who had yet to outgrow their martial self-image. In the crisis of that year, Bismarck's German government wanted war in confidence of victory, while the French government of Napoleon III could not avoid war, because it could not admit that Germany had become the stronger power.

The transformation of mentalities that creates war-inducing tensions between the current status of a country and its self-image, must have profound causes. But the effect is obvious: what was once considered acceptable becomes an intolerable vexation; the prestige once judged sufficient becomes a felt humiliation; what was once an impossible dream is viewed as a perfectly realistic aim. It was during the long post-Napoleonic peace that war-inhibiting military balances between the Great Powers were overthrown by the iron, coal, and steam engines of the industrial revolution. They yielded new, war-inducing balances between Prussia and the Hapsburg Empire by 1866; between Prussia and France by 1870; between imperial Russia and the Ottoman Empire by 1876; between imperial Japan and China by 1894; between the United States and Spain by 1898; and between imperial Japan and the Russian Empire in 1905. In each case, the greater beneficiary of industrial growth was strengthened to the point where it would no longer accept the division of power and control inherited from preindustrial days. In each case, the aggressor calculated that it would win; in each case those calculations proved correct. As this is written, China is the newly industrial country, and it too demands more than it has.

In war, the capacity to wage further war is ultimately limited by war's own destruction, whether by the systematic bombardment of industry or by the excess of killings over the natural increase of fighting-age populations, as in the struggles of nameless clans and tribes from the beginning of history. In peacetime, by contrast, every form of human progress except one (see below) tends to increase war-making capacities, and not in a symmetrical way, thus disturbing the military balances that once kept the peace. If peace did not induce war, there would be no war—for war cannot perpetuate itself.

The Advent of the Postheroic Era

The societal changes that dissuade combat in fear of its casualties (this is the exception) are secondary effects of the advance of prosperity, itself a secondary effect of peace. In the past, prosperity often encouraged war—it was the economically more advanced countries that were the aggressors: Prussia rather than the Hapsburg Empire in 1866, Prussia again rather than France in 1870, imperial Russia rather than the Ottoman Empire in 1876, imperial Japan rather than China by 1894, and the United States rather than Spain in 1898. But today's advancement is of a different order. It enriches not only nations but also a net majority of their populations; it not only enriches societies but also changes them demographically and culturally in profound ways.

By the classic definition, Great Powers were states strong enough to successfully wage war on their own, that is without allies. But that distinction is now outdated, for the issue today is not whether war can be fought with or without allies, but whether war can be fought at all—except in remote, technical ways that do not seriously risk any casualties. It turns out that all along there was a tacit precondition to Great Power status: a readiness to use force whenever it was advantageous to do so, accepting the resulting combat casualties with equanimity—as long as their number was proportionate to the gains of course.

In the past, this precondition was too blatantly obvious and too easily satisfied to deserve comment by either practitioners or theoreticians. While Great Powers would normally be able to rely on intimidation rather than actual combat, that was only so because it was taken for granted that they *would* use force whenever they desired—undeterred by the prospect of the ensuing casualties. Nor could a Great Power limit its use of force to situations in which genuinely "vital" interests, that is survival interests, were in danger. That was the unhappy predicament of threatened Small Powers, which might have to fight purely to defend themselves and could not hope to do more with their modest military strength. Great Powers were different. They could only remain "great" if they were seen to be willing and able to use force even to protect interests far from vital, and indeed to acquire more "nonvital" interests, whether in the form of distant possessions or further additions to their spheres of influence. To lose a few hundred soldiers in some minor venture or even some thousands in a small war or expeditionary campaign were routine events for the Great Powers of history.

It suffices to mention the abrupt American abandonment of Somalia after the loss of eighteen soldiers in October 1993 to expose the unreality of the Great Power concept in our own days. In pride or in shame, Americans might dispute any wider conclusion from that event (and the similar events in Haiti and Bosnia), reserving for themselves the special sensitivity that forces policy to change completely because eighteen volunteer professional soldiers are killed—soldiers, one might add, who come from a country in which deaths by gunfire were contemporaneously clocked at one every fourteen minutes. But in fact the virtue, or the malady as the case might be, is far from exclusively American.

At the time when the United States refused to fight in Mogadishu, Britain and France, not to mention that other putative Great Power, Germany, refused to risk their troops to resist aggression in the former Yugoslavia. Moreover, in fear of reprisals against their own troops, it was only with great reluctance, after almost two years of horrific outrages, that the two countries finally consented to the carefully circumscribed threat of UN-authorized air strikes by NATO aircraft that was issued in February

1994. To be sure, neither Britain nor France (nor any other European power) has any "vital" interests at stake in the former Yugoslavia, any more than the United States had in Somalia. But that is the essence of the matter: the Great Powers of history would have viewed the disintegration of Yugoslavia not as a noxious problem to be avoided but rather as an opportunity to be exploited. With the need to protect populations under attack as their propaganda excuse, with the restoration of law and order as their ostensible motive, they would have intervened to establish zones of influence for themselves, just as the genuine Great Powers of the past actually did in their time (even distant Russia, badly weakened by defeat and revolution, disputed the Austro-Hungarian annexation of Bosnia-Herzegovina in 1908). Thus the so-called power vacuum of disintegrating Yugoslavia would immediately have been filled, to the disappointment of local Small Power ambitions, and to the great advantage of local populations and of peace.

As for why nothing of the kind happened in the former Yugoslavia in the face of atrocities not seen since the Second World War, the reason is not in dispute: no European government was more willing than the U.S. government to risk its soldiers in combat.

Nor is the refusal to tolerate combat casualties confined to functioning democracies. The Soviet Union was still a functioning totalitarian dictatorship when it engaged in its ultraclassic Great Power venture of Afghanistan, only to find that even its tightly regimented society would not tolerate the resulting casualties. At the time, outside observers were distinctly puzzled by the minimalism of Soviet theater strategy in Afghanistan. After an initial effort to establish countrywide territorial control that was soon abandoned, the Soviet army settled down to defend only the largest towns and the highways that connected them, otherwise conceding almost the entire country to the guerillas. Likewise, expert observers were astonished by the inordinately prudent tactics of Soviet forces on the ground. Except for a few commando units, they mostly remained confined inside their fortified garrisons, often failing to sally out even when guerillas were visibly operating nearby. At the time, the explanation most commonly offered was that Soviet commanders were reluctant to rely on their poorly trained conscript troops. Actually they were under constant and intense pressure from Moscow to avoid casualties at all costs.

The same example allows us to eliminate another literally superficial explanation for the refusal to accept even modest numbers of combat casualties: the impact of television coverage. The American experience with full-color, instant-replay television reportage of visibly suffering wounded soldiers, body bags, and grieving relatives in every episode of combat from Vietnam to Somalia is widely thought to have been decisively important. Live human images relayed directly, it has been argued again and again, are much more compelling than the printed word, or even radio reportage. But the Soviet Union never allowed its population to see any U.S.-style television images of war, yet the reaction of Soviet society to the casualties of the Afghan war was identical to that of American society to the casualties of the Vietnam war. In both cases, cumulative totals over the span of ten years and more that did not reach the casualty figures of one day of battle in past wars were nevertheless deeply traumatic.

We must therefore look for a more fundamental explanation capable of being valid with or without democratic governance, with or without uncontrolled television reportage. And indeed there is one: the demographic base of modern, postindustrial societies. In the families that composed the populations of the Great Powers of history, four, five, or six live births were common, with seven, eight, or nine less rare than the present one, two, or three. Of course infant mortality rates were also high. When it was entirely normal to lose one or more children to disease, the loss of one more youngster in war had a different meaning than it has for today's American and European families, with their two children on average or less, all of whom are expected to survive, each of whom embodies a much larger share of the family's emotional capital.

As any number of historical studies have shown, death itself was a much more *normal* part of human experience when it was not yet confined mostly to the very old. To lose a young family member for any reason was always tragic no doubt, yet his death in combat was not the extraordinary and fundamentally unacceptable event it has now become. Parents and relatives who in the United States at least commonly approve when their children decide to join the armed forces, thus choosing a career dedicated to combat and its preparation, now often react with astonishment and anger when they are actually sent into situations where combat could take place. And they are apt to view wounds or death as an outrageous scandal rather than as an occupational hazard.

The Italians, perhaps more postindustrial than most in this particular sense, certainly possessing Europe's lowest birth rate, have a word for such reactions: *mammismo* ("motherism"). But with or without a word to define them, these are attitudes that have great political resonance, powerfully constraining the use of force. And the Soviet experience in

Afghanistan proves that the constraint can become operative even without mass media eager to publicize private grief or parliamentarians ready to act at the behest of mourning relatives. Indeed, the Soviet experience of Afghanistan shows that it hardly makes a difference if the casualty toll is kept secret by the strictest censorship—which only resulted in wild rumors of huge losses. In 1994, when the Russian Federation's democracy embraced both a free press and a loud parliament, the refusal to accept further combat losses interrupted the suppression of Chechnya's self-declared independence. Everything had changed in Russia except for a society no longer willing to accept thousands of casualties for any reason, not even the punishment of the widely detested Chechens. The 1999 version of Chechnya's reconquest was fought with a maximum of artillery and air bombardment, much reliance on heavy armor, very little infantry combat, and an absolute minimum of casualties.

Present attitudes toward life, death, and combat losses are not confined to the relatives and friends of servicemen on active duty. They are shared throughout society by and large—they were shared even within the Soviet elite it seems—so that there is an extreme reluctance to impose a possible sacrifice that has become so much greater than it was when total populations were perhaps much smaller but families were much larger. What of the Gulf war then, or for that matter of Britain's war to reconquer the Falklands? Do they not suggest a much simpler explanation: that it all depends on the perceived *importance* of the undertaking, on the objective value of what is at stake, or—more realistically—on the ability of political leaders to justify the necessity of combat? After all, even during the Second World War, servicemen greatly resented postings to what were described as secondary fronts, quickly dubbing any theater that was less than highly publicized as "forgotten" (almost an official name for the Burma front in 1944). Of course combat and its casualties are more likely to be opposed the less immediately compelling is their declared justification. It might therefore seem that the new family demography and the resulting *mammismo* are irrelevant after all, and that what counts is only what has always counted—namely, the importance of the interests at stake, the political orchestration of the event, and leadership.

There is undoubtedly some merit in these contentions, but not enough. In the first place, if lives can be placed at risk only in situations already dramatically prominent on the national scene, hence only when crises have reached their final extremities with war imminent or under way, that in itself rules out the most efficient uses of force—earlier rather later, on a scale smaller rather than a larger one, to prevent escalation rather than fight wars. More important, to use force only if there is an immediately compelling justification suits only threatened Small Powers. For a Great Power, that is a condition excessively restrictive. A Great Power cannot be that unless it asserts all sorts of claims that far exceed the needs of its own immediate security, to protect allies and clients as well as other less-than-vital interests. It must therefore risk combat for purposes that may be fairly recondite, perhaps in little-known distant lands, in situations in which it is not compelled to fight but rather deliberately chooses to do so.

Even now the exceptional effort of determined leaders skillful in the arts of political leadership can correspondingly widen their freedom of action, overcoming at least in small part the reluctance to accept casualties. That is obviously what happened in the Gulf intervention of 1990–91 and in the Falklands reconquest before it, impossible undertakings had it not been for the exceptional leadership of President Bush and Prime Minister Thatcher. And that indeed was the decisive factor, not the undoubted significance of keeping Iraq from controlling Saudi as well as Kuwaiti oil, or the insignificance of the Falklands for any practical purpose whatsoever (another illustration of the irrelevance of the "objective" value of the interests at stake).

Leadership is indeed important, but the routine functioning of a Great Power cannot depend on the fortuitous presence of exceptional wartime leadership. It will be recalled, moreover, that a low opinion of Argentinian military strength (indeed an underestimate of Argentinian air power at least) and the resulting belief that casualties would be low, was crucial to Britain's commitment to war in the Falklands. Likewise, the imperative of minimizing casualties was the leitmotiv of the entire Gulf intervention, from the initial Desert Shield deployment that was originally presented as purely defensive, to the sudden decision to call off the ground war as soon as the Iraqis had withdrawn from Kuwait, with Saddam Hussein still in power (although there were other reasons for stopping the attack on the Iraqi army, notably the fear that Iran would become the next threat if the former were utterly destroyed). In any case, it seems clear that the freedom of action gained by successful leadership is still rather narrow—it is not hard to guess what would have happened to President Bush if the casualties of the entire Gulf war would had reached the level of any one day of serious combat in either world war.

If the significance of new family demography is accepted, it follows that none of the advanced low-birth-rate countries of the world can play the role of a classic Great Power anymore, not the United States or Russia, not Britain or France, least of all Germany or Japan. They may still possess the physical attributes of military strength, or the economic base to develop significant military strength, but their societies are so allergic to casualties that they are effectively "de-bellicized," or nearly so.

Aside from self-defense and exceptional cases such as the Gulf war, only such combat as can take place by remote bombardment alone, without soldiers at risk on the ground, is still tolerated. Much can be done by air power with few lives at risk; sea power too can be useful at times; there are already some robotic weapons, and there will be more. But Bosnia, Somalia, and Haiti remind us that the typical Great Power business of "restoring order" still requires ground forces. In the end, the infantry, albeit mechanized, is still indispensable—and now mostly unavailable because of the fear of casualties. The high-birth-rate countries of the world can still fight wars by choice, and several have in recent years. But even those few among them that have competent armed forces lack other key Great Power capabilities such as a significant strategic reach or broad intelligence coverage.

As of this writing, the military authorities of the United States and of Europe have yet to contend with postheroic limitations, whose very existence they tend to deny. Army leaders and, in the case of the United States, those of the marines as well cannot admit that their manpower-intensive forces have become largely unusable in combat, except in the exceedingly unlikely event of a defensive war. Self-images and institutional cultures, as well as crass bureaucratic interests in undiminished budgets, all prohibit any recognition of postheroic realities. Instead, the pretense continues that forces classified as "combat ready" are truly ready for combat. Naturally that causes problems when combat is actually proposed, even on the smallest scale. In 1998 U.S. civilian officials requested the seizure for eventual trial of Radovan Karadzic and Ratko Mladic, respectively the political and military chiefs of the Bosnian Serbs during the Yugoslav civil war, both declared war criminals, accused of personal responsibility for major atrocities.

Within the framework of an ad hoc NATO planning unit code-named Amber Star, in typically elaborate fashion, the U.S. National Security Agency (specialized in remote electronic surveillance), the Balkan Task Force of the Central Intelligence Agency (in charge of field operatives), Federal Bureau of Investigation agents, and a unit of U.S. marshals (specialists in conveying prisoners) all set to work to provide continuous surveillance of the two targets. At times that was not a demanding task, for the easily recognizable Karadzic was repeatedly driven through U.S. army checkpoints in Bosnia at the time, quite unmolested because U.S. commanders were eager to avoid confrontation with the Bosnian Serbs. Concurrently, the U.S. Joint Chiefs of Staff authorized the Special Operations Command—in charge of commando units and assorted elite forces—to plan the seizures in conjunction with the British Director of Special Forces. A suitable plan was prepared in minute detail, with an amplitude of means. Although Karadzic habitually traveled about with a small escort armed only with light weapons, while Mladic was reported to be living a normal urban life in Belgrade, the Joint Chiefs of Staff insisted on a large-scale operation to avoid the danger that the commandos might be outmatched. The Joint Staff, which serves the chiefs and which institutionally represents all four services, army, navy, marines, and air force, demanded that the raids be conducted with "overwhelming force" to avoid the risks inherent in any small-scale commando operation. More than a year and tens of millions of dollars were consumed by these preparations. But when everything was ready for action at last, the Joint Chiefs refused to authorize the mission after all, on the grounds that the Bosnian Serbs might retaliate by attacking U.S. troops on peacekeeping duties in Bosnia.[11] From start to finish, the decisive consideration for the U.S. military chiefs was the possibility of casualties—even very few casualties.

Historically, societies unwilling to suffer combat casualties have turned to mercenaries, both foreign and "denationalized" local volunteers. It has duly been suggested that the United States as well as other postheroic societies should copy the Ghurkas of the British army, recruited in Nepal. Troops willing to fight can certainly be found where warrior cultures endure. They would be mercenaries of course, but they could be of high quality, while a common ethnic origin should assure their basic cohesion. In practice, Ghurkas or their equivalents would provide the infantry under "native" American or European officers, and natives would also provide the more technical forms of combat support normally much less exposed to combat risks. A variant suggestion is to copy the French Foreign Legion model, with native officers for units manned by foreign or denationalized volunteers. Under both schemes, political responsibility for any casualties would be much reduced, even if not entirely eliminated. The United States, incidentally, did raise ethnic mercenary units for its Indochina war, with satisfactory results, and the U.S. Army also recruited individual foreign volunteers for its Europe-based Special Forces, while Britain and France still have their Ghurkas and the Foreign Legion. Thus neither scheme is as bizarre as it may seem.

Military chiefs who deny the very existence of the problem of avoiding casualties at all costs can scarcely be expected to consider—let alone accept—such drastic and institutionally humiliating remedies. Instead, a partial solution has been found in the advent of routine precision in aerial bombardment both by remotely launched cruise missiles and by manned aircraft, themselves armed with guided weapons.

On March 24, 1999, when the United States and eight of its NATO allies started bombing the Yugoslav Federation of Serbia-Montenegro to force the evacuation of Kosovo, the world witnessed the beginning of the first war conducted under postheroic rules: no casualties for the fighting forces, which were no longer asked to do anything more dangerous than to launch cruise missiles from afar or release guided weapons from safe altitudes; and no deliberate attacks on enemy populations.

The outcome, after eleven weeks of aerial bombardment, was the first war victory ever won by air power alone, with no fighting whatever by ground forces—retrospectively illuminating the 1991 Gulf war, in which the substantive victory of air power was obscured by the belated intervention of ground forces. Moreover, the victory of air power in the Kosovo war was achieved by pilots that flew in greater safety than the passengers of some Third World airlines, as well by cruise-missile launching crews aboard warships and submarines that were far removed from any combat danger. The systematic jamming and spoofing of warning and missile-guidance radars, a great concentration of attacks on air defenses, and, above all, operating altitudes of fifteen thousand feet and higher, well above the maximum reach of visually aimed guns and hand-held missiles, were all meant to minimize pilot losses, albeit at the expense of hitting positive targets. As it happens, only one aircraft was shot down, a U.S. F-117 stealth fighter; its pilot ejected safely and was promptly rescued, so that the entire war was fought without a single combat casualty—a veritable triumph of postheroic warfare. But the Kosovo war also exposed the *strategic* limitations of fighting by remote bombardment alone, quite aside from the inevitable quota of errors in selecting targets and in aiming weapons, as well as purely technical malfunctions.

In the first place, as will later be discussed in detail, a war fought by precision bombardment alone is necessarily a slow and torturous process of identifying, selecting, and destroying single structures one by one. As the bombing continues, it cannot be known how many more structures must be identified, selected, and destroyed before the enemy decides to surrender, nor even if there is any correlation between the cumulative destruction achieved and progress toward the desired outcome. Unless the entire purpose of the bombing is to deprive the enemy of some specific facilities or weapons, so that it can be achieved *physically* and unilaterally, the success of a bombing campaign must depend on the enemy's decision to accept defeat. That decision can result only from a complex political process in which the impact of the bombing interacts with all sorts of other factors, including cultural determinants and historical memories, the inner politics of decision making, concurrent threats or reassurances from other powers if any, and more.

Because cultural determinants are hard to interpret, the enemy's decision making may be shrouded in secrecy, and other political pressures may be unknowns, there is no assurance that the political *theory* that guides the bombing—that destroying X targets will secure Y decision—is correct. Of course if one theory fails after much bombardment, another can be tried. For example, when the 1999 Kosovo war started on March 24, initially the bombing was mostly symbolic and largely aimed at air defenses, on the theory that the government of Slobodan Milosevic only needed to be convinced of NATO's determination to capitulate. When that failed to happen, in April the bombing became distinctly heavier and focused on weapon factories, depots, bases, and barracks, on the theory that Serbian military leaders would pressure the government to accept the abandonment of Kosovo in order to save their remaining institutional assets. By May 1999, however, civilian infrastructures such as power stations and bridges were being destroyed to make everyday life as difficult as possible, on the different theory that the Milosevic government was not undemocratic after all, that it would respond to pressures for surrender from an increasingly uncomfortable public.

One theory after another can be tried, but bombing inevitably evokes criticism and opposition. There are invariably tragic accidents to deplore even if there is no attempt to attack civilians directly and elaborate precautions are implemented to avoid incidental hits ("collateral damage"). Thus the political costs of persisting may not be sustainable, and even if they are, they may exceed the gains of the enterprise. As it was, the Kosovo war was won after eleven weeks of bombing, but at times the NATO alliance came close to fracture, which would have been an ironic outcome for a war fought chiefly to show that the alliance was still cohesive and effective in spite of the end of the Cold War.

A second limitation of remote bombardment, dramatically exposed by the Kosovo war, was that the absolute priority of avoiding any risk to NATO pilots made it impossible to protect the persecuted Albanians of Kosovo, on whose behalf the war was ostensibly being fought. Small groups of Serbian gendarmes and volunteer warriors, of two hundred men or less, were able to terrorize villages containing thousands of Albanians into fleeing the country because they were supported by a few tanks or other armored vehicles. As moving targets, those vehicles could not be identified and attacked effectively by cruise missiles or by NATO fighter bombers operating at altitudes of fifteen thousand feet or more. But of course they were vulnerable to aircraft that would fly low and slow, repeatedly circling to find them before diving down to attack. Any and all fighter bombers present on the scene could have performed the task, but NATO forces also included fixed-wing aircraft specialized for that very purpose, such as the American A-10, British Harrier, and Italian AMX, as well as armed helicopters such as the U.S. Army Apache and its British, French, German, and Italian counterparts, all designed originally as "anti-tank" helicopters. To use any of these specialized aircraft, however, would have exposed aircrew to antiaircraft fires; hence nothing was done.

The refusal of all other NATO forces to accept combat risks in order to protect the Albanians remains undocumented—inglorious episodes often are. But in the United States, where military secrecy is less easily invoked to conceal malpractice, the tale of the Apache helicopters that never flew in combat was quickly published.[12]

As soon as Serb police and militia started to expel Albanian villagers on the second day of the war, March 25, 1999, the NATO supreme commander General Wesley K. Clark requested authorization to employ 24 U.S. Army Apaches to attack armored vehicles in Kosovo. Although himself a U.S. Army general, Clark was evidently unaware of postheroic realities. The U.S. Joint Chiefs of Staff, including the U.S. Army Chief of Staff, General Dennis J. Reimer, opposed Clark's request, on the grounds that the Apaches would be excessively vulnerable to those air defenses that could not be neutralized systematically: highly mobile and scarcely identifiable machine guns, small-caliber cannons, and hand-held infrared homing missiles that cannot be neutralized by radar jamming or spoofing. It should be noted parenthetically that as of fiscal year 1999, the United States had spent a cumulative total of $15 billion on the Apache force (of which 743 were then in inventory), also in part to provide extensive armor protection and a full battery of electronic and infrared countermeasures that were presumed to be highly effective in protecting the aircraft. But of course no amount of self-protection can assure immunity in war. The commandant of the Marine Corps, General Charles C. Krulak, who participated in the rejection of General Clark's request, retroactively explained his opposition by evoking mothers, fathers, and "white crosses," in true postheroic style. It was not until April 3, 1999, the tenth day of the war, that the reluctance of the Joint Chiefs was partly overcome: Clark was authorized to send the Apaches from their German base to Albania, but not to employ them in combat without further authorization.

Reluctant bureaucracies ordered to act against their institutional preferences do not spring into action. It was found that the 24 Apaches, though till then expensively kept at the highest state of readiness by U.S. Army criteria, were "unready" to deploy from Germany to Albania. It was not until April 14 that the first Apaches of what was suggestively named Task Force Hawk left Germany, and it was not until April 26 that all 24 reached Tirana airport, thirty-three days after the start of the war, twenty-three days after the decision to send them. Among the many obstacles encountered was the deep mud—as if attack helicopters were not normally meant to be operated from unimproved terrain, the key advantage of helicopters in general, for which field-assembled pads are routinely provided. In reality much more than the placing of 24 expedient pads was involved, for the U.S. Army was determined to care for and protect the 24 Apaches and their crews more than adequately: 6,200 protective troops and command and service personnel with 26,000 tons of equipment were sent to Tirana in 550 flights by C-17 heavy transports, including a company of 14 M1A1 battle tanks, 42 Bradley infantry fighting vehicles, and 27 Black Hawk and Chinook helicopters for airmobile protective troops and for search and rescue. The expeditionary field headquarters of the force was itself large enough to require 20 mobile offices forty feet long, and 190 shipping containers with ammunition, replacement engines, and parts were sent—enough for a sustained campaign. To open the way for the Apaches by scattering bomblets against any hostiles in their flight paths, ATACMS tactical missiles were also provided. General Reimer's retrospective comment was exemplary of postheroic priorities: "We probably went in a little too heavy . . . I don't apologize for that . . . the people on the ground knew they were protected, and that gives them confidence"—the people in question being the Apache crews, rather than the Albanians then being terrorized with impunity.

Even then, with Task Force Hawk finally ready for action, there was none. The Joint Chiefs of Staff still feared that there would be too many casualties, a number whose theoretical maximum was of course 48, the Apache having a two-man crew, but that was variously estimated from a very prudent 5 percent per sortie to a fantastic 50 percent. In the meantime, however, another obstacle was found by the U.S. Army, an embarrassing one, to be sure, but one that served to delay combat: it was discovered that even though the Apache is primarily meant to operate at night, for which it has advanced forward-looking infrared scopes and sights already built in, none of the pilots in place were deemed qualified to fly with night-vision goggles. Training duly started, a little belatedly perhaps. On May 4, an Apache crashed, killing both crewmen. In addition, because of the absence of a ground force with its own organic intelligence capabilities, there was also the problem of finding targets without exposing the Apaches to greater danger by having them circle and look for them. U-2 reconnaissance aircraft, AWACS radar aircraft protected by fighters kept in the air by tankers, and Black Hawk helicopters in a scout role were all employed in a long series of target-finding exercises. These continued until the Kosovo war ended with not a single Apache combat mission flown: General Clark was never authorized to send them into action.

When in 1993 the United States abandoned combat in Somalia after eighteen soldiers were killed in a failed commando raid in Mogadishu, it was explained that no significant national interests justified the loss of more American lives. But when the commitments, political costs, and diplomatic risks of the war itself endowed Kosovo with the greatest possible strategic importance regardless of its prewar insignificance, it was found that the zero-casualty rule still applied, notwithstanding the interests at stake, including the survival of the NATO alliance. The notion that casualty tolerance is a function of the importance of the fight—a matter of rational cost-benefit calculations—was thus exposed as a mere rationalization. When institutions, political leaders, and societies still tolerate the casualties of combat, they will fight even for trivial reasons; when they no longer do so, all sorts of arguments are invented to explain why the combat at hand at any one time is not worthy of sacrifice.

This too is a way for peace to evolve into war. Peacetime conditions can induce societal and cultural changes that diminish effective military capabilities even as peacetime prosperity increases the resources that may be spent on the armed forces: in 1999, as the Apache saga was unfolding in Albania, the U.S. Army was in the process of spending $1.9 billion on minor upgrades to its Apaches.

The Defeat of Victory

If victory did not tend to evolve toward defeat by overextension, if growing power did not contain the cause of its own undoing, the swift expansion of Hitler's Third Reich from Normandy to Stalingrad and from Lapland to Egypt by November 1942 could never have culminated in a downfall just as swift, because all of Europe would have been ruled by a single power long before his birth. And the same would have been true of Napoleon's conquest and collapse, and those of all his lesser predecessors, going back across the centuries to the Roman Empire's own cycle of expansion and decline.

So great are the economies of scale that favor the larger military power over the smaller, so significant is the geometric advantage of reducing the proportion of frontier length to the space, population, and wealth enclosed, that the larger should have prevailed over the smaller in Europe's abundant wars until only one state remained, enclosing all the space that could advantageously be reached from a single center of power. Its extent would depend on the means of transport and communications available. But even in the technological circumstances of the Romans, when the horsed messenger was the fastest means of communication, and no form of transport outpaced marching troops, the space efficiently controllable by a single center of power extended right across Europe and far into Mesopotamia.

Yet the Roman Empire remained a unique exception. What happened instead of an unbroken sequence of vast empires was the "balancing" of power. The very strength of the power that was becoming the strongest at any one time provoked the fear and hostility of other large powers, turning yesterday's allies into suspicious neutrals, yesterday's neutrals into opponents. Or else it induced smaller powers to coalesce in order to form a barrier of resistance to the further expansion of the strongest.

Powers that were becoming stronger, because of rising population and prosperity, or because of a more efficient government better at mobilizing both, could employ their rising strength to expand, but only up to a certain point. That limit would be reached when the increasing economies of scale of the stronger power were matched by the increasing resistance of newly hostile opponents. A paralyzing equilibrium at that culminating point might then be accepted by the rising power, or else it might try to form an equilibrium-breaking alliance of its own, if it could find allies.

If, however, the rising power tried to break the barrier of resistance by war, the same logic of strategy would prevail whether the outcome were victory or defeat. If the rising power won its war against a rival or a coalition, its victory would evoke the fear and hostility of still other powers further away, which until then had been shielded by the defeated. Thus once again expansion would encounter a barrier of resistance. If the rising power lost its war, its defeat would be moderated by newfound allies concerned by the power of its victorious enemies. And if it was a coalition that won, its very victory would weaken it, by reviving the divergent interests that had been suppressed when it was imperative to join together to resist the rising power. A total victory can totally destroy a coalition, by the inevitable paradox.

So far only one arena of the power competition has been considered. But beyond the direct participants that face one another, there are always other powers large and small, nearby or remote. Normally they would be engaged in their own power competition within their own arena, but that changes if the rising power—or its enemies—becomes strong enough. The coalition of small powers formed to react defensively against a rising power in one region of the world might itself be threatening to others elsewhere. They might then seek an alliance with the rising power that the coalition wants to contain, overturning the equilibrium achieved by the coalition because there is no equilibrium for them.

The rules are simple, but the game can become complicated. By processes that were smoother when there were many powers and they all shared a common culture, and by processes that were clumsier when there were fewer powers less closely connected, Europe's disunity was preserved after the Roman downfall by many reversals of victory and defeat, of expansion and retreat. In still earlier days, the same dynamics were at work among the Greek city-states before the Macedonian primacy, and later among the Hellenistic kingdoms of Greece, Anatolia, Syria, and Egypt, which emerged from the division of Alexander's short-lived empire. And what we know of the dealings of the Gallic tribes with one another, of the Germanic tribes beyond the Rhine, and of the pre-Roman Italic states reveals the same paradoxical logic.

During the Cold War, the states of Western Europe gathered into a coalition commanded by the United States to maintain a barrier of resistance against Soviet power, with only the faintest suggestion of resistance to American power as well—a resistance that became somewhat more intense over the years as Europe itself was becoming stronger, the Soviet Union weaker, and American protection less urgently needed.

The North Atlantic Alliance and its NATO military command structure, which connected the United States, Canada, and thirteen Western European countries, resisted all Soviet threats and seductive offers for half a century. It will be interesting to see how long it can outlast the demise of the Soviet Union. At this time, there is as yet only the beginning of a fissure: under the European Defense Initiative launched in 1999 in the wake of the Kosovo war, the members of the European Union are forming a ministerial defense council with a designated head and general staff of their own that excludes the United States. Most of the countries involved are concurrently members of NATO, to which they still ostensibly defer, but it seems that the iron law of coalitions is already at work: formed to resist enemies, they do not long outlast them.

Europe holds no monopoly over the phenomena of strategy. Those who know of Japan before the centralization accomplished by the Tokugawa Shogunate; those who have studied the ancient China of the Warring States or the modern China of the warlords; those who are familiar with the history of the Indian powers before the British and before the Moguls; those who observe the abrupt alliances, sudden hostilities, and revolving coalitions of the contemporary Arab world; and indeed all who survey the dealings of rival powers and warring tribes at any time and in any place may usefully interpret events through the Italian Renaissance concept of the balance of power.*

Given the universality of the strategic predicament, it is the exceptions that demand explanation. Europe remained divided through the centuries and is still not united today, but China had long periods of unity in the past and is virtually united now. In Japan the rise and fall of warlords was finally brought to an end by the single government of the Togukawa Shoguns. In many other places, where before there were warring states there is now unity, as in Italy and Germany. And of course the European experience itself is still today heavily marked by the centuries of the Roman Empire, which could never have attained its dimensions unless expansion could in fact yield that much further expansion, instead of ending at a much earlier culminating point.

To note that the paradoxical logic of strategy reemerged as soon as a central power was weakened, if only by the personal failings of a ruler, diminishes the scope of what must be explained—but not the need to explain how culminating points were successfully exceeded.

The answer arises directly from the definition of strategy. When government is consensual, when conflict and strife are limited by law and custom, linear logic applies in full, and the paradoxical logic of strategy is irrelevant. Both stability and a steady progression are therefore possible, without need of an ultimately exhausting effort to resist the dissolution

---

* The first published references to the balance *(bilancia)* and the "weights" of power are found in the *Storia d'Italia* of the Florentine envoy and scholar Francesco Guicciardini (1483–1540).

of what is, and its replacement by its opposite. That is why rulers and regimes that have no natural claim to *legitimacy* are forever striving for it, whether by ideological or religious justification, by popular approval with or without elections, or even by dynastic right of inheritance. To the extent that legitimacy is secured, so is an exemption from the travails and reversals of the strategic predicament.

The provinces of the Roman Empire were gained one by one through often brutal conquest. But the empire was preserved by the legitimacy it obtained by successfully recruiting local elites of all cultures and races. All careers were opened to them in exchange for their loyalty; no position of power was closed to them, not even the imperial office itself. The Roman Empire thus evaded the strategic predicament. Instead of colliding with an early culminating point, the empire expanded in linear progression as each province successfully pacified provided men and resources for more conquest.

The Roman army conquered, but it was the Roman political culture of inclusion and co-optation that secured the legitimacy that long preserved the empire—and that is how all other prolonged exceptions to the strategic paradox have also been achieved.

Repression, by contrast, is fragile. Being itself in the realm of strategy, all its components—propaganda, police control, internal political intelligence—are continuously eroded by the reactions they evoke, undoing themselves, and thus require constant injections of effort not to decline toward impotence. Propaganda undermines itself as yesterday's boastful claims are denied by present realities; police control tends to become lax over time precisely because the regime seems secure, thus making it insecure; internal political intelligence functions until secrecy becomes integral to any opposition activity—undermining the value of informers.

Under Stalin, however, the stability of the Soviet Union was assured by *highly dynamic* forms of repression that overcame the paradoxical logic. As soon as a given propaganda campaign, say to establish Stalin as Lenin's designated successor, had reached its culminating point of success, it was not allowed to decline into ineffectual repetition. Instead it was replaced by a new propaganda campaign to further elevate Stalin. By the time of his death, Stalin had become stage by stage the supreme thinker and teacher of all time (academic books and articles on all subjects, from fluid dynamics to archaeology, started by quoting his sayings); the supreme warrior (he had won the Second World War with scant assistance); and the supreme builder of all of human history (he was reconstructing the Soviet Union into a paradise on earth).

Police control was not allowed to decline into mere routine, inevitably overlooking social interstices in which opposition might form. Of course any form of opposition by word or deed that was noticed or reported by informers would result in arrest, deportation, or execution. But that was merely reactive, and insufficient. By itself, it would only teach the opposition to adopt strict security precautions. Instead, to seize the initiative, the political police was employed to carry out a long sequence of "purges" against entire social categories: rich peasants and then middle peasants (when food was short), engineers (when the five-year plan was failing), military officers (when the arms build-up of the 1930s was empowering them overmuch), the high-ranking policemen themselves (grown too powerful), and many other categories large and small, down to plant geneticists and professors of linguistics, ending of course with the Jews, whose mass deportation was imminent when Stalin died in 1953.

Once a purge started, the political police had to arrest a given number of suspects—they had a quota to fill, fixed in advance. In some cases, for example high-ranking military officers in 1937–38, that quota amounted to a fairly large proportion of the entire category. Virtually all suspects arrested had to be found guilty by the investigators, who would routinely use torture to extract confessions of nonexistent opposition plots and treason in the service of foreign powers. Sometimes there were widely publicized demonstrative trials, though only when the accused were both important and willing to confess. Deportation to a labor camp was the usual sentence, though if there was any actual evidence of disloyalty, even if only verbal, the sentence was death. Sometimes there were no investigations but only arrests followed directly by mass executions. In any case, all those associated with the arrested were required to denounce them, including professional colleagues and coworkers, teachers, fellow students, parents, relatives, spouses, and their own children (young children who denounced their parents were elevated into highly publicized heroic models).

The aim was not merely to terrorize society but to reduce it into an inchoate mass of noncommunicating individuals deprived of any bonds of solidarity (all clubs and voluntary associations had long since been outlawed). Any personal opposition to the regime, any critical thought whatever, became a personal secret that could not be shared with anyone else, for fear of betrayal and arrest. In this way any potential opposition was inhibited at its source, instead of allowing individual opponents to talk with others and coalesce into groups. This system of repression was so effective that Stalin's regime was never threatened by any perceptible opposition. But it evidently exceeded the culminating point of effectiveness: after Stalin's death, it was deliberately dismantled by his successors, who feared for their own fate if their rivals were to seize control over the secret police.

A few dynastic rulers in the Arab world and southern Asia can still claim a measure of inherited legitimacy alongside many more democracies worldwide. But even after the downfall of European communism, many states are still ruled by repressive regimes of weak legitimacy or none. Although they differ greatly in every way, in all of them politics are war-like even if bloodless, and the paradoxical logic of strategy applies in full, requiring constant vigilance by the rulers and their active effort of repression to protect illegitimate power.

So far we have observed the logic of strategy in the setting of war, as well in political repression. Yet it embraces not merely warfare but all human conduct in the context of possible war (and possible political conflict). Insofar as states act to prepare for or avoid war, or use a capacity for war making to extort concessions from other states by intimidation without any actual use of force, the logic of strategy determines nonwar outcomes just as much as it does those of war itself, regardless of what instruments of statecraft are actually employed. Thus diplomacy, propaganda, secret operations, and conflictually motivated economic controls and initiatives ("geo-economics") are all subject to exactly the same logic of strategy.

PART II

THE LEVELS OF STRATEGY

We have seen how paradoxical logic—its sequence of action, culmination, de-cline, and reversal—pervades the realm of strategy. It conditions both the com-petition and struggle of entire nations and the most detailed interactions of weapons and countermeasures in exactly the same way, for the same logic applies on the largest scale as in the smallest, in all forms of war and in adver-sarial peacetime diplomacy as well.

The dynamic contention of opposed wills is the common source of this logic. But the subject matter conditioned by the logic of course varies with the level of the encounter, ranging from war and peace between nations down to highly technical encounters between specific subsystems, such as missile-control ra-dars against aircraft radar-warning receivers.

Each level has its own reality but is rarely independent of other levels above and below it. Thus the technical-level interplay of specific weapons with other weapons or countermeasures is subordinated to the tactical-level combat of the forces that employ those particular weapons. Obviously the strengths and weaknesses of those forces as a whole derive from all sorts of other factors as well, some material such as supply, some well-defined such as training, others mysteriously intangible: morale, cohesion, and leadership. The last are often more important in determining combat outcomes than the engineering factors that determine the capabilities and limitations of the weapons used. The tacti-cal level, moreover is itself subordinated to higher levels dominated by yet other factors.

Self-contained acts of combat are possible—indeed, that is the definition of "commando" operations (or "special operations," in U.S. military terminology). But normally the tactical-level actions of particular units of the armed forces on each side are merely subordinated parts of larger actions involving many other units. Then it is the operational-level interactions among the many units on both sides that determine the consequences of what is done or not done at the tactical level. If a unit bravely resists attack, its tactical success will merely ensure eventual capture or destruction if other units on both sides of it are retreating; if a unit fails in launching its own attack, it could still join a broader advance if the other attacking units are successful. Thus the operational level normally dominates the tactical—and the factors conditioned by the logic within the operational level are very different: details of topography and disposition for example, are now submerged while it is the overall interaction of the rival schemes of warfare that determines outcomes. Tactically weak forces can thus defeat stronger ones, if guided by a superior overall scheme; tactically strong forces can be defeated, if guided by an inferior operational scheme, which is more or less what happened in May 1940, when the Anglo-French armies were defeated by essentially fragile German columns.

Events at the operational level can be large in scale, but they are never autonomous. They are conditioned in turn by the broader interaction of the armed forces as a whole within an entire theater of warfare, just as battles are merely subordinate parts of entire campaigns. It is at this higher level of theater strategy that the consequences of single operations affect the overall conduct of offense and defense. Those broad military purposes hardly count at the operational level, at which defenders might choose to launch an attack to better defend their own sector, in which the attacker might remain on the defensive in a sector to concentrate his offensive action elsewhere. In most cases, the conduct of war operations at the theater level routinely includes both offensive and defensive operational-level actions, whether the overall aim is to attack or defend. And the key determinants are again very different. In ground warfare, for example, the detailed topography that is often decisive tactically and unimportant operationally is wholly submerged; what counts is rather the entire geography of the encounter, the length of frontages, the depths of territory of each side, the roads and other transport infrastructures. And it is at the theater level, where there is not only more space but also more time, that supply is decisive: a tactical fight can be won by a unit with its own ammunition, fuel, and food even if its future resupply has already been cut off; an operational-level battle can be won in the same conditions, perhaps capturing the enemy's fuel, food, and even weapons and ammunition to win one more battle—as the Germans did more than once in the North Africa in 1941–42 against the British. But supply at the theater level is needed for the many fights and battles of an entire campaign, so that the combat strength of the theater forces as whole ultimately cannot exceed their supply—and that is how the brilliant operational victories of the Germans in North Africa ended in utter defeat. Having outmaneuvered the British many times, in the end they were decisively outsupplied, being unable to transport enough fuel and ammunition across the Mediterranean and then across the vast desert against British naval and air interdiction.

The entire conduct of warfare in one or more theaters, as well as peacetime preparations for war, are in turn subordinate expressions of national struggles at the highest level of grand strategy, where all that is military happens within the much broader context of domestic politics, international diplomacy, economic activity, and all else that strengthens and weakens.

Because ultimate ends and means are both present only at the level of grand strategy, the outcome of military actions is determined only at that highest level: even a most successful conquest is only a provisional result that can be overturned by the diplomatic intervention of more powerful states; even a major military defeat can be redeemed by the intervention of new allies that weakness can attract under the usual workings of the balance of power.

The five levels of strategy form a definite hierarchy, but outcomes are not simply imposed in a one-way transmission from top to bottom because the levels interact with one another. Technical performance counts through its tactical consequences (good pilots can shoot down better aircraft; better tanks can be defeated by better tank crews), but of course tactical-level actions do depend in turn upon technical performance to some extent (even the best pilots can be outmatched by wholly superior aircraft), just as the many tactical events that form the operational level influence its results, while themselves being influenced by it. Similarly, operational-level actions have their effects at the level of theater strategy, which defines their purpose, while military activity as a whole affects what happens at the level of grand strategy, even though that is the level that determines final outcomes.

Strategy, therefore, has two different dimensions: the vertical dimension of the different levels that interact with one another; and the horizontal dimension in which the dynamic logic of action and reaction unfolds within each level. Our investigation began with the horizontal dimension, mentioning this or that level without attempting to define them. The aim was to avoid complications when first presenting the paradoxical logic in action with its often surprising results. But now a set of definitions of each of the five levels, each carefully worded and neatly presented in suggestive tabular form, might seem appropriate. Our subject, however, is as varied as human life, often charged with powerful emotions, shaped by institutional habits and urges, and clouded by the uncertain particulars of time and place of each encounter. Thus the verbal nets of abstract phrases can capture merely the hollow forms of strategy and not its turbulent contents. A great many definitions of tactics and of the other levels of strategy are already in circulation. But it is enough to look at any one of these definitions to visualize immediately many possible exceptions. And if these are remedied by formulating more definitions for various subcategories (aerial tactics, naval operations, and so on), an entire dictionary would eventually be needed to remind ourselves of what we mean by our own definitions—without really advancing our understanding of the real content of strategy.

Let us therefore proceed by plunging into the substance of strategical encounters, this time to dissect their component levels. As we focus on each level in turn before finally standing back to examine their dynamic totality at the level of grand strategy, we will uncover the boundary lines of the natural stratifications of conflict. When we do venture upon definitions, we will be expressing observed realities instead of erecting a hollow verbal edifice.

Given this purpose, we can consider just one large case, the defense of Western Europe during the later years of the Cold War. After the 1973 Arab-Israeli war, in which both antitank and antiaircraft missiles played a large role, some military experts claimed that the forces of the North Atlantic Treaty Organization (called the Alliance in what follows) could successfully resist a Soviet offensive against Western Europe by relying on "high-technology" nonnuclear defenses, so that the Alliance would no longer need the expensive ground forces it then fielded, mostly armored and mechanized divisions supported by self-propelled artillery. More important, the Alliance would no longer need to rely on nuclear weapons, except to dissuade the Soviet Union from using its own. The examination of this case is the guiding theme of what follows, with actual historical examples added to illustrate arguments—though never to prove them or disprove them, of course, because we already know enough of the complexity of strategy to know that history cannot be misused in that way.

5

The Technical Level

The varied nonnuclear defense proposals that were debated until the Cold War came to its sudden and peaceful end largely focused on the four hundred miles of the so-called central front, the border between West Germany and its unfriendly neighbors: the East Germany that no longer exists and Czechoslovakia, which is now divided. All those proposals were based on some combination of two ideas. One was that invading Soviet tank and "motor-rifle" (mechanized) divisions could be successfully resisted by infantry units abundantly equipped with antitank missiles. In some proposals, that infantry would consist of regular troops, which would wholly displace the armored and mechanized divisions then fielded, certainly costly, and also "provocative" according to some, because they could undoubtedly have been used to attack as well as defend. In other proposals, the new "antitank missile infantry" would consist of reserve or militia units that would be added to the extant armor-mechanized forces, to provide a further layer of defense.

The other idea, not quite so simple, was to combine satellite and airborne sensors, communications, computerized data-fusion and control centers, and long-range missiles with many separately aimed submunitions, into integrated "Deep Attack" systems. In sequence, the sensors would identify and locate Soviet armored vehicles and other moving targets even hundreds of miles behind the front; the data links would relay the information to the computerized data-fusion and control centers where the full picture of the entire target inventory would emerge, and engagement decisions could immediately be made; and finally the missiles would attack the identified targets en masse with their submunitions. A Deep Attack system could therefore delay, disorganize, and diminish advancing Soviet tank and mechanized columns long before they could add their mass, momentum, and firepower to the initial offensive launched by Soviet forces already on the front. That was already the major task of Western air forces after they had first won air superiority, but the whole purpose of Deep Attack was to act on a large scale as soon as a war started, without waiting for air superiority to be won, without risking delays if air bases were disrupted or if the weather was uncooperative. The Cold War is long ended, but Deep Attack lives on under the new label "Reconnaissance-Strike" systems, forming the most concrete expression of the so-called Revolution in Military Affairs—the famous RMA that preoccupied military bureaucrats on both sides of the Atlantic at the turn of the millennium. Interestingly, in spite of its suggestive Soviet-style name, many believe that the RMA is both an American idea and a new by-product of computer technology, while in fact the scheme originated in the Soviet General Staff of the 1970s, when the Soviet computer industry was famously backward.

As we contemplate the two ideas, we can already begin to imagine how the Soviet side could have reacted to negate or outmaneuver them, forcing them down the effectiveness curve from their culminating point of success. But our purpose is to uncover the general workings of strategy rather than to examine the ultimate merit of particular proposals. We must therefore examine the still-picture view of each level in sequence rather than the moving film of dynamic interactions within a single level. We begin with the first idea: antitank infantry.

The War of the Weapons

At the start we examine the confrontation between the weapons, assuming that all are manned by competent crews, of which we need know nothing else in this technical context. On the one side, we see the tanks and infantry combat carriers that form the cutting edge of advancing Soviet divisions as they seek to break through the Alliance front. On the other side, we see the defending infantry with its antitank missiles, perhaps deployed in the open, or more sensibly behind terrain cover, or more dubiously in concrete firing bunkers—but at this level of strategy we ignore the difference, just as we ignore how the Soviet tanks are moving, whether exposed in full view or cleverly probing forward within covered approaches offered by low-lying ground or forest margins (German forests, famously orderly since their nineteenth-century replanting, are cut by many fire-barrier roadways). At this level, it is enough to see just one antitank missile and one Soviet tank or combat carrier, and they might as well be facing each other on a featureless firing range.

We note that the antitank missile is a cheap weapon as compared to the tank or even the combat carrier, its cost (at say $20,000) perhaps 1 percent of the tank's or 10 percent at most of the combat carrier's. And while it takes no more than two men to form a missile-launcher crew, the tank will contain three or four men and so will the vehicle crew of the combat carrier, not counting the infantrymen inside. By whatever calculation of human service and life, that difference further improves the economic advantage of the antitank missile.

Next we see that the missile can assuredly be guided to its target, and if we test a number of them we find that they strike home 90 percent of the time. The hollow-charge warhead will easily penetrate the thin armor of the combat carrier with its stream of superhigh-velocity plasma, which will devastate everything and everybody inside. The tank might have thick plates of advanced ceramic-composite armor with "reactive armor" boxes on top of it, and all sorts of internal protection enhancements, but in our still-picture view we are examining missiles that are equally advanced, with stand-off precision warheads of sufficient diameter to penetrate the thickest tank armor. Reactive armor boxes can defeat many hollow-charge weapons, depending on the angle of attack, but the best missiles now available are in any case programmed to climb and dive vertically, bypassing the thickest frontal armor.

The tank crew is of course firing with its machine guns and even its main gun, perhaps with antipersonnel canister or fléchette rounds. Or, if it is a combat carrier, then both its infantry team and crew are firing, perhaps with a small mortar or grenade launcher in addition to several machine guns. But the missile has a longer range than any of those of weapons except for the main tank cannon. Its crew therefore has an excellent chance of destroying the target vehicle before its machine guns come within range or the tank gunner can spot the elusive missile launcher. At night matters do not change because both sides are using night-vision devices. True, because vehicles can supply power and refrigeration, they can have forward-looking infrared sights that are superior to the infantry's optical devices ("starlight scopes"), but compensating for that equipment difference there is the difference in "target contrast": tanks and combat carriers are much larger, very noisy, and thus far more easily detected at night.

Simple numbers can describe everything we can observe at the technical level of strategy. Using rough averages, we can estimate that 90 percent of all missiles will function correctly, 60 percent will in turn hit the target, and 80 percent will penetrate tank armor, of which 90 percent will cause immobilizing damage, to yield a 39 percent cumulative probability of success. In straight duels fought over our featureless range by competent, emotionless crews, 2.56 missiles will therefore destroy a tank that costs one hundred times as much, and 1.8 missiles will destroy a combat carrier that costs more than fifteen times as much—in that case, penetration and damage can be assumed, there being little armor, so that a hit is almost always a kill.

We can therefore see that the *cost-adjusted* effectiveness of the missile is categorically superior to that of the armored vehicle at this technical level (for example, $51,200 worth of missiles will destroy a $2 million tank). But that difference may mean little by itself, without taking into account the total military resources of each side: as of this writing, the rich United States is routinely using million-dollar-plus cruise missiles against hovels in Afghanistan or Iraqi radio huts. In our example, however, the Soviet Union did not have any superiority in total military resources; it certainly could not afford enough tanks or combat carriers to outmatch the missiles.

As some do, we might stop here and present this technical result as final—which it might be, if we were examining, say, an encounter between ballistic and antiballistic missiles in the vast and featureless firing range of space. Then indeed any advantage in cost-adjusted effectiveness would be a sufficient truth, to determine for example the sheer feasibility of the venture. For us, however, the examination of the technical-level duel between advancing armored vehicles and antitank missiles yields only a partial, highly provisional truth.

To be sure, the technical level does have an importance of its own, now more than in the historical past when differences in technical capacity were usually small. Today, the latest jet fighters, battle tanks, or submarines can significantly outclass less modern predecessors, whereas in the past there were only small quality differences between, say, any two competent swords or adequate shields. There were exceptions but only a few, such as the Huns, who first appeared at the end of the fourth century with a decisive technical advantage: their compound bows, short enough to be used on horseback yet of unprecedented range, accuracy, and penetrating power.

The boundaries of the technical level of strategy are not arbitrary. Within it, the weapons of war and their interactions can be observed with great clarity—but only as one slice of a much broader reality, because all other material and intangible factors that affect combat outcomes remain undetermined. By itself, the technical level is a sufficient reality only for scientists and engineers engaged in developing weapons. All they need to know to start working is what kinds of additional performance are most wanted; it is not their duty—nor is it their right—to decide *how much* performance is to be acquired at the expense of numbers or other military priorities.

Soldiers and Technicians

Scientists and engineers are rarely familiar with the detailed tactical contents of the military requirements that are imposed on them. In any case, their obedience to those requirements is often only formal: they know very well that military requirements change with each new tactical doctrine, each new "strategy," while the weapons they develop last for many years—thirty years and more for combat aircraft, even longer for tanks and guns. Scientists and engineers, moreover, tend to have little respect for requirements formulated by military authorities whom they often see as ignorant of the full range of technological possibilities open to them. They see military officers focusing on yesterday's "new-new" technologies, which are already not so new for scientists and engineers. The ever increasing technological education of military men (it started in the eighteenth century) has not closed the divide because the two sides are subject to different authorities: science itself for scientists and engineers, military institutions and hierarchies for soldiers.

Their purposes are essentially divergent. For military bureaucracies, the maximum quality that can be achieved in a single weapon is usually sacrificed for the sake of quantity: to reduce the magnitude of the forces is to reduce the base of the military hierarchy. For scientists and engineers, numbers have no value at all in themselves: maximum quality is the only goal of their ambition, so that they are always seeking to develop the most complete, the most perfect, the most versatile weapons with the highest possible performance, no matter how much the cost.

Before the First World War, it was the biggest and best-protected battleships, and the railway guns of longest range, that excited engineering ambitions. That suited navies well, because naval doctrine at the time stressed preparations for the single, all-out battle for global maritime superiority with the strongest possible warships, even if they were few, given that a big battleship could sink any number of cruisers. But huge railway guns were not at all consistent with contemporary artillery doctrines, which called for mobility; nevertheless, they were developed at great cost.

Before and during the Second World War, the paths of technological ambition diverged and proliferated to yield many different innovations, some of immediate military value (radar, for example, and eventually the fission bomb) and others of negative military value at the time, most famously the German V-1 and V-2 rockets that consumed vast resources without serving any worthwhile purpose. Many other innovations, such as the V-3 ramjet gun and the 100-ton Maus supertank also absorbed scarce German resources without even reaching the production stage.

At present, engineering ambitions focus on directed-energy weapons, such as airborne lasers powerful enough to burn through and destroy rocket boosters far below them; fighter aircraft that can cruise supersonically (today's so-called supersonic fighters use up their fuel quickly when they exceed Mach 1, on afterburner); "stealth" aircraft that are hard to detect with normal radars and whose infrared and sound emissions are also minimized; and—on a much larger scale—the RMA's Reconnaissance-Strike systems, whose most difficult challenge remains the fusion of all the information collected by many sensors into a single instantaneous picture of all the many targets of interest and their prioritization, so that their attack requires only the transmission of target coordinates to the cruise-missile launchers, bombing aircraft, or even artillery batteries.

In the meantime, yesterday's engineering ambitions have yielded today's nuclear-powered submarines, which are larger than Second World War cruisers and far more costly; nuclear-powered aircraft carriers that are even more enormous and enormously costly; and jet fighters themselves so elaborate that their annual output is smaller than the number that could be lost in a bad morning of air combat.

It has long been fashionable to deplore the tendency to pursue weapon quality at the expense of quantity, at least in the United States, but the paradoxical logic of strategy, at any of its levels, is irrelevant to the question, offering no guidance on the matter. It makes no difference if the technical-level action that evokes a reaction involves simpler weapons or a smaller number of more ambitious weapons. It is instead linear, commonsense, economic logic that imposes limits on the pursuit of quality at the expense of numbers, because the marginal utility of quality improvements must eventually diminish toward zero given the scientific-technological limitations of the time: the very best rifle producible, constructed of the most advanced materials with the latest techniques, can be only slightly more effective than any ordinary modern rifle based on the same scientific principles and of course costing much less. And so it is for bombers, missiles, submarines, or any other weapons we may compare.

We know that we are not in the realm of strategy when making such calculations because, as we add quality, the extra effectiveness gained can fall only to zero and not go below it (unless reliability is being sacrificed to complication, which should not occur if quality includes reliability). If strategy's dynamic paradox ruled the outcome, quality increments would actually begin to reduce the effectiveness of single weapons after a certain point.

Tensions between military priorities and engineering ambitions are constantly being negotiated by technically minded military men and militarily minded engineers, both marginal members of their respective groups. But when the products of technical development are finally handed over to the armed forces, it is mainstream views and institutional interests that will determine their employment. When the new is only an incremental improvement over the old, which is usually the case as somewhat better aircraft, tanks, or missiles replace essentially similar predecessors, military modernization is not impeded by institutional resistance: the new fits into the slots of the old, without requiring any change in the organization or its doctrines and established habits.

But if the new is a real innovation, not just a new model, so that the new equipment has no direct predecessor at all, as with remotely piloted air vehicles (or unmanned aerial vehicles), for example, then the armed forces must change their structure to absorb it, usually by creating new units, inevitably at the expense of previously established units. That is the great difficulty. Existing units such as fighter aircraft are represented in the councils of decision: even if those within them are of low rank, young pilots in this case, there will be high-ranking officers who come from that branch and that tradition, air force generals in this case. The units yet to be established obviously cannot already be represented by people with institutional power, as they have no bureaucratic advocates.

As a result, innovation will be significantly delayed even if potentially of great use, but it all depends: if the armed forces as a whole are expanding with an abundance of resources, they will accommodate the new more easily because established units lose only growth, not forces already in being. And of course wartime urgencies can overcome bureaucratic resistance. The reason the Israelis were the first to manufacture and use remotely piloted air vehicles seriously—really trying to make them work instead of testing them only to find shortcomings—was that when they were first proposed, the Israelis were fighting their 1968–1970 "War of Attrition." Their fighter pilots were exposed to surface-to-air missiles every time they flew over Egypt—and that made the idea of using pilotless aircraft very attractive.

By contrast, if there is scarcity when the new is being proposed, if the established forces are already starved for resources, with no war under way or imminent, bureaucratic resistance to the new will be intense—and mostly successful. Between 1990 and 2000, the arrival of cheap, reliable, and powerful small computers caused much *structural* change in the world: many businesses were drastically reorganized and many schoolchildren changed their habits of work and play. Those years, however, happened to coincide with the end of the Cold War and declining defense budgets, leaving military forces hardly changed at all. They did not adapt their structures and methods to exploit the many possible advantages of computer abundance; instead they merely added computers to their established organizational formats.

Innovation may be favored by historical circumstances, as with the amazingly rapid introduction of firearms in Japan,[1] or it can entirely fail when social resistance simply blocks innovation,* or when lack of organizational change causes the innovation to be utterly misapplied. A famous case of aborted innovation was the *mitrailleuse*, an early machine gun hurriedly adopted by the French army in 1869, in anticipation of war with Prussia. In a world of single-shot, bolt-action rifles, the *mitrailleuse* could fire three hundred rounds per minute with good accuracy out to at least five hundred meters. It was quite reliable; against infantry unprepared for its rapid fire, it should have had decisive effects. A Belgian invention, the *mitrailleuse* was manufactured in great secrecy by French arsenals at the behest of Napoleon III. Large numbers were ready when war with Prussia began in 1870.

But extreme secrecy had prevented field exercises and open tactical debate. Because the gun was too heavy to be manhandled and was therefore placed on a light two-wheel carriage, it resembled a piece of field artillery; because the infantry was not equipped to supply its ammunition needs at a time when one hundred rounds per man sufficed for weeks of campaigning, and each battalion could count on only a few horse-drawn wag-

---

* The Mamelukes of Egypt, descendants of Turkish warriors who were originally imported as military slaves, resisted firearms so rigidly that they would not even have commoner-musketeers serving alongside them when they rode into battle.

ons already burdened with tents, food, and impedimenta; and also perhaps because Napoleon III was himself an artillery expert, it was the artillery that received the *mitrailleuse*. When war came, French gunners naturally employed the new weapon as if it were a field piece, keeping it behind the infantry. That meant that it could not fire on its target, the German infantry.[2] It was too much to expect that the artillery gunners would abandon all their normal concepts to place the *mitrailleuse* among the infantry—to do so would have seemed a retrogression to seventeenth-century methods. Nor could the new weapon be handed over to the infantry without transferring the scarce artillery ammunition wagons as well. As it happened, in the battle of Gravelotte on August 18, 1870, the Prussian infantry advanced far enough to come within range of some *mitrailleuses*. Firing as many as twelve 25-round boxes of cartridges per minute (300 rounds per minute), the new weapons executed a massacre, accounting for many of the 20,163 Prussian casualties of that day.[3] But except at Gravelotte, the *mitrailleuse* had no impact on the outcome of the war. Had the innovation not been aborted by the failure to adapt organizationally, it might have averted the disastrous French defeat.

Political Masters and Technicians

While there are tensions between engineers and military men that only institutional change can resolve, chronic dissonance is merely the normal state of affairs between engineers and politicians. The political aims of the state are usually so distant and vague for the engineers that these aims hardly enter into the technical calculations. In rare cases, authority abruptly intervenes from above, to issue its orders, positive or negative. An American president may choose to close an avenue of development technically quite promising, simply because it offends his ethical sense or might perhaps hurt his public image. Another may order engineers to develop some new weapon that is beyond the contemporary boundary of scientific possibilities, without recognizing that scientific progress cannot be directed or accelerated by political decisions and additional funding. A Hitler or a Stalin could bring dictatorship into the laboratory, to order that ballistic rockets or fission bombs be built, and rapidly.

There are recorded cases of intrusion just as spectacular from the scientific side, most momentously on October 11, 1939, when the influential economist Alexander Sachs handed over to President Roosevelt a letter signed by the already eminent Albert Einstein. The letter introduced a memorandum signed by another refugee scientist, the then unknown Leo Szilard, whose idea it all was. Both documents invited the American government to investigate the possibility of initiating a uranium chain reaction "within a warlike device." Szilard's venture had been made possible by the assistance of two other refugee scientists, Eugene Wigner and Edward Teller. Each was destined for future fame, but their essential role just then was to drive Szilard to Einstein's Long Island beach cabin on successive occasions: Szilard did not have a driver's license. According to the account left by Sachs, Roosevelt seemed inattentive as he read the letter and memorandum, and it was only on the following day at breakfast that Sachs finally persuaded Roosevelt to take the matter seriously, by recounting an anecdote about Napoleon's refusal to finance Fulton's steamship project.[4]

In Nazi Germany, by contrast, circumstances just as fortuitous impeded the development of the fission bomb. Hitler's enthusiasm was readily kindled by the prospect of building rockets, fusiform and roaring, and his support of rocketry was both unstinting and tenacious. Nuclear physics, however, was a field notoriously filled with non-Aryan scientists (Szilard, Teller, and Wigner as well as Einstein were all Jews) and was further condemned by Nazi thinkers because it had disrupted many old certainties. Nor did the nuclear chain reaction find a German advocate as persistent as Leo Szilard. Thus matters of colossal importance were decided frivolously, because of the scientific ignorance of Adolf Hitler, who understood mechanical weapons quite well, electronic devices very little, and nuclear physics not all. Of course the American fission-bomb project would have started sooner or later, even if there had been no Szilard. But delay could have been decisive, if Hitler's tastes had been different.

In the aftermath of the Second World War, with its dramatic episodes of scientific warfare, and in the wake of Alamogordo, Hiroshima, and Nagasaki, the idea that political leaders should not disregard the possibilities offered by science became part of the conventional wisdom. Scientific offices proliferated within governments and armed forces, and scientific advisers were added to the staffs of presidents, prime ministers, and secretary-generals. That, however, did not do much to reduce the dissonance between science and politics. It turned out that there are only two kinds of scientific questions: routine matters, over which no political decision is needed at all, and controversial matters, over which scientists themselves also tend to disagree.[5] Politicians are still the captains of the ship of state, and military men are its deck crew, but now there are scientists and engineers in charge of the engine room, and they propel the ship toward unknown destinations.

6

The Tactical Level

Returning to our Cold War example, once we reexamine the fight between the antitank missile and the advancing armored forces at the next level of strategy, the picture before our eyes becomes both larger and fuller. It is larger, because we no longer simplify the encounter into a duel but must instead consider entire units facing one another, containing many missile teams and many armored vehicles. And the picture is fuller, because we are no longer comparing missiles and armored vehicles facing one another on a featureless test range, with crews who might as well be robots. At the tactical level we encounter all the human realities of combat.

First, however, there is the physical arena of the fight, its terrain and vegetation. There are no high mountains in central Germany where the front lines would have been, but in most places the land is contoured with hills and vales—and even mere folds in the ground can be important to the infantry, offering both concealment and protection. There are many covered approaches that smaller Soviet armored columns could have exploited to appear suddenly before the antitank missiles at short range, robbing them of their great range advantage over machine guns. In extreme cases, the emergence of visible targets might have occurred at such short range that the antitank missile could not be used at all; most designs have a minimum as well as a maximum range limit, because after its explosive launch, the missile must be "captured" by the guidance mechanism into the aiming line of sight (antitank rockets too have a minimum range set by time fuze, to protect their operators from the explosion).

Nor is Germany a desert. Everywhere there is vegetation that could have concealed the antitank infantry initially masking its presence. Along with even minimal terrain cover, it could offer critically important protection against direct-fire weapons. Moreover, with warning time before the fight, the terrain and its vegetation could not only be exploited in natural form but also enhanced by fortification and by minefields. Bulldozers and backhoes, or specialized combat-engineer vehicles with trench cutters and hole drillers, or even shovels and saws can transform exposed terrain into a fortified zone. No advance in weapon technology has eliminated the ancient advantage of fighting with overhead cover, to resist indirect-fire howitzers and mortars, and of entrenched firing positions and antivehicle ditches. With yet more time, continuous antimobility barriers fortified against breaching by firing bunkers in solid concrete could make an excellent contribution to the defense, contrary to all post–Maginot Line prejudice. Even less time is needed to add antitank mines to the defense; much can be done by hand, but mines can be emplaced far more rapidly by special layer vehicles or even projected by rockets in front of advancing armor. By contrast, firing positions that stand out from the natural surroundings as obvious targets, fragile fortifications too easily flattened by artillery, and minefields that are not covered by fire allowing their unimpeded clearance can be disastrous for the defense.

At this level of strategy, such things can be decisive in themselves. We therefore recognize that an entirely new factor affects failure and success: skill—not only the assumed technical skill to mechanically operate weapons, but the far more subtle tactical skill needed to exploit terrain advantages in moving forces and in positioning weapons against a particular enemy in a particular time and place. Now the natural aptitude and training of the men inside those armored vehicles, and of the missile infantry opposing them, become very important. Do they know how to act on the battlefield to protect themselves and hurt the enemy? Can their junior leaders quickly "read" the terrain and the immediate combat situation? Will they intuitively choose the better fields of fire or—on the other side—the better approaches of advance?

Leadership, Morale, Fortune

Skill must be an individual attribute, but it is vehicle crews and missile teams who are doing the fighting—in other words, groups, however small. What counts therefore is not personal skill but the skill effectively applied by groups as a whole—and that depends on the competence of their leaders. Are the commanders of missile-infantry teams selected for their tactical skill, or were they promoted more for their obedience than their ingenuity? Are the junior officers in command of armored units real leaders willing to act on their own initiative, or are they just followers of higher-ranking officers in the chain of command?

Nor is competent leadership sufficient without troops willing to face danger. As soon as the tactical encounter begins, with the shocking blast of the artillery, the sinister hammering of the machine guns, the deadly boom of mortar bombs, when the earth seems to explode from within to fly into the air; as soon as an armored carrier here or a tank there is hit, and starts to burn or explodes; as soon as the missile infantrymen discover their comrades of a moment ago dead or wounded—as soon as the fighting actually begins, that is, we discover that much more than skilled leadership determines outcomes.

Every natural instinct induces the attacking armored crews to pause in the safety of any shelter offered by the terrain, instead of continuing their advance into the unknown countryside before them, against an invisible enemy and his deadly missiles. And the same powerful instinct urges the infantrymen to flee, instead of holding their ground against the steel monsters relentlessly advancing upon them. Their missile launchers will now seem desperately flimsy and of uncertain effect—as opposed to the mathematical certainty that in a few minutes the defenders will be crushed under the tracks of advancing tanks and combat carriers, unless all of them are hit and stopped.

What overcomes instinct to make combat possible are the three great intangibles that all fighting armies strive to cultivate through parade-ground drills (to make obedience automatic); speeches, songs, and flags (to inspire pride); and punishments and rewards: individual morale, group discipline, and unit cohesion. Of these decisively important but unmeasurable attributes, small-unit cohesion is usually the most important, because the willingness of men to fight for one another survives the terrible impact of battle far better than any other source of morale.

At the tactical level of strategy, therefore, the intangibles of skill, leadership, morale, discipline, and unit cohesion enter into our picture, usually to dominate the outcome. That is why estimates of military balances that stop at the technical level are so systematically misleading: by comparing lists of weapons side by side, with seductive precision they exclude from the comparison the greater part of the whole.

There is another factor that powerfully influences outcomes within any one tactical encounter: fortune, that is, chance and probability—the chance that the troops on either side may be exhausted by lack of sleep, sickened by foul rations or unfed because of supply breakdowns, or badly frightened by some prior combat; and the probabilities of the weather. In central Europe, dense mist or thick ground fogs are common during many months of the year. This can allow the tanks and combat carriers to appear suddenly in front of the defenders, giving them almost no time to fire off even one missile—if they are still in place after the profoundly demoralizing experience of hearing the roaring approach of unseen armored vehicles.

Offense-Defense Asymmetries

All the things that count at the tactical level have their counterparts in other forms of warfare, in the air and at sea as well as on land. But do terrain factors, skill, leadership, morale, cohesion, and fortune affect the two sides differently? Does their addition to our picture modify the categorical conclusion reached at the technical level? Do they change the finding that infantry armed with antitank missiles could have been highly effective against Soviet armored forces in the defense of central Europe? The answer is a definite yes.

First, the needs of the two sides are unequal. Soviet armored forces only had to advance to execute their task. Most of the crews only had to operate their vehicles and fire their weapons through narrow-view sights, shielded from most of the terrorizing visions and sounds of battle by armor plate and roaring engines. To keep moving in the right direction, to make good use of the terrain, leadership is needed of course, and this has to be provided by junior officers at the head of the columns; but no such initiative is required from armor crews inside their vehicles.

The defending missile infantrymen, by contrast, cannot usefully participate in the fight by mere mechanical operation, in a state of diminished consciousness. They must stay active and alert to spot their targets at long range, in spite of intervening smoke, whether incidental or deliberate, and in spite of fog and mist. They must then calmly acquire the targets in their sights and then decide the moment of launch—a delicate matter because although the longest range is desirable, the greater the intervening distance the more likely it is that it will contain dead ground, in which the advancing tank might be hidden just long enough to evade the missile on its flight. After launch, the operator must keep the moving target in his sights during the long seconds of missile flight until impact (only now are the first fire-and-forget missiles being produced). And throughout the entire procedure, from the spotting to the hitting, the missile troops must perform their exacting tasks while all their senses are attacked by the sounds and sights of battle, with even the briefest distraction resulting in the loss of control over the missiles in flight.

Then there is the great asymmetry in physical protection, unless strong fortifications are provided. The armored force is only really vulnerable to the missiles, other tanks, or mines, but the defenders are vulnerable to every weapon on the battlefield: machine guns, mortars, grenade launchers, tank guns, and, most important of all, supporting artillery firing ahead of the advancing armor. In addition to killing and wounding, all these fires could incapacitate the missile infantry tactically, by forcing the men to seek cover instead of engaging their targets.

Actually not merely their senses but also their thoughts will conspire against the defenders. The advancing armor unit is driven forward by the units coming up from behind. Aside from following a given vector of advance, its task is open-ended, with the choices and fates of commanders and crewmen only loosely affected by the strength of the entire defense in front of them, of which they would know little and certainly could not calculate. But the defenders have ample opportunity to calculate: even with perfect visibility, their maximum range of engagement cannot exceed 4,000 meters; if enemy armor advances at a mere 15 kilometers an hour, they will have a total of only sixteen minutes of fighting time before the tanks and combat carriers will be upon them. If there is mist to reduce visibility in some degree or fog to reduce it much more, the engagement range declines and so does the available fighting time. In central Europe, even 1,500 meters and six minutes might be too optimistic. Theoretically, each missile-launcher team could engage a new target every minute, and such things are sometimes done on peacetime firing ranges. But in the actual sequence of combat, from spotting to hitting, one shot every two minutes is a high maximum, each with a 38 percent probability of killing its target, if no enemy fire is degrading crew performance.

To know if they can hold the line, or if retreat is the only alternative to death or capture, the defenders must therefore estimate how many tanks and combat carriers are actually advancing upon them. If that number is greater than one for each missile launcher that survives artillery bombardment and direct fire, then the infantry will know that their lives or liberty will be lost in the next several minutes. Because in our case study the enemy was the Soviet army, and because chance has placed them in front of one of its columns, the defenders had to expect the worst: the tanks and combat carriers they could actually see and engage may have been only a few, but many more would be coming up in short order. This abundance of armor—the reason why the antitank missile infantry concept had been proposed in the first place—could only result in a demoralizing tactical situation, from which the only escape was not to stand and fight but rather to launch a missile or two and then move smartly back.

For all these reasons, the initial finding at the technical level is now greatly changed. When we examine the encounter at the tactical level, we see that the defenders can no longer hope to destroy a tank costing one hundred times as much as a missile with 2.56 missiles, nor combat carriers costing at least fifteen times as much with 1.8 missiles per carrier. Instead, we see the missile infantry and their launchers lost to precursor artillery shells, mortar bombs, and direct fires before they can engage the enemy at all; others incapable of acquiring even one target during their few minutes of engagement time because of intervening smoke; and still others losing control of missiles already in flight to their targets, because of the blast and shock of the explosions around them.

How many missile launchers will therefore be required in tactical reality to destroy a tank or combat carrier? Is it ten or twenty, as some Middle East war experiences suggest? Or is it more, because central Europe does not have such splendid visibility? With the cost differences so great, the exchange ratios should remain favorable, but no longer by large margins. Our tactical-level finding, therefore, still provisional of course, is that the missile-infantry concept is much less promising than it first seemed at the technical level. And now we know that its success will depend to an unusually great extent on the qualities of the men involved. The intangibles of morale, discipline, and cohesion are almost always more important in combat than material factors, but especially so in this case, because the defense must withstand much more stress than the offense—a significant asymmetry that counts as a key disadvantage of the concept.

So we discover that the merits of the missile-infantry proposal were in fact critically dependent on what earlier might have seemed mere administrative detail. Will the missile infantry be manned by cohesive territorial units of friends and neighbors beholden to one another, and screened for aptitude, and trained as seriously as part-time training will allow? Or will reservists who once served as conscript soldiers years ago be assigned from all over the country, to meet for the first time just as the fighting is about to begin? Or is the missile infantry to be an elite corps of highly selected young men, trained and commanded to ensure the highest morale? And if so, by what sort of reasoning could the wealthy nations of the North Atlantic Alliance choose to use their best men to fight with cheap weapons against Warsaw Pact enemies much poorer yet far more heavily armed?

Thus at the tactical level of strategy we encounter the full complexities of the human dimension of combat, as we see the fighting unfold within a unique context of time and place. Because the unpredictables of the weather and of human circumstances vary, not even forces identically manned and armed, acting in identical ways on the very same ground, can twice fight exactly the same battle and get exactly the same result. True, chances cancel each other out, so that relying on probability estimates based on the observation of many events (accuracies of weapons, patterns of climate), we can reach tactical-level conclusions of broader validity, but even those apply only to particular forces with particular equipment and particular human characteristics, too.

The wisdom of tactical teachings in the detailed craft of war can neither travel very far nor last very long. There is no right or wrong that does not depend on the specific character of the antagonists and the specific performance of weapons. A given way of attacking an enemy outpost, flying an intercept or engaging an enemy warship, might be either suicidally bold or excessively timid, depending on the characteristics of the opposed forces. Manuals of tactics must therefore be rewritten whenever significant new weapons appear, turning what used to be impossible into mere routine, and making what was once quite safe impossibly dangerous. One may still read ancient texts on tactics for advice of enduring value, but it would be idle to pretend that they contain much more than the obvious. And if we read the far less interesting tactical manuals of the two world wars, we would find them just as outdated. Hence tactics are the proper subject of up-to-date professionals alone, just as any normative "strategics" that advocate this or that policy for one country or another can be of only contemporary validity at best—unlike strategy itself, which prescribes nothing and merely describes unchanging phenomena that exist whether we know them or not.

The Limits of the Tactical

In our still-picture view of the engagement between the missile infantry and advancing armored forces, we did not allow for any shift in tactics on either side. There was no reaction to success or failure that would then evoke further reactions on the other side and so on. It was simply assumed that both forces would execute simple tactics of frontal attack and frontal defense, although with proper attention to the terrain.

That simplification might be valid in the case of the initial collision between the first wave of advancing Soviet armor and the defensive line of antitank infantry. But if the defense succeeds in repelling that first attack, a reaction is bound to come, either to suppress the defense by greater artillery firepower or to circumvent it in some other way. The defense can also react, by using the time it gains with its first success to move to alternative positions, to send out hunting parties armed with antitank rockets if there is good terrain or vegetation cover for them, or to plan an ambush in which the next wave of the attack will be allowed passage before being engaged from behind. With that another round would begin.

The particular forces we have been examining are not, however, independent agents pursuing their own goals. What for them is the entire fight, indeed their entire existence at the time, is only a fragment of the entire battle for the higher echelons of command and the national authorities on both sides. They devised the plans and made the decisions that caused the fight. Once the battle begins, they strive to retain control over the course of the fighting by reacting to its emerging results. They might assign additional artillery or air support to the units already engaged in combat. They might sacrifice those units, letting them fight on unassisted, whether to exploit their remaining stopping power on the defensive or to keep up a vector of attack on the offensive, while their waning strength turns it into a feint. Once units already fielded are fully engaged in battle and perhaps absorbed in their own struggle for survival, higher echelons can fully assert their control only over the new forces they send in, which they can still freely direct into new defensive positions or, on the offensive, into new vectors of attack. Even with pervasive, instantaneous, communications there is no instantaneous control over units already engaged with the enemy, for then what can and cannot be done must depend on what the enemy can or cannot do.

The interplay of action and reaction is then no longer confined to the tactical level. We will need a quite different and much broader perspective to pursue the investigation. In it, the detailed particularities of the terrain and wider context lose their importance, as the full array of rival forces is examined on a much larger scale. For this we must ascend to the next level of strategy, after noting that although we have viewed an episode of ground combat, every other form of warfare past and present—at sea, in the air, or even in space-including warfare loosely described as "strategic"*—must have its own tactical level.

* Ever since the Second World War, the adjective "strategic" has been widely used to describe *long-range* aircraft and missiles as opposed to their shorter-range counterparts, in turn labeled "tactical," although, revealingly, there is no talk of strategic and tactical warships. This unfortunate terminology originated from the rhetoric of the early advocates of air power in a two-step process of transposition. First, the bomber aircraft they wanted to use against industrial and other homeland targets were called "strategic" to convey their ability to win wars on their own—as opposed to mere tactical bombing in support of ground forces. Then the adjective "strategic" became associated with the completely incidental quality of long range, which bombers might need to attack homeland targets in *some* geographic settings—and that in turn caused "tactical" to acquire the meaning of short range. It is a classic case of false distinctions that only serve to confuse. In the 1991 Gulf war, rather small "tactical" F-117 aircraft were employed to attack headquarters in Baghdad and other strategic targets, while huge "strategic" B-52 bombers were employed to attack troop concentrations in Kuwait and other tactical targets. In the 1999 Kosovo war, "strategic" B-52, B-1A, and B-2 bombers attacked Serbian ground forces, while all the strategic targets in Serbia were attacked by "tactical" F-15Es, F-117s, and others such. Nor is this a consequence of the new guidance equipment that allows routine precision, and therefore the replacement of massed bombing attacks with selective strikes on specific targets. Already in June 1941 the German Luftwaffe, which had already used short-range aircraft to bomb Warsaw, Rotterdam, and London in purely strategic attacks, would have needed aircraft of the longest range to attack Soviet troop concentrations behind the front.

7

The Operational Level

It is a peculiarity of English-language military terminology that it long had no word of its own to describe the middle level of thought and action between the tactical and the strategic—the level that embraces battles in their dynamic totality, in which generic methods of war are developed, debated, and applied. As we shall see, there was a good reason for this absence, a reason that no longer applied when I introduced the operational-level concept, now ubiquitous in both American and British field manuals and routinely employed in military writings.[1] It was hardly an original invention of mine of course. In the tradition of continental military thought, the German and Russian equivalents have a long history and a central importance.[2] Both traditions emphasize the "operational art of war" as a higher combination that is more than the sum of its tactical parts.

The weapons themselves interact at the technical level of strategy; the forces directly opposed fight one another at the tactical level; but at the operational level we encounter for the first time the struggle between the directing minds on both sides. That is the level at which overall methods of war are applied, as in the deep-penetration armored offensive or the defense-in-depth; the strategic bombing of key nodes as opposed to the battlefield interdiction of ground strength; layered naval air defense and other similar instances. It is at the operational level that the ongoing command of all the forces involved must unfold, and above all that is the level of the battle as a whole with all its adventures and misadventures.

The boundary between what is operational and what is tactical in methods, ongoing command, and the action itself is both difficult to define in the abstract and obvious in practice. Where single types of forces and their specific tactics—as, say, in submarines and submarine tactics, or artillery and artillery tactics—no longer determine outcomes by themselves, because other types of forces and other kinds of tactics are also involved, we have ascended to the operational level. Once again, there is no need for arbitrary definitions. As soon as we examine any episode of combat, we can recognize its natural stratification between the operational layer and what comes below or above. But of course the demarcation between tactical, operational, and strategic is also associated with a rising scale in the volume of the action and the variety of means.

At one extreme, for a primitive tribe whose entire force consists of warriors identically armed with shield and spear and always positioned in a single formation, the tactical, operational, and strategic must coincide for all practical purposes. Such a tribe cannot suffer a tactical defeat that is not also strategic, nor can it develop a method of war that is more than a tactic. By contrast, say, for the United States in the Second World War, quite different operational situations could coexist even within the same theater of war, so that each day could bring its share of both tactical victories and tactical defeats. And of course different operational methods were applied in the amphibious campaigns of the Pacific, in the strategic bombing of German industry, in the eleven months of continental warfare that began with the June 1944 Normandy landings, and in the struggle for naval supremacy in the Pacific.

Scale and variety are necessary conditions, but they are not sufficient: if the operational level is to have any substance of its own, the action must consist of more than the sum of the tactical parts. That in turn depends on the prevailing *style of war*, and more specifically on its place within the spectrum of attrition at one end and maneuver at the other.

Attrition and Maneuver in War

Attrition is war waged by industrial methods. The enemy is treated as nothing more than an array of targets, and the aim is to win by their cumulative destruction achieved with superior firepower and material strength in general. Eventually the full inventory of enemy targets could in theory be destroyed, unless retreat or surrender terminates the process, as almost always happens in practice.

The greater the attrition content of an overall style of war, the more will routinized techniques of target acquisition, attack, and resupply be sufficient, along with repetitive tactics, and the smaller is the opportunity—or need—to apply any operational method of war. Process replaces the art of war and all its ingenuities. As long as materially superior and abundantly supplied firepower-producing forces are brought within range of static targets (trenchlines, cities) or of enemy forces that must remain immobile and concentrated to achieve *their* purposes (not guerrillas, therefore), victory is mathematically assured. It is understood that if the enemy also has his firepower, the resulting reciprocal attrition will have to be absorbed. There can be no victory in this style of war without an overall material superiority, and there can be no cheap victories achieved by clever moves with few casualties and few resources expended.

There is no such thing as attrition warfare in pure form, without any cunning or artifice at all, truly reduced to an industrial process. But examples of warfare with a high attrition content are by no means rare. They include the trench fighting of the First World War, most of whose battles were symmetrical engagements between the rival artillery forces, along with infantry combat that opposed frontal attacks on foot against linear defenses anchored by machine guns and mortars; the Luftwaffe's attempt to defeat the Royal Air Force in June–August 1940 by deliberately seeking air-combat engagements, on the mistaken assumption that it had enough material superiority to win; Montgomery's battle of El Alamein, and most of his later battles, in which the enemy was first barraged by vastly superior artillery and then frontally assaulted by infantry, before being overrun by armored units in overwhelmingly superior numbers; the German submarine campaign of 1941–1943, whose goal was to win the war by reducing the total tonnage of oceanic shipping available to the Allies below the minimum needed for their war effort; the Allied campaign in Italy from 1943 to 1945, which degenerated into a series of grinding frontal offensives after the failure of the outmaneuvering attempt at Anzio; the air bombardment of Germany and Japan, in part aimed at industrial attrition and in part aimed at the attrition of urban areas in general; Eisenhower's broad-front offensive after the breakout from Normandy, which Patton subverted only occasionally with his deep-penetration maneuvers; Ridgeway's Korean offensives of 1951–52, in which ground forces slowly advanced in a solid front from coast to coast, against Chinese and North Korean forces systematically reduced by air power and artillery; much of the American fighting in Vietnam, even though the enemy stubbornly refused to assemble in conveniently targetable mass formations (despite concentric "search and destroy" actions to induce involuntary concentrations); and the notional case of the Cold War plans for the nuclear targeting of urban populations and industry, whose aim was to dissuade governments by threatening attrition on an colossal scale.

At the other end of the spectrum there is *relational maneuver*, in which the aim is not to destroy the enemy's physical substance as an end in itself, but rather to incapacitate by some form of systemic disruption—whether that "system" is the command structure of the enemy's forces, their logistic support, their own method of warfare, or even an actual technical system, as when radars are electronically deceived as opposed to subjected to brute-force jamming or outright physical attack.

Instead of seeking out the enemy's concentrations of strength to better find targets in bulk, the starting point of relational maneuver is the avoidance of the enemy's strengths, followed by the application of some particular superiority against presumed enemy weaknesses, be they physical, psychological, technical, or organizational.

While attrition resembles a physical process that guarantees results proportionate to the quality and quantity of the effort expended (unless the enemy can overturn the encounter), the results of relational maneuver depend first of all on the accuracy with which enemy strengths and weaknesses are identified. Beyond that precondition, success requires some combination of surprise and a faster speed of execution to attack the enemy's weakness effectively before he can react with his strength.

Two consequences follow. First, relational maneuver offers the possibility of obtaining results disproportionately greater than the resources applied to the effort, and thus offers a chance of victory for the materially weaker side. Second, relational maneuver can fail completely, if the selective strength narrowly applied against presumed weakness cannot perform its own task, or if it encounters unexpected strength because of misinformation. In the language of the engineer, attrition fails "gracefully," just as it can succeed only cumulatively: if a given target is misidentified or missed, that target will have to be attacked again, but the larger action is not endangered. Relational maneuver, by contrast, can fail "catastrophically" just as it can succeed with little strength, because an error of assessment or of execution can wreck the entire operation. Attrition is warfare paid at full cost but of low risk, while relational maneuver can be of low cost but may entail a high risk of failure.

There is one more consequence: because it requires accuracy in identifying enemy weaknesses, as well as speed and precision in acting against them, relational maneuver is qualitatively demanding. In the extreme case of commando operations, in which small forces seek to exploit specific enemy weaknesses, the required precision means that only units of high quality are of any use. More broadly, relational maneuver imposes irreducible standards, so that quantity cannot substitute for quality as freely as in attrition warfare.

Again, there is no warfare that consists purely of relational maneuver. As with attrition, what varies from case to case is the proportion of relational maneuver in the overall action. That proportion—here is the important point—defines the scope of operational-level methods. The more relational maneuver there is, the more important is the operational level. Modern examples of warfare with a high relational-maneuver content include the 1915 Gallipoli amphibious landings of the First World War, a failed attempt to force Ottoman Turkey out of the war by directly threatening its capital of Istanbul (in the event, Turkish armies in the fields had to be defeated in detail); the blitzkrieg offensives of the German army against Poland, Denmark, Norway, the Netherlands, Belgium, France, Yugoslavia, Greece, and the Soviet Union (until 1942), in which linear defenses, organized to defend national borders against broad-front offensives, were instead pierced by narrow-front attacks by infantry and artillery, whose breakthroughs were then exploited by rapid penetrations of motorized forces into the deep interior, which disrupted supply lines, command centers, and planning expectations; the Anglo-American response to Germany's submarines, which exploited their lack of air reconnaissance to deny them targets by grouping ships into convoys that occupied tiny fractions of the ocean space; the 1940 British campaign in North Africa, which defeated an Italian army vastly superior numerically by motorized penetrations of its desert flank, to cut off the Italians' only line of communications along the Libyan coastline; the 1941–42 Japanese campaign in Malaya, which defeated numerically and materially superior British forces by repeatedly outflanking their coastal-road communications through the jungle or amphibiously, each time forcing further hurried retreats down the peninsula; the deep-penetration offensive of Patton's Third Army in July and August of 1944, which rolled back the German forces in northwestern France after the Normandy landing; the failed attempt of September 1944 (Operation Market-Garden) to invade northern Germany through the Netherlands, by means of simultaneous parachute and glider landings to seize the successive bridges that would allow British armored and motorized forces to swiftly reach the Rhine at Arnhem (a plan undone by the slowness of British armor, among other things);

Patton's December 1944 counteroffensive, which outflanked the German forces that had advanced westward through the Ardennes; the failed attempts to disrupt the German war economy by the concentrated bombing of industrial "bottleneck" targets, as opposed to the generic bombing of urban areas; MacArthur's 1950 counteroffensive into central Korea by way of the Inchon landings, to cut off the invading North Korean forces in their deep rear, instead of laboriously pushing them back by frontal offensives from the south; the highly successful village-defense of the U.S. Marines in Vietnam, which energized numerous local militiamen with a handful of marines; the Israeli offensives of 1948, 1956, and 1967 in the Sinai, and of 1973 across the Suez Canal, which disrupted Egyptian defenses with fast penetration columns that exploited either surprise or hard-fought breakthrough battles at the front line to reach deep into the soft rear, where they cut supply lines, overran command posts, and in 1973 destroyed antiaircraft missile sites to give free rein to the air force; and the entire American use of air power against both Iraq in 1991 and the Serbia-Montenegro Federation in 1999, which circumvented both their relatively strong ground forces and the American inability to tolerate casualties.

National Styles in Policy and War

Nations and armed forces that see themselves as materially stronger than the enemy at hand—a perception that may or may not be accurate—will generally prefer to rely on the reliable methods of attrition: the frontal offensive, the systematic bombing campaign, the direct naval attack. Those who view themselves, rightly or wrongly, as materially weaker, or else fear the casualties of attrition even if successful, will instead seek to uncover enemy vulnerabilities that they can attack with the high-risk–high-payoff methods of relational maneuver. These propensities—they are not really choices of the moment—have even wider implications. Those who instinctively practice attrition develop their forces according to their own preferences and their own standards. Those who seek to practice relational maneuver must subordinate their own preferences to develop whatever capabilities they believe can best exploit enemy weaknesses. It follows that there is a profound difference in the approach to Intelligence as well. Both may use exactly the same techniques to gather and analyze data, but their attitude to the enemy is very different: the attrition-minded will primarily seek out targets to attack, paying no serious attention to the nature of enemy, while the maneuver-minded will also seek to understand the inner functioning of the enemy, looking for vulnerabilities that may be not material at all but rather political, cultural, or psychological. Moreover, because the attrition-minded must focus on enemy strengths to find their targets, they will tend to overestimate the strength of enemies they nevertheless consider inferior overall.* By contrast, because the maneuver-minded must focus on enemy weaknesses, they will tend to underestimate the strength of enemies they may consider superior overall. Each side's bias fits its intentions, to avoid risk and pay the price of attrition or to accept risk to win cheaply.

In shaping military policies in peacetime, as in the conduct of war, there are thus definite national styles, differentiated by their propensities toward attrition or maneuver. They do not arise from the permanent conditions of nations, and certainly not from any fixed ethnic characteristics. In fact, because they reflect self-images of *relative* material strength or weakness, they change with the specific enemy with which the comparison is made.

Britain, for example, followed a relational-maneuver approach in opposing continental great powers for more than two centuries until 1914, matching their greater strength in foot regiments not with its own scarce infantry, but by using diplomacy and gold to recruit continental allies with armies, while the Royal Navy precluded invasion, enforced naval blockades, and ensured that supplies as well as occasional British troop reinforcements could reach British allies in need. Diplomacy, much of it with petty chieftains, also played a large role in Britain's colonial wars, but when it came to actual fighting, plain attrition was dominant: troublesome potentates and hostile tribes were not elaborately outmaneuvered

---

* During the Cold War, U.S. military intelligence estimates (jointly produced by the Defense Intelligence Agency from the mid-1960s) invariably presented formidable inventories of Soviet forces, whose numbers and capabilities were maximized by including obsolete, obsolescent, and dubiously functioning weapons, along with all possible reserve forces regardless of their state of training, to portray U.S. and Allied forces as grossly outnumbered and outgunned. But after presenting such estimates to the U.S. Congress when military budgets were under consideration, in response to what became a ritual question ("would you want to swap their forces for ours?"), U.S. military chiefs would nevertheless declare that U.S. forces were superior. That was a logical necessity, because there was no inclination to restructure U.S. forces to fit Cold War conditions, notably by strengthening the grossly outnumbered ground forces in Europe at the expense of the chronically overbuilt but politically powerful U.S. Navy.

but instead confronted by frontal attacks and close-order musketry, until the Maxim gun arrived to make attrition much more efficient.

Israel between the wars of 1967 and 1973 provides an example of a national style that changed abruptly, only to change back again. The post-1967 self-image of material superiority led to a progressive abandonment of relational maneuver, so that when the October 1973 war began, frontal attack and linear defense were dominant—until the shock of severe tactical defeats during the first few days of fighting brought about an even faster reversion to relational maneuver.* And then there are the exceptions made by men and circumstances. In 1944, the American national style of war emphasized attrition (a sensible choice given both material superiority and ill-trained conscript forces), but that did not prevent Patton's deep-penetration maneuvers, calculated to exploit the inferior mobility of the Germans caused by chronic shortages of both trucks and fuel; and in 1951, Douglas MacArthur was the architect of a classic high-risk–high-payoff outflanking maneuver large enough to encompass the entire Korean peninsula south of his amphibious landing at Inchon.

National styles are stable enough to be worth defining, though neither all-pervasive nor permanent. It should be obvious by now that attrition and relational maneuver are not confined to the operational level. They are evident at each level of strategy, both below and above.

Their introduction at this particular level of strategy is nevertheless appropriate because *the significance of the operational level strictly depends on the extent that relational maneuver is present.* If the action is essentially characterized by attrition, as with much of the trench warfare of the First World War, a larger-scale operational view of the fighting can only show the same tactical episodes repeated again and again, on one segment of the front after another. In other words, the operational level is not more than the sum of its tactical parts. So we can learn nothing new, nothing that we would not already know by examining any one of the separate episodes at the tactical level.

That is true in all forms of warfare. The first stage of the Battle of Britain, dominated by the Luftwaffe's attrition campaign against the Royal Air

---

* This abrupt shift was exemplified by the exceedingly high-risk but highly successful crossing of the Suez Canal from October 15, 1973, to roll out behind the Egyptian forces that had crossed to the Sinai side of the canal, even though the Egyptians initially controlled both banks except for a narrow passage. As always in relational maneuver, the starting point was the detection of an enemy vulnerability, in this case the inability of the Egyptian high command to redeploy its forces in a timely fashion.

Force, consisted of daily bombing attacks against British airfields and aircraft factories, leading to the repetitive air combat of German escort fighters against the Hurricanes and Spitfires of Fighter Command, which were trying to intercept German bombers. The outcome was determined by nothing more than the arithmetic sum of the results of those encounters, with no operational (as opposed to strategic) goals on either side, and no operational-level methods of war being applied.[3]

When by contrast the relational-maneuver content is high, the operational level becomes correspondingly important. Of this the best illustration is perhaps the blitzkrieg, the classic form of offensive warfare of the Second World War, practiced not only by its German inventors but also by their Soviet and American enemies, and several times replicated after 1945 by the Israelis, the North Koreans, and the North Vietnamese, too, in their final offensive of 1975. No other method of war is so dependent on relational maneuver.

Blitzkrieg: The Rewards and Risks of Relational Maneuver

If we examine a deep-penetration offensive in a tactical-level picture, or rather a whole sequence of them as they unfold, we see meaningless and indeed misleading fragments of its totality. Looking at any one of its vectors of advance, we would see a long column of tanks, infantry carriers, and trucks moving in single file deep into enemy territory, advancing almost unresisted. We might think that we are not watching a war at all but only a triumphant victory march, because we see no fighting to speak of, except for the odd skirmish when tanks at the head of the advancing column crash through checkpoints of the enemy's military police or collide with his supply convoys whose trucks are innocently driving toward the front. We can be certain, it seems, that the invaders will soon reach their goal, even the enemy's capital city, perhaps to win the war as soon as they get there.

When we redirect our view back to the original front line, we discover how the column succeeded in penetrating through the solid barrier of troops and weapons all along the border: there is a break in the front, made just a short time earlier by infantry assaults supported by both artillery and air strikes. While the enemy spread his strength all along the front, the attack was concentrated against that one segment. But the breach is no more than a narrow passage. On either side of it, the enemy's forces remain strong. They are distracted by feints and minor attacks from the troops thinly distributed to face them all along the front; they are harassed by some air attacks, but essentially they are intact.

The narrow breach in the front now seems a very vulnerable passage indeed: the defensive forces on each side need only move over a little to link up again and close the gap. We might therefore conclude that the long, thin, deep-penetration column is not marching to victory but instead advancing to its own destruction. The column is already far from its own territory on the other side of the front line, where all its depots remain, from where all its supplies must come. We see trucks traveling down the one route opened by the pencil-thin advance to bring fuel and ammunition to the column, but those strong defensive forces on either side of the breach will surely bring that traffic to an end as soon as they converge to close the gap in the front. Then the tanks, troop carriers, artillery, and the rest can no longer be resupplied. Even if there is little combat and therefore no need for ammunition resupply, the column will soon run out of fuel.

If the column is forced to stop, its extreme tactical-level vulnerability will be revealed: the long thin line of vehicles is all soft flank and no hard front, open as it is to attack from either side all along its length. Any enemy force in the vicinity, no matter how small, can attack the nearest segment of the stalled column. It seems that the spectacularly imprudent attackers are themselves accomplishing a complete victory for the defense. To encircle such a large force would normally be difficult, but by driving so deep inside enemy territory, the attackers have in effect encircled themselves; their striving to advance has merely transported them toward the enemy's prisoner-of-war camps.

But if we stand back from this narrow tactical-level view to examine the broader operational-level situation, the picture before our eyes is entirely transformed. First, we discover that the deep-penetration column we earlier saw in isolation is only one thrust of the advance. There is at least another, and perhaps several. Each, it is true, originates in a breach of the front that remains quite narrow and potentially vulnerable. But the different columns are converging, and it is no longer clear who is encircling whom, because the penetrations are segmenting the territory of the defense as so many slices in a cake.

Moreover, when we look at how the defense is actually reacting, we discover that those intact frontal forces on either side of each breakthrough are not converging toward one another to strangle the penetrations. They have been ordered to withdraw as rapidly as possible, in order to reconstitute an entirely new defended front deep behind the original front line. Clearly the intention is to confront the advancing columns with solid strength to protect the entire supporting rear with all its military bases and barracks, storage depots, supply convoys, service units and headquarters.

Once we look inside those headquarters, of corps, armies, and army groups, we see that there is much confusion and some excusable panic: enemy tanks are approaching fast, and the new front, which is supposed to be reconstituted ahead of them, still exists only on the paper of planning maps. Actually the withdrawing forces of the defense are losing the race. Instead of outpacing the attackers to set up their new front line, they are themselves outpaced—they cannot retreat fast enough. Having been deployed originally to ensure a determined resistance against frontal attack, the forces of the defense were simply not structured for rapid movement. Their infantry had been distributed along the front by companies and battalions, and much of the field artillery was likewise distributed in many scattered batteries to provide each frontal unit with its supporting fire. As for the tanks and armored carriers of the defense, they were not grouped by the hundreds in divisional columns ready to move; they too were distributed along the front, all set to counterattack locally in support of the infantry holding each segment of the front. These scattered forces must gather to form road columns before they can begin the retreat, and that will take time, even if there is no hesitation at all. But when the unexpected order to withdraw arrives, the commanders and staffs of frontal forces that have not been attacked—most of them, in fact, given that the enemy's penetrations are narrow and few—are shocked by the idea that they should retreat even though the enemy in front of them is not advancing at all. There is also a reluctance to abandon the well-protected front, with its minefields, dug-in weapon positions, and perhaps elaborate fortifications.

Still, orders are orders, and the withdrawal reluctantly begins. Even then there are delays. The trucks now urgently needed at the front are still scattered in transport pools all over the country. There are certainly not enough of them on the spot to move all the troops in one wave. The shortage of tractor-transporters for tanks, armored carriers, and self-propelled artillery is even more acute, and if they travel all the way on their own tracks, many of them will break down before they can reach the new front line. Besides, except for armored units and forces kept back from the very first line of defense, it is difficult to withdraw units that are firing and being fired upon by the enemy. His forces, it is true, seem rather weak, for clearly the main effort is being made elsewhere by those deep-penetration columns, but still to disengage troops actually in combat is very hard.

Nevertheless we see that the frontal forces of the defense are beginning to withdraw. They are on their way to the new positions they are to hold quite far in the rear, whose separate segments are to connect with each other to form the new front line. But as they move, they encounter new delays. Naturally the support and service units had started to move before the frontline combat forces, and now their heavy traffic of trucks and jeeps is blocking the roads. Deeper behind the front, the congestion becomes even worse: civilians too are evacuating, in cars, carts, and buses and on foot. Moreover, the forces in retreat do not only have to fight their way through traffic. Quite unexpectedly, they have to fight in earnest. We now see that combat teams had peeled off the deep-penetration columns to move sideways across the country and await all comers in ambush positions on major roads. The combat teams are actually quite small, but the retreating forces that suddenly encounter them cannot know that. All they know is that they were supposed to be in safe territory, in their own homeland in fact, that they were supposed to move as fast possible, without slowing down to let advance guards explore ahead. Driving straight into the ambush, they suffer heavy losses because at first the enemy can open fire unresisted against troops sitting inside trucks and combat carriers, artillery towed by its tractors, and even tanks caught by surprise with their guns still braced to the rear, convoy fashion. Thus forces in retreat, physically and mentally organized to move fast rather than to fight, must attack to be able to continue their retreat. If they are determined and have good leadership, they will fight their way through the ambush, but not without losing time, materiel, and men. Although they were on the offensive operationally, the ambushing combat teams had all the advantage of the tactical defensive—it was they who could choose optimal firing positions after studying the terrain. Although the defense is retreating operationally, its ambushed forces must overcome shock and surprise to generate the will to attack. Losses are bound to be unequal, and after-fight exhaustion adds to the demoralization of retreat

One more shock awaits those forces that do reach their assigned positions. They find nothing ready for them, no trenches or gun positions, no food or field kitchens, no wire communications for their headquarters, and above all no ammunition dumps to replace those left behind at the front for lack of transport. Aside from the sheer lack of time, there is another cause of unpreparedness: the enemy's deep-penetration advance, slicing through the rear zones, has overrun many transport units, capturing and destroying many of their trucks and scattering the rest. Depots and logistic centers have also been overrun, and many support and service units cannot reach their assigned positions on the new line, because enemy combat forces stand between them and their assigned destinations.

The newly arrived forces of the defense nevertheless begin to settle in. The troops work hard to dig trenches and excavate gun positions, mustering what ammunition they have. Enemy aircraft make occasional raids, which interrupt the work, kill or wound some men, and demoralize more. Food is a problem, which prompts unit commanders to resort to an ancient expedient: they send off foraging parties into nearby villages to take what they can. Yet the situation seems to be improving. The new defensive front in the deep rear, which was nothing more than a line drawn on headquarter maps, is becoming a reality as more and more forces arrive to take up their assigned positions. Only a few segments remain uncovered, though it is true that many are manned only by small units thinly spread. Of necessity the new frontal defense is weaker than the original one because so much has been left behind or lost in transit, but the high command is energetically mustering reinforcements and fresh supplies wherever it can, sending them forward as fast as possible.

The abandonment of the original front and the loss of all the territory between it and the new front line are most unfortunate of course, but the defense in retreat starts benefiting from the paradoxical logic that can reverse defeat into victory: the high command finds that less time and fuel are needed to reinforce and supply the new front, which is so much closer than the original front line. That too is a reason for some cautious optimism. All the defense needs is a little time to reorganize its forces.

But there is no time, it is already too late. The leading units of the deep-penetration columns have already reached well beyond the new front line and are now overrunning central bases and depots, as well as higher headquarters, whose staff officers, communicators, clerks, cooks, and military police guards must engage in hopeless combat against attacking teams of tanks and mechanized infantry.

In the confusion, the high command of the defense strives to restore control over the situation by redeploying its frontal combat forces once again: it sees no alternative to another retreat, to form a new front line even deeper in the rear. When the orders are sent out over surviving communication links, some of the frontal combat forces are still stranded on the original front line. Others are still in transit, perhaps caught in traffic jams. Only the troops that had been digging in on the new front line can act quickly. They are now ordered to retreat once again, to establish a new new front. Perhaps they still have the energy and determination to obey promptly, but even those that have their vehicles ready cannot out-race the enemy columns that have bypassed them some time ago and are rolling steadily ahead.

Thus the entire wrenching process may have to be repeated yet again, until little combat power remains among the mass of increasingly disorga-nized defensive forces, scattered all over the map, disconnected from their support units, cut off from resupply, and increasingly demoralized. Mass surrenders begin, as soon as any enemy troops are actually encountered. Capitulation, or else retreat on a continental scale if the defenders have that much land to lose, are the only options that remain for the high command. All those things happened to the Poles in 1939, to the French in 1940, to the Russians in 1941, and then to the U.S. Army in Korea in 1950, to the Egyptians in 1967, and to the South Vietnamese in 1975.

It is only now that the tactical parts once again become consistent with the operational whole, to yield an unexpected outcome. Until the forces of the defense are actually thrown in chaotic disarray, any tactical-level view of the fighting continues to mislead because nothing has remedied the extreme tactical-level vulnerability of the long, thin deep-penetration columns of the offense. The decisive material and psychological impact of their concerted advance is evident only at the operational level. In that broader and fuller view of the fighting, we see that the vulnerability of the deep-penetration columns is only theoretical, while the increasing paralysis of the defense is fatal.

In hindsight, we know that the great mistake of the high command was to order the very first withdrawal, instead of ordering the strongest possi-ble counterattacks against the narrow breakthrough passages. If a large proportion of the forces had been kept back from the front line for that very purpose, the breaches in the front would soon have been sealed, and the deep-penetration columns would have been cut off from resupply, making it easier to destroy them in detail.

But the high command of the defense never had this clear operational-level view of the fighting. At the beginning, and for some time afterward, it could not even know that the enemy was intent on deep penetrations—his initial attacks were indistinguishable from a conventional attempt to advance in linear fashion all along the front. Reports of attacks large and small were in fact coming in from every sector of the front, but the emerg-ing picture of the situation formed at headquarters was actually very reassuring. The enemy had apparently launched a general offensive. In most places, his attacks were surprisingly weak and had failed. Unit commanders were eagerly reporting defensive victories in many sectors, with the usual overstatement of the magnitude of the enemy forces they had repelled. The enemy had managed to advance in only a few places, achieving a few, narrow breaches of the front. Of course further attacks had to be expected, because the enemy would undoubtedly try to advance more broadly—otherwise he would have to pull back those few attacking forces that had been successful, whose flanks were so dangerously exposed.

That is how a linear-front mentality shapes perceptions. Those "surprisingly weak" enemy attacks are not recognized as feints, whose only purpose is to divert attention from the main forces seeking to break right through the front. Because its own method of war is to defend a front line with forces distributed all along its length, the defense high command assumes that the enemy also means to fight in linear fashion, to push back the entire front by a broad offensive.

The deep-penetration maneuver exploits this linear mentality by supplying facts to reinforce its misconceptions. The best attacking forces are of course massed opposite a few, narrow sectors of the front to fight their breakthrough battles, with the armored columns waiting behind them to start their own advance. But in addition there are at least weak forces opposite every sector of the front, all under orders to stage whatever small attacks they can, or at least to open fire as if they were about to attack.

The linear operational method has been drilled into the minds of the defenders during years of planning and field exercises. It has a powerful hold. So when they first hear of enemy forces that have broken through their front, they assume that the enemy has decided to launch a limited offensive or just some raids. Unless intercepted, raiding forces will have to withdraw back to the safety of their own side of the front before they run out of supplies. Or if it was a limited-front offensive, its exposed flanks would soon offer a good opportunity for counterattacks. That is how the British and French high commands interpreted the initial German penetration into Belgium on May 10, 1940, before there was a clear understanding of the methods and purposes of the blitzkrieg, Hitler's version of deep-penetration warfare. But that is also how the first North Korean tank attacks of June 1950 were analyzed before it was understood that a full-scale invasion was under way, and again how the crossing of the Suez Canal by Ariel Sharon's forces on October 15–16, 1973, was interpreted by the Egyptian high command. Having themselves successfully crossed in great strength, holding as they did a solid front on the eastern or Sinai side of the canal after repelling a series of Israeli counterattacks, the Egyptians assumed that a small Israeli unit had somehow infiltrated across the canal through a gap in their front that would soon be sealed. They thought that it was nothing more than a morale-boosting commando raid that would soon be withdrawn, or else intercepted and destroyed. By the time the Egyptians realized that the Israelis were inserting large armored forces west of the canal, that they were intent on rolling out behind the Egyptian front on the Sinai side to cut it off from its sustaining rear, it was too late: the Israelis had already sent two armored divisions across, which were advancing both south and west—threatening Cairo itself after cutting off the southern portion of the Egyptian front.

The linear mentality retains its hold even when reports of substantial enemy forces deep behind the front start to come in. Such reports, after all, will not come from the senior commanders of the frontal forces, who are still focused on the enemy opposite their sectors, most of which are still firmly held. Instead, they mostly originate from air force pilots, who are quite capable of mistaking a friendly transport column for an enemy armored division, or else from military police checkpoints, shocked remnants of road convoys and service units that have been smashed, civilian police, village mayors, and others. There is a war on and nerves are taut, so that a great many hysterical reports are coming in anyway, of enemy parachutists supposedly landing everywhere, and indeed of enemy tanks not merely deep behind the front but altogether too deep to be there at all.

At this point, information both valid and timely becomes war's most powerful weapon—and it is desperately scarce for the defenders. Ownership of observation satellites is still limited to a few countries and is of no great help anyway for current, minute-by-minute intelligence—unless a satellite happens to be overhead at exactly the right time, and the data is analyzed both correctly and fast enough. The United States has by far the best satellite observation of any country, but it was of no use at all on August 2, 1990, when the Iraqi army swiftly invaded Kuwait (had it invaded Yemen in a two-week transit, the satellite would have served very well). Aerial reconnaissance photography is far more likely to yield information in useful time, and far less likely to be misinterpreted, but it does require overflight—which in turn presumes basing within reach and a preexisting state of war. Signals intelligence, normally the fullest and most reliable source of information, is far better suited to uncover the enemy's general capabilities and intentions than to keep track of tactical movements—especially because deep-penetration warfare can be remarkably uncommunicative.

The columns are advancing as rapidly as they can, toward the war-winning objectives marked on their maps; they curtly report progress by place code, but headquarters in the rear have no need to issue further orders if all goes well. The commanders riding at the head of each column decide on the spot whether to attack resisting forces astride their path or bypass them to continue advancing rapidly. Progress reports are collated as they come in, to show ever deeper penetrations on the map—crucial to prevent the air force from bombing friendly forces and to focus its efforts against defending units that could block the columns or even attack their exposed flanks. Actually the headquarters of the offense need little information. Communications are mostly one-way, from the front to the rear, with orders going the other way, from rear commands to the columns only when they need to be redirected, to avoid their convergence (and traffic jams) or to secure convergence (for a greater mass).

The needs of the defense are entirely different. When its commanders finally understand that the attacks are no mere raids, nor a limited-front offensive, nor the opening stage of a linear broad-front offensive, timely and accurate information about the movements of the deep-penetration columns becomes decisively important. If only defense headquarters could obtain a clear operational-level picture of the unfolding battle, the remedy would be obvious: first, close the gaps in the front with all-out attacks from each side by the mass of still intact frontal forces; second, order all secondary and service units of minor or negligible striking power that are well behind the front to form roadblocks wherever they are—they are bound to be useful, either to slow down the enemy's advancing columns or to impede reinforcement and resupply; third, send any combat formation still in the rear to attack the exposed flank of the nearest enemy penetration.

By now, however, the channels of communication into defense headquarters are saturated by the mass of reports coming in. Most were reasonably accurate when originally sent but are outdated by the enemy's rapid movements. Others are overstated, understated, or simply mistaken. Others still are the product of fearful fantasies (in both the Spanish civil war and the May 1940 invasion of France, reports of "fifth columnists"—enemies in disguise—were ubiquitous). As the information is sorted out, to try to determine where the enemy is and how fast he is moving and in which direction, commanders and their staffs are swamped by the sheer volume of incoming messages. Moreover, while they try to sort out how matters really stand, matters are not standing at all because the enemy is continuing to advance. As noted, modern intelligence techniques do not help that much, and neither do modern telecommunications, judging by the experiences of recent wars. As soon as movement begins, so does the fog of war. In the 1991 Gulf war, Iraq was blanketed with every manner of surveillance, but its mobile Scud missile launchers could not be found except by chance. In the 1999 Kosovo war, fixed targets could be located and attacked with extreme precision, but mobile targets such as Serbian armored units remained elusive. In the 1973 Arab-Israeli war, the Egyptian high command was unable to find a fairly large Israeli force that was much nearer to Cairo than Tel Aviv.[4]

What is actually happening is an information *race*, which preconditions the redeployment race that is usually decisive. On one side, the advancing deep-penetration columns are generating all kinds of reports by their very movement. On the other, defense commanders strive to process the information quickly enough to obtain a valid if not totally current ("real-time") picture of events. If the defense wins the race, if its ability to assimilate and analyze information is not overwhelmed, there is a good chance of outright victory: if the vectors of enemy road columns can be identified correctly, even modest forces can accomplish much because the enemy columns are so inherently vulnerable at the tactical level. But if the information battle is lost, if the operational-level view of the situation remains too confused to aim counterattacks correctly and in good time, then even strong forces can accomplish little or nothing. Instead of smashing into the enemy flanks to force strung-out road columns to laboriously assemble their own counterattack, defense forces of perhaps considerable striking power will only exhaust themselves in fruitless movements to find the elusive enemy, before themselves falling victims to ambush. If the defense loses the information race, its entire service structure behind the front will be disrupted by the deep-penetration offense, leaving the frontal forces bereft. They might still try to fight with their integral supplies, but at a hopeless disadvantage.

Until that final stage, there is still the possibility of a linear solution: the defense withdraws into its interior to reconstitute a hard front. That would of course leave the enemy in control of much territory, but resistance could still continue effectively *if* the frontal combat forces can disengage, regroup in columns, and move faster than the enemy, to quickly redeploy along with any fresh forces to create an entirely new front. This scenario presumes that there is enough territory to yield—without losing the resources needed to keep fighting. For to be successful, the withdrawal must exceed the one-bound penetration range of the enemy, beyond which his armored columns must stop to allow supplies to catch up with them, to refit vehicles, and to rest the men.[5] With that, the outcome no longer depends on the dynamic interaction of the rival forces at the operational level but rather hinges on the geographic depth of the theater of war—and to consider that aspect of war we must ascend to the next and higher level of strategy.

The Case Study Resumed

After this illustration of relational maneuver, we are ready to reconsider the antitank infantry proposals of the Cold War years, this time at the operational level. We now know that the technically excellent and tactically adequate (no more than that) antitank missile defense must also be effective at the operational level if it is to be effective at all. And we also know that the encounter of armor and antiarmor can no longer be examined in isolation, but must be seen in the context of all the forces on both sides that would interact on the entire battlefield: artillery of different categories (mortars, howitzers, guns, barrage rockets, bombardment missiles), the line-holding frontal infantry, the mechanized infantry of the attackers, combat engineers and their doings, all such air power as affects the battlefield itself, helicopter troops, and also any barriers and fortifications.

Moreover, if it is the less radical proposal that we are considering, which would add an additional frontal layer of antitank missile infantry to the armored and mechanized forces of the defense instead of replacing them altogether, the latter too must be considered—indeed, they would remain the most important part of the entire defense.

As we seek to estimate the effect of the antitank missile infantry among the many-sided interactions of the operational level, we now know that the fight between the armor unit and the missile unit that we examined at the tactical level must be inconclusive by itself. The same is true of any one air duel in a much wider struggle for air superiority, of any one hide-and-seek sequence between a submarine and the aircraft, destroyers, and submarines of an antisub task force.

For in the wider operational-level view, we can see what remained invisible at the tactical level: behind that first unit of advancing tanks and mechanized infantry, there are many more such units, forming a deep column waiting to fight their way through the front.

What we learned at the tactical level continues to be true, but the meaning of that truth is transformed: the armored vehicles that the missiles are destroying are there, in a sense, precisely to be destroyed, while they in turn destroy or scatter launcher teams, or simply exhaust their stock of missiles. In other words, the tanks and combat carriers are not only firing ammunition, they themselves *are* ammunition, expended by the advancing army to open the way for its further advance. Although the attackers would rather lose less than more in breaking through the line, as long as passage through the front is achieved, the tactical "exchange rate" between missile teams and first-wave armored vehicles is not so important at the operational level. The success or failure of the ensuing deep-penetration offensive will not depend on whether a few advanced units suffered 5, 10, or even 50 percent losses to break open the front—the price of entry into the soft rear.

The operational method of each side now becomes the critical factor. Just as tactics are aimed at maximizing outcomes at the tactical level, operational methods seek to maximize outcomes at the operational level, but in both cases prescriptions cannot be absolute: it all depends on who is fighting whom, and in what circumstances. Only one operational method has been discussed above, deep-penetration maneuver. But there are several others, needless to say, and as long as the attritional content is less than total, there is scope for air and naval operational methods as well, just as there are tactics for each.

In air warfare, for example, interception and airfield attack are two distinct operational methods that may be used to win air superiority, each of which may be implemented with a variety of different tactics. Equally, the use of air power against ground forces may employ different operational methods. One is "battlefield interdiction"—strikes against the more concentrated formations that have not yet reached the battlefield (where they must disperse to deploy, becoming less vulnerable to air attack). Another is "close air support," in which air forces attack units on the battlefield itself, on the calculation that the loss of efficiency will be outweighed by the gain in air-ground synergism: if air strikes are immediately followed by ground attacks, they may find the enemy still paralyzed by shock and surprise. Also there are different operational methods of air bombardment: the "area bombing" of the Second World War in its post-1945 nuclear form, precision bombing as discussed below, and "deep interdiction," aimed at overland communications, whose main purpose is to strangle the flow of reinforcements and supplies to the combat zone. Similarly, to cite a naval example, the protection of shipping against submarines may be accomplished by different operational methods, which include the use of minefields, picket ships, and submarines in ambush to keep the enemy from reaching the sea lanes of interest; area defense, by the active hunting of submarines in transit with long-range aircraft and mixed task forces of destroyers, aircraft carriers, and submarines; and finally convoy protection by immediate escort. In each case the dividing line between tactics and operational methods is obvious.

Reverting to our case study and the critical role of the operational methods of each side, we already know that the putative attackers are trying to achieve the blitzkrieg effect[6]: the disruption of the entire supporting structure of the defense, the forced evacuation of forward airbases and nuclear storage sites, and above all the unbalancing of command decisions, to misdirect any counterattacks and impose a disorganizing retreat. As for the defense and its choice of operational methods, we already know that frontal attrition by missile troops alone cannot be successful against a deep-column attack. It is not that attrition is an inferior form of warfare but rather that its material demands are directly proportionate to the task. And in this case the task of each defensive unit is impossibly demanding, because offensive forces highly concentrated against narrow segments of the front will grossly outnumber defensive forces distributed all along that front.

Attrition is a matter of arithmetic, and it could succeed, but only with a much more elaborate defensive system than just a line of missile infantry. First, antitank barriers such as minefields, sharp-sided ditches, and concrete obstacles—all duly overwatched to prevent breaching—would be needed to slow the enemy's rate of approach, so as to keep the number of incoming vehicles below the engagement capacity of the missile troops. One can substitute for the other, within limits: the more resistant the barriers, the fewer the number of surviving antitank missile teams that is needed to keep the enemy from advancing. That is a function of successful hits against both the engineer vehicles trying to demolish the barriers and the tanks and combat carriers that can cross them. Second, in another trade-off, fortified firing positions would be needed to ensure high exchange rates between missile teams lost and vehicles destroyed. Of course, the economy of such a fortified frontal defense would depend on the length of frontage that must be covered, not an operational-level question at all but rather one that belongs to the level of theater strategy. In any case, without overwatched barriers and fortifications far more costly than the missile launchers themselves, the antitank infantry has no chance of success. Thus the technically superior and tactically adequate missile infantry is found to be ineffective by itself at the operational level.

When we next consider the less radical version of the proposal, which calls for the addition of a frontal layer of antitank troops to the armored and mechanized forces of the defense, we see that its attrition would have a definite value. In part, that results from the sum of two tactical effects: first, the delay imposed on the offense, which could be valuable in itself to gain mobilization time, if the enemy had originally achieved surprise; second, the actual attrition that can be exacted, because if there is mobile warfare still to come, a reduction in the enemy's numbers is no longer irrelevant to the outcome. But the value of an added frontal layer of fortified missile infantry could be much greater than the sum of those tactical parts. By clearly revealing the enemy's major vectors of advance where he does achieve breakthroughs, and by continuing to shield all the other segments of the front, a strong first line anchored by missile troops can allow the mobile forces of the defense to be that much more effective at the operational level: they can counterattack the flanks of the invasion columns while themselves being protected from flanking attacks by the intact segments of the front.

This scenario presumes either a timely mobilization or a frontal defense sufficiently robust to gain enough time for the mobile forces to muster out of their bases, reach the front, and deploy properly to mount their counterattacks. With either of those things, the defense is far better placed than it would be without a frontal layer of fortified antitank troops. Unless vastly superior, an all-mobile defense would initially be engaged in defending the front instead of being free to launch its own counterattacks. And if the enemy does achieve surprise, once the armor and mechanized forces of the defense do reach the front, they would have to engage the advancing enemy head-on in "meeting engagements," instead of being able to attack the flanks of enemy columns.

In the case of the less radical proposal, therefore, the technically superior and tactically adequate frontal defense by missile infantry is operationally valid after all. The next question is just how valid it is in comparison with the alternative of adding more armored and mechanized forces instead. It is then a question of opportunity costs, that is, the amount of mobile strength that is given up to acquire the frontal layer of missile troops, with the required barriers and their overwatching forces. The answer will depend in part on how the force is manned, whether by scarce regular troops taken from the mobile forces or by more abundant reserve troops. Institutional specifics that were irrelevant at the technical level, which were then discovered to be important at the tactical level, turn out to be decisive at the operational level.

Because they are static, there are only two operational methods for the employment of the missile troops: frontal defense on their own or in combination with counterattacking mobile forces. Obviously there are other ways of employing the missile troops, in settings more favorable than those of frontal defense, where they have to absorb the undiminished momentum of the offensive. One possibility, already mentioned, would be an "elastic defense," which would seriously oppose the enemy's advance only after it had penetrated deep enough to exhaust its initial reach. That requires a correspondingly deep retreat in good order—and enough territory that can be lost without losing the war. Another possibility would be a defense-in-depth, either in the form of multiple lines, to impose successive delays as well as attrition, or in the form of strong islands of resistance, to channel enemy movements into prepared fire zones setting the stage for counterattacks.

But those are not operational-level choices, for the factors at work are determined not by the interaction of the forces in combat but rather by the extent, depth, and character of the theater of war, at the next level of strategy. Moreover, as soon as the question of giving up territory for military reasons becomes an issue, so do all the attached political considerations, as we shall see.

Attrition and Maneuver in Peacetime Military Policy

By now it will have become obvious that attrition and relational maneuver are present not only in war but also in peacetime preparations for it, as for example in the research and development of weapons. Under an attritional approach, the aim is simply to improve weapons, to gain any and all technical advantages that science offers and that the available resources and talent can develop. There is no particular tactical or operational focus; the goal is simply to develop the "best" weapons in all-around performance that can be produced and deployed at tolerable cost. Accordingly, instead of seeking to update or add to existing weapons, brand new equipment is developed to avoid inherited design constraints. When the new weapons replace what was there before, large and often costly changes are needed in maintenance procedures and facilities; for example, old stocks of replacement parts will no longer serve, and new ones will have to be accumulated. Completely new equipment will also require new training for both maintenance and operating personnel, and that too may be costly.

Therefore, only major gains in performance can justify the effort—and they are unlikely unless large engineering advances are achieved. That stipulation in turn not only makes research and development expensive but also requires many years for the initial studies and calculations, proto-typing, tests, recalculations, further prototyping, and more tests. Finally, because the period of gestation is so long, it is only by coincidence that the particular characteristics of the new weapon will match the specific configuration of enemy vulnerabilities or the specific tactical require-ments of the forces that will use that weapon. By the time the equipment arrives in service, former enemy weaknesses may well have become strengths and vice versa, while the operational methods of the users them-selves may have changed.[7]

Under a relational-maneuver approach, by contrast, the aim of research and development is to obtain specific capabilities that would exploit equally specific enemy vulnerabilities and suit the tactics and operational methods designed for that purpose. To have the new equipment in good time, while the presumed enemy weaknesses still persist, it cannot be totally new and must instead be developed by updating, modifying, or recombining existing subsystems, components, and parts. That obviously imposes design constraints that prevent the full exploitation of all the pos-sibilities theoretically offered by the current state of scientific and tech-nical progress. The equipment cannot be totally new and thus will not reflect the "state of the art," as technologists say. Moreover, because up-dated or improved designs are introduced at relatively short intervals, overall maintenance and training compatibility with prior equipment is essential to avoid ruinous integration costs—and that imposes further de-sign constraints. In other words, truly major technical advances ("break-throughs") are much less likely to be achieved. But what is lost at the technical level may well be less than what is gained at the tactical and operational levels. For example, the all-new M1 tank initially developed by the U.S. Army in the 1970s, primarily for war on the NATO central front, was first employed in combat in 1991, not in the rolling meadows of Germany but in the Arabian desert, not defensively against masses of Soviet tanks but offensively against Iraqi forces withdrawing from Kuwait. Because the Iraqis were by then badly battered and demoralized by weeks of air bombardment, any and all battle tanks would have been just as effective against them (the French Foreign Legion advanced successfully with light armored cars). The shortcomings of the M1, notably the huge fuel consumption of its gas turbine engine and the vulnerability of its ammunition magazine high in the turret, made no difference at all, any more than its strengths did. By contrast, the Israelis have been producing successive variants of their Merkava tank over the years: they progressively introduced new engines to increase its agility while leaving armor and gun unchanged; then substituted a much more powerful 120 mm gun for the original 105 mm, while leaving engine and armor unchanged; then added a low-light TV tracking device (for antihelicopter use); then increased armor protection against antitank missiles; and so on. Each time, these changes were complicated by the need to fit the preexisting design, but they also presented the opportunity to respond quite quickly to new threats and developments, incorporating the lessons not only of field exercises and technical tests but also of combat experience.

What is true of research and development applies to all other aspects of military policy. Attrition implies the independent pursuit of the best in general, whether in the training of armed forces, the construction of bases and facilities, or the acquisition of equipment. In relational maneuver, by contrast, "best" solutions are sacrificed to capabilities that exploit the vulnerabilities and limitations of specific enemies. Neither attrition nor relational maneuver is ever present in pure form, but their relative weight will usually reflect national self-images as well as the overall approach to the business of war.

A First Vision of Strategy Whole

In focusing on the step-by-step climb from one level of strategy to the next, I have ignored the horizontal dimension—the ebb and flow of action and reaction within each separate level. This is not just an abridgment of reality but an actual distortion, because vertical interactions between the levels influence, and are influenced by, the paradoxical logic within each horizontal dimension to cause the sequence of success, culmination, and decline. If for example a new weapon appears in combat, the enemy reaction at the technical level in the form of countermeasures or competing weapons may be answered by tactical reactions, which could in turn induce an operational-level response by the enemy. Thus if the enemy introduces better antiaircraft missiles when war is actually under way, there is no time to react at the same technical level, by developing electronic countermeasures over months or years. Instead, the only possible reaction is tactical—to fly at ultralow altitudes below the minimum engagement altitude of those missiles, in the first place to attack the missiles themselves. The enemy too has no time to respond technically, by acquiring new missiles that can engage targets more rapidly at lower altitudes, while the tactical response of adding rapid-fire antiaircraft cannon to each missile site is unlikely to be adequate. The enemy's major response may therefore be operational, to switch from an area defense provided by fixed missile sites to a fluid point defense provided by antiaircraft missiles frequently moved from place to place (some are actually mobile on self-propelled vehicles, but virtually all antiaircraft missiles can be moved overnight). Then, unless real-time intelligence coverage of the entire area of interest can somehow be assured—a difficult task if the enemy is skilled in camouflage and disciplined in using his radars and radios—it will no longer be possible to send fighter bombers fast and low on carefully evasive flight paths that avoid overflying all missile sites except the one to be attacked at ultralow altitude.

In other cases, the sequence could go the other way, the first action may be operational, the enemy response may be tactical, and the further reaction may be technical. Obviously there are endless combinations in the interaction of the vertical levels and their horizontal dimensions.

Even though our vertical progress from level to level is far from complete, we can no longer visualize strategy only in its horizontal dimension, as an agitated sea in which the waves and counterwaves of the paradoxical logic negate one another, in a perpetual striving for an impossible equilibrium. Nor can we see strategy as a multilevel edifice, offering a different truth on every floor. We must instead accept the complexity of combining both images in our minds: the floors are not solid, as in a building, but in agitated motion, sometimes to the point of breaking through into another level, just as in the dynamic reality of war the interactions of the vertical levels themselves combine and collide with the horizontal dimensions of strategy.

8

Theater Strategy I:
Military Options and Political Choices

Because the logic of strategy at the theater level relates military strength to territorial space, we can understand much of it in visual terms, examining forces and their movements in a bird's eye view, or perhaps one should say in a satellite overview. Of course strategy has a spatial aspect at every level, but at the tactical level it is the detailed nature of the terrain that matters, while the combat encounters of the operational level could be much the same in any number of different geographical settings. At the theater level, however, some *specific* territory is the very object of the struggle. It may be as large as a continent or as small as an island; it can be a province, a region, an entire country, or a group of countries; but in any case a "theater of war" must form a reasonably self-contained space rather than just one part of a larger whole.*

While conditioning the interaction of the adversary forces in spatial terms, the logic of strategy at the theater level encompasses only factors of military significance: the length of fronts and the barrier-value of their terrain, the depth of territories, all aspects of access and transit, and so on. By contrast, it totally ignores the political, economic, and moral character of the territory in question, treating cherished homelands rich in resources or production exactly on the same footing as alien deserts. It is not surprising therefore that in the making of military policies, the logic of strategy at the theater level is often ignored, even if it is fully understood.

In the case of Korea, for example, the concentration of powerful North Korean forces with many tanks and much artillery near the border, the known ability of North Korean infantry to infiltrate in depth, and the

---

* As Clausewitz notes (*On War*, book 5, chap. 2), the defining characteristic of a theater is that even in a larger war, events outside its boundaries should have no direct effect within it, only the indirect effect of generally weakening or strengthening the adversaries.

bellicosity of the North Korean regime, all suggest that a war would begin with a surprise offensive of extreme intensity. Such an assault, however, could neither be long sustained nor progress far into South Korean territory, because much North Korean artillery is immobile and the foot infantry would soon run out of energy and supplies. In the circumstances, the logic of strategy at the theater level has the effect of greatly weakening a South Korean defense that would seek to protect all of the country's territory right up to the armistice line, while strengthening a defense that would await the enemy further back. An "elastic defense" of the first fifty kilometers of South Korean territory, with delaying actions and fire ambushes behind terrain barriers, but with no attempt to hold a rigid front, would allow the North Koreans to defeat themselves by advancing too far. Once fully mobilized and deployed, the South Korean army could counterattack in superior strength all the way to the border and then across it, while U.S. and South Korean air forces could inflict heavy losses on the North Koreans, when both advancing and retreating.

The logic of strategy at the theater level certainly favors an *elastic* defense, which defends no specific tract of territory in order to better defend all of it, by releasing forces from any protective duties. But it ignores the nature of the territory that would twice be fought over and occupied by the ungentle North Koreans in between. It is not a desert but rather a densely populated area that includes the northern edge of Seoul, the vast metropolis where some 9 million Koreans live, which contains the seat of all national institutions and a substantial part of the country's industry. Especially because both Korean governments claim exclusive sovereignty over the entire peninsula, the loss of those first fifty kilometers might induce a collapse of public confidence in the South Korean government and would demoralize the armed forces. Not surprisingly, South Korea's military policy therefore spurns strategic logic, instead seeking to provide the Seoul national capital area with a *preclusive* defense, which aims to deny any enemy intrusions whatsoever.

The logic can be ignored at will, but of course that does nothing to diminish its *consequences*. For South Korea, they include both costs and risks. Large forces must be kept at a high state of readiness at all times; elaborate barriers of minefields, vehicular obstacles, and long reinforced-concrete walls have to be built and maintained; and both are costly. Yet even so, the preclusive defense remains much more fragile than an elastic defense would be, given the same balance of forces. But nothing in the logic of theater strategy as such can dictate another order of priorities, nor indeed any priorities at all, no more than a known relationship between unemployment and inflation can dictate political choices between the two: in some countries, high inflation is tolerated but not high unemployment; in others, it is the other way around. The economic logic that defines the relationship between the two does not prescribe the choice of economic policy. Likewise, in the Korean case the logic of theater strategy determines the relationship between the elasticity of the defense and its costs and risks, but political priorities demand an inelastic defense, overriding all other considerations.

Europe's Central Front during the Cold War Years

During the Cold War, the North Atlantic Treaty Organization faced its greatest threat in what is now peaceful central Germany. And just like the South Korean government, NATO was politically committed to a preclusive defense in geographic circumstances that would have favored a far more elastic defense. In a retrospective view of the situation at the level of theater strategy, we would see the eastern edge of the Federal Republic ("West Germany") extending from the Baltic coast all the way south to Austria. For some 625 miles, the border would divide East Germany and Czechoslovakia, at the time both basing areas for the Soviet army. Upon mobilization, as units of the Belgian, British, Canadian, Dutch, German, and American armies would move out of their barracks and bases to deploy into their assigned positions, NATO's "central front" would acquire a physical form. We would see not a solid line with units stationed shoulder to shoulder but rather a series of deployments of men, vehicles, and weapons within a band of territory running from north to south. Roughly one-third of NATO's tank and mechanized formations (the "covering forces") would have advanced to within a few miles from the border, with the rest kept some distance behind. Even though the front held by the covering forces would not follow each twist and turn of the border, it would still be stretched out over some 600 miles. In addition, at least the low-lying tracts of the border with neutral Austria would also have to be protected, because Soviet invasion forces from Hungary could pass up the Danube valley quite quickly.

We can now finally dispose of the missile-infantry proposal. Given the length of the frontage that the Alliance was committed to protect, we can immediately understand why a frontal defense by missile troops would have been very weak, even if elaborately shielded by properly overwatched barriers. For we discover that in those narrow sectors of the front where the two sides would actually collide in combat, the antitank missiles would be greatly outnumbered by Soviet armored vehicles, even though the missiles were so much cheaper. As matters stood during the last two decades of the Cold War, more than 10,000 tanks, an even larger number of infantry combat vehicles, much self-propelled artillery, and all manner of support units could attack from a standing start from East Germany and Czechoslovakia, with much greater forces moving up behind them from Poland and the Soviet Union.[1] That great mass of vehicles would not of course be distributed evenly from north to south opposite every segment of the front, but instead be concentrated into four or five vectors of advance, each moving westward in a phalanx as broad as the terrain would allow. Some might be constricted into an approach as narrow as a two-lane road, while others might advance on a width of as much as ten miles. But summing all the vectors and the width of every phalanx, Soviet armor would still be attacking only a fraction of the entire 600-mile line. Thus even if a huge force of missile troops were raised, with tens of thousands of launchers, Soviet armor rolling forward would easily outnumber them in every combat encounter.

The arithmetic of attrition must therefore guarantee defeat. It cannot be otherwise when the number of missile launchers must be distributed to cover all the frontage, while invading armored forces attack in concentrated force.[2] Of course the missile troops could also be concentrated, in fact they could outconcentrate the invasion columns, if they were mobile enough. But that cannot be done just by supplying trucks to transport them up and down the front along the border patrol roads, because any movements that far forward would be much too vulnerable to artillery fires. It can only be done by keeping the bulk of the missile troops in wait at rearward crossroads, ready to rush forward on their trucks to reinforce sectors of the front under attack. Incapable of cross-country movement and thus road-bound, motorized missile troops in transit would be highly vulnerable to air attack and quite unable to move forward against the artillery fires running ahead of each invading phalanx. Helicopters could assure an even faster response. Enough of them could allow the missile troops to outconcentrate the invasion columns every time, but that is no longer the cheap alternative originally proposed—and why carry missile troops with antitank launchers anyway, when helicopters can have their own missiles without need of troops to launch them? In either case, those most fragile of aircraft would be highly vulnerable to the antiaircraft weapons that accompany armored forces and to the descending curtains of artillery fire of a large-scale offensive.

With trucks much too vulnerable as well as road-bound, and with helicopters too vulnerable as well as too expensive, only well-armored ground vehicles, fit to go across country, can provide mobility under fire for the missile troops, to allow them to meet the concentrated attack. Armored and tracked, such vehicles could certainly bring the missile troops where they would be needed. They would of course replicate the present carriers of the mechanized infantry . . . which of course includes antitank missiles among its weapons. And if armored vehicles are to be acquired, why not arm them with built-in missile launchers that can be used without dismounting? And if there are to be built-in weapons anyway, why have only bulky missile-launchers with their slow rates of fire, when guns remain superior for antiarmor combat at closer ranges? If taken that far, the original proposal dissolves into a mere variant of the existing mechanized forces, or even into a re-creation of the tank itself. We have come full circle, back to the conventional solution of fighting armor with armor. We can now recognize that the persistence of armored forces is not just the result of institutional rigidity, the force of tradition, the power of entrenched military bureaucracies. Without protected mobility there is no concentration, and without concentration there is no strength.

Offense-Defense Force Ratios

No mention has been made so far of the supposed advantage of any defense, the often quoted ratio of three to one that the offense supposedly needs to win. At the tactical level, it is true, because defensive troops holding a line can dig trenches, foxholes, parapets, and other protective structures, they can kill and wound the exposed attackers more easily than the attackers can kill or wound them. For frontal attacks against entrenched defenses, a ratio of three to one is therefore a reasonable rough average.

In the wider view of the operational level, however, we see that the offense need not attack that particular line at all. It can instead bypass the line on one side or both—the simplest of relational maneuvers. If the entrenched troops remain where they are, the defense fails absolutely and may be destroyed in the process by enfilading fire down the line. The defense can react against the outflanking move only by thinning out the line to extend it far enough or by abandoning the entrenched line altogether to intercept the attackers. In the first case, the ratio advantage is preserved, but the balance of strength shifts in the attackers' favor because there will be fewer defenders in each segment of the line. In the second, the balance of strength where the forces clash is unchanged, but the ratio advantage is lost. In either case, three units will no longer be needed to defeat just one.

In the setting of the western front in the First World War, the tactical ratio advantage was obtained at the level of theater strategy as well, because the continuity of trenchlines all the way from the Belgian coast to the Swiss border prevented any simple bypassing. And the ratio advantage was also preserved at the operational level, because column attacks focused against narrow segments of the front could not outconcentrate the defense. With field telephones, railways, and trucks available to gather its forces, the defensive counterconcentration was faster than the advance of foot soldiers against artillery fires, barbed wire, and machine guns. The intellectuals who dominated the post-1918 French general staff,[3] in fact, could prove mathematically the counterconcentration superiority of defense over offense, inexorably derived from the speed advantage of lateral railway and truck movements along the front, over the slow rate of the foot-infantry's advance against fire. It was only necessary to offset the initial start that the enemy might have, if intelligence failed to uncover preparations until an offensive was imminent. That, however, could assuredly be done, for an uninterrupted defensive line would have the tactical advantage of entrenched troops who cannot be bypassed, thus allowing one unit to hold three or more at least temporarily, until reinforcements arrived.

By this calculation, so long as German mothers did not breed more than three times as many sons, the French would be able to resist any offensive, unless first weakened by futile offensives of their own. Victory was therefore assured if a purely defensive theater strategy was rigidly followed. But one more element was added to the defense to reduce its price in blood: prepared fortifications. Once again, it was a matter of common sense: concrete-lined trenches and fortified weapon positions already built in peacetime were obviously much better than unsanitary, less resistant mud trenches and dugouts improvised under fire; likewise, elaborate forts to shield the artillery would enhance its potential, both for counter-battery fires to prevent the enemy's artillery from crushing the line infantry and for attacks on the enemy's own advancing foot soldiers.

Such were the seemingly compelling reasons to build the formidable Maginot Line all along the Franco-German border. Those fortifications did achieve their maximum possible success in May and June 1940, when the German offensive bypassed them by way of Belgium to evade the

formidable strength of its barriers, solidly entrenched infantry, and fortified artillery. By the usual paradox of strategy, the Maginot Line failed
to protect France because it was oversuccessful: no defensive system can
possibly achieve more than to dissuade the enemy from even trying to
attack it. In retrospect, one may speculate that a less formidable defensive
system, an incomplete solution with attractive gaps, might have served
France better, by offering the possibility at least that the Germans would
choose to attack it, becoming entangled in positional warfare as in the
First World War. As it was, the Maginot Line, deemed impassable at both
the tactical and operational levels, was countered at the level of theater
strategy: in May 1940, the German offensive penetrated the unfortified
Belgian Ardennes all the way to the Channel coast. With the Maginot
Line bypassed, the arithmetic of concentration and counterconcentration
was overthrown by the blitzkrieg. Led by the tanks and half-track carriers
of Panzer divisions, the German deep-penetration columns moved at motor speed to outrace the lateral gathering of defensive strength. That nullified whatever tactical ratio advantage entrenched infantry might have
had, even if equipped with many antitank weapons. One can only wonder
at the deep-seated emotional preferences that have completely reversed
the twin lessons of 1940, to condemn the fully successful Maginot Line,
while upholding three-to-one ratios valid only at the tactical level.

Battlefield Nuclear Weapons

During the decades of the Cold War, the military plans of the Western
Alliance for the defense of the central front in Germany changed several
times. But almost till the very end, they continued to rely on "battlefield"
nuclear weapons. The larger role of nuclear weapons has always derived
from their function as instruments of suasion* at the higher level of grand
strategy. For now, however, it is their role in theater strategy that concerns us. Battlefield nuclear weapons, with explosive yields and radiation
effects that were quite modest by intercontinental nuclear standards in
the form of shorter-range missiles, artillery shells, demolition charges, and
tactical aircraft bombs,[4] were meant to provide a technical-level response
to the power of the Soviet army. They offered an economical way of defeating a large-scale offensive that threatened the collapse of the front.

* The term is meant to describe both persuasion and dissuasion, in all their forms.
The subject is discussed in Part III.

Under the Alliance policy of the 1970s and 1980s, a Soviet nonnuclear offensive would be resisted by a nonnuclear defense for as long as possible; but if Soviet formations continued to reach the front and the defense could no longer hold them, then battlefield nuclear weapons would be used.

When first fielded in 1952–53,[5] U.S. nuclear weapons for battlefield use quickly rose on the curve of effectiveness. They were easily integrated into the planned frontal defenses of those days: a chain of small forces in shallow deployments that almost formed a true line all along the border. There were just enough forces to distinguish between a border incident and an offensive—which could be answered only by nuclear counterattack. Nonnuclear weakness yielded strength, by making the use of nuclear weapons more credible. But this technical-level reaction to nonnuclear Soviet strength reached its culminating point of success quite soon, for by the later 1950s the Soviet army had acquired its own battlefield nuclear weapons. Thus if the defenders tried to shield crumbling sectors of their front by attacking Soviet invasion columns with nuclear weapons, the Soviet command could reply by breaking open other sectors of the front with its own nuclear weapons.

Yet action and reaction did not nullify each other in this case. If nuclear weapons were employed, the Soviet army could no longer conquer rich lands by invasion but would instead preside over their devastation. Thus if the Alliance could persuasively threaten to use its battlefield nuclear weapons if attacked, it should have been able to dissuade any Soviet attempt at conquest, whose only possible outcomes were either nonnuclear defeat or nuclear destruction. As always with suasion, it is the adversary leaders who control the process; deterrence can succeed only if they believe the threat and then calculate the punishment as greater than the reward. It follows that security obtained by suasion is inherently less reliable than adequate defensive strength would be ("deterrence by denial"). As against that, nuclear weapons present a threat much less easily minimized than that of any number of armored divisions, because their effects are accurately predictable.

In this case, however, the effectiveness of suasion would depend on the motive: if the Soviet leaders had attacked the Alliance out of desperation rather than in the hope of conquest, they would not have been dissuaded by the prospect of causing a belt of nuclear destruction down the middle of Germany. Illegitimate power is forever insecure. One much-feared Cold War scenario started with a general revolt in Eastern Europe caused by the subversive example of Western European freedom and prosperity. At that point, an attack on Western Europe would have been a plausible countermove, to deprive unrest of its impulse by threatening consequences even worse than continued oppression.

Another possibility was that the Soviet Union would attack for defensive reasons, to defeat an Alliance offensive that its leaders believed to be imminent. The idea that aggression could be concerted in secret by the Dutch parliament, the West German chancellor, the grand duke of Luxembourg, and the Belgian cabinet, as well as the White House and Whitehall, might seem fantastic. But the Kremlin leaders presided over a government that had a seemingly infinite capacity for suspicion, and no date in history was more clearly remembered in the Soviet Union than June 22, 1941, when invasion came as a dreadful surprise. If what was perceived as self-defense had been the motive of aggression, Alliance battlefield nuclear weapons would have retained their physical capacity to nullify an impeding Soviet nonnuclear victory but would not have dissuaded attack altogether.

It was from German territory that most of the shorter-range nuclear weapons of both sides would have been launched, and it was German frontal zones that would have suffered nuclear devastation. Because it would have been so damaging, the Alliance nuclear counterthreat could therefore have been self-inhibiting. Yet even the government of West Germany continued to reaffirm the threat of battlefield nuclear attack in the event of an impending Soviet nonnuclear victory.[6] It preferred that risk to the cost of keeping nonnuclear forces capable of defeating a nonnuclear invasion without appealing to the higher court of nuclear war.

The risks of relying on nuclear weapons became increasingly obvious as the Cold War continued, but for the Alliance the consequences of increasing *non*nuclear strength could have been paradoxically negative. The refusal of the European allies of the United States to increase their nonnuclear forces was certainly motivated by opposition to greater military expenditures. But it could also have been justified by strategic reasoning. True, if the nonnuclear forces of the Alliance had been strong enough to defend the central front against a Soviet nonnuclear invasion, there would have been no need to employ battlefield nuclear weapons. In the event of war, therefore, the world would have been spared the ultimate danger of a step-by-step progression from battlefield to intercontinental nuclear war. But if nuclear use is absent in a war, nonnuclear combat must occur in a war still enormously damaging for the affected European populations, but not for either Russians or Americans. It seemed wise at the time to equalize the risk.

9

Theater Strategy II: Offense and Defense

On the offensive, the largest choice at the level of theater strategy is between the broad-front advance, which only the very strong can attempt—for otherwise the army advancing everywhere must everywhere be outnumbered—and the narrow advance, which offers the opportunity of victory even to the weak, by focusing their strength. On the one hand, the broad-front advance with no relational maneuver, no operational ingenuity, is likely to be that much more costly in casualties. On the other hand, its simplicity reduces risks: parallel forward movements are much more easily coordinated than converging penetrations, and of course there are no exposed flanks. By contrast, risks and rewards both inexorably increase as advance is more focused, culminating in the pencil-thin penetrations of the classic German blitzkrieg of 1939–1942, part bold maneuver, part confidence trick. By the usual reversal of the logic, only those who already have a safe margin of superiority can afford the cautious broad advance, while those already at risk must accept yet more risk to have any chance of success at all.

On the defensive, however, the choices of theater strategy determine not only the deployment of military forces but also the fate of the territories exposed to danger. That often results in a clash between the linear logic of politics, which equates defense with protection, and the paradoxical logic of strategy, which routinely trades off protection against defense. The clash is especially apparent in the case of an elastic defense. The resulting freedom of action to evade the enemy's main thrusts, to move at will and concentrate in full, gives the defenders every advantage of the offense, while they still retain their inherent advantage of fighting in a known and presumably friendly environment. Often regarded as ideal from a purely military viewpoint, this is the least desirable of defensive strategies for those who govern, regardless of whether it is wealth, welfare, or control they seek to maximize. Likewise, in the opposite case of a preclusive defense, the political best and the military worst again coincide.

Both extremes are of course rarities. In practice, only approximations are encountered: even when Stalin's high command decided to elude the renewed German offensive of 1942 with a defense so elastic that hundreds of towns were abandoned, it would not abandon Stalingrad; and even the Cold War commitment of the North Atlantic Alliance to defend West Germany preclusively did not require the protection of every inch of its territory.* Compromises are inevitable. More scope is allowed to political priorities when the sense of security is greater (justifiably or not), while military priorities are likely to dominate the decisions of theater strategy only when imminent disaster is feared.

There is obviously an entire spectrum of choices between the extremes of an elastic defense that does not resist at all but rather saves its full strength for counterattacks and a fully preclusive frontal defense. Only political decisions—including emergency responses to shifting situations—can define the boundary between what is to be protected at all costs and what may be abandoned at least temporarily. But there is another format that diverges from this spectrum, a "defense-in-depth," in which a frontal zone more or less deep is neither preclusively protected nor abandoned. Instead that zone is selectively defended by self-contained forces that operate as islands of resistance, forming a grid rather than a line. Historically, defense-in-depth strategies have served to protect castle towns and fortified cities near hostile frontiers on a permanent basis; that was part of the strategy of the Roman Empire from the time of Diocletian in the later third century. In modern wars, they have been applied in zones of maneuver. Shielded by favorable terrain or artificial barriers, organized and supplied to fight on their own, such islands of resistance serve to hold important passages along major avenues of approach or to shield valuable infrastructures such as airfields and major depots. But if there is to be a chance of victory, their main function must be to offer protected bases from which disruptive incursions and counterattacks can be launched, ideally in coordination with the main forces kept behind the frontal zone defended only in depth.

If the islands of resistance are to be strong enough, and if they are to be laid out in sufficient depth, they certainly cannot form a continuous front. The enemy can therefore advance without pausing to attack them

* The one-bound reach of Soviet armored forces was so deep that a defense sufficiently elastic to absorb their momentum would scarcely have defended West Germany at all.

if he so chooses, bypassing every island of resistance to reach his objectives in the deep rear. But that opportunity is also a potential trap: just as in the past an advancing column could not simply bypass an unsubdued fortress holding forces ready to sally forth without grave risk, so even today an armor-mechanized penetration cannot simply ignore enemy forces that remain free to attack its vulnerable flanks. Yet to pause in order to reduce each island of resistance in turn must interrupt the critical tempo of the advance, while to leave containment forces around each one results in a growing dispersion of strength.

The dilemma thus created for the attackers by a defense-in-depth can be accentuated if the defenders have the means and moral capacity to launch raids against the supply columns, service units, and lesser detachments that the enemy advance itself brings within their reach. To the extent that the terrain confines the offensive to narrow avenues of advance that can actually be blocked, it is not a dilemma that faces the attackers, who must instead overcome the resistance of each successive defended island along their path. But strategy allows no unlimited linear progression in this matter either: the more the terrain of the theater of war confines movements, the more valid a defense-in-depth becomes, but only until a culminating point is reached. Beyond that, in truly restrictive Himalayan-type mountain terrain, for example, a linear defense of mutually supporting positions that block every passage becomes preferable to any defense-in-depth. Of course no defense-in-depth or linear defense for that matter can succeed on its own, without offensive forces that can eventually counterattack the enemy; without offensive forces, the forces of the defense will be imprisoned in their positions, nowhere more so that in high mountain terrain.

For the North Atlantic Alliance during the Cold War, there was no danger of overshooting the terrain limits of a defense-in-depth on the central front. Some sectors in central Germany did contain mountains but nothing of Himalayan or Alpine caliber. There was no possibility of blocking the major avenues of penetration with a few strong positions. Still, even in the north German plain and the so-called Fulda Gap, there were significant terrain obstacles, both wooded ridges and urban areas that could have accommodated a grid of islands of resistance. A defense-in-depth theater strategy would certainly have been a relational-maneuver response to the Soviet threat of those days, for it would have served well to absorb and diffuse the armored "mailed-fist" momentum of the Soviet army. Deprived of the solid obstacle of the central front to break through, the invasion columns would instead have had to fight their way through the entire defended belt, all the while exposed to flanking attacks. Manned as it was by conscript and reserve forces perfectly capable of pushing ahead but lacking in tactical skill, the Soviet army would have suffered greatly even from local counterattacks by relatively small forces—as long as enough of them were mounted to make a difference.

During the Cold War many schemes for the defense-in-depth of the Alliance central front were circulated. Some advocated retaining the existing armored and mechanized forces but keeping them back to maneuver freely instead of being locked into frontal positions.[1] Others called for a combination of the same forces with missile light infantry in small units to be moved about by helicopters,[2] or with local militias that would fight in guerrilla fashion, alongside regular light infantry units,[3] or with small units of standard infantry distributed in local garrisons to defend the stone-built villages that dot the German countryside.[4] In some variants, continuous lines of fixed antitank barriers were to be added, to slow down Soviet armored columns; in others, with or without fixed barriers, fortified positions were to be provided for some of the troops, to enable them to delay passage through roads and terrain corridors in a deep zone behind the front. In all these schemes, the purpose was to delay indefinitely the deep penetrations that Soviet armored columns would seek to achieve after fighting one hard frontal battle. Instead, the Soviet columns were to be entangled within the deep defense, until they could be cut off and defeated piecemeal or counterattacked in strength.[5]

The defense-in-depth alternatives suggested for the central front differed in detail, but they had one thing in common: they were all examples of original military thought, which arguably diverged not only from ossified bureaucratic plans but also from political realities. Moreover, all the schemes suffered from the classic delusion of the "final move": in reacting to the deep-penetration theater strategy imputed to the Soviet army, they failed to allow for the likely reaction—a new and different Soviet theater strategy designed to overcome a defense-in-depth. In other words, they ignored strategy's fundamental phenomenon.

But before addressing these criticisms, we should recall the considerable merits of these schemes in purely military terms. They still represent the state of the art. At the tactical level, as we have seen, troops fighting from within fortifications against attackers who must move in the open benefit from favorable "exchange ratios," as their fire acts with full effect while the attackers' fire does not. Likewise, small, agile units trained to raid Soviet columns opportunistically, and to pull back as soon as they were counterattacked, would also experience favorable exchange ratios. Moreover, as long as the units that cover them with their weapons can endure under fire, barriers such as antitank ditches, solid obstacles, and minefields can improve the tactical effectiveness of blocking positions, by reducing the enemy's rate of advance, ideally down to the target-engagement capacity of the defensive weapons in place.

At the operational level, the combined effect of barriers and road-blocking fortifications reduces the *relative mobility* of attackers, making it that much more likely that sufficiently strong counterattacking forces can be positioned advantageously to engage their flanks. At the theater level, any and all of these schemes would have circumvented the Soviet army's greatest strength, its ability to break through solid fronts, while exploiting its greatest presumed weakness, its lack of small-unit flexibility.[6]

Defense-in-depth schemes were nevertheless rejected by successive West German governments and therefore by the Alliance as a whole. That they diverged from established policy was not conclusive—policy can change at any time. But their political unrealism was of a more fundamental order. At the technical level of strategy, or the tactical or operational, the goals pursued are self-evident, material, and beyond debate: higher kill probabilities, better exchange ratios, and victory in battle are certainly more desirable than their opposites. At the theater level, however, the very meaning of success and failure is a matter of political decision. Defense-in-depth schemes could defeat a Soviet invasion without defending West Germany in the meanwhile—and whether the concurrent ruin of both the Soviet army and of much German territory would have been a success or a failure is an open question. The amount of territory that would have been given over to prolonged warfare varied with each specific scheme, but none could offer a preclusive defense of the entire national territory, as the "forward" defense was meant to do.

The advocates of the different schemes of defense-in-depth argued that the danger of exposing some part of West German territory to nonnuclear destruction was far preferable to the ultimate danger of exposing all of it, including cities, to nuclear devastation. The choice was complicated by the different risk levels associated with the two dangers: it could certainly be argued that battlefield nuclear dissuasion was more reliable than its nonnuclear counterpart. But actually the terms of the choice were themselves questionable, because there was always a third option: the West German government could prohibit at any time the use of nuclear weapons based on its territory. Hence if dissuasion failed, a Soviet invasion began, and the front could not hold, the West German government could refuse to authorize nuclear counterattacks and ask for an armistice instead. Even the harshest Soviet terms could reasonably be preferred to the use of nuclear weapons on German soil or to the widespread destruction that prolonged nonnuclear warfare would inflict on Germany's crowded lands. Defense-in-depth schemes were far more attractive as an alternative to declared peacetime policy than to actual wartime policy.

The Cold War is over, and so are all the debates over the best way of defending the central front. But the lessons of the experience are enduring. Once the level of theater strategy is reached, military decisions are no longer separable from political imperatives. That introduces two unavoidable complications. First, the paradoxical logic of warfare (he who defends all can defend nothing, or, victory can be excessive) inevitably clashes with the linear logic of politics, which calls for maximum protection or maximum conquest as the case might be. Almost all military men therefore consider almost all politicians too bold or too timid. Second, the military striving to obtain the best possible outcome—even if short of victory—can be at odds with the ever present political option of pursuing a negotiated outcome instead. It is only at the level of grand strategy that these collisions are unresolved one way or another.

Nonterritorial Warfare

Guerrilla (from the Spanish "little war") refers to the combat of small units that do not seek to hold territory and describes a *tactic* that can be employed by anyone, including the strongest armies. It can also denote the combat dimension of *revolutionary war*.[7] Guerrilla combat as an adjunct of regular operations is as old as war: any form of unstructured raiding qualifies. Armies used to have light cavalry and skirmishers for that. Now they have commando or "special operations" units. The principle is the same: with or without main-force engagements, smaller self-contained units that can operate without supply lines behind them are sent to attack targets in the soft rear. In revolutionary war, by contrast, the dominating context is the internal struggle for the control of government. Guerrilla combat is one of its tools, designed to humiliate and weaken the government in power by attacking its soldiers, policemen, and civil administrators. But the major instrument of revolutionary war is subversion—the undermining and displacement of the official administrative machinery by propaganda and terrorism. The relative proportions of propaganda and terrorism are a good indicator of intentions: when much terrorism is employed and not much propaganda, a democratic form of government cannot be the aim of the insurgents.

Guerrilla fighters cannot normally have a technical-level advantage over regular armies, and they rarely have a tactical advantage. But they certainly have an operational advantage: insofar as they fight elusively, without trying to defend terrain against determined attack, guerillas remain free to do as much or as little fighting as they choose, when and where they choose. They can harass regular forces, ambush road columns, attack small detachments, and sabotage infrastructures and supply facilities, each time dispersing before superior strength. The guerrilla is thus a relational-maneuver response to superior military strength, and one of the weaknesses it seeks to exploit in many cases is the self-restraint of regular forces bound by the norms of the official government. Jewish, Kikuyu, Chinese communist, Greek, and Arab guerrillas fighting British troops in Palestine, Kenya, Malaya, Cyprus, and Aden, Vietnamese and Algerians fighting French troops in Indochina and Algeria, and certainly the Vietcong fighting Americans, could rely on their enemy's self-restraint in dealing with the civilian population at large. There were exceptions of course, with harsh behavior by some troops here and there and even the occasional act of deadly violence, but no systematic retaliation was countenanced by the military authorities, let alone by the governments at home, acting under the scrutiny of parliaments and press.

If, by contrast, such inhibitions are absent or weak, the freedom of action of guerrillas can be greatly restricted by the threat of violent reprisals against the civilian population at large, which contains their families and friends. When each guerrilla assassination results in the execution of several innocent civilians held hostage just for that purpose; when each successful ambush is followed by the annihilation of the nearest village; and when each raid on a headquarters or depot is followed by massacres, not many guerrillas will feel free to assassinate, ambush, and raid whenever opportunity offers. Their emotional tie to the civilian population from which they derive is a potential weakness, which ruthless occupation forces can exploit in their own relational-maneuver response.

The reprisal policy of the German forces during the Second World War was very effective in minimizing the results that guerrillas could achieve, in most places, most of the time. The mere diversion of German manpower to oppose them must be the largest part of any estimate, but with that duly included, it is now generally agreed that the military impact of the Norwegian, Danish, Dutch, Belgian, French, Italian, and Greek resistance was unimpressive.[8] The Polish resistance was more an effort to organize a secret army for the eventual control of Poland after a German with-drawal than an ongoing guerrilla campaign, and when that army did emerge to fight, it did so in perfectly conventional form, by attempting to secure Warsaw in August 1944, when the arrival of the Soviet army seemed imminent.[9] Only Tito's communists and the Soviet partisans were truly effective as guerrillas during the war, precisely because they were willing to compete with the Germans in ruthlessness, at great cost to the civilian population.*

The post-1945 guerrillas fighting colonial rule did not face that dilemma as we have seen, but as of this writing, armed separatists in Kashmir, Sri Lanka, and Sudan are following the Soviet partisan model, attacking government forces whenever and wherever they can, without being re-strained in any way by the plight of the civilian population.

Point Defense

It may seem strange that to harm civilians at large and to arm them can be equivalent responses, but this is true in the paradoxical realm of strat-egy. The symmetrical theater-level response to guerrillas is to emulate their dispersion. Instead of providing an area defense with large forma-tions ready to sally out to engage the enemy—an ineffectual procedure against elusive opponents—many small units are detached to provide a "point defense" of as many vulnerable targets as possible. Guards on bridges, dams, and power stations, as well as town and village garrisons, road checkpoints, and patrols, compete with the diffused strength of the guerrillas, and do so advantageously in most cases because regular troops are apt to be better disciplined, better trained, and better armed. Naturally, if a conventional war is also under way, the opportunity cost of many point defenses in rear areas is the loss of combat strength at the front, and indeed that is one of the causes of the paradoxical convergence between uninterrupted advances and defeat.[†]

---

* In Yugoslavia the usual divergence between community protection and ideologi-cal resistance was particularly acute: the Serbian nationalist Cetniks were virtually incapacitated by the German reprisal policy and eventually driven into forms of collab-oration.

† Historically, the needs of point defense have restrained the expansion of military empires, as the quantum of total unrest continued to accumulate. The Roman rule, more or less, was to pacify one province and obtain its taxes (or recruits) before conquering another, but, even so, security requirements grew because the secular tranquillity of

In the context of revolutionary war, however, point defense is the most important function of the armed forces, to safeguard the workings of society and state until the motives of insurgency are removed by reforms, counterpropaganda, or surrender.

The obvious operational-level guerrilla response is to adopt a more concentrated form of warfare. Having initially resorted to dispersion because of their inability to match the strength of large government formations, when point defenses are organized to oppose their small bands, the guerrillas discover that guards, village garrisons, checkpoints, and patrols are all vulnerable to their larger bands, gathered to attack specific objectives. As the process develops, a distinction often emerges between guerrillas who remain in small localized bands and "main forces" that operate in wider areas, perhaps countrywide. At this stage the guerrillas could defeat the point defense in detail, by employing their main forces for successive attacks against smaller regular units. But as the guerrillas try to do so, they become rather less elusive in their larger groupings, both because hundreds cannot hide in nature as a few can and because the ingathering of main forces removes individual guerrillas from their home habitat (and as strangers they are less likely to be assisted by the locals). This shift allows the government to engage the guerrillas in a concentration-counterconcentration contest, on terms that vary according to the respective means of supply, communication, and mobility. If there is no great difference between the two sides in such capabilities, the spiral may continue to ascend until both are fielding large formations, and *guerra* displaces the guerrilla.

This is unlikely, however, because guerrillas will rarely be able to gather all their localized bands into main forces, and will not usually want to do so anyway, because the advantage in supply, communications, and mobility will generally remain with the government.* Hence main forces

---

some provinces was accompanied by recurrent uprisings in others. Some such calculation must have motivated the injunction against further conquest in the testament of Augustus. Recorded by Tacitus, *Annals* I.11, and criticized in his *Agricola* XIII.

* This was the case long before the advent of modern logistics, radios, and helicopters. The Romans, whose physical mobility was not superior to insurgent enemies, already derived an advantage at the level of theater strategy from their signal-tower networks, whose smoke (day) and flame (night) signals relayed warnings and orders; from their well-made roads, whose full use by insurgents was denied by road forts; and from their granaries, also fortified, from which troops could obtain food and fodder available only to insurgents after time-consuming sieges.

and their battles are likely to coexist with elusive small bands and their opportunistic attacks on any targets of value left undefended. The result is that the government is confronted with the concurrent need for both large formations—to fight main forces—and point defenses. This places it in exactly the same position as an army engaged in conventional war at the front that has conquered actively hostile populations and seeks to minimize the diversion of its forces to provide point defenses in the rear. For an army of occupation, the cheapest solution is to dissuade guerrilla attacks by reprisals, deadly or not (property destruction can be just as effective), rather than to preclude them by distributing small units throughout the resisting areas.[10] In fighting domestic insurgents, the equivalent solution is to induce the inhabitants of insecure areas to form self-defense militias for point defense, thus releasing detachments on garrison and guard duty to revert to their formations for larger-scale actions against the insurgent main forces. That was the solution successfully adopted in El Salvador during the 1980s, when the Defensa Civil armed and trained villagers to defend themselves against guerilla bands. Once a mobile training team had taught the villagers how to use the M.1 carbines issued to them along with simple tactics, a single army sergeant with a field radio was left behind to provide leadership and summon help if needed; the system worked remarkably well and was indeed far more effective than the attempts of the regular army to find and engage the guerrillas with its noisy and slow 1,200-man battalions.[11]

During those same years, the Soviet army was fighting its last war, in Afghanistan. Facing elusive insurgents all the more fragmented because the resistance was politically divided, the Soviet army and its Afghan government allies heavily relied on reprisals to contain the insurgents: the area bombing of nearby villages was the normal Soviet response to insurgent attacks, and there were many reports of executions of fighting-age men rounded up in the vicinity. Obviously the deterrent effect was small—products of a warrior culture inflamed by religion, the insurgents were not dissuaded by the plight of the civilian population. Yet over time, the bombing was quite effective, by changing the demography of Afghanistan. Areas in which insurgent activity was intense were gradually depopulated. Where the rural population was undiminished, by contrast, the volume of insurgent action remained low. Increasingly, guerrillas in the field no longer had their families and clans nearby. Having moved to refugee camps inside Pakistan and Iran, the civilians were safe from Soviet reprisals, but they left the insurgents without supporters nearby to provide food and information. Aside from occasional commando operations, the Soviet army—mostly manned by young conscripts—avoided offensive action, to minimize casualties. The number of casualties indeed remained small, well below 1,000 killed in action per year. But in the end that too proved to be excessive. It turned out that the closed and censored Soviet society was even less willing to accept casualties than American society had been at the time of the Vietnam war.

10

Theater Strategy III:
Interdiction and the Surprise Attack

We have seen that the different formats of theater defense are not freely available options but modes preordained by fundamental political and cultural attitudes. Normally it is a preclusive defense that is desired, even if some shallow form of defense-in-depth is accepted in practice. As for its deeper versions, and certainly any sort of elastic defense, these are hardly ever deliberately planned; they are accepted only reluctantly, to avert imminent defeat.

Actually there is a format even more desirable in theory than a preclusive defense: an *active* defense, whereby a theater is defended by launching an immediate counteroffensive, without any defensive fighting at all. Thus the inherent tactical advantages of the defense are deliberately sacrificed, either to spare the national territory from damage or because there is a lack of geographic depth in which to carry out effective defensive operations; that was Israel's predicament in 1973, when concerted Arab offensives were launched. Further, it is organizationally easier to launch preplanned offensives than to cope defensively with a variety of surprise attacks. In all cases, however, if both the attacker and the defender choose the offensive, one or the other must have seriously misread the balance of power. One reason an active defense is a rarity at the strategic level is that it requires an offensive elan more likely to be encountered among aggressors than among victims. In fact no modern example in pure form can be cited except for Israel's 1973 war, and the nearest case before that, the advance of the French and British armies into Belgium in immediate reaction to the German offensive of May 10, 1940, was not an encouraging precedent.

The advent of long-range means of attack has made it possible for both sides to wage war deep in the enemy's territory, but certainly theater depth continues to favor the defense, if there is disposable space. France, though a large country by European standards, lacked depth in its rail-way-age warfare with Germany from 1870 to 1940 because supremely valued Paris is not at the center of the country but rather in its northwest corner, a mere one hundred well-roaded miles from the Belgian frontier, with no major terrain barriers in between. That being so, the size of the country was actually a disadvantage since most French reserves and garrison forces had to come from afar to stand between Paris and the frontier. That obviously made Paris and France vulnerable to surprise attack. It was to compensate for this weakness that there was so much French fortress building on the frontiers long before the Maginot Line.

The same geography was favorable for French offensive action in a northerly direction, into the Low Countries and the German lands. With its political center so well positioned to serve as a forward command post, and with the frontier fortresses in place to serve as depots and jump-off bases, France could readily mount surprise offensives and frequently did, until the unification of Germany nullified the advantage.

The Soviet Union, like the tsars' Russia before it and the Russian Federation since, was in exactly the opposite situation. With almost eight hundred scarcely roaded miles to shield Moscow in a westward direction, measuring only to Warsaw, there was ample theater depth to absorb the strength of Swedish, French, and German invaders from Charles XII to Hitler. Peter the Great's foundation of his capital did not change matters fundamentally. While the city's defensive depth to the north was much smaller than Moscow's, by the time St. Petersburg was built Swedish power was in sharp decline, and no new northern great power had arisen in its place. As for westward depth, the shorter distance from East Prussia, still almost five hundred straight-line miles, was offset by the watery terrain in between, which imposed large detours around swamps and lakes.

Moscow's geographic depth is even greater to the east, across a strategical vacuum of several thousand miles to the centers of Chinese power and Japan, neither of them in any case containing more than a peripheral threat, if that, to this day. Only to the south was Muscovy exposed, as long as what is now Ukraine remained a no-man's-land, part of the steppe corridor open to Turkic and Mongol invasions—and that danger was finally removed by Russian expansion and Ottoman decline during the time of Peter the Great.

By the same token, however, the offensive potential of Russian armies mustered out of Moscow was greatly diminished by distance; until the railway age, their strength and supplies would be consumed in marching long before they even reached their own frontier. St. Petersburg's foundation did not change matters much, for Russian forces were still mostly mustered out of Moscow and the surrounding regions. Hence the preparation of any major Russian offensive before the railway age was a lengthy affair, with one year's campaigning season best used to prepare for the next, by moving forward armies and their supplies to the advancing front. Even during the Second World War, the Soviet army needed several months to rebuild its strength from one offensive to the next, once the war turned to its advantage in the summer of 1943. Even now, in spite of air transport as well as railways and a few paved roads, considerable time and resources are needed to overcome distance, and the long lines of communications are subject to a novel vulnerability, from air attack.

The other side of the coin of the Soviet Union's formidable defensive depth was therefore the inability of its armies to launch offensives in full strength from a standing start. In a westward direction, except for forces already stationed well forward in East Germany, as it then was, even Soviet formations at full readiness faced long transits before they could have gone into action. It was in that context that one more defensive concept for the Alliance central front was proposed: a *deep-attack* theater strategy, to be superimposed on the frontal defense to delay, disrupt, and diminish Soviet forces moving toward the combat zones by aerial strikes. The peacetime array of Alliance forces stationed in West Germany might or might not have managed to hold the first wave of Soviet armies. But certainly it could not offer a reliable nonnuclear defense against the mobilized Soviet formations that would next have reached the scene, at a much faster rate than Alliance reinforcements could arrive.

Interdiction as a Substitute for Depth

A number of different deep-attack schemes were proposed,[1] all of them anticipations in one way or other of the so-called Revolution in Military Affairs, much discussed since the 1990s. What they had in common was a reliance on cruise or ballistic missiles armed with many small submunitions as well as manned aircraft, to attack targets far behind the front over ranges of hundreds of miles.

Already in those days there was nothing new about the air attack of fixed targets in the rear, be they bridges or airfields, and only detailed calculation could or can evaluate the relative merits of doing so with guided missiles rather than manned aircraft. During the Cold War, the overall Soviet reaction to the technical superiority of Western air power was an exceptionally broad and intense effort to develop air defenses. The result was a broad array of mobile antiaircraft missiles that are still scattered around the world. They in turn duly evoked an Alliance reaction, both in the form of evasive tactics now obsolete (ultralow altitude penetration that virtually precludes the use of precision-guided weapons) and electronic countermeasures that have continued to develop. But after decades of reciprocal preparation, the ability of Western pilots to attack targets deep in the rear remained uncertain. Missiles therefore offered an attractive alternative, though one that raised a number of technical, military, and political difficulties.[2] It was, however, the deep attack of Soviet reinforcements moving toward the combat zones that was the novel idea. It presented technical difficulties and raised questions that remain important even now. In the wake of the 1999 Kosovo air war, the ability of air power to effectively attack mobile targets remains an unfulfilled promise, in sharp contrast to the routine precision with which fixed "high-contrast" targets such as bridges and power stations can be identified, designated, and destroyed.

Artillery and Air Interdiction

Again, there was nothing new about the interdiction of reinforcements as such. The systematic shelling of approach roads to the front was already much employed during the First World War, when this long-range artillery tactic was an important element in both front-holding and front-breaking theater strategies. Along with the unnatural obstacle of the no-man's-land between the opposed trenchlines, with its shell craters often filled with water and barbed-wire obstacles, and the decisive arithmetical advantage of entrenched machine guns against troops advancing on foot, artillery interdiction allowed defenders to outconcentrate the offense.*

---

* The advantage of the defense in First World War conditions derived from the relative ease with which trenchlines could be reinforced by troops marching from the nearest railway siding, albeit under artillery fire, as compared to the multiple obstacles in the path of attackers also on foot who were trying to fight their way to those same trenchlines against machine-gun fire. The initial, tactical-level purpose of the tank, armored against machine-gun fire and provided with tracks to cross shell craters and crush barbed wire, was precisely to overcome this asymmetry. It was only later that the tank's operational-level potential for deep-penetration offensives was recognized.

With much less success long-range artillery was often used in attempts to break fronts, by preventing the gathering of reinforcements into sectors under attack.

Artillery shelling against points on the map, typically crossroads on the approaches to the front, did not kill or wound many men nor destroy much equipment. But neither did it have to do so in order to achieve the delay that was its purpose (heavy casualties by artillery interdiction did happen sometimes, as when thousands of troops converged each day for months on end into the small salient of Verdun).

During the Second World War, and later in Korea, Vietnam, and then Iraq in 1991, the long-range interdiction of supplies and reinforcements by air attack replaced or supplemented the shelling of approach roads. Deeper forms of air attack require larger and more costly aircraft, or at least more fuel and therefore smaller bomb loads than attacks at the front; as a result, they must be justified by a compensating advantage. That there is, because of the different dispositions of the enemy behind the front and upon the front. Reinforcements moving to the combat zone in road convoys or by rail offer more visible, more concentrated, and therefore more profitable targets for air attacks than forces deployed for combat— especially if they are on the defensive. But the richness of targets is one thing and the ability to exploit it quite another: fighter bombers cannot range freely in the deep rear, flying along roads and rail lines to strafe and bomb military traffic at will, unless the logic of strategy is suspended by a nonreacting enemy. That was almost true of Iraq in 1991, for only localized air defenses remained active; by contrast, NATO air forces remained notably cautious in the 1999 Kosovo war, fearing the low-tech but proliferated air defenses of the Yugoslav forces.

As always, there is a paradox at work. If the enemy's own air power and antiaircraft forces are formidable, then his troops and supplies in transit can be crowded in dense convoys in broad daylight, for then air interdiction is not likely to be attempted in any great depth by large numbers of attacking aircraft (partly because many fighters would be needed to escort the few armed for bombing and strafing). But if the enemy's air defenses are weak, allowing a free hand for interdiction aircraft, then they are not likely to encounter dense military traffic they can profitably attack. For in that case the enemy would strive to move his troops and supplies at night, or in dispersed order, or both. Thus air power that is too strong undermines its own potential utility. To be sure, night movements and dispersal both impose delays in themselves, if not actual destruction, and the remaining question for the attackers is whether the time won justifies the cost of air interdiction. Will it delay the arrival of a particular body of troops that might tip the outcome of a given battle? Or will air interdiction merely lengthen a routine one-week transit by a number of days?[3] In the context of the defense of the central front during the Cold War, it was unlikely that Soviet reinforcements and supplies moving toward the front could have been seriously hampered by the bombing of bridges, viaducts, railway yards, and roads. The increasing multiplicity of roads and greater rail density going from east to west, from the Soviet Union to West Germany as it then was, and the Soviet army's primacy in combat bridging would have ensured the failure of an interdiction campaign aimed at the transport network itself.[4]

Deep Interdiction Schemes

In current RMA schemes as in their Cold War deep-attack predecessors, the bombing of transport infrastructures is only a secondary effort, though now very efficient in the age of routine precision. The main effort, however, is to be made against the moving traffic itself—targets much harder to find, identify, designate, and hit. So far, up to and including the 1999 Kosovo war, only fixed targets have ever been bombed efficiently, that is, expending a small number of weapons for each target destroyed. But it is the claim of RMA optimists that recent advances in sensors and computing offer a way to break out of the strategic paradox, by nullifying the protection of the night and—more dubiously—of dispersed mobility. Satellite observation cannot be continuous, but high-altitude air observation by remotely piloted vehicles can be. Instantly relayed, the data can be assessed semiautomatically to select specific targets and the means of attacking them, directing missiles or manned aircraft with advanced munitions to their targets. That offers the technical possibility of attacking forces in transit, even by night, even if they are dispersed—but only if each component works just right.[5]

There is still nevertheless much controversy about the feasibility, economy, and resilience of "systems of systems" that would identify and track moving targets, send missiles and manned aircraft of one sort or another against them, and achieve the necessary aiming corrections as targets continued to move. Leaving detailed computations to others, we can examine the matter in strategical terms, discovering once more that Clausewitz has preceded us. There were no combat aircraft or guided missiles in his days, but the fundamental asymmetry between supplies en route behind the front and forces deployed for combat, was already present. So was the attraction of striking behind the lines with deep-raiding cavalry. As usual, Clausewitz depicts the favorable prospect before revealing the difficulties:

> An average convoy of three to four hundred wagons . . . will be two miles long; a major convoy will be considerably longer. How can one hope to defend this length with the handful of men that are normally assigned as escorts? Added to this difficulty is the ponderousness of the whole, which crawls slowly along and is always in danger of ending up in confusion. [Today's convoys are longer: a single mechanized division with four thousand vehicles or more, requires at least forty miles of road track.] Moreover, every part requires the same degree of cover, other-wise the whole train would stop and fall into disarray if any part were attacked. One may well ask how the protection of such a convoy is possi-ble at all . . . Why is not every convoy seized once it has been attacked, and why is not every convoy attacked if it is worth an escort at all . . . ?
>
> The explanation lies in the fact that most convoys are better protected by their general strategic situation [in the rear] than is any other part of the army that the enemy may attack, and hence their limited means of defense are decisively more effective. We may therefore conclude that while it may seem easy tactically, attacking a convoy is . . . not very advantageous.[6]

In other words, once the operational disadvantages of any action per-formed outside one's own area of control, deep inside the enemy's space, is subtracted from the tactical advantage of engaging targets that are con-centrated, visible, and vulnerable as they move on roads and rail lines, the remaining benefit may not suffice to offset the costs and risk of at-tacking at longer range in depth. Clausewitz reminds us of a third and more subtle consideration: the "general strategic situation" of convoys in the rear is operationally advantageous to the defending forces as a whole both because they can more easily observe the unfolding combat and be-cause all their strength is in place. In the days of Clausewitz, the fate of a cavalry raid would not be known until the raiders returned to tell their tale; the rest of the army could not assist the raid in any way for lack of current knowledge of its vicissitudes. And only a small part of the entire army could be sent on raids: a few hundred horsemen would amount to a large raiding force even for an army of tens of thousands.

Today there are technical means of observation that can monitor the action as it unfolds, but it is still the defense that can best assess the ongoing results of aerial attack within its own area of control. Unless and until they are destroyed, observation satellites can relay back imagery, but puffs of smoke and exploding debris would both reveal the effects of air strikes and conceal them. High-altitude radar aircraft can look sideways to a considerable distance, and aerial photography may continue throughout a war, but the totality of the information thus collected still cannot compare with the exact detail of a multiplicity of situation reports, if the defense still has its telecommunications and can receive them. That information advantage, and the possession of all means in place, can enable the defenders to react with broad means against the narrow effort of the deep attack, whether by engaging raiding cavalry with its own, as in the time of Clausewitz, or by using today's air power and electronic warfare.

We cannot predict the outcome of interacting measures and countermeasures that would ensue if deep-attack systems were actually deployed. But sensors, transmission relays, control centers, primary air vehicles, and terminal munitions are all potentially vulnerable to countermeasures. Although the sensors that initially detect the targets for relay back to the control centers can have broad abilities on their varied platforms (satellites as well as manned and unmanned aircraft, with radar, infrared, optical, and other sensors), the guidance of the individual munitions that finally attack each separate target must be narrowly simple if the system as a whole is to be economical.

There is nothing to prevent the use of several different types of terminal guidance for as many different types of munitions, so that road convoys and other targets in the rear could be attacked with mixed batches of guided munitions resilient as a whole against any one countermeasure. But there is no obstacle either to the combined use of different countermeasures by the defense. Not all terminal munitions must be guided, of course; the many small bomblets of cluster weapons are aimed at areas not points. But then it is their lethality itself that is a narrow capability subject to countermeasuring.*

---

* The notion that very small, very economical, hollow-charge bomblets or self-forging fragment devices can be lethal against otherwise well-armored battle tanks because they would strike at their thin topside armor is reminiscent of the belief that torpedoes would be effective because warship armor was thin or absent below the waterline. Just as that weakness was remedied as soon as the attempt was made to exploit it, so also spaced-armor roofs were added to tanks, in a typical broad-capability response to a narrow threat.

The Fragility of Consecutive Systems

The technical contest between terminal munitions and terminal counter-measures is more or less symmetrical, but there is a fundamental asymmetry in the contest between deep-attack systems as a whole and the countermeasure efforts against them. To succeed, the raiding cavalry of the days of Clausewitz had to elude front-watching pickets, maneuver around larger forces in its path, find a convoy isolated on its own, and scatter its escort in order to attack effectively—and all those things had to be achieved in sequence. Likewise, in deep-attack systems the initial sensors and the relay transmissions and the control centers and the missiles or manned aircraft and the terminal munitions must all function correctly one after the other in exact sequence. The defenders can defeat the system's ability to attack any given set of targets by successfully neutralizing just one of the components. True, redundancy can diminish the disadvantage, but only at a price—and even then the risks of friction, requiring no effort by the defender, will be multiplied by the consecutive nature of deep-attack systems.

When we stand back from all technical speculations, what remains before us is the sheer uncertainty of the results that deep-attack systems can offer, as countermeasures invisibly evolve over time. Uncertainty is war's constant companion, but there is a large difference between the uncertainty that attends the use of a sword (which might break), a plain rifle (which can jam), or a tank (which might break down) and the use of a complicated consecutive system of many separate devices, each separately fallible.

The most straightforward response to deep-attack systems is simply to attack them, but as of this writing only the United States could build them and only the Russian Federation could attack them. Antisatellite missiles and long-range fighters can seek out and destroy the unmanned platforms of the initial sensors (concurrently with electronic interference against their relay transmissions); manned strike aircraft, bombardment missiles, and commando raids could be launched against the computerized control centers (concurrently with the attempt to confound their workings by camouflage and simulations); the missile "farms" and airbases of the primary vehicles could likewise be attacked (concurrently with the attempt to jam or sever their communications from the control centers); air defenses of all kinds, in the form of fighters, missiles, and antiaircraft guns, would strive to interfere with the delivery of the terminal munitions (concurrently with the use of deceptive and protective countermeasures against them); and in combining all these forms of attack, the asymmetrical vulnerability of consecutive systems could weigh heavily in the outcome. If fortune or a successful intelligence penetration assisted the neutralizing effort, the destruction of some sensor platforms, some control centers, and some primary vehicles at their source or in transit might suffice to neutralize a complete deep-attack sequence, and then the next one, and so on.

11

Nonstrategies: Naval, Air, Nuclear

Before proceeding to examine the level of grand strategy, we must first pause to dispose of the confused and confusing question of one-force "strategies," whether naval, air, or nuclear. Mere looseness of language and the innocent exuberance of one-force enthusiasts are both present. But if there really were such a thing as naval strategy or air strategy or nuclear strategy in any sense other than a combination of the technical, tactical, and operational levels within the same universal strategy, then each should have its own peculiar logic, or else exist as a separate counterpart to theater strategy, which would then be limited to ground warfare. The first is impossible, the second unnecessary.

To argue the matter in order, I will begin by noting that at the technical, tactical, and operational levels it is self-evident that the same paradoxical logic applies. Accordingly, in exploring those three levels, I freely cited naval and air war examples along with those drawn from ground warfare. At the level of theater strategy, it is true, the focus of the inquiry was on ground warfare, with air power discussed only incidentally,* and with no naval examples cited at all. But there is a reason for that.

---

* That would have been "tactical" air power in the current English-language official terminology, which embraces all forms of air power that affect a given theater, as opposed to "strategic" air power, aimed at homeland targets, such as civil infrastructures and industry as well as the state apparatus, both civil and military. The modes of tactical air power include: "air superiority," performed by fighters for command of the air over a theater of war; "close support," performed by fighter bombers, light bombers, or specialized ground-attack aircraft to directly assist the ground forces; "battlefield interdiction," performed by fighter bombers and light bombers, to attack ground forces in the immediate rear of the battle zones; and "interdiction," performed by fighter bombers and light bombers to attack infrastructures and supplies and forces in transit in the depth of the theater of war.

Space and Mobility

The omission of naval examples and the slighting of air warfare in the discussion of theater strategy were not accidental. To be sure, the same *spatial* expression of the paradoxical logic is present in naval and air warfare as well. Naval and air forces also have both forward and rearward dispositions, forward defenses, defenses-in-depth, and so on—all of which could also apply to extra-atmospheric or space warfare for that matter. Air and naval forces interact spatially within the level of theater strategy exactly as ground forces do. But because of their superior mobility, the spatial phenomena are much less important. Dispositions can be changed so swiftly that they do not precondition outcomes; in fact, they are often so transitory that they are trivial.

Thus the concept of naval superiority popularized by the eminent naval historian Alfred Thayer Mahan,[1] which guided the conduct of both the British and the German navies in the First World War, and of the Japanese navy in the Second World War, amounted to an outright nullification of all spatial considerations. The superior fleet would control the oceans of the entire world while remaining concentrated at a location of its own choosing, mostly quite inactive. With the torpedo boat already virtually neutralized by 1914, and the submarine (wrongly) disregarded, the ultimate ability to defeat the enemy's battleship squadron, *if* there were a battle in some location at some time, would assure all the benefits of naval supremacy everywhere and continuously. The stronger navy would gain free use of oceanic sea lanes for commerce and military transport while their use was denied to the enemy—and without need to blockade his ports.

It was the hierarchy of naval strength that was to ensure this outcome: being inferior, the enemy battleship squadron could not risk battle; nor could his battle cruisers venture out. Hence enemy cruisers could not steam about to attack shipping on the high seas, nor provide support for destroyer flotillas to do so, because if intercepted they would be defeated with ease by battle cruisers just as fast, of greater endurance, and with bigger guns and stronger armor. The cruisers of the stronger fleet could therefore operate unchallenged, and the enemy could neither secure nor deny sea lanes with his destroyers because they could not withstand battle with the superior fleet's cruisers.

Thus the remote and inactive battleship squadron concentrated in one location could indirectly exert its domination over the oceans regardless of distance—as far and as wide as the unchallenged cruisers could reach. There was nothing to prevent an enemy destroyer from dashing out of secure harbors to intercept a stray merchant ship passing nearby, but that was all: except for sheltered coastal passages and closed seas such as the Baltic, the side inferior in battleships would find itself excluded from navigation on the high seas, as indeed was the case for Germany during the First World War.

Once the submarine was introduced, however, the superior squadron of battleships could no longer assure the safety of *its own* commercial shipping. In the presence of strong enemy submarine forces, to focus exclusively on the hypothetical clash of the battleships would condemn the fleet to passivity because the capital ships would need their escort of cruisers (against destroyers) and destroyers (against torpedo boats), leaving nothing to protect shipping from submarine attacks.[2]

At worst, the result could be a symmetrical denial of navigation, a poor outcome for the side more dependent on oceanic commerce. This indeed almost happened at the peak of the German U-boat campaigns of both world wars, in 1917 and 1942 respectively, when Allied battle fleets prevented German maritime commerce, while German submarines greatly impeded Allied shipping—with both forces almost unlimited by spatial considerations.

It is not the medium of warfare that makes the difference, then, but rather the degree of mobility of the respective forces: the greater the mobility, the less consequential the locations of the forces at any one time. If ground forces could also move freely and quickly across the full expanse of theaters of war and between them, the level of theater strategy would lose its importance for them as well. The railways had that effect to some degree, but motorization was more consequential. With trucks to carry them, troops and weapons could move from one sector to another in "tactical" time, that is, in the course of a single battle, thereby diminishing the importance of prebattle deployments. Air transport intensified the effect for intratheater movements by the time of the Second World War; since then, its range has been extended to intertheater movements as well, though only for the relatively small and light forces that can be airlifted over long distances.

Important phenomena persist within the level of theater strategy only because of the mobility limits of ground forces; the vulnerability, limited capacity, and airfield dependence of air transport, and the geographic constraints, slow speed, and port dependence of sea transport. A parallel may be drawn with the insignificance of the operational level of strategy if attrition is the dominant mode of combat. There is no need to define separate naval and air counterparts to theater strategy merely because the phenomena of ground warfare are the most important within that level. Nor can there be some other level of strategy that would apply only to a single form of military strength and that would stand above the operational level yet below the level of grand strategy.

The Contents of Nonstrategy

If there are no distinct phenomena, what then is the content of the many writings that carry "naval strategy," "air strategy," "nuclear strategy," or, most recently, "space strategy" in their titles? With the interesting exception of Mahan's claim for sea power, we find that it is mainly technical, tactical, or operational issues that are examined in that literature, or else that it advocates some particular policy, usually at the level of grand strategy.[3]

Questions of force composition, for example, loom large in what is described as naval strategy. But the old debate between the advocates of battleships and those of aircraft carriers, or the newer argument among the advocates of submarines, missile magazine ("arsenal") ships, and classic warships, clearly belong to the operational level of analysis, just as in actual warfare such forces would interact competitively at the operational level. As for even narrower debates over such things as the merits of larger and smaller aircraft carriers, they belong to the technical level of analysis, just as in reality the matter depends on differences in technical performance and cost. To be sure, technical preferences often reflect broader considerations as well—but then they will be considerations of grand strategy, such as how large carriers are better for offensive warfare and small ones for defensive escort.

When it comes to air power, choices of force composition are also conditioned at the technical, tactical, or operational levels, rather that at the level of theater strategy. That was true of the 1945–1955 debate (in both the United States and Britain) between the advocates of "balanced" bomber forces (heavy, medium, and light) and those who argued that all resources should be devoted to heavy bombers alone. And it was true of the 1955–1965 debate between the advocates of guided missiles and those who saw continued value in manned bombers. It also applies to the current debate between the advocates of unmanned aircraft (remotely piloted vehicles, cruise missiles) and those who insist that manned aircraft should continue to claim all available resources. Spatial considerations have played no role in these debates, so dominant are cost-effectiveness calculations and the silent force of institutional preferences: air forces commanded by pilots are not enthusiastic about unmanned aircraft.

Questions of targeting, which have traditionally been important in what is described as "air strategy,"[4] do not belong to theater strategy either but rather to the level of grand strategy. Of course any military or civilian targets might be bombed for any reason. But the *consequences* of bombing will be manifest at the level of grand strategy. Hence the choice between target categories is a fit subject for national policy, as indeed the victims' response will be a national response, again at the level of grand strategy.

The same considerations apply to the purposes for which naval power is employed. Only the results of amphibious landings will be conditioned at the level of theater strategy. But when it comes to blockades or long-range sea denial, or the projection of naval air power on land, grand strategy will be the more relevant level of action and response. True, the effectiveness of sea denial or projection may depend on geographic factors and thus the level of theater strategy, but the operational and tactical interactions of the forces on each side will tend to be more important. Certainly if navigation is denied, the consequences will be determined by the self-sufficiency of the affected state; once again, action and response will be manifest at the level of grand strategy.

Claims of Autonomy: Sea Power

There can be only one valid justification for defining a strategy confined to just one form of military power: that it is decisive in itself. That was precisely Mahan's claim: in his interpretation of history, sea power was the determining factor in the rise and fall of nations.[5] Actually Mahan employed the term "sea power" in two different senses, to mean either dominant armed strength at sea ("which drives the enemy's flag from it, or allows it to appear only as a fugitive") or, more widely, to describe the full range of benefits that maritime efforts could secure: commerce, shipping, colonies, and access to markets.[6] Mahan's sea power I was the short-term determinant that decided the outcome of wars, by blockade and sea raids. His sea power II was the long-term determinant of the prosperity of nations. That Mahan overgeneralized from his interpretation of British history is obvious: he equated sea power in both meanings with power as such, ignoring the continental states that did not rely on long-distance navigation to any great extent, including Germany in both World Wars and the Soviet Union in its day.

Somewhat less obvious perhaps, and more interesting from the viewpoint of our strategical inquiry, was Mahan's fallacy of composition in explaining British success against its continental enemies as the result of British strength at sea.

That for the British sea power I was an essential instrument, and sea power II the source of much wealth, is beyond question. But the real cause of Britain's naval supremacy was the success of its foreign policy in preserving a balance of power in Europe.[7] By intervening to oppose any one Great Power or coalition that seemed on the verge of dominating continental Europe, the British ensured continued strife. That forced the continental powers to keep large armies, which in turn prevented them from keeping large navies as well. Sea power I and II were both required to keep the continental powers well balanced, and at each other's throats. But that was not Mahan's sequence or intent.[8] We can therefore recognize that superior sea power was the *result* of a successful strategy, rather than its cause. It was a very active diplomacy, and the ability to subsidize willing but poor allies, that received priority in British policy, not the upkeep of the Royal Navy. Once the conditions that made it relatively easy to have naval superiority were established by successfully upholding the balance of power, the navy was given the modest means it required to have sea power I, which in turn yielded sea power II.

Had the British neglected diplomacy and subsidies in a straightforward attempt to achieve superiority at sea by outbuilding all seafaring continental rivals, the immediate result would have been to consume the capital needed for sea power II, and the longer-term result would have been to undermine the balance of power. That in turn would have reduced the diversion of continental efforts to land warfare—and British resources would have been insufficient to compete with all the seafaring talent of a united Western Europe.

That British naval supremacy coexisted with the notoriously ungenerous funding of the Royal Navy reflected the logic of strategy. By contrast, it would have contradicted the paradoxical logic if Britain could have achieved supremacy just by adding more and more frigates to the Royal Navy. European adversaries left free to react by an exclusive British focus on naval strength would have built their own frigates, instead of being forced to devote their resources to their armies. Contemporaries who deplored the neglect of the Royal Navy, and admirals who bitterly complained that British gold was being given away to foreigners while their own ships were in need, had common sense on their side but not strategy.

Ironically, by the time Mahan published his book, the British government had abandoned its historic policy. Instead of arming Germany's continental adversaries, especially the undersupplied Russians, to keep its power well entangled on land, substantial funds were finally granted to the Royal Navy to preserve sea power I in a direct shipbuilding competition with imperial Germany. Common sense and popular opinion were both satisfied. It was not as a guide to policy but rather as the propagandist of a policy already formed that Mahan was so greatly acclaimed in Britain: the National Defence Act, which mandated "parity" with the two strongest continental navies combined, was passed in 1889—before Mahan's first "influence" book was published.

In the end, sea power II, the capital it had accumulated, and much blood were all sacrificed in fighting the First World War. That was Britain's first truly costly continental engagement, which a less intense concentration on sea power I might have alleviated if not prevented. Whether it was the rigidity of public opinion that turned British leaders from emulating their predecessors (who would have financed railways and arsenals for tsarist Russia in lieu of building more battleships) or simply their own lack of strategic clarity, there is little doubt that Britain's agony of decline was much accelerated by a policy that was reflected in the Mahanist delusion.

Strategic Bombardment

An entirely new claim of strategic autonomy emerged just after the First World War. By then, the limitations of naval strength in modern war had been exposed, with blockade agonizingly slow, sea raids hardly possible (land forces could reach the scene too quickly), and the one large amphibious offensive at Gallipoli a costly fiasco. Because the tactical advantage of sheer height was so universally understood, the heavier-than-air aircraft had been adopted for military use within a few years of its first appearance. By 1914 aircraft for general observation and for artillery-fire correction were present in all the major armies, and by 1918 air forces had emerged on a large scale: the Royal Air Force had 22,000 aircraft in its inventory and 293,532 men in uniform by November 11, 1918, Armi-

stice Day. Navies too had acquired their aircraft, mostly floaters precari-
ously launched from warship decks and recovered from the water; but
the first true aircraft carrier was already completed before the end of
the war.

Aircraft were therefore well established but mostly as ancillaries to armies and navies. Among the pioneer flying officers and publicists of military aviation who demanded independence for the new arm, some did so
on the grounds of efficiency, stressing the savings that could be obtained if
the acquisition of aircraft and the training of pilots were centralized, instead of being fragmented between armies and navies. Others, however,
went much further, proclaiming the strategic autonomy of the new arm.

Three men who promoted air power as the wave of the future achieved
wide resonance for their views, advancing similar arguments quite independently: Giulio Douhet, a leader of the Italian air force even before
1914, published his *Il dominio dell'aria* (The command of the air) in 1921;
the American William (Billy) Mitchell, also a flying officer, published his
Winged Defense in 1925, long before Douhet's book was translated into
English in 1942, when Mitchell had just bombed Tokyo; and Hugh Mon-
tague Trenchard, founder of the Royal Air Force, mostly disseminated his
views in Royal Air Force internal papers.

The common argument of Douhet, Mitchell, and Trenchard was that
aircraft offered the possibility of penetrating directly into the heart of enemy territory, overflying defended fronts and all geographic barriers; that
large fleets of bombers could therefore circumvent the slow processes of
land and naval warfare by destroying the industry upon which all modern
forms of military power depend; and that victory could thus be achieved
quickly by superior air power alone,[9] without the enormous casualties of
land warfare and the long years of naval blockade. Douhet, Trenchard,
and their followers differed from Mitchell in claiming that bombers could
virtually disregard air defenses, thereby equating air power with *offensive*
strength alone.[10] But all three agreed that all other forms of military
strength had been made obsolescent by air power.

As it turned out, strategic air power was afflicted in the Second World
War both by its own shortcomings and by the reaction it evoked—a reaction all the more powerful because the large claims made for bombardment had been generally accepted before the war, while its shortcomings
of precision and volume had been overlooked. One reaction to the threat
of massed air raids on capital cities (with gas-filled bombs, it was thought)
was the intense search for a means of long-range detection that would
give some hope of intercepting enemy bombers. By 1939, Britain, Ger-

many, and the United States had all developed long-range radar, over-turning the Douhet-Trenchard assumption that the bomber would always get through.[11]

Air Defense

Fighter defenses were almost useless before radar, yet they had not been abandoned on the fragile hope that a multitude of telephoned reports from air spotters and sound-location devices would permit interception. Both high-speed fighters and suitable organizational schemes for their direction by ground controllers were therefore already in place when radar arrived on the scene. In the meantime, because they were meant to be "strategic" and therefore required large weapon loads to destroy industry and cities, bombers had evolved into much larger and rather slower aircraft than the fighters of their day, against which they could hardly maneuver.*

The bomber advocates recognized this tactical weakness and offered the remedy of massed formations well-armed with machine guns. Before radar, moreover, they could expect to outconcentrate the stray fighters they might encounter on their way. In accordance with classical military principles, the advantage of the initiative would yield numerical superiority over enemy fighters within the time and space of the encounter. The concerted fire of the tail gunners, dorsal gunners, belly gunners, and front-firing guns of bomber formation would negate the fighter's advantage in maneuverability, by denying every vector of attack no matter how quickly the fighter could switch from one to another. In other words, the operational-level advantage of the massed bomber formation was to overcome the expected tactical-level inferiority of the single bomber.

This is where radar-assisted ground control intervened. It allowed the purposeful interception of bomber formations by entire groups of fighters instead of having to rely on standing patrols and their chance encounters.† Air space could therefore be defended systematically, as land space had long been defended, with the radar net forming a front line and

---

* The exception was the Luftwaffe bombers, which had to be maneuverable because they were designed for dive-bombing as well. Their greater structural strength and acceleration diminished range and payload—and without reducing their vulnerability significantly.

† But at night, until radar-equipped fighters became available around 1943, each fighter had to be individually directed until it entered into visual contact with its target, precluding mass interception—though even radarless fighters could operate if illumination was provided by moonlight, searchlights, or fires on the ground below.

fighter squadrons acting as mobile forces that could converge to match the degree of offensive concentration. The bombers' advantage in the initiative was reduced to whatever delay radar limitations, deliberate countermeasures, and organizational frictions might impose on interception. The defense for its part would have the classic advantage of fighting within its own air space, notably the ability to prepare the "terrain" with antiaircraft guns, searchlights, and balloon barrages. The defense, moreover, could hope to make repeated intercepts with the same aircraft, each time refueled and rearmed for action while the bomber formation was coming and going back over a period of hours. Thus air defenses were also superior at the level of theater strategy, adding to the tactical advantage of fighters, no longer offset by the operational-level advantage of bomber formations that could now be matched by fighter formations.

That sequence ensured the defeat by attrition of the Luftwaffe's 1940 bombing campaign against Britain. It could not break the will to fight of the British, as no bombing campaign would ever break the will of any other nation thereafter, while the Luftwaffe bomber force lacked the explosive and fire-raising payloads to destroy much British industrial capacity quickly, as no bombing campaign was ever to do thereafter against any other major industrial nation.

There was irony in the fact that the Luftwaffe was the first air force to attempt "strategic" bombardment in the Second World War, and the first to fail at it, because its leaders had not believed in its value and had not made the bombing of cities and industry their top priority.[12] Instead of heavy bombers, the Germans were building medium and light bombers that emphasized precision for battlefield use, achieved by dive-bombing, which in turn precluded large bomb loads. Given the aircraft it had, the Luftwaffe's bombing of British cities, as of Warsaw and Rotterdam before them, had been an improvisation. As an incidental consequence, Germany's losses greatly understated the vulnerability of bombers as such, because its own bombers were especially maneuverable and also rather fast.

Because the Luftwaffe had no four-engine heavy bombers, of the kind that were to be produced in great numbers by both Britain and the United States, its failure against Britain was discounted by the bomber advocates, who continued to proclaim the strategic autonomy of their preferred weapon. It was only after British and American heavy bombers had attacked Germany on a large scale that the Douhet-Mitchell-Trenchard theory was finally abandoned, first by the British and then by the Americans. To be sure, bombing was not repudiated as an effective means of war, but evidently it could not be a self-sufficient and swift instrument of victory.

The long and bloody process of attrition by ground fighting and naval blockade that the bombers were supposed to circumvent was instead translated into the air war—in which the chances of survival of bomber crews were actually smaller than those of the infantry in the trench warfare of the First World War.

In the end, it was only the technical superiority of British electronic warfare and the superior performance of American escort fighters (especially the P-51 Mustang, which achieved a seemingly impossible combination of long range and maneuverability) that enabled the bombers sent against Germany to destroy as much as they did. But against the sheer scale and flexibility of German industry and infrastructures, even the vast scale of British and American bombing, which dwarfed all Luftwaffe raids against Britain, could have only a slow cumulative effect, no more rapid than that of blockade. Bombing could not even achieve swift results against Japan's much smaller and less flexible industrial production, which suffered more from the lack of raw materials (caused by shipping losses) than it did from the bombing.[13] Quite simply, the advocates of "strategic" bombardment had grossly overestimated its physical effects and greatly underestimated the political and industrial resilience of its victims.

The Advent of Nuclear Weapons

When the fission ("atomic") bomb literally exploded on the scene in 1945, it seemed that the claim of strategic autonomy for air bombardment, just disproved by the experience of war, had most unexpectedly been rehabilitated. All the shortcomings of the bomber (technical, tactical, and theater-strategic) and all the resilience of its victims would be nullified by the new weapon.

The bomber, it had been learned, would not always take off as planned because of technical failures; it would not always survive against air defenses; it would not always navigate correctly to reach its target; the bombs would not all be aimed accurately, and not all would explode. It was the multiplication of these "degradation factors" that had made destruction by air bombardment so much more difficult to achieve than had been expected, even while the amount of destruction needed was much greater than had been foreseen.

But with fission bombs, the destruction of cities and industry became easy work. Douhet and his colleagues had thus been rescued from their greatest errors,[14] and it seemed that nothing could prevent the fulfillment of their prediction: once fission bombs were produced in reasonable numbers, the air arm—or whichever arm transported them—would become utterly dominant, making all other military forces unnecessary. Strategy, it seemed, would itself be unnecessary, except for nuclear strategy, that is.

It was of course the *nonuse* of the new weapon in a diplomacy of deterrence that was most relevant to the planners of a satisfied status quo power such as the United States, for which it was enough to avert aggression in order to win. Upon this conjunction of the large destructive potential of the fission bomb and the particular American view of the world shaped by political circumstances and cultural preferences, the entire concept of deterrence was quickly built. Initially, it was confidently expected that the "absolute weapon" would deter all forms of aggression, all wars.[15] If the Soviet Union had been the first to acquire the bomb, it too would no doubt have focused on ways of exploiting its nonuse, but then the concept would have stressed "compellence" to change the status quo in its favor, rather than to protect it by deterrence.[16]

Naturally, the paralyzing dissuasion that could satisfy a satisfied power such as the United States was not equally satisfactory to the Soviet leaders, who still wanted to change the state of the world. Their reaction guaranteed that even nuclear weapons would share the paradoxical fate of all technical innovations in the realm of strategy: the greater the increment of strength they offer when originally introduced, the greater the disturbance of the prior equilibrium and therefore the greater the reactions evoked, which reduce the net effect of the new weapon over time. When originally introduced in the form of fission bombs that only one country could produce—and only in small numbers—nuclear weapons promised to transform strategy. They were eminently usable: the city centers of Hiroshima and Nagasaki had been devastated with no perceptible ill effects on the rest of the planet. It followed that five or ten Soviet cities could also be devastated. And the United States of course was not exposed to comparable retaliation because it had the only nuclear weapons in existence. Therefore the threat of nuclear attack, even if unspoken, even if unformed in the minds of American leaders, could reasonably be expected to dissuade any outright aggression.

Nuclear Autonomy Diminished I: Subversion

But inaction is a success only for satisfied powers. While in the Soviet Union every effort was being made to react competitively, by developing not only fission but also fusion weapons, an outmaneuvering reaction also emerged. As it happened, the first Soviet priority at the time was to establish *political* control over the eastern half of Europe, by establishing local communist governments subservient to Moscow. Local communist parties, however, were defeated in the first postwar elections, while the overt use of force would have provoked the United States excessively. The wall of dissuasion was instead outmaneuvered by subversion.*

In the intimidating presence of Soviet occupation forces, between 1945 and 1948 the leaders of the majority political parties of Hungary, Romania, and finally Czechoslovakia were intimidated into forming coalitions with local communist parties. Police forces were invariably placed under the communist ministers in these broad coalitions. Soon, noncommunist government ministers, still in the majority but under personal duress, voted to outlaw the remaining political parties on the right outside the coalition, which were accused of "fascism." Then a new coalition was formed, excluding the most conservative party, which was outlawed in turn or dissolved by its own leaders in fear for their lives. The process was repeated, narrowing the coalition slice by slice, until only the communists and their controlled subparties remained in office. By the end of 1948, the process was completed: the wall of nuclear dissuasion was intact, but Soviet power had tunneled underneath it, to assert full control over Eastern Europe with no overt use of force.

At first, therefore, the strategic autonomy of nuclear weapons was diminished only in nonmilitary ways that were almost invisible. As the United States and Britain reacted first in Europe and then beyond it with their own countersubversion (financing anticommunist parties, mass media, and trade unions), more and more tunnels were bored under the wall of nuclear dissuasion. The pattern persisted for decades, until the end of the Cold War, assuming varied forms as client military forces and secret services, the supply of insurgencies, and the support of transnational terrorists were added to the repertoire.

The first effect of nuclear deterrence was thus to divert warlike energies into indirect or less visible forms of conflict, always excluding direct American-Soviet combat but not armed violence. While indirect and deniable forms of conflict became part of the everyday reality of international politics, nuclear weapons evoked a much more prosaic defensive reaction.

---

* The covert manipulation of politics was achieved by the physical intimidation of leaders, bribery, infiltration, secret subsidies, false-front propaganda, and deniable paramilitary action, to induce political groups in and out of office to act in a manner contrary to their declared purposes.

The Soviet response to the threat of fission bombs carried by American long-range bombers was to give the highest priority to antiaircraft defenses. Huge numbers of antiaircraft guns left over from the war but still perfectly adequate, radars copied from models originally supplied by the United States under Lend-Lease, and the first jet fighters and missiles were all harnessed to new air defenses to resist American bombers.

Usually it is the defensive reaction that does the most to diminish the net effect of new weapons, but that was not so with nuclear weapons. Even air defenses far more capable than those of the Soviet Union in the first postwar years could not be capable enough, because any one surviving bomber could destroy so much. With the inevitable bomber-protecting response in action as well, the net effect of the new weapon was scarcely diminished by air defenses.

Nuclear Autonomy Diminished II: Inhibition and Retaliation

Even before the United States faced any danger of retaliation in kind (1945–1949), self-imposed inhibitions set limits to the use of the fission bomb. It was not a world destroyer, as the fusion bomb could be, but several fission bombs together could devastate a large city, and the sheer dimensions of one bomb's destructive strength exceeded the culminating point of military utility in many cases, quite independently of whatever retaliation might be evoked. Such great destruction inflicted even on declared enemies would be politically acceptable at home and abroad only if interests broadly recognized as highly important were at stake. Thus even while the American nuclear monopoly lasted, the excessive destructive power of the fission bomb left room for an entire category of possible wars that might have to be fought by "conventional" armed forces. They would be small wars of course, in remote locations no doubt, against secondary enemies, on behalf of marginal allies, wars still worth fighting perhaps—but not with atomic bombs. Thus the strategic autonomy that some had eagerly attributed to the fission bomb, which was already of no avail against indirect and deniable forms of attack, was further diminished by aggressions insufficiently provocative.

A much greater reduction in the strategic autonomy of the fission bomb was imminent. The symmetrical reaction evoked by the American nuclear monopoly even before 1945 (when Soviet spies penetrated the Manhattan Project) yielded its first fruits by 1949, when the Soviet Union tested its first fission device. Although there was no parity between the two bomber forces—one still small, the other no more than embryonic—the scope of nuclear deterrence was immediately affected: the present value of future money is discounted, but future military strength is anticipated.[17]

Once retaliation in kind became possible, war planners had to be much more circumspect in their envisaged use of fission bombs, and political leaders much more careful in issuing threats—even deterrent threats.

What suasion with fission bombs could achieve in imposing action (compellence) or inaction (deterrence) had always been limited by the other side's assessment of the likelihood of actual use, which was inevitably diminished when a nuclear response became possible. Up to a point, opinions about the character of the leadership of the would-be persuading power had to figure in the assessment: those deemed especially prudent would be less intimidating than those deemed reckless. Speculation on the political uses of madness notwithstanding, what suasion could achieve would not be greatly influenced by variations in the prudence attributed to generally prudent American and Soviet leaders. Instead, the scope and limits of suasion with fission bombs would largely be determined by perceptions of the importance of the interests at stake for the other party. Exactly the same threat might be fully plausible in seeking to deter a direct Soviet attack on American territory but much less convincing when issued to shield a marginal ally from a peripheral Soviet intrusion.

The "balance of perceived interests" thus joined the balance of technical capabilities in defining what nuclear threats could achieve, breaking any simple relationship between the nuclear strength in hand and its value for suasion. Soviet assessments of American interests in American eyes, and American assessments of Soviet interests as the Kremlin saw them, might be manipulated on either side by skillful posturing,[18] but only within limits: not every locality in danger could be made into a Berlin to be defended at all costs; not every international connection of the Soviet Union could be elevated to the status of a sacrosanct alliance.

As a result, another category of possible wars fought by conventional forces came into existence, reducing further the strategic autonomy once attributed to the nuclear weapon. True, the possibility that the loser would resort to the use of fission bombs virtually prohibited direct warfare, even on the smallest scale, between American and Soviet forces for any interests regarded as secondary by both sides. Hence expeditionary adventures, raids, and counterraids by American and Soviet forces against each other played no role in the Cold War. Prior possession affirmed by a physical military presence became more important than ever before, because where one was, the other would not go.

What was true for marginal interests, however, would not be true of interests truly important to both sides, over which war might erupt in spite of the risk of an eventual resort to fission bombs by the loser. Those interests had to be protected by conventional armed forces in place. The post-1949 stationing of American troops and air power in Europe and the conduct of war in Korea from June 25, 1950, marked the retreat of suasion with fission bombs alone.

The Excessive Weapon

Nuclear capabilities were transformed in two different ways during the early 1950s. Alongside the development of fusion devices yielding fifty or even five hundred times as much energy as the first fission bombs, there was also the arrival of mass production for smaller "tactical" bombs, nuclear artillery shells, depth charges, sea and land mines, and rocket and missile warheads. The effects on the strategic autonomy of the nuclear weapon were contradictory. On the one hand, the destructive potential of large fusion bombs, with retaliation in kind duly included, exceed by far any culminating point of utility for the purposes of suasion. Indeed, the curve declined so steeply that less could be expected from those weapons than from the earlier fission bombs, which had only a fraction of their destructive energy. The interests that can warrant the risk of starting a war that could destroy civilization are naturally fewer than those that could earlier justify the risk of a war with fission weapons. On the other hand, the incorporation of nuclear weapons into every part of the armed forces greatly diminished the significance of nonnuclear imbalances. With nuclear weapons present in the inventory of air wings and army corps, warships and submarines, a direct mechanism was in place to convert imminent nonnuclear defeat into nuclear combat, nullifying the victor's achievement until then.

Both of these effects were evident in the experience of the nuclear powers from the start of nuclear abundance in the mid-1950s till the end of the Cold War. The Soviet Union never succeeded in excluding nuclear weapons from the balance of nonnuclear forces on land, in which its numerical advantages therefore remained without effect. The American policy of "massive retaliation" (1954–1961), which was meant to nullify the entire balance of nonnuclear strength by relying "primarily upon a great capacity to retaliate, instantly, by means and at places of our own choosing," also failed.[19] Massive retaliation would certainly have affirmed the strategic autonomy of nuclear weapons, had it been successful. But it will never be known if the Soviet leaders could have been dissuaded by nuclear threats alone, because the policy was declared but never implemented: the United States did not reduce its nonnuclear forces to the very low levels needed as regional trip wires for its "great capacity to retaliate." Instead, over the decades, through cycles of rearmament, war, disarmament, inflation, and more rearmament, the American nonnuclear military effort became the best evidence of the erosion of nuclear suasion.

As the decline in military utility caused by their own excessive destructive power shows so clearly, nuclear weapons are fully subject to the paradoxical logic of strategy. A struggle fought with many large fusion warheads would certainly have been different enough from all previous wars to warrant description in its own terms. War economics or war poetry, war propaganda or war legislation, and all the other familiar ancillaries of war, could have no place in the resulting annihilation. But there is no distinct logic that would apply. The same strategic logic that we have examined through its technical, tactical, operational, and theater levels, also explains the self-negation of nuclear war, as well shall see when we reach the level of grand strategy.

12

The Renaissance of Strategic Air Power

In January 1945, after five years of increasingly heavy Anglo-American air bombardment, Berlin was devastated, with many office buildings and apartment houses in the central districts reduced to burnt-out shells, and many factories and warehouses left roofless and ruined in the outlying areas. Yet Nazi Germany's minister of propaganda, Josef Goebbels, could still broadcast nationwide, as well as internationally by shortwave radio heard around the world. Hitler in his bunker and the Wehrmacht High Command in nearby Zossen could still send out orders and receive reports from all fronts by teleprinter and telephone land-lines and by radio, and the German army could still move and supply its forces by rail right through the often bombed but soon repaired Berlin marshaling yards. As for the city's population, many were living in rudely patched-up housing, but electrical power, the telephone service, public transport, the postal service, piped water, sewage disposal, and the supply of all basic necessities were still functioning with only brief interruptions, as did many cinemas: on January 30, 1945, the great color spectacular *Kolberg* had its well-attended gala premiere.

Less than forty-eight hours after the air offensive against Iraq started on January 17, 1991, Baghdad was still mostly intact as it was to remain throughout the Gulf war, but Saddam Hussein and his spokesmen could no longer broadcast on television or nationwide radio, all major military headquarters in the city with their land-line and radio communications were wrecked, and in Baghdad the population at large was left without electricity, telephone service, public transport, piped water, or sewer disposal. With the war hardly begun, Iraq's leader and his military commanders were already blind, deaf, and mute in their paralyzed capital city, unable to find out what was happening outside Baghdad soon enough to react usefully, and unable to send out orders in any case, except by dis-

185

patch riders and a surviving fiber-optic network that reached only a few locations.

The immediate effect of this aerial decapitation was to incapacitate Iraq's abundantly equipped air defenses. Each air force base with its fighters, each missile or gun antiaircraft battery was left to its own devices, deprived of the early warning necessary to alert them and of centralized direction. To keep track of intruding aircraft in order to attack them again and again, to exploit the menace of high-altitude missiles to drive intruders down within range of mobile missiles and guns, to meet concentrated air attacks with a concentrated defensive effort, air defenses must be "integrated," but Iraq's no longer were because all its national and regional control centers were already wrecked. The major early-warning radar stations had been destroyed from the start of the air campaign, while the runways of many air bases had been damaged. Yet there were still some Iraqi search radars, countless observation posts remained intact, and runways were soon repaired in most cases—but all to no avail, because there was no centralized command to combine the information, order fighters into action when they could take off, and coordinate the vast number of intact antiaircraft guns and missiles.

As for the vast Iraqi army, the effect of the air offensive was cumulative rather than immediate. But within two weeks it too was paralyzed, unable to supply food, water, fuel, and ammunition to the large forces in and around Kuwait because of the destruction of rail and road bridges, ammunition dumps, oil refineries, petroleum product tank farms, and most larger depots for supplies of all kinds, including bombs, shells, and warheads for rockets and missiles. Nor could the army move its forces back into Iraq or forward into Saudi Arabia, because they would have been detected and heavily attacked. Yet even if they remained in their camouflaged and dug-in positions, tanks, troop carriers, and artillery pieces could be destroyed by the direct hits of guided weapons,[1] along with aircraft in or out of concrete shelters, missile batteries, command posts, naval craft, and much else. The pride of the regime—its vast complex of military industries—was also heavily damaged in the course of the air campaign. Postwar UN inspectors found much that survived, but many assembly lines, factories, and repair workshops; missile and nuclear development centers; chemical and biological-warfare laboratories; and production plants and storage bunkers had been bombed quite effectively.

The Anglo-American air offensive against Germany ravaged all major cities and many towns without *directly* incapacitating German military strength. By contrast, the 1991 air offensive against Iraq left its cities and towns almost intact but thoroughly defeated Iraq's armed forces, so that the final ground offensive did not have to be fought in earnest—it was mostly unopposed. Iraqi troops already immobilized, often hungry and thirsty, diminished by desertions,[2] and with many of their heavy weapons already destroyed,[3] hardly resisted the one-hundred-hour advance of the American and allied ground forces around and through Kuwait. Heavily armored U.S. Army M.1 battle tanks advanced unscathed, but so did lightly protected troop carriers, the jeeps of the French Foreign Legion, even the rented cars of adventurous journalists. The very nature of the ground offensive was a tribute to air power: U.S. and coalition forces advanced in columns much too widely separated to help one another, because it was confidently assumed that air attacks would immediately break up any Iraqi attempt to converge against any one of them.

Air power had finally won a war—or as much of it as the United States wanted to win—for it was President George Bush who unilaterally proclaimed a cease-fire on February 27, 1991, while Saddam Hussein remained in power with large forces still at his disposal. Only the conquest of the whole of Iraq by ground forces could have guaranteed the elimination of Saddam Hussein's regime. But if the planners of the air campaign had been charged with the task, they might have succeeded by simple perseverance given enough time. If all road movements in and out of Baghdad and the repair of utilities and telecommunications had been prevented by continuing air attacks, Iraq's highly centralized dictatorship would have been totally isolated from the rest of the country. As a fugitive in his own besieged capital, forced to remain in hiding for fear of an air strike, Saddam Hussein would eventually have lost control of the nationwide security and propaganda machine that kept him in power. Long before that, any part of the country at all removed from the capital would have been free of his oppression, and full-blown independent powers would have emerged in both the Shi'ite south and the Kurdish north. That of course was the very prospect that induced President Bush to stop the war when he did. Had Iraq disintegrated, a permanent U.S. military presence in Mesopotamia would have been needed to contain Iran.

Assessing What Happened

To understand what actually happened in a war—even if short, mostly one-sided, and confined to a single theater—is notoriously very hard, for the actual course of events must be discerned through the dazzling refractions of war's distinct levels: political, strategic, operational, tactical, and technical—each diverse, some contradictory. To cite an obvious example, the participation of the Arab forces in the coalition was politically valuable, operationally insignificant, and potentially useful at the level of theater strategy—for the Egyptians, Syrians, and Saudis were at least present in the middle sectors between the U.S. Marines on the coast and the major U.S. Army and British forces much deeper inland. Had there been real fighting instead of a cavalcade, that might have made a difference.

The multiplicity of different levels offers ample scope for confusion and controversy, as the endless rewriting of military history shows. It also offers easy opportunities for misrepresentation, whether to serve personal prejudices or the claims of rival military bureaucracies. By selecting the one level that best fits the case—tactical or political, operational or strategic—any number of propositions can be argued persuasively, and almost any "lesson" can be drawn, often to justify military choices made long before or to argue the merits of one service or branch or weapon. When venturing into this methodological swamp, the only remedy is to firmly refrain from any attempt to learn supposed lessons from any war until it has been comprehended tolerably well on all its diverse levels and dimensions—a task normally accomplished after the passage of two generations or so, with protagonists safely dead, the last secrets revealed, and all passions spent.

Only one finding about the 1991 Gulf war can already be safely presented: the fighting unfolded without the ebb and flow of alternate fortunes that mark any serious war because of the immediate success of the historically unprecedented aerial "decapitation" offensive. For the rest, what follows is no more than an initial attempt to understand what happened without attempting to extract findings of general validity. Offensive air power is especially *situational*, highly dependent on the intensity of conflict. In the extreme case of a pure guerilla war—without any identifiable structural targets of value, with the guerillas themselves much too elusive to be bombed usefully, and with their propagandists, suppliers, and chiefs indistinguishable from the population at large—air bombardment is bound to be futile, regardless of its lethality or precision. By contrast, as the intensity of the conflict increases, so does the potential value of offensive air power, eventually to reach the opposite extreme of a war that can be won by aerial weapons alone. Both the 1991 Gulf war and the 1999 Kosovo war were in that category insofar as it is accepted that their only goal was to secure the withdrawal of the offending party from Kuwait and Kosovo respectively.

With due caution, two further findings about these wars can be presented: first, their outcomes depended on air power to an extent entirely unprecedented in the annals of warfare; and, second, their air offensives differed in kind rather than degree from all previous air campaigns. For it was certainly not the sheer weight of ordnance that accounted for the results obtained.

As far as the Gulf war is concerned, contrary to the impression left by triumphalist press briefings, which proclaimed each day the total number of sorties flown as if each one was a bombing strike, less than half of the roughly 110,000 flights recorded from the start on January 17, 1991, till the cease-fire on February 27, 1991, were "strike" sorties.[4] And those aircraft were not heavily loaded. Even the huge, ancient B-52s carried only half the bomb loads of their predecessors of the Vietnam war, dropping a total of 25,700 tons in 1,624 sorties,[5] 15.8 short tons per sortie. As for the mass of fighter bombers and attack aircraft (that is, light bombers), average bomb loads were much smaller than their theoretical capacity. The F-16 fighter bomber, for example—the most numerous of all U.S. aircraft present—was typically armed with two Mk.84 bombs for a total of 4,000 pounds, almost exactly one-third of the aircraft's maximum weapon load.[6] As for the F-117 "stealth" (low observable) light bombers—the only manned aircraft that attacked targets in central Baghdad—they averaged 1.5 tons in the 1,300 combat sorties of the war.[7] Actually the average bomb load for all U.S. aircraft that carried out strike sorties omitting the B-52s was just under 1 ton.[8] All in all, the total weight of aerial weapons used against Iraq was less than 90,000 tons, counting all the coalition forces that took part and all classes of weapons, guided and unguided.[9] That may seem a huge amount—but only until it is compared to the 134,000 tons dropped by heavy bombers alone on Germany during the one month of March 1945, not including the uncounted bombs and rockets of more than 3,000 American, British, and Soviet fighter bombers.

We therefore reach a deceptively simple conclusion that is in reality full of complications: it was the unprecedented precision of the air campaign rather than its volume that yielded the spectacular result. A more controversial proposition is also tentatively offered in what follows: that only precision attacks with guided weapons were decisive, while the rest of the bombing was no more effective than in previous air wars, that is, it was mostly ineffective.

Guided and Unguided Air Weapons

For all the talk and imagery of high-technology "smart" weapons that characterized media reportage of both the Gulf war and the Kosovo war, they accounted for only a fraction of the aerial weapons used. Of all the different weapons dropped or launched by U.S. forces in the Gulf war, only 17,109 were guided to their targets as against 177,999 plain unguided bombs—some of the cluster variety, but most simple "iron" bombs similar to their predecessors of the Second World War. A large portion of the latter (72,000)[10] were dropped in bulk by B-52s, but the greater part were delivered by fighter bombers, many of which could have been armed with precision weapons.[11] Similarly, the warheads of guided weapons of all kinds accounted for only 6,631 tons out of the total of 71,627 tons of ordnance dropped or launched by U.S. forces.[12] Going by the number of weapons, therefore, we would call 91.2 percent of the aerial campaign against Iraq old-style bombing; going by the tonnage, that percentage declines to 90.74 percent; but either way old-style bombing dominated the air campaign even without taking into account the allied air forces, of which only the French used a fair proportion of guided weapons. In the Kosovo war, the guided proportion was higher but still very far from the total tonnage.

We know exactly what the successful precision attacks of the Gulf war achieved—in some cases the results were shown on television (the broadcasting of failed attacks would have been too much to expect). Each missile or guided bomb that reached its target—a *very* high proportion in excess of 50 percent—destroyed or damaged some building, installation, or major weapon specifically selected for attack, immediately depriving Iraq of whatever function that particular object was supposed to provide. We also know the specific consequences that ensued: the end of telephone service after Baghdad's central exchange was hit; the mass flight of aircraft to Iran, after the supposedly bomb-proof shelters of the Iraqi air force began to be penetrated one by one; the interruption of supply road traffic to the Iraqi forces in Kuwait after the rail and highway bridges were cut.

Such direct and specific results were of course entirely different from those of old-style bombing, in which each weapon, even if successfully dropped in the general proximity of the target, could only contribute in some unknown degree to the damage later seen in postattack photographs—or to the craters left by the bombs that had landed harmlessly round about.

Nor did it have to be claimed in the aftermath of guided-weapon attacks that a "morale" effect had somehow been achieved even if nothing of substance was hit. And even that is only the lesser part of the difference, for as we know from the record of all previous bombing campaigns, aerial devastation inflicted by the random fall of bombs need not specifically weaken the war capacity of the enemy. There are exceptions, of course, as in one dramatic episode of the Gulf war, when unguided bombs were purposefully scattered over an equally dispersed Iraqi ammunition dump, whose spectacular chain of explosions deprived the Iraqi forces in and near Kuwait of a large part of their ammunition reserves. But with old-style unguided bombing such a direct relationship between action and result is very unusual.

It is true that even the most precise of guided weapons can be useful only against a "point" target, that is, some structure or object that can actually be destroyed or incapacitated by one explosion. That may be something as obviously destroyable as an artillery piece, a single-aircraft shelter or a fairly compact building. In the Gulf war, such point targets included the office towers that housed the headquarters of military intelligence, the Ministry of Defense, and assorted other ministries in Baghdad, all left outwardly almost intact but with their floors collapsed one on top of another all the way down to street level. Likewise, even sturdy steel and concrete four-lane bridges were rendered useless by just two bombs accurately delivered to cut their full width. In Belgrade, Novi Sad, and elsewhere in the Yugoslav Federation there was a list of similar point targets that could be and were incapacitated by single hits in the 1999 Kosovo war.

But that still leaves the "extensive" targets,[13] which are not compact enough to be incapacitated by one hit, or even two or three. They are the targets held to justify unguided free-fall bombing. But just how common are they—and can they be effectively attacked at all? In the case of the Gulf war the question may seem idle because the entire vast deployment of Iraqi ground forces in and near Kuwait was represented as a multitude of extensive targets. Certainly, the Iraqis were spread out over the terrain, as any ground force of even minimal competence must be. Platoon positions were well separated from one another and from their company command post, just as the cluster of companies was well separated from regimental headquarters and the regimental artillery.

It is true, moreover, that the separate units of such an array of forces cannot realistically be attacked individually. A platoon is an abstract concept rather than a physical object that a guided weapon can attack. When a pilot—or, better still, a remotely piloted vehicle—flies over a platoon, the scene below will reveal three or four separate tanks if it is an armored unit, as many armored troop carriers if it is a mechanized unit, or a dozen foxholes and a dugout or two if it is an infantry platoon. Guided-weapon strikes are still profitable in the first case: even Saddam Hussein's enormous number of tanks did not make them too abundant to be individually attacked with GBU-12 laser-guided bombs at $9,000 apiece. The second case is already doubtful: armored troop carriers are much cheaper than tanks and were even more abundant in Iraq's lavishly equipped army. Unless the aim was tactical rather than strategic, say to stop an advance under way that included them, armored troop carriers do not warrant individual attack. There is no ambiguity in the third case: scattered foxholes and dugouts are not worth attacking even with the cheapest guided weapons.

Because ground forces deployed to hold terrain are indeed "extensive" targets, the prevalence of old-style bombing in the Gulf war may thereby seem fully justified, and so also for the unguided bombing of the Kosovo war. But just because attacks with costly guided weapons are impractical against dispersed troops, it does not follow that air strikes with cheap unguided bombs are therefore effective. On the contrary, the evidence old and new is overwhelmingly on the other side. Most famously at Monte Cassino in 1943, and in Normandy in 1944, the largest bombardments of ground forces of the Second World War yielded miserable results, as did all other bombardments of that kind before and since.[14] To the pilots over Monte Cassino who looked down at the mayhem they had wrought such an outcome seemed incredible, as it was for the Allied troops who marched up there in 1943 convinced that no Germans could have survived the cascading bombs that left the ancient abbey in ruins, only to be cut down by machine-gun fire. It was the same for the British tanks that advanced on Caen after its destruction, till stopped cold by the vast majority of German antitank gunners that had survived. In the 1999 Kosovo war, the rather small Yugoslav army deployment in Kosovo (less than 25,000 men in all) was heavily bombed for several weeks, but when the NATO troops arrived and Yugoslav units withdrew to Serbia, it was found that their losses of men and equipment had been on the order of 2 percent rather than the estimated 25 percent.

It is always the same. The bombs land with awesome explosions, the earth trembles, the upcast of craters jets in the air, the troops are shocked by the blast waves, many bleed from noses or perforated ear drums, they are terrorized into apathy or outright panic. But unless the enemy is nearby and ready to advance immediately,[15] the moment passes. The explosions cease, the ground stops heaving, the troops calm down, and the number of dead and wounded is finally found to be very small, indeed so small that if a count is done the counters declare their astonishment— though what is more astonishing is that anyone should still be surprised by the amply proven fact that bombs rarely kill deployed troops. It is their natural dispersal that protects ground forces so well, even if not deeply dug-in, as most of the Iraqis in and near Kuwait (or the Yugoslavs in Kosovo) were not, in spite of fantastic tales of bomb-proof shelters relayed by the press complete with imaginative diagrams.[16]

One might be inclined to dismiss the historical evidence because nowadays there is a technical remedy for dispersal: the cluster bomb—a canister that scatters a large number of bomblets whose joint lethal effect extends over a much larger area than an equivalent bomb of classic form. Of the 177,999 unguided bombs dropped by American aircraft during the air campaign against Iraq, one-third were of the cluster variety, 27,735 of them Mk.20 Rockeyes with 247 one-pound bomblets each, and others even better suited for use against infantry.[17] Such "antipersonnel" weapons are presumed to be so terribly lethal that in the later 1970s, the U.S. government stopped supplying them to some countries that continued to receive all sorts of other weapons. And their apparent effects as shown in test-range films are so impressive that again one would conclude that there would hardly be any survivors if troops had been present on the scene.

Geometry dominates imagery, however. In interventionist rhetoric, Kuwait was invariably described as "tiny," while Saddam Hussein's army was huge; and situation maps duly showed the "Kuwait Theater of Operations" crowded with the sausage-shaped graphics of Iraqi divisions and lesser units. But the ratio of occupied space to empty sand within each unit zone was still so low that not even bomblets by the million could overcome the geometry of dispersal.[18] Only the number of Iraqi casualties during the air campaign would provide conclusive evidence that not even cluster bombs can make the bombardment of ground forces effective, except when the shock effect can be exploited immediately by ground action, that is, when the bombing is not strategic but tactical and for close air support.[19] No comprehensive statistics are available, but in the case of four Iraqi divisions stationed in Kuwait that were bombed repeatedly and especially heavily, the estimates are as follows: Division 1, 100 killed, 300 wounded, out of 11,400 troops in all, totaling 3.5 percent casualties; Division 2, 300 killed, 500 wounded, out of 5,000 troops, 16 percent casualties; Division 3, 100 killed, 150 wounded, out of 8,000 troops, 3.1 percent casualties; Division 4, 100 killed, 230 wounded, out of 7,980 troops, 4.1 percent casualties.[20] Because the bombardment was so intensive in these cases, its results were not miserable, but they were not brilliant either. For the rule-of-thumb estimate is that at least 25 percent casualties are required to incapacitate a *tactically defensive* unit in mediocre armies, and twice that is required in armies of good quality. In the battle of Stalingrad the best units on both sides continued to fight defensively even after losing 75 percent casualties. On the offense, even the finest troops will stop attacking in earnest if they suffer even as little as 5 percent casualties in a short span of time (hours rather than days).

Bombing "Morale"

As against unforgiving numbers there is always the infinitely malleable "morale effect," invariably claimed when bombardment does not hit anything significant that can be photographed and evaluated against the political and military costs of bombing.

During the formative years of air power theorizing between the two world wars, the presumed morale effect of strategic bombing—almost any bombing it seemed—was constantly invoked. Even later, during the first two years of the Second World War, the leaders of the Royal Air Force confidently asserted that their inaccurate and scant bombing was on the verge of breaking the morale of the German populace ("cowering in shelters, plotting revolt"). In the case of the Gulf war, morale effects were also claimed, with apparently much stronger justification, for it is known that many Iraqi troops did desert their units. In the same battered four divisions cited above, the proportion of deserters was reportedly huge: 5,000 (out of 11,400) troops in Division 1; 1,000 (out of 5,000) in Division 2; 4,000 (out of 8,000) in Division 3; and 2,500 (out of 7,980) in Division 4.

The issue seems settled: it would appear that bombing in bulk with unguided weapons (even "carpet bombing") is effective after all, even though casualties remain very small in spite of the use of cluster bombs. Perhaps the historical evidence that bombing inflicts only a transitory shock, and does not permanently demoralize even mediocre troops, should be ignored. The bombing of Iraqi forces in Kuwait was certainly both heavy and prolonged—imagine how the troops must have felt: immobile for weeks on end under bombardment, without any active mission of their own to absorb their attention, always exposed to attack from their air yet rarely able to fight back with antiaircraft fire, and entirely impotent against the B-52s flying invisibly high. It is disconcerting to find that the historical evidence of all prior air wars was thus outdated, but it seems that the facts leave no other choice. Or do they? For those facts are open to an entirely different interpretation: the Iraqi troops that may or may not have been "demoralized" by inaccurate bombing were certainly starved by the *guided-weapon* strikes that stopped the flow of trucks bringing them food and water in the desert. The same document that cites the desertions and attributes them to the morale effect of carpet bombing also includes the following: "Many prisoners complained of only receiving a handful of rice and flour for a single meal each day. Water had to be trucked into camp and became scarce as the air campaign continued and large numbers of water tankers were destroyed. Drinking unpurified water resulted in constant [health] problems."[21]

This statement suggests that perhaps there is no need to invoke elusive morale effects. In first-class armies, troops have been known to keep fighting till they literally faint with hunger, but even the finest troops cannot fight on without water. When the tanker trucks stopped coming, the Iraqi troops out in the desert were doomed. Some could still find unpurified water, but for the rest the only alternatives were death in place, perilous defection to Saudi Arabia for those in forward positions, or desertion—the best choice of all. And it *was* a matter of choice: "The Iraqi army gave its troops seven days of leave for every 28 days of service on the front . . . In February, [during the bombing] soldiers who had missed their January leave [when leave was suspended after the war started on the seventeenth] were given a four day leave. Most failed to return."[22] In other words, it was hard for many Iraqi troops *not* to desert. The systematic destruction of road and rail bridges from Baghdad to Basrah, the prompt attacks on the pontoon bridges that the Iraqis attempted to assemble, and the ceaseless strafing of road traffic especially between Kuwait and Basrah not only reduced the flow of supplies but also made travel slow, perilous, or simply impossible.

We therefore find that the supposed morale effect of unguided bombing was irrelevant: the Iraqi soldiers who went home on leave could not have rejoined their units in any case, regardless of the state of their morale. Hence we can disregard even eyewitness reportage at ground level—which has a familiar ring, for in this matter there are established literary conventions: "The aircraft held most in fear was the B-52. Attacks by these aircraft were described by one officer as 'Something extraordinary.'

The officer related that troops would be horrified when they heard the heavy bombers commence their bombing runs . . . the sound and vibrations of the bombing could be heard and felt . . . many miles away. The sound effects spawned suspense and fear among the soldiers because they dreaded they would be the next target."[23]

We dismiss this evidence not because we suspect its veracity but because it is misleading even if true. Of course the bombs scattered among Iraqi troops spread horror, suspense, and fear—the same temporary effects recorded in Vietnam as in prior air wars, which dissipate once the bombing ceases. But the effects of the guided-weapon attacks that interrupted Iraqi road and rail traffic were neither psychological nor temporary; they were physical and cumulative. When road and rail bridges were cut by the bombing, the former could at first be circumvented, or partly repaired, or substituted by pontoons, but the Baghdad-Basrah railway that conveyed the army's supplies in bulk stopped operating altogether. That increased Iraqi reliance on road transport. Next, a repaired road bridge or floating pontoon bridge was cut, backing up the traffic in a congested mass. Next, tactical aircraft would attack the long line of vehicles. After that fewer drivers would risk the journey, and there were fewer vehicles to drive anyway.

The morale of individual Iraqi troops was therefore doubly irrelevant. Whether Iraqi soldiers were totally demoralized by the bombing, or as fanatically determined as the Waffen SS in its best days, their *units* could not advance, retreat, or survive in place once their supplies were stopped by the interdiction of Iraqi transport. That made the bombing of "morale" a redundant cruelty and a wasted effort.

Why Precision Bombing Is Different

That the interdiction of their supply traffic would inevitably force the withdrawal of Iraqi forces from Kuwait, or else cause their internal collapse because of hunger and thirst, seems obvious enough in retrospect. Yet both before and during the Gulf war, the advocates of an early ground offensive vehemently insisted that air interdiction "never works," often citing the experience of the Vietnam war as their evidence. Thus the circumstances of Vietnam, with its multiplicity of north-south routes by way of Laos and Cambodia, with its dense jungle cover to shroud most road segments from observation and attack, with its multitudes of porters and bicycle haulers as well as truck convoys, were equated with the situation of Iraq and Kuwait. Iraqi forces were much too large to be supplied by elusive camels in the night. They had to rely on the rail line to Basrah and on a two possible highways with several major bridges each, outlined in stark clarity against the desert terrain with no natural cover at all, and therefore fully exposed to air surveillance and attack. Vietnam, moreover, was not an arid wasteland but a country full of rice and water, so that even if their supply lines could have been totally cut, North Vietnamese troops would still not have lacked food or water, but would have lost only their ammunition resupply—and that too is a need that can be controlled, except in defending against *ground* forces.* In the case of the Iraqis in Kuwait, by contrast, resupply was needed even in the absence of ground combat but was far more easily interrupted. The logistic vulnerability of the Yugoslav army in Kosovo was even lower than that of the North Vietnamese in Indochina, in spite of the lack of dense jungle cover, because there was no ground combat that required ammunition resupply.

It was also argued before the Gulf war that interdiction would be ineffectual because the supply stocks of the Iraqi forces in Kuwait were enormous—some accounts claimed six months' worth of food and water. That would have been a unique logistic feat, but the claim was simply untrue. Some Iraqi divisions had as much as a full month's worth of essential supplies. But the air interdiction that can stop rail and road traffic can also attack stocks of supplies—and it did: "Another officer stated that his division had available one month's worth of food, water, and ammunition pre-stocked. Air attacks destroyed 80% of this stockpile."[24]

The air interdiction of Iraqi supply lines into Kuwait was thus very effective, and it might have made a ground offensive unnecessary given enough time—always assuming, as perhaps one should not, that the strategic goal was only to obtain Iraq's evacuation of Kuwait. But while the Vietnam analogy was entirely inappropriate, it reminds us that air interdiction can be useless, useful, very useful, or even a self-sufficient method of war, depending on the specific circumstances that obtain at the level of theater strategy: the density and exposure of transport nets, the extent of cross-country trafficability, the distances involved, and above all the composition and magnitude of supply needs. It is for this reason among

---

* Interdiction in Vietnam was always insufficient but never useless. It imposed both actual and "virtual" losses: to evade the air attack, the North Vietnamese had to use circuitous routes and much manpower was thereby lost to their combat forces.

others that the value of air power in war is so highly *situational*—a crucial consideration in defining the overall role of air power in national strategy.

To be sure, not all the bombing with old-style unguided weapons in the Gulf war was directed against the Iraqi forces in Kuwait for "battlefield preparation." Even the B-52s, which could not aim their unguided bombs individually as fighter bombers can with some accuracy,[25] were used to attack airfields, industrial complexes, and open-air supply dumps. Unlike dispersed troops, such targets can be usefully attacked without having to claim morale effects. But these targets also constitute a rather restricted category now that there is the alternative of precision. For example, even open-air supply dumps can best be attacked by guided weapons aimed at the separate clusters; as it was, in the Gulf war most of the bombs aimed at supply dumps fell harmlessly between the clusters. Of all possible types of industrial complex, only a few are best attacked by an extensive scattering of bombs. Heavy engineering factories for example are not seriously damaged by bringing down their roofs: once the rubble is removed, the machines remain almost intact, unless fires are also started to ignite their lubricants and cause meltdowns. Even refineries and chemical works can be attacked much more economically with a few guided weapons if their processes are known well enough to uncover the critical modules.

As for military airfields, only guided weapons can destroy the key facilities that are likely to be protected by thick concrete: aircraft shelters, ordnance bunkers, command posts, ready rooms, and electronics repair workshops. Unguided bombs can only damage unprotected ancillary buildings and runways. That may be useful to briefly keep enemy aircraft grounded, but during the Gulf war even the exceptionally passive Iraqi air force was quick enough with the runway-repair remedies that are now in general use: quick-setting concrete to fill bomb craters, expedient platforms to cover them and replace fractured aprons, perforated metal slats, and more.

The appropriate deduction is not that unguided weapons have become worthless but rather that a reversal of roles has taken place. While the official designation for unguided bombs is still "general purpose" ("Mk.83, 1,000 lb. G.P."), they have in effect become today's *specialized weapons,* while the various types of guided weapons became the standard weapons of air bombardment after the Gulf war, as indeed they were in the Kosovo war. It was the *generalization* of air attacks with the 3-feet median inaccuracies of laser-guided bombs, versus the 30 feet of past best efforts, the 400 feet that was averaged in the Vietnam war, and the 3,000 feet of much Second World War bombing, that yielded the transformed, war-winning, air power whose results were first manifest in the Gulf war of 1991 and better proven in the 1999 Kosovo war, when there was no ground combat at all.

Structuring an Optimal Air Campaign—in Theory

We may therefore conclude that if the overall circumstances of a conflict permit its success at all, an air campaign can nowadays be planned as a combination of three distinct efforts: *strategic bombing,* to incapacitate the essential physical components of the enemy's overall ability to pursue political or military goals,[26] including headquarter organizations and command centers, information-gathering and information-disseminating structures with their telecommunication adjuncts, related public infrastructures, and military-industrial and military facilities; *supply interdiction,* to deny transport infrastructures, their traffic, and stocks; and *independent, direct force attacks,* to disrupt the enemy's operational methods of war by destroying the particular classes of military equipment they require (as opposed to equipment most valuable in the abstract)—such attacks are "independent" for they are not designed to support particular operations on the ground. In addition, logically last but operationally first there is the *air combat and defense suppression* needed to facilitate all of the above, by establishing air combat superiority and by systematically attacking air-defense radars and other sensors, related communications and command centers, fighter bases, antiaircraft missile forces, and other antiaircraft weapons.

The very different mission of *close air support,* to directly assist ground forces in combat, may also become a necessity in conducting an air campaign, even if no offensive ground action is intended. In defending territory it may not be possible to await the cumulative but far from instantaneous results of strategic bombing, supply interdiction, and independent direct attacks on the enemy forces. If there is enough strategic depth, it may still be possible to rely on frontal air attacks alone to contain the momentum of an enemy offensive. But otherwise resistance on the ground will also be necessary, and therefore close air support too. An air campaign may thus include some unguided bombing (even "area" bombing) and also close air support as highly specialized lesser adjuncts, but otherwise it amounts to a specific sequence of guided-weapon attacks, much as a bridge is built in a specific sequence of precalculated steps.

There is however a huge complication: success in guiding weapons precisely to their targets is worthless unless the right targets have been chosen. Area bombing as practiced in the Second World War may often have been ineffectual or even counterproductive, but it required no special knowledge or talent in selecting targets—a list of enemy cities with their geographic coordinates was quite enough. But to defeat an enemy of any substance by a finite number of high-precision attacks, the inner workings of its civil and military institutions must be intimately understood—and that requires cultural insight as much as factual intelligence information. And then there is an obvious trap, because no air campaign or any other act of war is at all like building a bridge. No river of nature has ever deliberately changed its course to evade the spans of a bridge, yet circumvention as well as direct opposition are integral to the conduct of war. An air campaign may begin with a carefully planned sequence of guided-weapon attacks, but when the enemy reacts, the chosen sequence, or the preferred modes of attack, or the target selection, or all of those things must also change to keep up. Sheer persistence is the key to success in all things, except in war, when only those who persist flexibly can hope to prevail.

Air Campaigns in Practice

Largely because it was guided by a plan both sound and insightful,[27] the air campaign that determined the outcome of the Gulf war was a great success. Yet it must still be considered a transitional mixture, including much old-style bombing of dubious efficacy and lacking a responsive mechanism to change the original plan, which was followed very rigidly. Organizational innovation had failed to keep pace with the advancement of aerial munitions and surveillance systems, so that there was routine precision in the use of weapons but great confusion in targeting. More than the mere technicalities were involved. The ability to reliably direct bombs to within three feet of their aim point is wasted unless enough is known about the functioning of their targets in the total scheme of things. Highly developed by the end of the Second World War, "vulnerability analysis" became a lost art in the aftermath, because the advent of all-destroying nuclear weapons seemingly made it unnecessary. This is not so in the "postnuclear" present, especially now that weapons can aimed at discrete parts of even small structures (the air shafts of bunkers, outdoor auxiliary generators, and so on). To some extent, vulnerability analysis is a matter of engineering, but to a greater extent it must remain an art. Often it is the processes contained inside structures, rather than the structures themselves, that offer the most profitable vulnerabilities—and those might be managerial and bureaucratic rather than technical processes.

Before all the technicalities, there is the strategy of a campaign. Even in a most uneven encounter, the planners of a bombing campaign must contend with scarcity—they cannot attack all possible targets immediately and concurrently. Some, including key air-defense installations, automatically warrant the highest priority. Others, notably urban areas as such, can be dismissed as useless or even counterproductive. It is in between that planners have to select what to bomb and in what sequence. Science is everywhere applied in air warfare, but no scientific theory can guide the choice and prioritization of targets, on which the success of bombardment must entirely depend. There is no other recourse but to study as broadly as possible the country and its political culture, its leadership, all that is known of current goals in the conflict at hand, the peculiar strengths and weaknesses of the armed forces and their presumed methods at every level. All that and more are needed to construct an "anatomical chart" that identifies the key elements of the enemy as an operating system, or rather as a combination of operating systems. Yet as soon as the bombing starts, enemy "operating systems" will begin to change because of it, as attempts are made to circumvent the effects of the bombing already absorbed and of whatever subsequent bombing the enemy anticipates, rightly or wrongly. Hence, the usual paradox awaits: precisely in the degree that the "anatomical chart" *was* accurate and the bombing *was* effective, prewar planning will be undone insofar as the enemy can and does react. A peculiar danger is concealed in the reassuring spectacle of enemy passivity: the bombing may be wonderfully precise yet ineffectual from the perspective of enemy leaders. Neither Saddam Hussein in the Gulf war nor Slobodan Milosevic in the Kosovo war seemed especially concerned to react to the air campaigns against their regimes; perhaps both saw the destruction as actually useful or at least neutral in keeping them in power. Both did remain in power in the aftermath.

Because the continued effectiveness of an air campaign requires the continuous reassessment of the target list, it follows that any delay between the execution of air attacks and the reverse flow of damage assessments exacts a penalty. In fact, the most serious organizational weakness uncovered by the Gulf war was precisely in the collection, analysis, evaluation, and dissemination of bomb damage assessments.[28] It was a short-coming hardly remedied by the time of the Kosovo war, in the first place because of a shortage of photographic reconnaissance aircraft: it seems that airmen always prefer to buy one more fighter rather than its recon-naissance variant, one more manned aircraft rather than a dozen remotely piloted air observation vehicles (a mere handful reluctantly bought from Israel were deemed essential during the Gulf war, but hardly any more were bought in subsequent years in time for the Kosovo war, when only *two* of the larger U.S. machines were available). The results were to delay needed changes in campaign plans, resisted in any case by command rigid-ities; the needless duplication or triplication of attacks against well-destroyed targets; and the failure to reattack undestroyed targets. That is why even the best air weapons, with an 85 percent probability of hitting their targets, can never be anywhere near as effective operationally in actually incapacitating relevant targets.

It was the Israeli air force that first demonstrated the new art of *system-atic* air-defense suppression on June 10, 1982. Sixteen batteries of then modern Soviet antiaircraft missiles (enough to equip a fair-sized army) were destroyed in less than one hour without any aircraft lost by the combined use of a broad array of U.S. and Israeli electronic-warfare de-vices (radiation-homing missiles, jammers, and decoys) and unmanned weapons (remotely piloted strike vehicles, surface-to-surface missiles) as well as ultralow-altitude air strikes with cluster bombs. The key was that all these means were employed simultaneously in a single operational-level attack, itself made possible by intelligence preparation that yielded the complete electronic order of battle of the Syrians. It was a new way of fighting against air defenses: not the sequential attrition of radars, mis-siles, and gun positions of the Vietnam war but rather an electronic ver-sion of an idealized commando raid, in which every separate action is preplanned for concurrent execution, to finish the job before the enemy even fully recognizes that an attack is under way. When the Syrians re-acted by sending in their best jet fighter squadrons, the Israelis used the same integrated approach to intercept them. In the past, dogfights with Syrian jet fighters had resulted in 10:1 or at most 16:1 ratios in favor of the Israelis. On June 10, 1982, however, the tactical skill of individual Israeli pilots was complemented by airborne radar surveillance that tracked Syrian fighters as soon as they took off and by the task-force direc-tion of the interceptors to achieve operational synergisms. The result was a wholly unprecedented kill ratio of 85 to 0.

In the Gulf war, the concerted suppression of Iraqi air defenses from the very start of the air campaign did more than minimize U.S. and coalition aircraft losses. It also allowed the reconquest of the middle altitudes most suitable for precision bombing. By flying fairly high—usually well in excess of 10,000 feet—aircrew had the perspective to find and recognize their assigned target, launch their weapons with deliberation, and observe if the target was hit. (The damage, however, could only be assessed by others after the detonation and secondary explosions, if any.) By contrast, the ultralow-altitude, high-speed penetration tactics of the Royal Air Force, developed over the years to circumvent Soviet antiaircraft missile defenses in Europe, were misapplied against Iraq. Its antiaircraft missiles could hardly operate anyway, while antiaircraft gunfire was most abundant. Needless British losses—six aircraft in six days—were the result. Worse still, to fly manned aircraft as if they were missiles prevented the use of the most effective precision weapons, notably laser-guided bombs. British Tornados flying low and fast could only drop unguided bombs or scatter area munitions by preset commands from their navigation computers—their crews could see nothing below them except indistinct terrain flashing past.

Another discovery of the Gulf war air campaign that was confirmed in the Kosovo war is that stealth aircraft, designed to evade radar and infrared detection, can be wonderfully economical, even though each one is much more costly than a nonstealth equivalent. The reason is simply that they can operate on their own. By contrast, nonstealth strike aircraft are usually escorted by fighters flying top cover, other fighters armed with antiradiation missiles, active jamming aircraft, and often tankers for them all, so that only a fraction of the aircraft that go into action actually carry any offensive weapons. During the Gulf war, the use of as many as eight or ten fighter bombers to deliver six bombs was quite common.[29] In the Kosovo war, the proportion of strikers to supporting aircraft was not much higher. Inevitably the overall economy of air power as a form of war is degraded as the ratio of escorting aircraft increases. The striving to avoid air losses altogether can all too easily overshoot the culminating point of utility. Virtual attrition—the diversion of resources from positive action to self-protection—can be more costly than actual attrition in lost offensive effectiveness. As noted earlier, in the Kosovo war, NATO strike aircraft were so well escorted and protected that their pilots flew more safely than the passengers of some Third World airlines, but the air campaign was weakened in proportion.

Having *immediate* information on the outcome of air attacks already performed is of such importance that guided weapons that allow at least a partial review of their video-recorded results are correspondingly valuable. Conversely, the value of weapons that reduce the backflow of information to target acquisition only (notably air-to-surface missiles) is reduced in proportion. As for cruise missiles, sent safely to their presumed destinations without risking any aircrew but also without any immediate knowledge of the results if any, their value must be degraded even more.

The cruise missiles employed during the Gulf war[30] had much larger median inaccuracies (15–45 feet) than the best of the air-launched weapons, the laser-guided bombs (3 feet), and that difference was highly significant in the case of many types of targets. That disadvantage was largely remedied by the time of the Kosovo war, when cruise-missile median inaccuracies were below 10 feet. As against that, cruise missiles cannot lose their important operational-level advantage: large numbers can be launched simultaneously from the very start of an air campaign. During the Gulf war, a total of 52 were launched on the first day and another 52 on the second day; 196 had been launched by the end of the third day out of the total of 284 launched in the entire air campaign. In the Kosovo war, the total launched was greater, but there was less simultaneity at the outset, because only a few targets were initially authorized by the councils of NATO.

Evaluating Offensive Air Power

Why did the grand promises of the air pioneers of the 1920s remain unfulfilled until the 1991 Gulf war? Had they expected too much technical progress too soon? Actually the opposite was true: they had entirely failed to anticipate that air power could regress instead of advancing. When the Italian Giulio Douhet, the American Billy Mitchell, and the future Lord Trenchard variously claimed that future wars could be won by air bombardment alone, they had implicitly assumed a high degree of accuracy in identifying and hitting targets. All three had flown biplanes in the First World War, when the only means of navigating were purely visual, often by following known roads, railway lines, and rivers. This method of course depended entirely on good visibility, but when practicable at all, it virtually guaranteed that one target area would not easily be mistaken for another. No doubt it never occurred to them that in subsequent decades much more elaborate means of navigation would be used that could provide no such assurance of accuracy.

Likewise, they had dropped their bombs at speeds below ninety miles per hour and at low altitudes, often under one thousand feet. That was perilous even in those days, but it was also inherently quite accurate, at least in attacking extensive targets such as marshaling yards. Again, the air pioneers of the 1920s did not anticipate that in subsequent decades fighters and bombers would chase one another to much higher speeds and altitudes and then into the night, precluding any hope of accuracy even with fairly elaborate bombsights. Finally, the crews of the First World War could almost always see if they had hit their targets, if their bombs had exploded, and if there were any immediate signs that damage had actually been inflicted—a far cry from the hopeful and usually deluded presumptions of those who bombed after them in decades to come.

Thus the F-117s that were precisely navigated over specific buildings in Baghdad from January 17, 1991, to direct laser-guided bombs to within three feet of their aim points with the concurrent filming of the attack sequence, finally recovered the lost qualities of offensive air power that Douhet, Mitchell, and Trenchard had taken for granted. That is why their promise was finally redeemed in the Gulf war, after a seventy-year detour through competitively increasing speeds, tentative target acquisition, and often gross imprecision.

PART III

OUTCOMES: GRAND STRATEGY

Now at last we are ready to encounter grand strategy, the level of final results. This is also the everyday form of strategy, because the dynamic workings of the paradoxical logic are constantly present in international politics, even when war in any form is only a highly theoretical possibility.

In examining the prior levels of strategy from the technical to the theater-strategic, we had convenient labels to differentiate among the normative doctrines of military institution, the analyses of interested observers, and the objective reality of each level. There are for example the tactics prescribed by the manuals of a given military service or meant for a specific type of force ("armor tactics") or perhaps for a particular setting ("jungle tactics"); there is tactical analysis performed to evaluate a weapon or explain a combat episode; and then there is the tactical level of strategy itself as it exists in reality, whether or not any particular tactics have ever been recommended or any analysis performed. It was the same for the trio of prescribed and applied techniques, the technical analysis of combat encounters, and the technical level of strategy itself. And there was no great difficulty in differentiating among prescribed operational methods, such as defense-in-depth; the operational-level analysis of, say, Patton's 1944 deep-penetration offensive in France; and the operational level itself—whose importance, we discovered, depended on how much relational maneuver it contained. At the next level, the need for clarity imposed rather clumsier distinctions, for example, between the "theater strategy of NATO" (theater-level analysis) and the level of theater strategy itself, in which military phenomena are conditioned spatially.

At the highest level of strategy, however, we have no convenient terms to differentiate among grand strategy as the doctrine declared by a given state or imputed to it ("Chinese grand strategy"); grand strategy as a level of analysis, in which we examine the totality of what happens between states in peace and in war; and the reality of grand strategy, the conclusive level of strategy as a whole. Of course only the latter exists universally, because very few of the states that participate in international politics have a thought-out grand strategy of their own. My purpose, as always, is not to recommend any particular grand strategy for any particular country but rather to uncover the inner reality of the paradoxical logic at the level of grand strategy.

13

The Scope of Grand Strategy

If we recall the earlier image of strategy as a sort of multilevel edifice, with floors set in motion by the waves and counterwaves of action and reaction, we would find that its highest level is much more spacious than all those below it, in a way that no feasible architecture would allow. For at the level of grand strategy, the interactions of the lower, military levels yield final results within the broad setting of international politics, in further interactions with the nonmilitary relations of states: the formal exchanges of diplomacy, the public communications of propaganda, secret operations, the perceptions of others formed by intelligence, and all economic transactions of more than purely private significance. On this disproportionate top floor, therefore, the net outcome of the technical, tactical, operational, and theater-strategic emerges in continuous interaction with all those dealings between states that are affected by, and in turn affect, what is done or not done in the militarily sphere within any one state.

In a different image, which captures the dynamic reality of our subject, grand strategy may be seen as a confluence of the military interactions that flow up and down level by level, forming strategy's "vertical" dimension, with the varied external relations among states forming strategy's "horizontal" dimension.

Strategy in International Politics

The boundaries of grand strategy are wide, but they do not encompass all the relationships of all participants in the totality of international politics. Whatever dealings may exist between Sweden and Guatemala, for example, are unlikely to be influenced by reciprocal fears of attack or by reciprocal expectations of warlike assistance. It follows that Swedish-Guatemalan relations are not conditioned by the logic of strategy, though of course both Sweden and Guatemala do have strategical relationships with potential enemies and potential allies that may intersect at some point. Grand strategy thus exists within international politics but does not coincide with its boundaries. We may note incidentally that one way of evaluating the state of global politics on some normative index of progress is to examine how many of its relationships are significantly strategical. To be sure, grand strategy also exists outside international politics, for it includes the highest level of interaction between any parties capable of using force against each other, including criminal and terrorist groups.

The same paradoxical logic is manifest at the level of grand strategy in domestic settings as well, as long as the state's monopoly of force is incomplete, whether in civil wars or in criminal activity. In fact, one could identify the level of grand strategy even in a knife fight between two cutthroats in an alley: their grunts and screams may be seen as forms of diplomacy and propaganda; one or the other may attempt to employ economic inducements, offering money to stop the fight; some intelligence and deception will be present as each tries to misdirect the other by feints. And we may recognize in the fight a tactical level, formed by their reciprocal thrusts and parries, and a technical level, in the qualities of their knives. Even the participants themselves recognize distinctions between the levels, because they may plead, threaten, and bargain with each other as they continue to fight. So grand strategy may be present even on the smallest scale, at least until the police arrive.

But if the logic at work in the knife fight is the same as that of international politics, the phenomena it conditions are very different, not only because they are trivial but because they are made of individual acts and individual thoughts. The entire institutional and political aspect that characterizes the conduct of states is therefore absent, and with it the permanent contradiction between linear-logical political arrangements and the paradoxical logic that rules conflict. My inquiry will be confined to the dealings of states with one another not because strategy has a more natural place within them, but precisely for the opposite reason: only states ruled by strategists-kings could emulate the spontaneously strategical conduct of two cutthroats going at each other in an alley, for whom paradoxical action to deceive and outmaneuver comes quite naturally.

Whether we imagine it in static terms as an edifice or in dynamic terms as a sort of complicated fountain, grand strategy is the conclusive level, where all that happens in the vertical and horizontal dimensions finally comes together to determine outcomes. Brilliant victories at the technical, tactical, operational, or theater-strategic level, or for that matter diplomatic blunders, may have the opposite effect or even remain without consequence in the confluence of grand strategy.

Linear Goals in a Paradoxical Medium

Whether the results that grand strategy yields are deemed good or bad is a matter of subjective interpretation: how outcomes are seen depends on the goals being pursued. Whether goals are set by tradition, dictatorial whim, bureaucratic preference, or democratic choice, the logic of strategy has no role in shaping them. At the level of grand strategy, some governments seek power over other states, or even territorial expansion; others desire only to keep what external power and influence they have, while focusing on domestic goals, including the increase of prosperity; some governments are active on the world scene primarily to claim economic aid in various forms and can measure their achievement with rare precision; others see a fullness of success if they are simply left alone; and still others seek external support precisely to be left alone by their enemies. Each government has its own goals, if only implicit, and each therefore measures results differently so that the same outcome, say, the preservation of an unchanged status quo, may be deemed highly successful by one government and a crushing failure by another.

Much effort is wasted in defining "national interests," as if they had an objective existence that could be identified and measured. It should be obvious that so-called national interests emerge in a political process that owes nothing to the logic of strategy. When contending parties in domestic politics seek approval for their own particular goals by presenting them as "national" interests, they must do so by commonsense arguments, in which good is good, bad is bad, and larger gains are better than smaller, with no paradoxes.

There is no need to cite an infinity of examples to show the consequences of the pervasive contradiction between commonsense aims and strategic logic. It has made history into a record of the follies of mankind. It also explains why many political leaders successful in domestic governance fail in foreign policy, why many conquering heroes of war or diplomacy fail when attempting to govern at home. In a few specific matters, the repetition of tragic error time after time over the centuries has left some impression, so that the pursuit of linear-logical aims is at least questioned. If x army divisions or y missiles are thought necessary for national security, it is now possible that twice as many will not be automatically accepted as even better. It may at least be suspected that additional divisions or missiles could evoke adversary reactions either competitive or, worse, preemptive. It is fittingly ironic that such enlightenment derives from the simplistic, in fact mechanistic, idea that "arms races" are self-propelled and closely interactive. The clash of political ambitions that is the true cause of competition in all categories of weapons, and in many other things as well, is thus ignored.

A more obvious category of exceptions to the unthinking pursuit of linear-logical aims is evident to any traveler in lands of ancient conflict. Around the coasts of the Mediterranean, countless villages are perched on mountains, now picturesque and easily reached by car and tractor, but for centuries most uncomfortably removed from their own fields in the valleys below. The ruins of lowland settlements dating back to many different periods show that it was only through bitter experience that survivors learned that the good place is bad and the bad place is good in times of war. As long as the Romans ruled, common sense favored convenient valley sites. In recent times of peace, the valley can again be chosen for its convenience. But during the centuries in between, the villagers were constantly exposed to the fatal temptation of leaving their mountain to settle in the lowland, where the weary climb would no longer be added to each day's labor. The ruins still visible show how often they yielded to temptation.

Matters are no different for rival states entrapped in conflict. Divided by common interests that are not mutual, they are usually in perfect agreement on the goodness of peace and the badness of war, but they cannot act on those commonsense findings because the one-sided pursuit of peace and disarmament would be a powerful incentive to the adversary to intensify its own pursuit of war.

But that is the rule of survivors, not the universal rule. Attempts to project linear logic into the realm of conflict, in search of commonsense cooperative solutions, are fairly frequent. If we want peace, why not simply have it? If we agree that weapons are costly and dangerous, why not simply disarm? And if there is a quarrel over substantive interests, why not resolve it by all the procedures of law, arbitration, and bargaining that daily resolve many such quarrels within the domestic sphere? The persistence with which such cooperative solutions are proposed is not surprising, for the notion that the very pursuit of peace or disarmament logically leads to their opposites is simply bizarre from the viewpoint of linear logic.

But of course it is not intellectual error that induces these attempts to descend into the comfortable valley, but rather the acute temptation to escape from the cruel paradoxical logic. The modern annals of diplomacy are filled with attempts to negotiate commonsense solutions and with attempts to dissolve hostility by demonstrations of goodwill, as if expressions of hostility were not a mere symptom of colliding purposes. Only when the causes of conflict have been removed can cooperative diplomacy and gestures of goodwill be productive. Thus post-1945 Franco-German diplomacy successfully propelled joint initiatives in many fields, setting in motion the unification of Western Europe. Starting soon after the war, many summit meetings, state visits with mass participation, youth exchanges, and more such all helped to dissipate an outdated hostility. But it was only the suppression of the old conflict by the new, much wider East-West conflict that ensured the success of Franco-German diplomacy and of all the gestures of goodwill. When exactly the same procedures were tried before the Second World War, with continuous formal diplomacy, summit meetings (notably at Munich), arms-control negotiations, and a great many gestures of goodwill, including friendly reunions of veterans of the trenches, the only effect of so much gazing at the tempting valley below was to weaken French defenses while Nazi Germany was rearming.

From this famous failure of statecraft, and the parallel British-German case that was to cast the ancient and honorable practice of appeasement* into disrepute, a most influential exception arose to the temptation of projecting linear-logical solutions into the realm of conflict. The arms-control negotiations of the interwar years, the summit meetings, the goodwill gestures, and even the process of diplomatic communication itself were all condemned as harmful because they weakened efforts to prepare for the war they could not possibly avert. Accordingly, for many years after the Second World War, Western diplomacy with the Soviet Union was conducted with great, perhaps excessive, caution in the shadow of the "lesson of Munich." It is possible to argue that in the pro-

---

* "Appeasement" implies that the causes of conflict can be identified and removed by cooperative diplomatic surgery. That is often possible, though not when the cause of conflict is the very character of one of the adversaries. Some states (Hitler's Germany, Stalin's Soviet Union, Saddam Hussein's Iraq, and North Korea at present) absolutely require conflict to maintain their own internal political equilibrium.

cess useful opportunities for mutual accommodations may have been missed, at least during the Khrushchev years (1954–1964). It has rightly been said that history teaches nothing except that it teaches nothing, for we now know that after Stalin, Soviet leaders were not intent on war as Hitler had been, and their timetable in the pursuit of their ambitions certainly lacked Hitler's urgency.[1]

To be sure, diplomacy can serve many purposes even if conflict cannot be diminished, and indeed it can be especially productive in the midst of war, not necessarily to bring it to an end. The intermingling of warfare and direct negotiations in both the Korean and Vietnamese wars was a return to classical procedures. It was rather the absence of direct diplomacy during the two world wars that was untypical. In the case of the First World War, the abandonment of diplomacy was an elite concession to mass sentiment (inflamed from the start by elite-directed propaganda) and is now seen as evidence of the special ferocity of "democratic" war. In the Second World War, diplomacy did have its role but only with Japan and only at the very end, because the perpetuation of the imperial role was accepted by the Allies, which did not even contemplate the possibility of perpetuating Hitler's rule.

The Case of Arms Control

If confined to narrow and well-defined issues, even an outrightly cooperative, linear-logical diplomacy can coexist with the persistence of unresolved conflict over larger interests. Such diplomacy can serve one side or all sides by channeling the continuing rivalry away from paths deemed undesirable by all. In territorial conflicts, one form of cooperation has been the reciprocal acceptance of "buffer" states, left alone by both sides even if they continue to seek expansion elsewhere. In the context of the largely nonterritorial American-Soviet conflict—a warlike struggle without war—the 1955 State Treaty that left Austria as a neutral state was a rare and atypical example of cooperative diplomacy on a large scale. Much more typical was the 1962 Atmospheric Test-Ban Treaty, which inaugurated a long series of arms-control agreements that continues still, with the Russian Federation. The energies engaged in the nuclear competition, which served as a substitute for active warfare, were not diminished at all. But the agreed channeling of competitive efforts away from nuclear detonations in the atmosphere was of benefit to both sides, and to the rest of humanity as well. The error hidden in that diplomatic success was to misunderstand the *diversion* of conflictual energies as a partial solution of the conflict itself, thus wrongly suggesting that a progression of further partial agreements might bring the conflict to an end. Throughout the Cold War, arms-control negotiations were often misinterpreted as a form of conflict resolution, when in fact they only affected a symptom of conflict.

The process of negotiations in itself was often seen as having a useful calming effect. So it did, but that is only half the story. Because arms limitations as such do not restrain the competitive impulse but merely divert it, the consequences of agreed limits depend on the specific features of the weapons restrained and of the new weapons that are built with the resources thus released. While the former weapons are known, the latter are not. Therefore the pursuit of arms control is a gamble for each side, though it systematically favors the side best placed to innovate (that was generally the United States in the American-Soviet competition). In any case, the development of new weapons caused by agreed limitations on those that already exist must generate further stresses in the conflictual relationship. New weapons often have novel configurations that disturb established patterns of interaction between the forces on each side. The resulting "innovation shocks" easily overcame the calming effect of arms-control negotiations during the Cold War, explaining why celebrated agreements were followed by periods of acute tension.

The pursuit of arms control is itself conditioned by the paradoxical logic, when effective agreements that limit the competition in some way are successfully negotiated. Specifically, as with any other activity in the realm of strategy, arms control steadily pursued must eventually become self-defeating after a culminating point, in this case after a certain accumulation of agreed limitations. It is the mechanism of "verification"— the procedures and devices used to assure compliance with negotiated restrictions—that is the vehicle (not the cause) of the self-annihilation of arms control.

Dependent on satellite observation, radar tracking, and signals intelligence, verification is the sine qua non of arms control: what cannot be verified cannot be limited. Not all weapons are sufficiently visible to be detected and reliably counted, and not all forms of performance are sufficiently transparent to be assessed. If all existing weapons whose number and characteristics could be verified are successfully restrained by mutual agreement, developmental energies and production resources would be diverted to the acquisition of new weapons not yet controlled, some sufficiently visible to be assessed and counted remotely, and others not. If the new weapons that are verifiable were then limited in turn, the result would be a further diversion of effort into newer weapons, some verifiable and others not. Eventually, as the process continues and all verifiable weapons are duly subjected to effective limitations, all developmental and production resources will have been diverted to the acquisition of weapons that cannot be verified for one reason or another, which therefore cannot be the subject of limitations. At that point, the competition in arms would continue. But arms control would have come to an end, annihilated by its own success, just like the perfect antitank weapon that would cause the disappearance of tanks from all battlefields, or the army that advances so far that it marches to its own self-destruction.

That arms-control diplomacy can at best achieve only specific restraints on particular weapons hardly condemns its pursuit, for that is precisely its purpose. Certainly the process itself cannot be blamed for the chronic propensity to misconstrue it as a device for the resolution of the underlying hostility and as a prelude to disarmament. Yet no error is more natural in the domestic politics of prosperity-seeking countries of consensual government, where the reconciliation of conflicting interests is the everyday business of politics.

The tension between the goals formed domestically by linear thinking and the conflictual dimension of international politics is not a universal condition. Governments that rule by warlike methods at home are much less likely to pursue inappropriately cooperative goals on the international scene. Their leaders need not have any greater intellectual understanding of the paradoxical logic; indeed they may be primitives who do not think in such terms at all. But habitual reliance on secrecy, deception, intimidation, and force at home contains its own education in strategy, as patterns of failure and success themselves suggest the outlines of the logic. Just as consensual politics at home inspires a linear-logical outlook in foreign policy, the domestic politics of dictatorships prepares them for the logic of conflict abroad. No particular predisposition to aggressive conduct follows. As the historical record shows, dictatorships can be impeccably peaceful and democracies can be fiercely aggressive. It was an increasingly democratic Britain that was increasingly aggressive during the nineteenth century in subduing much of south Asia and Africa, and its leading competitor in imperial expansion was France, especially after the advent of democratic government in 1871. Nor can the spirit of the times be invoked to explain all: the electorates of both countries still favor the use of force overseas when the opportunity arises. British popular enthusiasm for the 1982 Falklands war amazed other Europeans, and it was with ample public support that France tried to play a leading role in the Kosovo war of 1999.

There is no asymmetry of intentions, therefore, but there can be one of effectiveness. Its consequences are manifest in struggles between prosperity-maximizing countries and power-maximizing regimes that try to apply abroad what they daily practice at home. The former easily prevail in production and technical advancement, but in the use of secrecy, deception, and intimidation, the more practiced governments naturally show greater skill. Prolonged war can nullify the difference, however. In the Second World War, the Anglo-American democracies proved superior precisely in secrecy and deception, to the point of making the Germans and Japanese seem almost naive in retrospect. Yet in coping with the conflictual aspects of peacetime international politics, linear-logical attitudes are an undeniable source of weakness that can weigh heavily in the balance of power. The defeat of Iraq in 1991 and of Serbia in 1999 by primarily democratic coalitions illustrated both their enormous material superiority and also the vast effort required to overcome unimpressive opponents when they are hardened by dictatorship. In both cases, moreover, the democratic victory was insufficient at the time to remove the rulers, one of whom indeed remains in power at this writing.

14

Armed Suasion

War is a dramatic rarity in interstate relations, as opposed to the endless low-level warfare of internal conflicts. Thus the normal results that emerge at the level of grand strategy are not those of war but of "armed suasion," as I call it. They are no less substantial for the absence of any visible clash of arms, for armed suasion is nothing less than power, or more precisely that portion of the power of states that derives from their military strength.

Armed suasion is inherent to the possession of strength: there can be no capacity for the use of force that does not evoke some response from those who hope it might be used on their behalf, or from those who fear it might be used against them. I introduced the new term to overcome the political and cultural bias that so greatly emphasizes "deterrence," just one form of armed suasion, obscuring the more general phenomenon: armed suasion is to "deterrence" (or "dissuasion") what strength in general is to defensive strength. And having introduced the general concept, now I can revert to plain language to describe its various forms, with dissuasion being the negative form as persuasion is the positive, manifest both when adversaries feel themselves compelled to act as they are told to do and when friends are encouraged to persist in friendship by their expectation of armed help if needed.

Whether adversaries and friends are persuaded, or adversaries are dissuaded, it is always by their own doing that the action unfolds. It is not the keeping of armed strength that generates armed suasion but the response of others to their own perceptions of that armed strength. It is the result of decisions *they* make, shaped by *their* calculations and emotions, which inevitably reflect entire worldviews, including opinions of the armed strength before them, visions of the likelihood and circumstances of combat, and estimates of the willingness to use force for or against them. Descriptions of this or that military force as a "deterrent," which imply that the act of dissuasion is accomplished by the upkeep of a given force, entail a confusion between subject and object that can be dangerously misleading. The would-be deterrent is the passive object, and the party to be influenced is the sentient, active subject, who may or may not choose to be dissuaded.

Perceptions of potential military strength also evoke suasion. Subject to the envisaged duration of whatever warfare is deemed possible, the mobilization capacity of nations can induce anticipatory suasion at par, at a discount, or not at all. For example, the widespread belief in the 1950s that any American-Soviet war would be nuclear from the start and very short, may well have reduced the suasion that the United States obtained from its vastly superior capacity for industrial mobilization. In the 1960s, by contrast, while Soviet military policy increasingly emphasized preparations for a protracted nonnuclear war, American mobilization capacity was in fact rapidly eroding (because weapons became increasingly complex and decreasingly producible).

In combat, force is an objective reality in action, whose only valid and totally unambiguous measure is in the results achieved. With armed suasion, however, there is only the subjective estimate of a given potential for combat in the eyes of others, friends and enemies alike. The accuracy of such estimates is not merely uncertain but actually indeterminate, because that combat potential is measurable only in the reality of specific forms of warfare that may never happen. Even then, combat outcome will be influenced by all the unpredictables of time, space, and circumstance.

To be sure, it is easy to think of extreme cases in which uncertainties and indeterminacy are both nullified by overwhelming material imbalances, as in the case of a nuclear war between China and nonnuclear Vietnam, or a naval war between the United States and some tiny island state. But the record of military history shows that as soon as one contemplates less extreme cases that are not entirely absurd, uncertainty and indeterminacy begin, and far sooner than any reasonable reading of the precombat evidence would suggest. But then, if the outcome of wars were less uncertain, there would be much less war, because defeats would be anticipated and then avoided by reaching accommodations in one way or another.

Nothing can be done to overcome the essential indeterminacy of combat, but great efforts are made to reduce uncertainty in estimating military balances. Numbers are dutifully counted for men, weapons, and supplies, and there is much striving to evaluate the quality of weapons and their ancillaries. But there still remains the far larger part of the unknown, the intangibles of organization, operating skills, morale, cohesion, and leadership that count for so much more than the material factors. When it comes to tactics, operational methods, and theater strategies, other uncertainties intrude: are they only prescribed on paper or will they actually be executed? And if executed, will they be done well? Again the answer depends on human intangibles that cannot be measured at all and that can be assessed only on the basis of prejudices that may be perfectly sound or totally wrong: until 1870 France, not Germany, was considered the warrior nation of Europe; until the establishment of the state of Israel, the Jews were widely viewed as incapable of combat.

Diplomacy, Propaganda, and Deception

In the absence of objective measures for armed strength, strategy outside war is therefore a commerce conducted in as many currencies as there are interested parties. Inevitably, different values—sometimes greatly divergent—are assigned to the same military forces. An important function of both diplomacy and propaganda is precisely to manipulate those subjective evaluations. Sometimes, very rarely, the aim is to devalue forces about to be unleashed so that they may be launched with unexpected strength, but much more often the purpose is to intimidate, to evoke as much armed suasion as possible. That is why even a pervasively secretive Soviet government chose to display its weapons in Red Square parades to which Western military attaches were invited, to view and photograph the latest aircraft, tanks, guns, and missiles. At the time, ironically, it was forbidden to photograph even prosaic railway stations.

If secrecy can undercut the potential for evoking armed suasion and appropriate advertisement can secure it in true proportion, even more can be obtained by outright manipulation. During the 1930s the diplomacy of Mussolini's Italy was greatly enhanced by a stance of restless bellicosity and by a contrived facade of great military strength. Mussolini talked of an army of "eight million bayonets," and his parades were dashing affairs of running *bersaglieri* and roaring motorized columns. The Italian air force was greatly respected because of its spectacular long-range flights to the North Pole and South America; and the Italian navy could afford many impressive ships because so little of its money was wasted on gunnery trials and fleet exercises. By a military policy in which stage management was far more important than the sordid needs of war preparation, Mussolini sacrificed real combat strength for the sake of hugely magnified images of military power.*

But the results of the suasion evoked by those images were very real: Britain and France were both successfully dissuaded from interfering with Italy's conquest of Ethiopia, its intervention in Spain, and the subjection of Albania. And none dared to oppose Italy's claim that it was a Great Power, whose interests had to be accommodated sometimes in tangible ways (such as the licenses obtained by Italian commercial banks in Bulgaria, Hungary, Romania, and Yugoslavia). Only Mussolini's last-minute decision to enter the war in June 1940—when his own considerable prudence was overcome by the irresistible temptation of sharing in the spoils of the French collapse—brought years of successful deception (and self-deception) to an end.

What Mussolini did, and many others before him, has also been done since his day, with Nasser of Egypt being his closest imitator and Khrushchev during the missile-gap years an even more successful practitioner. As we now know, between 1955 and 1962 the Soviet Union's supposedly great strength first in bombers and then in "atomic rockets" consisted of a few bombers and a mere handful of intercontinental ballistic missiles. Carefully orchestrated talk and the spectacular imagery of Soviet space exploration were systematically employed to magnify Soviet nuclear capabilities. But that is how matters are with armed suasion: when there is no objective truth but only a mass of impressions there is room for much error, and for deception as well.

"National Will"

Because military power can dissuade or persuade only if its actual use is considered possible, that great subject of metapolitical speculation, the "will" of leaders and nations, is reduced to simple mathematics when it comes to armed suasion. Aside from all else that is of consequence, the effect that armed forces induce in others depends on their perceived strength multiplied by the perceived will to use that strength. And if that will is believed to be absent, even the strongest forces, whose strength is fully recognized, may not dissuade or persuade at all. Nations that successfully present themselves as relentlessly peaceful cannot expect to obtain

* Among other things, the number of Italian army divisions was increased by one-third when the standard three regiments were reduced to two, to form supposedly more agile "binary" divisions; the only result was to increase divisional overheads.

much armed suasion from the forces they keep. Sweden, for example, although a considerable military power by European standards, was apparently unable to dissuade violations of its territorial waters by Soviet submarines during the Cold War. At least from the narrow viewpoint of armed suasion, a demonstrative peace policy can be too successful.

But few countries are willing to display an easily provoked bellicosity just to maximize their potential for armed suasion. Most are confronted by one of strategy's typical dilemmas: to avoid the actual use of force and still protect their interests, they must maintain a reputation for violence if they are to persuade or dissuade by armed suasion—and that is not the kind of reputation that countries intent on avoiding war want to present. Domestic political imperatives and urges derived from unstrategical sentiments and self-images often undercut the potential for armed suasion, sometimes with costly results. The usual way out of the dilemma is to present a Januslike appearance, proclaiming both a dedication to peace that rules out all aggression and also a great readiness to fight if attacked. Valid enough for countries that have to protect only themselves, this simple formula will not serve for Great Powers that must do more than just protect themselves. They are forced back into the dilemma and accordingly must keep a declaratory stance carefully balanced between a reassuringly peaceful attitude and one that reassures lesser allies precisely because it is not wholly peaceful.

Multilateral alliances complicate the striving to avoid the use of force by obtaining its results from suasion, with some allies contemplating separation because they are frightened off by an excessive bellicosity, while others are in exactly the same position because of exactly the opposite reason. Ultimately, by the usual paradox, it is those considered most willing to use force that are least likely to have to use force. That was the secret of the great military empires of history, whose widespread intrusions on other nations could only have resulted in constant war on all fronts, were it not for the eagerness with which their desires were accommodated without war.

Overt attempts to exploit armed suasion, positive or negative, by declared demands are quite rare, but *latent* suasion is a common phenomenon. In fact, the suasion that perceived armed strength silently evokes largely preserves such world order as there is, just as the ultimate existence of courts and police officers is the preserver of private property. That silently continuous effect is not only undirected but mostly unconscious. Armed forces are maintained to preserve institutional continuity, for possible future war, for internal repression, or even for the sake of tradition. Only rarely are they deliberately kept for the purpose of suasion.

The Paradoxical Logic in Armed Suasion

Whether or not there is conscious intent, if there are governments that choose to see the military strength of others as reassuring, or adversaries who consider it a threat and are therefore dissuaded from some hostile act, armed suasion is at work. Because it is a conflictual phenomenon, whose existence derives entirely from the possibility of war, even if most improbable, armed suasion is conditioned by the paradoxical logic. Just as warlike actions lead to reactions that set in train strategy's distinct logic, so too armed suasion evokes not only desired responses but also opposing reactions, and it does not matter at all if the suasion is spontaneously induced by military strength meant for quite other purposes.

With linear logic out and paradoxical logic in, the usual results follow. In the static view, more can be less and vice versa, as in the common case of the less extreme threat that elicits suasion all the more because it is that much more plausible. In dynamic terms, we encounter again the coming together of opposites that may reach the point of becoming a full reversal. The more an attempt at dissuasion is effective in achieving its goal, the more likely it is that it will be circumvented or even directly attacked by the frustrated aggressor: if the Soviet Union had not been so well dissuaded in the immediate post-1945 period from the outright use of force in Eastern Europe, it would not have engaged in so much subversion. And during the Cold War, if the Soviet Union had not been so well dissuaded from attacking Western Europe, it would not have pursued so many adventures in the Middle East.

More generally, we have already seen how nuclear dissuasion was circumvented on a global scale by indirect and deniable forms of aggression, both covert-political and paramilitary, both bloodless and very bloody indeed. While the United States and the Soviet Union were dissuaded from direct warfare with each other throughout the Cold War because of the presence of nuclear weapons, their hostility found outlets in the wars fought by their allies, clients, and agents. The counterpart of the unprecedented peace of the Great Powers was therefore the prevalence and intensity of Small-Power wars, some 144 of them during the Cold War years 1948–1991. Moreover, they were often much more than desultory affrays fought with obsolete weapons. Some were intense, exemplified by the post-1967 Arab-Israeli wars in which high-quality weapons were increasingly used; or else they became endlessly protracted conflicts of attrition, as in Cambodia, and between Iraq and Iran during the much of the 1980s. Thus the triumph of nuclear dissuasion was paradoxically evident in nonnuclear violence.

Second-Strike Attack as a Paradoxical Remedy

The December 7, 1941, attack of imperial Japan on the U.S. fleet at Pearl Harbor embodied the confluence of success and failure in suasion. Had the deployment of the fleet to that forward base been ineffective in dissuading a Japanese invasion of British Malaya and the Dutch East Indies, it would not itself have been attacked to make those invasions possible.[1]

Understandably, the Pearl Harbor attack left a deep and enduring impression on American strategic culture. Yet it was not considered a "lesson" of Pearl Harbor that antagonists should not be deprived of choices other than war—as Japan certainly was by the April 1941 trade embargo that essentially cut off its oil supplies. Nor was a lesson learned from the refusal of the United States to wage war to oppose Germany's conquests, or Japan's before 1941, even as they respectively subjected most of continental Europe and much of China. In the end it was Japan's war cabinet that made the decision to intervene on America's behalf.

What was learned from the Pearl Harbor experience was that an armed force sufficiently threatening to dissuade attacks against other targets positively invites attack upon itself—unless even its residual postattack strength is calculated by potential aggressors as sufficiently great to dissuade them. From this lesson came the concept of "second-strike capability," which played a large role in shaping American and then Soviet military policy during the Cold War.[2] The recognition that only postattack, not preattack, strength can dissuade, and that vulnerable forces can provoke war, greatly influenced the design and deployment of nuclear weapons. Its practical consequence was the elaborate protection and abundant multiplication of nuclear weapons and of their means of command.

Patterns of Suasion

Aside from its everyday effects, silent, undirected, and mostly invisible, armed suasion also has its clear-cut victories and defeats. The Romans had to fight for two centuries to subject Carthage and every part of the Iberian peninsula, but the domination of the larger and richer Hellenistic lands was obtained with one battle and a great deal of intimidation.*

Similarly, Hitler won Czechoslovakia without a fight entirely by armed suasion, whereas he had to fight for Poland. Aside from the damage inflicted in the process, there was no difference in the aftermath because both were conquered. We may note the equality of results between the successful defense of Korea by war in the years 1950–1953 and its equally successful and far less costly protection by armed dissuasion in all the years since.

The Korean example is especially instructive, not because it typifies dissuasion at work but precisely because it does not: in the Korean context, the distorted, quasi-mechanical view of "deterrence" as an action of one's own, rather than an intended political response, is much less misleading than usual. In the first place, the perceived danger that emanates from North Korea is not a conceptualized threat, derived from computations of the enemy's military potential in imagined, perhaps highly hypothetical circumstances. Instead the threat has an immediate physical form: much of the huge North Korean army is massed near the front line, visibly ready to attack. As for the intent of the North Korean leaders to invade, before the economic collapse of the 1990s, it was frequently proclaimed and confirmed by actual invasion preparations including tunnels dug underneath the demilitarized line, sporadic commando attacks, and repeated assassination attempts against South Korean officials[3]—the last a rare form of war that even the Arab states and Israel have always avoided. Moreover, the South Korean view of the threat was not a self-centered mental construct, imposed on a military threat that might be directed in quite other

---

* Intimidation was mostly masked by pieties: subjected and obedient clients-rulers such as Herod were dubbed "friend of the Roman people," and it was the Roman consul C. Flaminius who proclaimed the "freedom of all Greeks." But intimidation could be brutally direct, as when the Seleucid ruler Antiochus Epiphanes IV was curtly ordered out of Egypt and Judea in 168 B.C. by C. Laenas Popilius, who confronted him as he was advancing with his troops. Popilius had no troops with him, only the text of a senate resolution that offered a stark choice between immediate retreat and war with Rome. Antiochus asked for time to consider the matter, but Popilius traced a circle in the sand around his feet with a stick and demanded an immediate reply. The humiliation was intense and the loss huge, for Egypt's great wealth was within his grasp, but Antiochus obeyed: the Romans had just defeated and ruined one Hellenistic king, Perseus of Macedon, and they might easily have chosen to destroy another. This episode, vividly described by Polybius (book 29), would fall within the current definition of "compellence."

directions (such as the Iraqi military buildup in 1989–1990, which the Israelis wrongly viewed as directed against themselves, never imagining that it might be used against Kuwait). Because of geography alone, the North Korean forces can fight only against the South; they can serve no other external purpose. Thus the North Korean threat can actually be described accurately by that word, because it is both continuous and can only be aimed in one specific direction—just as the mechanical view of deterrence always implies, even if it is seldom the case. Normally the danger is not continuous but rather a possibility that could materialize in the hypothetical circumstances of a severe crisis; and it is not specific in form, intensity, or direction, so that no countering effort is self-evidently appropriate.[4]

In the Korean case, dissuasion is unusual in another way as well. Although the possibility remains of bombardment after the fact, to punish North Korea for having launched an invasion, it is primarily the prospect of a successful defense of the South that is meant to dissuade invasion. An element of dissuasion by denial, as opposed to dissuasion by punishment (or "retaliation"), is inherent in any defense, just as an element of persuasion is inherent in any offensive strength. But the two forms of intended dissuasion are separable in principle, and the difference is reflected in the detailed composition of the forces involved.

A policy of dissuasion by denial seems at first glance altogether preferable to the alternative of dissuasion by punishment, and not only in the particular case of Korea. Similarly, a policy of nonnuclear dissuasion by denial seems even more clearly preferable in principle to dissuasion by nuclear punishment.

In the first place, under a policy of dissuasion by denial, all available military resources can be used to provide the most effective defense possible against invasion. If those preparations dissuade the attempt, so much the better. But if they do not, the invasion can still be resisted physically. In other words, no military resources have to be diverted from the defensive effort to maintain retaliatory forces, of vast destructive capacity perhaps but of small value in physically resisting advancing enemy forces.

Above all, dissuasion by denial does not have to rely on the tenuous psychological calculus that is the essential mechanism of dissuasion by punishment. In the classic formulation, in order to dissuade, the punishment has to be certain and capable of inflicting "unacceptable damage." Aside from its physical requirements—namely, the ability to strike after an attack—this certainty of punishment also implies a peculiar and indeed paradoxical reversal in the usual characteristics of victims and aggressors.

The victim has to proclaim his will to attack most destructively, and because counterpunishment is to be expected the victim must actually appear reckless, ready to act in a self-destructive manner, in order to dissuade. The aggressor by contrast must be a prudent calculator to be dissuaded, and certainly must not be self-destructive. In the case of the NATO Alliance during the Cold War, a gathering of democratic countries on the defensive, it was especially difficult to simulate a reckless collective personality.

Then there is the question of the magnitude of the punishment. It must be large enough to be "unacceptable," we have seen, but how much is that and for whom? Hitler at the end declared that the destruction of the German nation was acceptable and even desirable, because the Germans had shown themselves to be racially degenerate by failing to win the war for him. Hitler could not have been deterred by punishment at that point, because he might actually have welcomed the nuclear destruction of Germany. Stalin was never driven to the point of self-destruction, but he evidently considered the deaths of many millions of his subjects perfectly acceptable. Mao likewise presided over the deaths of tens of millions of Chinese, many killed because they were two-acre landlords.

How much damage, then, must be threatened to exceed the limits of the acceptable? Reasonable people are easily dissuaded—one nuclear weapon on one small town will already be unacceptable damage. But it is the Hitlers, Stalins, Maos, Pol Pots, and Saddam Husseins who must be dissuaded, not gentler souls who would find aggression unthinkable anyway. Yet such men are the very ones who might find any amount of damage acceptable as the price of aggression, as long as their own power survived. Because moderates are excluded from consideration in any event, Hitler, Stalin, Mao, Pol Pot, and Saddam Hussein are not unrepresentative exceptions that can be overlooked. They are typical of those who must be dissuaded—and only attacks on "leadership targets" (their residences, their headquarters, and themselves) are likely to be unacceptable enough for them. But to attack the leaders, as we saw, precludes any realistic hope of dissuasion to stop a war before its destruction exceeds all limits.

As for leaders and governing groups that are not so murderous, for whom the destruction of, say, a few cities would be quite unacceptable in normal circumstances, they too may not be dissuaded by such punishment in the midst of an intense crisis. Prudence can be overcome by the sheer dynamics of commitment making, as each side is maneuvered into positions from which retreat is emotionally difficult and politically dangerous. Crises are unusual, and those with any large element of emotional intensity have been few indeed,* but again it is not for normal times that dissuasion is needed, but precisely for abnormal times when even reasonable leaders may act unreasonably.

As against all the shortcomings of nuclear dissuasion by punishment, nonnuclear dissuasion by denial has one great defect: it has often failed and can fail again whenever an aggressor comes to believe, rightly or wrongly, that he can win. Of course he might lose, but a war must still be waged and suffered—a war that dissuasion by punishment could have avoided, though at the risk of catastrophic failure.

Nuclear Dissuasion in Europe

In Korea, demography and geography allow each side to man the narrow front from sea to sea in great strength. But in the case of Europe during the Cold War, the ratio of ground forces to front lines was not favorable for the defense, and any advantage in battlefield air power was not large enough to offset the deficit, once Soviet air defenses were included in the calculation. Even if the Alliance had greatly increased its forces, it would still have been inferior at the level of theater strategy, because it had to provide a "forward defense" of the entire territory, while the Soviet offense could concentrate against narrow sectors. Even if the forward defense could have been abandoned, and the ratio of forces to frontages greatly improved, nonnuclear dissuasion by denial could still have failed, if Soviet military and political leaders were sufficiently optimistic. Like others before them, they might have come to believe that a cleverly prepared surprise attack could defeat the Alliance.

With dissuasion by denial so unreliable, and dissuasion by punishment riddled with uncertainties, it is not surprising that the Alliance attempted to combine both forms of dissuasion from 1967 until the end of the Cold War. Actually the Alliance relied on a combination of means: inadequate nonnuclear frontal defense forces, a rather vulnerable complement of battlefield nuclear weapons (also meant for dissuasion by denial), theater-range nuclear forces that were also somewhat vulnerable, and American

* The standard list of Cold War crises serious enough to raise nuclear considerations includes Iran 1946, Berlin 1948, Korea 1951, Korea 1953, Quemoy/Matsu 1954, Indochina 1954, Suez 1956, Quemoy/Matsu 1958, Berlin 1959, Berlin 1961, Cuba 1962, Pueblo/Korea 1968, India/Pakistan 1971, Egypt/Israel 1973. Of these, only the three Berlin crises and the Cuban Missile Crisis were emotionally intense.

long-range nuclear forces, the last larger and much less vulnerable than either battlefield or theater-range nuclear forces but whose use on Europe's behalf could not be certain.

Yet the sum of inadequacies was an impressive deterrent: because the nonnuclear frontal defenses were inadequate, the use of battlefield nuclear weapons could be credible. In the course of a desperate losing fight, with Soviet invasion columns breaking through, the firing of nuclear artillery and short-range nuclear missiles about to be overrun was not implausible. By contrast, with stronger frontal-defense forces, the initial wave of invaders could have been contained; once given the opportunity to deliberate, governments would likely prohibit the use of nuclear weapons—even if there was no other response to the imminent arrival of Soviet second-echelon formations. If, however, the nonnuclear frontal defense forces had become much stronger, making the use of battlefield nuclear weapons unnecessary, the Soviet Union could no longer have hoped for a quick nonnuclear victory and would have reverted to its theater strategy of the 1960s, based on the early use of its own battlefield nuclear weapons to break open gaps in the front.

In the usual paradoxical way, therefore, if the strength of Alliance nonnuclear forces had been increased beyond the culminating point of a defense that could stop intrusions but not an all-out offensive, the result would have been to *weaken* dissuasion, by reducing the credibility of battlefield nuclear use. If the strength of the nonnuclear forces were then further increased to much higher levels, to make the use of battlefield nuclear weapons unnecessary, the result would not have been to avoid nuclear warfare but rather to ensure it in the event of war—because if the Soviet Union became desperate enough to attack, it would have had to attack with nuclear weapons. Of course the Soviet Union would lose any chance of a quick and clean nonnuclear victory, but that was only relevant if the Soviet Union attacked the Alliance by calculated choice rather than in desperation. It is possible, then, that the refusal of Alliance governments to keep larger nonnuclear forces throughout the Cold War era reflected an awareness, however unsystematic, of strategy's paradoxical logic: once again, more can be less.

Likewise, the vulnerability of the theater-range missiles and nuclear-strike aircraft of the Alliance was not necessarily a disadvantage; nor was their limited range, which was insufficient to reach deeply into the Soviet Union. As matters stood during the Cold War, the theater-range nuclear weapons of the Alliance were meant to deter by threatened punishment rather than denial, specifically to dissuade Soviet nuclear attacks against air bases, entry ports, command centers, and other military targets . . . including battlefield nuclear weapons. But they could not reach the most important Soviet cities, while Soviet theater-range weapons could reach all European cities. It followed that the Soviet Union could threaten European cities to dissuade the Alliance from using its own theater-range nuclear weapons to resist invasion, while the latter could not threaten the Soviet Union itself without a high risk of attracting a Soviet first strike against those theater-range nuclear weapons.

Only American intercontinental nuclear weapons had the range, protection, and numbers to destroy all Soviet cities even after absorbing the full impact of a first strike. And that counterthreat was the essence of the American nuclear guarantee to the European members of the Alliance: American cities were placed at risk by the threat against Soviet cities, in order to negate Soviet threats against European cities, meant in turn to dissuade the use of Alliance nuclear weapons against an invading Soviet army.

The fundamental bargain that sustained the Alliance was therefore the exchange of the European promise to resist Soviet military intimidation in peacetime and oppose invasion in wartime, for the American promise to share in the risks of nuclear war if it went beyond battlefield nuclear attacks. If the theater-range nuclear weapons of the Alliance were made strong enough to counter *all* Soviet nuclear threats, there would have been no need to rely on American intercontinental weapons, breaking the link between European and American survival. Once again, more would have been less, as the paradox dictates.

Asymmetrical Nuclear Suasion

In Korea, dissuasion is an almost mechanical application of potential military strength against a continuous threat of attack. But that is unusual. In most cases, there is no continuous threat to be averted but only a possibility, perhaps remote, of an eventual threat. That was certainly true of the central axis of the worldwide balance of military strength during the Cold War: the reciprocal striving for nuclear suasion of the Soviet Union and the United States. Images such as "two scorpions in a bottle" and the very idea of the "Balance of Terror" suggested that there were symmetrical threats to the respective populations. Actually it was asymmetry that characterized the Cold War. For the Soviet Union, the threat of an American nuclear attack could become a danger only in the event of a prior

Soviet attack, nonnuclear perhaps (an invasion of Europe) but not resistible by nonnuclear forces alone. For the United States, the threat of a Soviet nuclear attack could become a danger only in the event of a prior American nuclear attack against Soviet military targets, in the context of impending defeat in Europe.

Thus it was only in a second stage of nuclear war that attacks against cities would become an imminent danger, with American and European cities threatened by the Soviet Union in the attempt to dissuade the United States and the Alliance from launching further nuclear attacks against advancing Soviet military forces. This underlying asymmetry governed the interplay of implicit nuclear threats step by step. Because of their presumed nonnuclear weakness, it was the United States and its allies that were the first to threaten nuclear attack, although not against cities. And because of that, in turn, it was the Soviet Union, though devoted to the accumulation of operationally usable military power, that had to be the first to threaten nuclear attacks against American and European cities.

But it was the middle stage of reciprocal "counterforce" threats that was actually the engine of the American-Soviet nuclear competition. For the majority of their nuclear weapons were aimed at each other's nuclear weapons—and that was the function that drove the effort to increase missile accuracy. Once again there was no symmetry, and no "mindless" quest for supremacy, but rather the pursuit of substantive aims. The purpose of the Soviet counterforce threat to American nuclear weapons of intercontinental range was to dissuade their *selective* use, by threatening to destroy them en masse if any were employed at all. The Soviet aim was to deny all flexibility in the use of American nuclear forces of intercontinental range, in order to make them useless as purposeful instruments of war. (No Soviet counterforce attack could possibly leave the United States without enough functioning weapons to destroy Soviet cities.) The purpose of the American threat to Soviet nuclear weapons of intercontinental range was precisely to allow their selective use, by threatening to offset Soviet counterforce attacks by destroying Soviet weapons in turn.

In other words, it was to be able to use very few nuclear weapons that many were built. Were it not for the counterforce targeting requirements of each side, the intercontinental-range nuclear forces of the Soviet Union and the United States could not possibly have become as large as they became, with more than 20,000 warheads on both sides at the peak of the Cold War.[5] If the nuclear weapons themselves had been removed from the target lists of each side, there would have been no worthwhile targets at all for most of the intercontinental nuclear weapons acquired by each side.

The easy, unilateral American solution to the arms race was to renounce the use of intercontinental nuclear weapons—except to retaliate against a prior Soviet nuclear attack upon the United States by attacking (only) Soviet cities. With such a policy, the United States could have reduced the number of its intercontinental weapons quite drastically. Counting fifty city targets at most (enough to deter anyone), making a healthy allowance for weapons lost to a prior would-be disarming Soviet attack, and allowing for technical malfunctions, a maximum of, say, 500 nuclear warheads distributed for safety among bombers and missiles, both cruise and ballistic, both land-based and sea-based, would have sufficed. (Even as of this writing, with the Cold War only a memory, some 3,000 intercontinental nuclear weapons remain in the U.S. inventory.) Such an American policy of "no first use" would have undone decades of accumulation: out of more than 10,000 American intercontinental nuclear weapons deployed at the peak of the Cold War, all but 500 could have been dismantled. And there would have been no need to negotiate any agreement to obtain reciprocity, because most Soviet weapons would have been made unusable anyway since they would no longer have had any worthwhile targets.[6]

What prevented this ready solution was the very structure of the Cold War military balance, in which it was only the asymmetrical American threat to use nuclear weapons *selectively,* in response to a nonnuclear Soviet attack, that linked nuclear strength with nonnuclear, allowing the former to offset weakness in the latter. And it was the threat of selective use that embodied the vital connection between the United States and its European allies, to offset the natural, territorial proximity of the Soviet Union, which would otherwise have been decisive. The relatively few warheads involved thus had a significance that transcended their numbers, because they propelled the counterforce competition that finally resulted in huge nuclear inventories. But those few weapons could not be eliminated without severing the Alliance connection that both exposed the United States to nuclear danger and also made its nuclear strength relevant on the world scene.

During the Cold War, nuclear war was frequently imagined in just one of its possible forms, as a relentless escalation of move and countermove that would inevitably reach the ultimate stage of all-out attacks on the respective populations. In that extreme eventuality, the conditioning effect of the paradoxical logic would have been correspondingly extreme:

the full use of nuclear strength would have overshot the culminating point of utility so completely that the result would have evolved into a full reversal, with the most devastating attacks equivalent to no attack at all from the perspective of each attacker-victim. Had the destruction of all large population centers been carried out, neither side could have identified any benefit from the parallel catastrophe inflicted on the other, even if there were survivors interested in calculating the matter.

15

Harmony and Disharmony in War

We have recognized that there is no automatic harmony among the vertical levels of strategy, but we have yet to confront the full implications of disharmony. When a weapon is technically inefficient, tactically inadequate, of slight operational value, and ineffective at the level of theater strategy, we can safely predict what will happen at the conclusive level of grand strategy, where that particular weapon achieves its final effect. Subject to errors of assessment by others, and subject also to deliberate and successful deception, that weapon should add very little to the suasion that the armed forces as a whole can hope to evoke. And subject to all the contingencies of combat, that weapon could not do much to increase the chances of victory in war. It is just as obvious that an equally harmonious sequence of success level by level, can be expected to produce good results at the level of grand strategy, both for suasion and in war.

When first introduced at the end of the seventeenth century, even the humble bayonet made a significant difference, by finally allowing all foot soldiers to be equipped with firearms. Until then, each infantry force had to have a proportion of pikemen to hold back cavalry charges while the musketeers tended to the slow reloading of their weapons. For the French army, which was the first to use the new device in large numbers, the bayonet actually won battles at first because its infantry could have more firepower than equal numbers of enemy troops, as long as many of them were still armed with the pike. Although honored as the "puissant pike," that ancient weapon lacked a social group to defend it, as the Mamelukes of Egypt once saved their swords by resisting the introduction of firearms.

The bayonet was readily adopted because it required so little innovation—it was fully compatible with existing tactics and operational methods, as well as with the established regimental organization. Former pikemen could quickly be drilled to become musketeers, and the strain on supply was insignificant at a time when a hundred shots per man was ample allowance for an entire campaigning season. Therefore the technical advance was not contradicted or diminished at the higher levels of the vertical interaction, and its effect could be fully manifest at the level of grand strategy—until the bayonet was universally adopted and the initial French advantage was entirely lost.

In the twentieth century, the introduction of the British Chain Home network of early warning radar stations in time for the 1940 Battle of Britain had similar results. The task of air defense did not change at the level of theater strategy, and there was no difference at the tactical or operational levels either: with or without the radar detection of hostile aircraft, the fighter mission itself, the nature of combat maneuvers, and the teamwork of squadrons and groups were exactly the same. Once again, the technical innovation was unimpeded at the three higher levels of strategy, and once again its effect was fully manifest at the level of grand strategy, in the form of a *numerical* gain. Because they could be sent where and when they were needed on the basis of radar information, the fighters of the Royal Air Force did not have to patrol the skies in search of enemy intruders. The aircraft could remain on the ground until they were sent toward their targets by the radar-informed tracking room of Fighter Command. The Luftwaffe could be resisted in full force with all machines fueled and ready, and pilots as rested as prior combat would allow. Just as the number of French musketeers was effectively increased by the bayonet, so too the number of British fighters ready to fly intercepts was increased by radar, whose technical effect reached up to the level of grand strategy at full value.

But what about disharmony? We have already encountered its simple and conclusive form, that of achievement at one level totally negated at the next, as in the case of the French *mitrailleuse* of 1870, a significant technical innovation with its high rate of fire, whose effect was nullified at the tactical level. As a result of this extreme disharmony, the effect of that early machine gun was not perceptible at all at the level of grand strategy.

When weapons are really new, such total negation is not rare. Technical innovation and organizational change proceed at different rates, driven by different impulses, and it is easy enough for a fatal dissonance to persist between the two. For example, remotely piloted air vehicles (or unmanned air vehicles) for overhead observation were first introduced by the Israelis in the 1970s and used extensively by them in the 1982 Lebanon war. But because these vehicles did not belong to the established repertoire of ground forces—they are not tanks or guns—and were seen as competitive by air forces (they can displace piloted reconnaissance aircraft), there was no great enthusiasm for their adoption. The U.S. forces had very few in the Gulf war, and even in the Kosovo war only a handful were in service, mostly imported from Israel. The ability to monitor enemy forces continuously has revolutionary implications both tactically and operationally; costs are moderate, and there is no casualty exposure, but none of those advantages could overcome the bureaucratic aversion to new equipment that does not fit the established order of things.

Normally the effects of disharmony are more subtle and more measured, with no absolute negation but instead a complex interpenetration of failure and success. In our image of strategy, the waves and counterwaves of action and reaction at any one level can intrude on the levels above and below at the extremes of failure and success.

Interpenetrations

Consider a classic case of disharmony in recent military history, that of the German expeditionary force that fought in North Africa during the middle years of the Second World War. By the time Lieutenant General Erwin Rommel was sent to Tripoli, capital of Italian Libya in February 1941, at first with just one partly armored division, Hitler had decided that Egypt was not worth conquering and preparations for Barbarossa—the invasion of the Soviet Union—were far advanced.[1]

Accordingly, Rommel's task was strictly limited by the orders he received: he was to help the Italians resist the British offensive that was seemingly on the verge of expelling them from North Africa, but he was not to advance into Egypt. Even the reconquest of Cyrenaica, the huge eastern half of Libya, was not to be attempted until the autumn, if then.

Such restraining orders should hardly have been necessary. Rommel's force was much too small for offensive action; he himself had never been in North Africa before and had no experience whatever of desert warfare; and the German army was in any case wholly unprepared for that harsh environment, having neither the necessary equipment nor desert training.[2] Its vehicles did not have sand filters, and the Germans did not even know that a low-fat diet was essential to keep troops healthy in the torrid desert climate.[3] The German Army High Command (OKH) had already calculated that an offensive to conquer Egypt would require at least four armored divisions with commensurate air power. A force of that size could not be spared from Barbarossa, and in any case it could not be supplied by scarce motor transport across the vastness of Libya—the one and only road, the Via Balbia, followed the Mediterranean coast for more than a thousand miles from Tripoli to the Egyptian frontier.[4] Moreover, the sea route from Italian embarkation ports was precarious, with steady losses of shipping to British submarines as well as aircraft based in Malta. Finally, the handling capacity of the port at Tripoli was insufficient for the tonnage that would have been required.[5] OKH had done its sums and concluded that the conquest of Egypt was a logistic impossibility.

At the level of theater strategy, the British were in a vastly superior position. From west to east, the lands under their control extended across Egypt to Palestine, Transjordan, Iraq, and the Persian Gulf. From north to south, their control extended from Egypt and Sudan all the way across Africa to Capetown. British forces in North Africa, with their Indian, Australian, New Zealand, and South African contingents, were already much larger than any that Germany could possibly send, and they were much superior in quality to the Italian forces with Rommel.

The British advantage in supply was even greater, with a long but safe sea route around the Cape, secure access to ports at both ends of the Suez Canal, a good road and a railway from the canal to Cairo and Alexandria, well-equipped bases and workshops, and ample motor transport unaffected by fuel shortages. At the level of theater strategy, therefore, given his means nothing more could be expected from Rommel than a modest defensive effort.

Rommel arrived in Tripoli on February 12, 1941, with a small staff and the title of commander in chief of German troops in Libya.[6] Two days later, troopships brought the reconnaissance and the antitank battalion of the Fifth "Light" Division, some two thousand troops in all, with guns and armored cars but no tanks. In spite of the danger of air attack, Rommel ordered the ships to be unloaded overnight, under floodlights. The next day, February 15, the small German force paraded through the streets of Tripoli before driving directly to the east. The British had taken Benghazi, capital of the Cyrenaican half of Libya, 600 miles from Tripoli, and had advanced another 100 miles beyond it, but they showed no inclination to advance any further. (The Greek campaign was about to begin, and British units were being withdrawn for shipment to Greece.) Rommel could therefore have carried out his mission of defending Tripoli without attacking at all. He was supposed to wait for a second division, the Fifteenth Panzer, due in mid-May, before attempting an offensive, and even then he was not supposed to go beyond Agedabia, at the gates of Cyrenaica, without further orders.

Rommel did not obey OKH. Without waiting to stockpile supplies or organize his transport, without pausing to acclimatize the troops, Rommel drove his small force forward as fast as it could move. On February 26, 1941, when the Germans encountered the British for the first time in a minor skirmish, they were already 470 miles east of Tripoli. One week later, the only Panzer regiment of the Fifth Light arrived, with some fifty tanks in all. It too was paraded through the streets of Tripoli and sent directly to the east. One month later, on April 2, 1941, Rommel fought his first battle to seize Agedabia, 500 miles east of Tripoli, at the base of the great bulge of Cyrenaica held by British forces stretched out along the coastal road. From Agedabia, where he was supposed to stop, desert tracks cut across the base of the bulge to reach the coast next to the Egyptian frontier.

Acting directly against an order from Hitler himself, Rommel divided his already small one-division army.[7] One part pressed the retreating British forces along the interminable coastal road. A stronger outmaneuvering force in the meantime advanced across the base of the Cyrenaican bulge on rock-strewn camel paths to cut off the British retreat. Rommel led his troops in person, often riding in an open car at the head of the column. Two days later, on April 4, 1941, the Germans advancing along the coast entered Benghazi. By April 9, the outmaneuvering force had emerged from the desert to stand before Tobruk, the port of eastern Cyrenaica, by then the main British base, some 1,000 miles from Tripoli. At that point, Rommel was still supposed to be in Tripoli to await the arrival of his second division. To reach the coastal road and Tobruk so quickly, Rommel had driven his forces long past the breaking point of the embryonic supply lines that originated in Tripoli. His units had to obtain fuel by sending back scarce troop trucks for it or by capture; half of his tanks had broken down along the way, the men were so exhausted that they could hardly stay awake, and the entire force, very small to begin with, was scattered across the desert.

The Germans moved so fast and so far that all British forces in Cyrenaica west of Tobruk were outmaneuvered, cut off or forced into a panic retreat during which they left behind much more equipment than the Germans had to begin with, along with large quantities of food, fuel, and ammunition.[8] Again and again, small German teams of truck-borne infantry and artillery with a mere handful of tanks would emerge unexpectedly out of the desert to surprise and capture, destroy, or scatter British truck columns, artillery trains, and infantry units retreating along the coastal road. British armor units, though numerically superior, never seemed to be in the right place at the right time to assist the infantry and artillery; and they would fall prey to German antitank guns when trying to fight on their own without infantry or artillery support.[9] It is clear that Rommel's "follow me" method of command and his sheer dynamism conferred a huge operational-level advantage on the German forces. With Rommel leading them in person, the Germans could act and react much faster than the British, just as a better fighter pilot can turn inside the circle of a more sluggish opponent in a classic dogfight, to fire at his tail with impunity while his opponent is still trying to react to the turn.

Yet Rommel's headlong advance in the spring of 1941 did not end with victory in Cairo. Instead, it inaugurated almost two years of dramatic offensives and hurried withdrawals by one side and then the other, as each overshot its culminating point of success. Great as it was, the operational-level advantage of the Germans in North Africa could only diminish in part their extreme disadvantage at the level of theater strategy; it could not penetrate to the level of grand strategy to give them a decisive victory. The obvious reason is that for the Germans the entire North African campaign was a mere sideshow in a worldwide war. Its outcome was bound to be dominated by what would happen in the more central theaters of war: at the eastern front, where the Germans had almost a hundred times as many troops as in North Africa; in Western Europe after the June 1944 Normandy landings; in the Asian-Pacific theaters that detained additional American strength; in the North Atlantic theater, where the struggle between Allied shipping and German submarines would determine how much supply the Allies could have in Europe; and in the air theater over Germany, where the war of the bombers against industry was unfolding.

Vertical Success and Horizontal Failure

Actually all those military struggles in the "vertical" dimension that dominated the outcome of the fighting in North Africa were themselves dominated by Hitler's utter failure of statecraft in the horizontal dimension. Because his entire conduct united the strongest industrial powers of the world against Germany, Italy, and their distant Japanese ally, the defeat of Germany was virtually certain in spite of any number of battlefield victories. Having chosen the British Empire, the United States, and the Soviet Union as his enemies, and Italy, Slovakia, Croatia, Hungary, and Romania as his allies, Hitler had preordained his defeat. Only colossal success in the vertical dimension could have overcome the consequences of colossal error in the horizontal dimension. And that much military success was impossible because of Germany's inferiority in material resources—itself the most obvious consequence of its inferiority in the horizontal dimension.

In the confluence of both dimensions at the level of grand strategy, the early German and Japanese military successes in the vertical dimension did diminish at first the impact of fundamental weakness in the horizontal dimension. Specifically, the German occupation of much of Western Europe and of the western regions of the Soviet Union with their large industrial capacity, as well as the Japanese seizure of Malayan rubber and tin production and of oil in the Dutch East Indies, reduced the imbalance in material resources caused by the failure of German and Japanese statecraft. At the level of grand strategy, therefore, during the early years of the war the Axis advantage in the vertical dimension, derived from prewar preparations and superior competence, was reducing the huge Allied advantage in the horizontal dimension. In that regard, the successful cooperation of a conservative British government with Stalin's Soviet Union may be compared to Hitler's gratuitous declaration of war upon the United States after Pearl Harbor, and to Japan's own gross miscalculation that led to the attack on the American fleet when it was Southeast Asia that was Japan's actual objective.

Once the Allies mobilized their human and material resources in earnest, their superiority derived from success in the horizontal dimension began to condition the military struggles of the vertical dimension in one theater of war after another. With that, the Germans and Japanese could no longer achieve further gains at the level of grand strategy: their qualitative military superiority had become insufficient to offset numerical inferiority. At a later stage, the rising skill of Allied soldiers, sailors, and airmen, the emergence of competent military leaders, technological advancement, and the development of appropriate tactics and methods all deprived the Germans and Japanese even of their former superiority at the tactical and operational levels, in one form of war after another, in one theater after another.

With quality in their favor in addition to quantity, the Allies no longer lost in battle the advantages that they were obtaining from their superiority in the horizontal dimension. In the confluence of grand strategy, the result was the reoccupation of some lost territory, increasing damage to German and Japanese industries by bombing, and eventually the submarine interdiction of Japanese shipping routes. Thus the countries that had picked the wrong allies and made the wrong enemies to begin with, started to lose what they had earlier gained by the bold aggressions of 1939–1942, which exemplified their peculiar conjunction of military talent and incompetent statecraft. In the end, the final victories of 1945 were so absolute because of the mutually reinforcing effects of superiority in both dimensions: Axis forces increasingly outmatched technically, tactically, and operationally were also in sharp numerical decline within each theater of war, because of all their prior losses in the multiplicity of theaters that itself expressed their complete and continuing failure in the horizontal dimension.

Where was the logic of strategy in the outcome of 1945? After all, according to the paradoxical logic, the increasing weakness of the Germans and Japanese in the vertical dimension should actually have been advantageous to them in the horizontal dimension, to slow down or even interrupt their decline. As the Allies were progressing toward total victory in the major theaters of war, as the profile of the postwar distribution of power was beginning to emerge, the alliance was ripe for fragmentation. If the war simply continued on a straight path, it would eventually leave the British and Americans facing the Soviet Union in a new confrontation, in which each side would need the Germans and Japanese as allies.

Technically and industrially inferior, the Soviet Union needed German and Japanese industrial talents. For the British and Americans, it would be German and Japanese troops that would make all the difference in facing a continental power as rich in ground strength as the Soviet Union. And neither side could hope to have what it would need in the emerging postwar world if Germany and Japan were completely defeated and destroyed as major powers.

That was the opening that German and Japanese statecraft might have exploited, had the two regimes not previously followed paths so extreme that any accommodation with them was virtually ruled out. Had it not been for the effect upon American opinion of the traumatic Pearl Harbor attack, with all its sinister connotations that racism amplified; had it not been for the effect of all that the Nazis had done, the Germans and Japanese could have auctioned their remaining strength and future potential, to induce one side or the other to adopt them as allies. Such was the breakdown of statecraft in Berlin and Tokyo that the attempt was not even made, though Japan did succeed in remaining at peace with the Soviet Union until the very eve of its surrender.

Stalin, it appears, was convinced that the British would strive to persuade the more innocent Americans to secure an alliance with Nazi Germany before its defeat became complete, making German support against the Soviet Union useless. From Stalin's point of view, it was simply illogical for the British and Americans to reach the forthcoming postwar confrontation without securing the valuable alliance they could so easily obtain. He himself had been preparing for the new postwar struggle since 1943, and had already overlooked Nazi crimes easily enough to make a profitable alliance with Germany in 1939. Stalin therefore assumed that the British and Americans would do what he would have done in their place, probably behind the fig leaf of a new German military government that would remove Hitler while continuing the war—but only against the Soviet Union. That is why news of the abortive military coup against Hitler of July 20, 1944, merely aroused Soviet suspicions, as did any British or American contacts with German officers (which did eventually take place during the last weeks of war, in conjunction with localized surrender negotiations.)*

Stalin was wrong in his suspicions of the British and Americans but perfectly right in his conscious understanding of the logic of strategy. The American alliance with the Germans and Japanese did materialize just as he (and Hitler in his final days) had expected, though only after the war had ended, and the political character of the new partners had entirely changed. During the war itself, however, the alliance-breaking tendency manifest in the horizontal dimension was willfully resisted, so that no contrary force intervened to impede the Axis defeat, eventually fully accomplished in the vertical dimension of each form of war, in every major theater of war.

---

* After being informed by the *British* of the American negotiations in Berne with commanders of the German forces in Italy intent on surrender, the Soviet government vehemently denounced the talks as an anti-Soviet conspiracy in a note of March 22, 1945, to the British ambassador in Moscow. In a message of April 3, 1945, to Roosevelt, Stalin wrote, "I also cannot understand the silence of the British . . . although it is known that the initiative in this whole affair with the negotiations in Berne belongs to the British."

The Limits of Interpenetration

It follows that if Rommel had won his own fight in North Africa, he would merely have shared the fate of the unchallenged German garrisons in the Channel Islands, Denmark, and Norway, which had to surrender anyway on May 7, 1945. But of course Rommel did not win his own fight. Great as it was, the operational-level superiority of the German forces over the British did not fully overcome the conditioning effect of the spatial factors at the level of theater strategy. One must look beyond North Africa to recognize the magnitude of the inferiority against which the Germans were striving. We may speculate that if Rommel had received larger forces, and if they had been properly supplied, he might have reached his own ultimate objectives, Cairo and the Suez Canal, some fifteen hundred miles from Tripoli. That would have been a great victory indeed for a general whose talents did not extend beyond the operational level and who obviously did not comprehend theater strategy at all.[10] But that would still have been only a battle victory, or rather the result of several battle victories, not a campaign victory—for the campaign would not have ended.

Had Rommel reached Cairo and the Suez Canal, the British would have continued to fight, no doubt forming a new front south of Cairo from bases in Upper Egypt and the Sudan, and another new front on the Sinai edge of the Suez Canal, from bases in Palestine and Transjordan, with resupply for both fronts by way of the Red Sea. If left alone, the British would have developed bases, workshops, field hospitals, roads, rail lines, and ports with American assistance, to accumulate reinforcements for an eventual reconquest. Unable to force a British surrender, which could be obtained only in London and not in Cairo, the Germans would then have had to choose between waiting passively as the British buildup increasingly threatened their hold on Egypt and launching further offensives, to capture the base areas in which the British counteroffensive was being prepared. Further epic conquests of Upper Egypt and Sinai would have made Rommel even more famous than he is, but so long as London did not surrender, a campaign victory would still have eluded him. Just as they did when the loss of Malaya, Singapore, and Burma to the Japanese threw them right out of Southeast Asia into India, the British would have continued to fight, resisting in the vast deserts of Transjordan as well as in Syria, and also in the vaster expanse of Sudan, with supply to their eastern front by way of the Persian Gulf and Iraq, and supply to their southern front by way of the Cape and East Africa. As before, the British would have started to accumulate reinforcements, eventually going over to the offensive, just as they reinforced in India after 1942 and then set out to reconquer Burma in 1944, on their way to Malaya and Singapore (whose impending reconquest was made unnecessary by Japan's surrender).

With their forces by then stretched out across a huge area from Libya to Transjordan and down into the Sudan, the Germans would once again have been faced with the choice between indefinite fighting on two fronts against an enemy of growing strength and another round of offensives to advance into the space from which the British continued to threaten all their conquests. So long as the campaign did not end, everything from Tripoli onward would still be at stake and could be held only by more fighting—which had to be offensive fighting for the Germans, swimming as they were against the tidal wave of material strength coming upon them, the result of their fundamental failure in the horizontal dimension of statecraft. Ultimately Rommel would have had to advance through East Africa all the way to Capetown, and also eastward beyond Iraq and across Iran to conquer the whole immensity of India, in order truly to win his campaign. Only then would there be no more open fronts for the British to fight from. Unless they were totally expelled from Africa and squeezed out of India by a German advance to meet the Japanese on the Burmese frontier, the British would have continued to challenge all previous conquests, still with faraway Tripoli as their final objective.

When Rommel was at the very peak of his success well inside Egypt in the late summer fighting of 1942, and the German summer offensive in Russia had reached the Caucasus, while the Japanese seemed on the verge of invading India, there were in fact fears of a concerted Axis offensive on a scale more than Napoleonic, to achieve a link between German and Japanese forces somewhere between Iran and India. As we now know, the Germans and Japanese had no such plan, or indeed any other plan of concerted action, fighting as they did as cobelligerents rather than as allies in the full sense. As we also know, all three offensives had already exceeded their culminating point of success: what was actually to be found at the spearheads of those spectacular advances of 1942 were Rommel's badly outnumbered tanks running out of fuel, a thin wedge of German infantry stalled in the Caucasian mountains, and starving Japanese troops at the end of badly overstretched supply lines.

But even if there had been real strength in those offensives, even if they had somehow been supplied to advance much farther than they did, even if India had been conquered from either side, the major war effort of the Allies would have continued essentially undiminished. No matter how enormous in scale, the entire war from Tripoli to India would still have been a mere sideshow. To be sure, much would have been lost to the Allies: the manpower of the Indian army, whose well-drilled regiments added significantly to British strength outside India as well; the more dubious contribution of the Chinese army against the Japanese; the oil of Iraq and Iran, insofar as the tanker shortage allowed it to be used outside the Middle East (the Germans could hardly have used much of it themselves); and the rising though still small war production of India itself. Still, most of what the Middle East and India added to Allied resources was consumed locally, while both required strength from the outside to defend them. Therefore the overall balance of forces and resources for the main Allied efforts against Germany and Japan would not have worsened by much and may even have improved.

In accordance with the paradoxical logic, failure at the theater level can become net gain at the level of grand strategy—as long as defeat is not too costly in forces lost in the process—whenever efforts are being expended on secondary theaters that cannot yield victory anyway. That was true for both sides during the Second World War, as in any war, but more so for Germany and Japan than for the Allies, owing to the fundamental asymmetry in their situations at the level of grand strategy.

Victory and Defeat in Two Dimensions

Because of their great superiority in war resources, the Allies could benefit from any military encounter that reduced German and Japanese military strength, even if their own losses were higher—as long as the loss ratio did not exceed the overall ratio of their superiority (or, more precisely, as long as Allied losses did not reduce the gap in the respective growth rates of their armed strength). For example, at a time when Germany was producing, say, five hundred fighter aircraft and pilots per month while British and American fighter production destined for the European theater was three times larger, even the loss of three Allied fighters for every two German fighters shot down would eventually accumulate to yield victory. For the Allies, moreover, such attrition could be profitable anywhere: there are no sideshows in attrition.

It was nevertheless undesirable for the Allies to divert efforts from the main theaters. To do so would not make victory less certain, because cumulative attrition could proceed anyway, but it would slow down the Allied progress toward victory simply because it was not in secondary theaters that enemy forces could be encountered in the greatest numbers. Further, it was only in the most important theaters of all, the German and Japanese homelands, that military strength in the vertical dimension of strategy could be applied to intensify German and Japanese weakness in the horizontal dimension, by blockade and by bombing industry and infrastructures.

The Germans and Japanese were in a very different situation. Military victories, that is, successes in the vertical dimension, could help them to win the war only if those victories could reshape the horizontal dimension as well. The defeat of Allied forces in battle, as happened again and again during the early years of the war, was not enough. It did not diminish the central Allied advantage in the horizontal dimension: their superior ability to generate trained men and equipment for their fighting forces.*

The Axis powers could finally benefit from military success only when it could serve as a substitute for statecraft, by undoing the alliances ranged against them. This in fact did happen, when Germany totally defeated Poland, Belgium, and France, forcing them out of the war altogether, thus greatly improving the German situation in the horizontal dimension. No such vertically induced gains in the German position could possibly be achieved in North Africa, which contained neither allies that could be totally overrun nor war resources of any value.

The German Army High Command was therefore quite correct in opposing Rommel's adventure in Egypt. Though Hitler overruled his generals as he often did, otherwise, he sent only small forces to Rommel, appreciating his exploits mainly for their publicity value: the dashing general in the romantic desert made for excellent copy, especially in contrast to news from the Russian front, sinister even in victory.[11]

Rommel's advance into Egypt could serve no greater purpose. Nor did it help that the effort to defeat him absorbed disproportionately large British forces—the British had no main theater of war in 1941 and 1942, while the Germans did from June 22, 1941, a few weeks after Rommel's arrival in Tripoli. It was only on the Russian front that Germany could have

---

* To win by battle victories alone, the Germans and Japanese would have had to inflict more and more losses as time went on, to overtake the increasing capacity of the Allies to field new forces. Britain and the Soviet Union did not reach their maximum force-generating capacity until 1943, while the United States never reached its limit at all. And of course the German and Japanese ability to inflict losses was already in decline by 1943.

achieved definitive results at the level of grand strategy. By fighting the Soviet Union, the Germans did have at least a possibility of victory, since vertical success could have horizontal consequences in that theater: any German conquest of inhabitants and resources would diminish the Soviet Union just as if an ally were being detached by diplomacy, and it could simultaneously enhance Germany just as if an ally had been gained, to the extent that people and resources could be harnessed to the German war effort. A total conquest of the Soviet Union would have eliminated the consequences of Hitler's greatest failure of statecraft, enabling Germany to cope with the additional failure of statecraft represented by the American entry into the war alongside Britain.

While the German investment in North Africa was at least kept quite small, imperial Japan compounded fundamental failure in the horizontal dimension—a failure of intelligence in every sense—by dissipating its military strength in secondary theaters. After the Pearl Harbor attack, the Japanese occupied Malaya, Singapore, and the Dutch East Indies, achieving solid gains in the horizontal dimension. Though there were no Allies to defeat and detach in those countries, there were important resources: the rubber, tin, and palm oil of Malaya and, above all, the petroleum of the Dutch East Indies. As for the conquest of the Philippines, accomplished as it was with small forces, it too was well justified to drive the Americans away from the Western Pacific; those islands could have provided airfields for heavy bombers to attack Japan from the first, as well as a staging base for a broader counteroffensive in due course. But the invasion of Burma that followed, the island seizures in the South Pacific, the attempt to conquer New Guinea, and the continued war in China were all vast diversions of effort from the one and only theater where in theory the Japanese could have won the war: the United States itself.

Having done for the Americans what the Americans could not do for themselves, by resolving their deep differences and forcing them to fight, the Japanese could have overcome this huge failure of statecraft only by invading the United States. To convert their temporary naval-air superiority demonstrated at Pearl Harbor into a conclusive victory at the level of grand strategy, the Japanese had to incapacitate American military strength at its source, because it was bound to grow far beyond their own. It was not in China, Burma, the South Pacific, or New Guinea that the Japanese could strangle American mobilization. The one campaign that could have secured victory for them would have been an invasion of California, followed by the conquest of the major centers of American life, culminating in an imposed peace dictated in Washington. To be sure, the forces of imperial Japan, even if pulled back from China and everywhere else, could never have been successful in conquering the United States, if only for logistic reasons, and of course no such invasion was even contemplated. Yet there was no other way of winning the war.

It follows that the *only* good Japanese option immediately after Pearl Harbor was to sue for peace, bargaining away Japan's ability to resist eventual defeat for some years in exchange for whatever indulgence the United States would offer to avoid having to fight for its victory. In the final negotiations before Pearl Harbor, the Roosevelt administration had asked a great deal from imperial Japan, including the withdrawal of its forces from China and also from French Indochina. After Pearl Harbor, the United States would undoubtedly have demanded more, perhaps Japan's withdrawal from its new colony of Manchuria and very likely from the older colony of Korea as well, if not Taiwan. Moreover, having discovered how effective the Japanese armed forces could be, the Americans would have insisted on a partial disarmament at least. To accept all that immediately after splendid combat success would have been impossible psychologically and politically, yet it was the only way of saving Japan from certain and total defeat.

That logic measures the true strategic value of the tremendous tactical and operational success of the Pearl Harbor attack: it was pure loss. Japan would have been far better off if all its pilots had lost their way over the Pacific or missed their mark. Had Japanese naval aviators achieved a pleasing comical effect in failing to inflict any damage, the Americans would have been all the more generous in the subsequent peace settlement. At the level of grand strategy, the confluence of the vertical dimension with the horizontal dimension was so adverse for Japan that tactical and operational success at Pearl Harbor was actually much worse than failure would have been.

The case is far from unique. Tactical achievements can easily become counterproductive at the level of grand strategy. All that is needed to make more into less is a sufficient disharmony between the two dimensions. If, for example, the diplomatic and propaganda effects of a bombing campaign are adverse, more bombing is worse than less bombing, and destructive bombing is worse than ineffectual bombing.

If there is a severe disharmony between the different levels of the vertical dimension, then military actions simply fail. But when there is disharmony between the two dimensions, vertical success can be worse than failure.

Because imperial Japan was defeated to begin with, once it failed to march on Washington immediately after Pearl Harbor, there were no genuinely decisive battles in the Pacific war. The only difference that the naval and ground battles of the Coral Sea, Midway, New Guinea, and Guadalcanal could make was to change the speed of Japan's decline toward complete defeat. None of those battles, dramatic as they were, could be decisive at the level of grand strategy because none of them could have changed the outcome of the war, as some of the German-Soviet battles on the eastern front could have done. Even a complete victory of the Japanese navy in the 1942 battle of Midway could only have had a temporary result: had American aircraft carriers been destroyed instead of the Japanese, those losses would not have deprived the United States of the naval supremacy that ships and aircraft in production and personnel in training would have ensured in any case by 1944. And had the Japanese defeat at Midway been even greater than it was, that too could only have accelerated an outcome that was inevitable in any case, once the fully mobilized military forces of the United States arrived on the scene.

The Rewards of Harmony

The North Vietnamese, who did not have to live down a counterproductive initial military exploit like Pearl Harbor, won their war by modest military achievements in the vertical dimension, coupled with highly effective propaganda and diplomacy in the horizontal dimension. They could never have won by succeeding in the vertical dimension alone, even though they were adequate at the tactical and operational levels, and only slightly inferior at the level of theater strategy.* As for the technical level, the elusive Vietnamese style of war diminished its importance for both sides, in spite of the peculiar American enthusiasm for anything technical, especially if new and somehow advanced. Once the United States intervened, the North Vietnamese could no longer win by accumulating tactical victories because Vietnam ceased to be the main theater of the war—it was only the scene of the fighting. The strength ranged against the North

* The ability of the North Vietnamese to redeploy their forces on foot from one end of Vietnam to the other was mechanically much inferior to the American-South Vietnamese ability to do so by road transport, air, and sea. But elusiveness gave them the initiative at each remove, so that they were not inferior in their ability to concentrate forces for any one engagement. Their ability to reinforce an ongoing engagement was vastly inferior, to be sure, but in their style of war, prepared engagements were followed by dispersal.

Vietnamese was coming from a quite different theater, the United States itself, source of equipment and supplies for the South Vietnamese from start to finish, as well as of all American military forces that operated in Vietnam between 1966 and 1972. Even if the North Vietnamese could have defeated every single force sent against them, victories in the vertical dimension alone would only have enabled them to resist until the arrival of yet more forces, eventually to lose.

Nor could the North Vietnamese interdict the flow of American strength across the Pacific. They had no submarines or aircraft that could operate over the open ocean, while their ground strength in Vietnam itself did not suffice to seize and close South Vietnam's ports and airfields until the very end of the war. Still less could North Vietnam have applied strength in the vertical dimension against the United States itself: while the Americans bombed North Vietnam whenever they chose to do so, the North Vietnamese could not bomb or otherwise attack the United States—it was simply too far away for them. But their diplomacy and propaganda had unlimited strategic reach: they started off by damaging American relations with major allies in Europe, before reaching into the United States itself, with powerful consequences.

Without ever defeating any large body of American troops in battle, without coming close to exhausting American material strength, the North Vietnamese won by successfully exploiting diplomacy and propaganda to fragment the American political consensus that sustained the war effort, first to induce the withdrawal of American forces, and then to bring about a drastic decline in the flow of equipment and supplies to South Vietnam. Military achievement was indispensable for the North Vietnamese, not to win battles that were bound to be inconclusive anyway, but simply to prolong the war, creating the conditions in which diplomacy and propaganda could be successful.

As the example of North Vietnam's victory shows, in the confluence of grand strategy even modest achievement in the vertical dimension can be sufficient to yield victory, if it is harmoniously combined with success in the horizontal dimension. That is the counterpart of the impossibility of winning in either the vertical or the horizontal dimension alone (as Mussolini tried to do with diplomacy, propaganda, and no real military strength). The success of Anwar Sadat's October 1973 war against Israel is an even sharper demonstration of the principle.

The Egyptians recognized that they could not win by straightforward military action alone. They could reasonably hope to cross the Suez Canal, overcoming its tiny garrison of some four hundred and fifty troops, but they knew that they could not defeat the Israeli army in the Sinai, to then impose a settlement or simply proceed to invade Israel itself. The deployed forces of the Egyptian army were much larger than the active-duty standing forces of the Israelis. But when the Israelis mobilized their reservists, they could field as many as seven divisions and could send enough of them to the Sinai to defeat the eight Egyptian divisions, given Israeli superiority in air power and in armor-mobile combat at the operational level.[12] In other words, Egypt could not do much in the vertical dimension of strategy.

By contrast, in the horizontal dimension, the international situation was potentially favorable for Egypt in 1973. The United States had just disengaged from Vietnam and was in no mood to wage war anywhere else. The Soviet Union was far more inclined to be active, to claim in the reality of world politics the "strategic parity" that the United States had recently conceded in the 1972 Strategic Arms Limitation accords. Beyond that imbalance, there was the "oil weapon." With falling production within the United States and other sources scant, the Arab oil exporters of the Persian Gulf and North Africa had become the price-setting marginal suppliers. Rising worldwide demand for oil was beginning to drive up prices, but they were still contained by long-term supply contracts and established profit-sharing arrangements between rulers and oil companies. Only a dramatic reduction in exports could release the new market power of the Arab oil producers, to set a new price plateau well above the traditional U.S.\$ 1.80 per barrel. When Sadat asked them to impose an embargo on all countries friendly to Israel, the Arab oil producers were more than happy to comply—instead of having to sacrifice for the sake of Arab solidarity, they could serve the cause very profitably indeed.

Israel, by contrast, was in a weak position diplomatically. It had neither oil nor any other source of wealth. In the United Nations, it was isolated in facing the huge Arab, Muslim, and communist voting blocs, to which the African states added their votes in the hope of rewards from the Arab oil producers. In Europe, Israel was criticized for being uncooperative in resolving the conflict with Egypt to reopen the Suez Canal, and the lure of Arab export markets also played its part in isolating Israel.

Strength in the vertical dimension may yield little benefit in adverse circumstances as we have seen, but *potential* strength in the horizontal dimension may yield no benefit at all. True, even if Egypt had done nothing, rising diplomatic pressures might eventually have induced the Israelis to give up conquered territory without the peace treaty they demanded in exchange. And the sheer passage of time would have increased American as well as European and Japanese dependence on Arab oil, further increasing diplomatic pressure on Israel in the long run. Those, however, were processes both prolonged and also uncertain: if the United States reverted to activism after overcoming its trauma of Vietnam, while the Soviet Union became distracted by its own difficulties, the Arab producers would not brave the consequences of imposing an embargo on Egypt's behalf. Nor would their control over the oil market endure forever.

Only military action could activate Egypt's potential strength in the horizontal dimension. That was not industrial strength as with the Allies in the Second World War but rather diplomatic strength—the ability to use the strengths of others, both the Soviet Union's weight in world affairs and the Arab "oil weapon." Yet, as we have seen, the Egyptians could not actually win a war, and they knew it. But they did not need a total victory to activate diplomatic pressures on Israel; in fact, if the Egyptians could have marched all the way to Tel Aviv they would not have needed diplomatic support in the first place. But they could not hope to interest the Soviet Union and the United States without some fairly major military action; commando raids and artillery shelling were not enough. Only a crossing of the Suez Canal could do it, and not an overnight affair either, since that would be followed by an Israeli counterattack that might force the Egyptians back in humiliating fashion. Sadat needed an actual battle victory, even if it would not develop into a campaign victory at the theater level.

The Suez Canal, a hundred yards of still water, was not itself a serious obstacle. In any case, the Israelis no longer manned their canal-side fortifications, having switched to an armor-mobile defense based on the prompt deployment of a reinforced tank division against any attempted crossing. As always, they also relied heavily on their air power.[13] The Egyptians could therefore cross the canal easily enough, but that would not solve their immediate problem of coping with counterattacking Israeli tanks. Still less could they hope to resist the full force of the Israeli army once it mobilized its reserve forces, within three or days of a canal crossing. In the meantime, the Israeli air force, which Egyptian fighters could not successfully engage in air combat, would systematically attack Egyptian forces on both sides of the canal.

The Egyptian plan that solved these seemingly insoluble problems is a model of its kind because of the harmony it achieved both within the vertical and the horizontal dimensions and also between them.

In the horizontal dimension, one important element was diplomatic: the Syrian military dictatorship with which Egypt's relations were far from close, was nevertheless persuaded to launch a simultaneous offensive. Israel would therefore have to divert some of its forces to the Golan Heights instead of the Sinai front. In the event, two of the five reserve tank divisions were sent to fight the Syrians during the first week of the war.

An equally important element of the plan in the horizontal dimension combined propaganda and deception to achieve total surprise for the planned offensive. The massing of Egyptian forces and bridging equipment near the canal could not be concealed, but the Israelis were successfully persuaded that it was all done for an armywide exercise, as often before. The Israelis did not receive a clear indication that an offensive was imminent until the early morning of October 6, 1973. They did not overcome residual doubts and send out mobilization orders until 9:20 A.M. Some armies require weeks to recall civilians, fit them out, and form up their units for combat. The Israelis were able to do it in twenty-four hours or less, and complete armored brigades could reach the Sinai front in one more day. But by 9.20 A.M. on October 6 they had less than five hours left before the outbreak of war.

According to the standard theory, surprise is achieved when "signals" conveying true information are masked by "noise"—the greater mass of outdated, erroneous, and deceptive information; a variant stresses the importance of deliberate deception.[14] But there may be a deeper truth in the matter: deception deceives when there is a strong predisposition to self-deception. By October 6, 1973, Israeli Intelligence had been monitoring the Egyptian buildup in front of the canal for several months, just as Stalin had closely followed German preparations for the surprise attack of June 22, 1941, and U.S. officials knew that Japan would attack *somewhere* long before the Pearl Harbor attack of December 7, 1941.

But the Israelis did not attack to disrupt Egyptian preparations. There was a cease-fire in effect, the population was enjoying its tranquillity, and Israel's diplomatic position was weak: an attack would have provoked vehement criticism and perhaps substantive penalties. In the circumstances, only the certainty that an Egyptian offensive was imminent could have persuaded the Israeli government to order a preemptive attack.[15]

When an enemy is allowed, for whatever reasons, to build up his readiness to attack, appropriate excuses invariably emerge to justify inaction. For the Israelis in 1973, it was that Sadat was only bluffing, as he had bluffed before. For Stalin in 1941, it was that Hitler would issue an ultimatum and make territorial demands before launching an attack—which Stalin would avert by accepting Hitler's demands, even surrendering the Ukraine if necessary (that way, it would be the British and eventually the Americans who would have to pay the price of defeating Hitler). For Roosevelt in December 1941, inaction was justified by the conscious calculation that war had to be started by the Japanese to unify the country—though of course he did not expect an attack on the U.S. fleet at Pearl Harbor.

But there is more to it than that. When true warnings are *not* ignored because of political inhibitions or suppressed by misleading theories, they become false warnings after the fact. This too is one of strategy's reversals. If the Israelis could have placed a microphone in Sadat's desk to actually overhear his orders to launch the offensive of October 6, 1973, if they had therefore mobilized their reserves to send three or four divisions to the front, Sadat would have had to cancel his offensive. So nothing would have happened on October 6, 1973, converting the true warning into false information. In the aftermath, the source might be validated nonetheless, but it is more likely to be discredited as deceptive (it is standard procedure to "turn around" detected listening devices). Next time, the surprise could succeed *because* it had once failed.

Sadat's prudent planners did not believe that their forces would be able to withstand a full-scale counteroffensive once the delayed Israeli mobilization was completed, even if part of the Israeli army was diverted to the Syrian front. For that seemingly insurmountable problem yet another horizontal-dimension solution was found: after several days of fighting, once the "oil weapon" and Soviet diplomatic support were both activated and the United States was duly alarmed, Egypt would obtain an imposed cease-fire in the Security Council of the United Nations, to freeze the post–October 6 lines and secure its gains.

Even with the mobilization of Israeli reserve forces delayed by surprise, the Egyptians still had to face from the start both Israeli air power and the two hundred or so Israeli tanks of the canal garrison. They were few, but the Egyptians had bitter memories of what fast-moving, fast-thinking Israeli armored forces could do to their rigidly-by-the-numbers army. The harmony of the dimensions would not help; the Egyptians had to find a military solution in the vertical dimension alone.

Sadat's planners successfully overcame that challenge too, in a carefully coordinated multilevel response. The most obvious remedy was the deployment of many antitank and antiaircraft weapons, a technical-level solution. Specialized antitank infantry teams equipped with both hand-held rockets and portable wire-guided missiles were added to each standard unit, while the Egyptians followed the Soviet model in elevating their air-defense forces into a separate service and also supplied many portable antiaircraft missiles to the infantry. As it happened, the antiaircraft missiles were much more successful than expected, and the antitank weapons also outperformed expectations, at least at the beginning of the war.

Still the weapons themselves were not enough. The Egyptians also had a tactical-level response for counterattacking Israeli tanks, the most immediate threat they faced. Tank-hunting teams of foot soldiers with hand-held rockets were assigned to attack Israeli tanks in their reverse-slope firing positions, to exploit their lack of infantry escorts for close-in defense. In the event, Israeli tanks were late in moving into their positions, so that the Egyptian teams found themselves ambushing arriving tanks in conditions even more favorable than expected.

More important still was the operational-level solution, aimed at Israeli air power as well as armor. Contrary to the textbook prescription that calls for mostly armored forces in river-crossing offensives (a great Soviet specialty), the Egyptians sent foot and motorized infantry across the canal rather than tank units. By so doing, Sadat's planners hoped to deprive the Israeli tanks of the best targets for their guns and to dilute the effect of Israeli air strikes. In the event, Israeli tanks were reduced to firing at infantry with their scarce armor-piercing rounds, after quickly running out of both high-explosive shells and machine-gun ammunition. As for Israeli fighter bombers, instead of being able to attack well-delineated armored vehicles, they found themselves under constant threat from missiles while wasting their bombs on dispersed infantry.

The dilution of Israeli strength was compounded at the level of theater strategy because the Egyptians did not concentrate their effort in textbook fashion but instead crossed at many points all along the seventy miles of the Suez Canal. The Israeli air force, already facing amorphous infantry forces it could hardly bomb usefully, could not therefore be efficient in attacking the crossing medium either: instead of a few major bridges, easily seen, easily destroyed, and hard to repair, its pilots had to attack a great number of light pontoon bridges whose damaged sections could be replaced in minutes, as well as a large traffic of boats and amphibious vehicles hardly worth bombing at all.

The opening of Sadat's offensive went off exactly as planned, a rare occurrence in military history. The crossing of the Suez Canal was duly accomplished in a few hours on October 6, 1973, and the Egyptian forces resisted quite easily both the counterattacking Israeli tanks and the Israeli air force, whose fighters were harried by large numbers of antiaircraft missiles. On the rising curve of their success, the Egyptians defeated the first arrivals of mobilized Israeli reserve forces on October 8.[16]

By then the "oil weapon" was already being activated as one Arab producer after another stopped tanker loadings, the United States was duly alarmed, and the Soviet Union started to play its appointed role, denouncing Israeli aggression and asking for an Israeli withdrawal from the entire Sinai.

But having achieved much success, the Egyptians who had resisted both tanks and aircraft could not resist temptation. Instead of seeking a cease-fire-in-place to hold his gains, as urged by the Syrians (already hard-pressed after brief success), Sadat risked the fortunes of war by exceeding the prudent limits of the initial plan. On October 14 the Egyptian army launched an armored offensive into the Sinai, attempting to fight a war of maneuver beyond its competence, overshooting its culminating point of success. Many Egyptian tanks were destroyed, while Israeli losses were insignificant. The defeat of the offensive marked the turning point of the campaign. On the following night, the Israelis reached and started crossing the Suez Canal through a gap between the Egyptian forces, boldly sending an expanding torrent of armor that rolled out behind the Egyptian forces on the Sinai side. Many Egyptian antiaircraft missile sites were overrun, allowing the Israeli air force to operate far more effectively than before. Within a week, the Egyptians were reduced to pleading for a cease-fire-in-place that left an important part of their army surrounded, while the Israelis had reached within seventy miles of Cairo. It was a splendid feat of arms but only an operational-level victory, not a victory of grand strategy, because the Israelis could not advance to occupy Cairo and impose a peace on their terms. The Soviet Union was threatening to intervene, the United States demanded a cease-fire, and in any case the Israelis had neither the strength nor the will to conquer Egypt.

Instead it was Sadat who achieved a definite if strictly limited victory at the level of grand strategy, formally recognized by all in the 1974 "disengagement" agreement that left Egypt in control of both banks of the Suez Canal. Egypt's diplomatic superiority—derived from its alliance with the oil producers, Soviet support, and American interest in becoming its new patron—had prevailed over Israeli military superiority. The Israelis had survived initial failure to win impressive victories, but once again achievements in the vertical dimension alone could not overcome weakness in the horizontal dimension. Such contradictions are far more common than the coupling of superiority in both dimensions of the 1991 Gulf war and the 1999 Kosovo war, both conducted by the United States with many allies against isolated enemies.

When vast military superiority is combined with vast diplomatic superiority, there is no room for doubt about the outcome, and not much room for strategy either. The bombing of both Iraq in 1991 and Serbia in 1999 was largely one-sided combat against enemies that could hardly react. It was a management challenge more than an act of war, for the enemy largely functioned as an inert set of targets, feebly defended by small-caliber antiaircraft guns and uncoordinated missile batteries. Of the Kosovo war it might be said that it would have been better if packaging and handling costs had been saved by having the aerospace contractors deliver their cruise missiles directly on target.

If the enemy cannot react, the paradoxical logic loses its impulse—but not entirely. It emerged sufficiently to save both Saddam Hussein and Slobodan Milosevic: precisely because the United States was much too strong to be threatened by either Iraq or Serbia, it did not have the moral energy to risk the casualties of removing them from power by conquest. Both continued to preside unmolested over the countries their recklessness had ruined, Milosevic till removed by domestic revolution, Saddam Hussein till now.

16

Can Strategy Be Useful?

My purpose has been to uncover the workings of the paradoxical logic in its five levels and two dimensions, offering a general theory of strategy in the process. Readers may find that it explains the twists and turns of history more persuasively and with fewer discrepancies than mere common sense, though of course the only real test of any theory is its ability to predict, given enough information. The one thing that no theory can do is to prescribe what should be done, for that depends on values and goals. I leave the derivation of rules of conduct, practical schemes of action, and complete grand strategies to those who have powers of decision in a specific time and place. Theory can only suggest how their decisions should be made: not by narrowing down complex realities to identify simple choices and ''best'' answers for each separate problem, but rather by comprehending all five levels in both dimensions, to find solutions that achieve a tolerable harmony among them all. Then mere adequacy is enough to prevail, without need of superlative strengths or skills. The greatest captains of military history, from Alexander the Great to Napoleon and beyond, were all defeated by less famous enemies, just as the brilliant Rommel was defeated by the infinitely mediocre Montgomery.

Yet there are serious reasons to be cautious in applying even that much wisdom. To begin with, there is the sheer complexity of the required harmonization. It makes even the choice of a single weapon into an elaborate undertaking. Cost calculations and technical tests, themselves already quite elaborate, no longer suffice. The weapon has to be evaluated at the tactical level also, to examine how it would be employed initially, then to anticipate enemy reactions, and finally to determine its net value in the aftermath. And this is only the prelude to analysis at the operational level, and next at the level of theater strategy—perhaps to be repeated for each separate theater of interest. If a new weapon is important enough, because of novel characteristics, dramatic aspect, or magnitude of effects, the likely reactions by allies and enemies alike in the horizontal dimension must also be evaluated before the definitive decision to acquire it can be made at the level of grand strategy. That applies for example to the proposed deployment of "thin" ballistic-missile defenses to guard against attacks by rogue states that acquire a few ballistic missiles or contrive their own. Will a U.S. deployment set off a new arms race with the Russian Federation or even China, not the intended targets at all? Will it induce rogue states to place their nuclear weapons or biological agents in suitcases for hand delivery—a threat much harder to control even for their own purposes? Will it separate a protected United States from unprotected allies, or to the contrary, will it reassure them because a protected United States could be more steadfast on their behalf? Only when those questions are answered is it worthwhile to call in the engineers to find out how effective ballistic-missile defenses could be and the bookkeepers to find out the cost.

All such calculations are already supposed to be included in the decision process. Yet there is a wide gap between current practices and the full iteration through levels and dimensions that the theory would require. Often enough, what happens now is that advocates and critics of this or that decision focus on just one or two levels—the levels that correspond to their own expertise and where analysis can yield congenial results.

That is why in the annals of military history there are so many cases of technically impressive weapons that would never have been built if the most elementary tactical reactions had been considered. In the 1943 battle of Kursk, for example, the Germans lost their entire production of costly Ferdinand heavy tanks because they lacked machine guns to resist Russian infantry—a failure that could have been predicted by any soldier on that front. Likewise, there are many cases of weapons both technically and tactically successful whose decisive operational failure should have been expected. For example, the United States spent hundreds of millions of dollars on specialized antitank aircraft needed only against *massed* armor, which are never used because massed antiaircraft guns are then present as well—and that too was a fully predictable outcome. And there are cases of weapons successful at all military levels but counterproductive at the level of grand strategy because they fail in the horizontal dimension. German pre-1914 battleships were wonderfully advanced and did well in combat, but all they ever gained for Germany was Britain's lethal hostility—once again a wholly predictable result.

Much greater complications arise if the theory is to be used to construct an entire scheme of grand strategy. In the first place, whether its goals are set by tradition, bureaucratic compromise, a dictator's whim, or democratic choice, they must be consistent. It does not matter if they are wise or foolish in anyone's opinion, but they cannot be mutually exclusive or ranked inconsistently, for otherwise the definition of a grand strategy cannot even begin. Next, precise norms of conduct must be worked out for both the vertical and the horizontal dimensions of strategy. Whatever elegant ingenuity the scheme may contain, its implementation will depend on a myriad of detailed bureaucratic decisions. In military policy, the specific priorities set by the scheme will inevitably encounter the resistance of the different branches and services of the armed forces, because there is never enough for everybody. For example, all attempts to restructure and not just reduce the U.S. armed forces after the end of the Cold War were blocked by military insistence that budget cuts should be shared equally. It was obvious that army and marine ground forces left over from Cold War garrison duties should be cut disproportionally to pay for more air power, but all efforts to do that were successfully resisted. The Joint Chiefs of Staff were thus spared unpleasant quarrels—but when the United States fought the 1999 Kosovo war the shortage of air power was acute, while there was an abundance of unused and unusable ground forces.

Above all, any scheme of grand strategy will require coordinated action in diplomacy, propaganda, secret operations, and the entire economic sphere, as well as in military policy. Even if there is no elected parliament to challenge the executive and its scheme of grand strategy, even if there are no interest groups capable of opposing the required policies, the highly diversified bureaucratic apparatus of modern states is itself a major obstacle to the implementation of any comprehensive scheme of grand strategy. Each civil and military department is structured to pursue its own distinct goals, and each has its own institutional culture. Consciously or not, the separate departments are likely to resist a concerted scheme whenever it clashes with their particular bureaucratic interests, habits, and aims. For the implementation of a normative grand strategy, the organization of modern states is both the essential instrument and a powerful impediment.

In any case it is not easy to devise harmonious strategic solutions that are actually superior to mere pragmatic improvisations. Insight into the paradoxical logic in its five levels and two dimensions readily exposes the error of decisions that suit only one level or that ignore the reactions of others. But to proceed from the negative to the positive it is necessary to confront *all* relevant aspects at each level and in both dimensions, first to understand and decide, then to act. The resulting complexity allows that much more room for error. The theoretical superiority of properly strategical conduct may thus be overturned in practice, just as in war a clever and complicated maneuver can be so burdened with friction that it fares less well than a brutally simple frontal attack.

There are frequent calls in public life for "coherent" or "consistent" national policies. It is often taken for granted that the actions of each part of the government should be tightly coordinated to form a national policy that is logical in commonsense terms. That is fine for economic and social policy, but when it comes to the realm of conflict in foreign affairs as in war itself, only seemingly contradictory policies can circumvent the self-defeating effect of the paradoxical logic. If, for example, in considering grand strategy a point is reached when some growth in current war readiness is held to be necessary but total military spending cannot grow, manpower levels, stocks, and training would all have to be increased at the expense of long-term weapon development, construction, and so on. Because the result is to enhance present strength at the expense of future strength, such a military policy would mandate a conciliatory foreign policy to diminish future conflict, restraint in current operations if any, or outright concessions. Subject to many other variables here ignored, a "hard" military policy of immediate strength would thus require a "soft" foreign policy. As a result, the overall conduct of national policy would seem neither coherent nor consistent, precisely because it does achieve harmony in both dimensions of strategy.

This particular example suggests another grave obstacle to strategical conduct at the national level: it is hard for democratic political leaders to follow policies that can so easily be condemned as illogical and contradictory; and in this example, as so often, the charge of appeasement can also be made. More generally, it would be hard to maintain public support for paradoxical policies when the latter, inevitably, could only be explained through the adverse medium of commonsense discourse. Only dictatorships can pursue deliberately contradictory policies with little or no need for explanation. They can and do combine conciliatory diplomacy, and even concessions meant to relax the vigilance of their adversaries, with an accelerated armament effort. They can thunder and threaten in one direction while preparing to act in another; and they can launch surprise attacks even on the largest scale. Democratic governments also have their military buildups but cannot mask them because the public must be informed to justify the sacrifices. Democratic governments can also threaten other countries or even attack them outright, as the rump Yugoslav Federation of Serbia and Montenegro was attacked in 1999, but again any such action must be justified in advance, precluding political surprise at least and often tactical surprise as well.

Democracies cannot function as cunning warriors stalking their enemies in the night. Nor can modern pluralist democracies achieve coherence in their foreign policies, shaped as they are by the contending forces of voluntary pressure groups, organized lobbies, contending bureaucracies, and political factions. Yet there is much to be said for the resulting incoherence. Consider the case of the United States after the end of the Cold War. Its foreign policies certainly drifted into numerous contradictions as NATO was expanded even while trying to cultivate Russian friendship, as China was treated as both ally and enemy on alternate days. Only if all incoherence and all contradictions had been eliminated could the United States have pursued consistent priorities in its dealings with each country, regional grouping, or issue, each time combining promises and threats, punishments and inducements so as to maximize American leverage.

That is the result that the critics of incoherence presumably hope for. The effective power of the United States on the global scene would certainly be increased, exploiting the potential of its current economic, technological, military, and informational primacy to a far greater degree than is now the case. The United States, in other words, would become the ultimate Great Power of all history, with far more control over global events than any predecessor could have dreamed of.

That state of affairs, however, would not last for very long. During the Cold War, when the United States had a coherent strategy to maximize its own power, the Soviet Union was also present on the scene to absorb and counter much of that power with its own initiatives and responses. The result was some sort of equilibrium.

Moreover, in spite of the relative magnitude of two greatest powers as compared to all others, Cold War conditions created patterns of mutual dependence. The United States was needed by its allies for their protection but itself constantly needed the active cooperation of its allies. As for the Soviet Union, it was forever eager to court any friendly state it could not outrightly control. While that species of pretended neutrality called nonalignment meant little, even firmly aligned countries could exercise a great deal of independence.

It was out of the reciprocal power of the United States and the Soviet Union that third parties extracted their own independence and their own leverage. The Soviet Union's few allies could bargain for its aid because they were of use in the Soviet struggle against American power. The much greater number of American allies feared the Soviet Union, yet it was because of Soviet power that the United States had to rely on their cooperation. But now that the Soviet Union is no more, there is no equilibrium at all. There is now a multidimensional American supremacy that is quite unprecedented in all of human history and that awaits only the determined pursuit of a power-maximizing global strategy to become fully effective for the United States, and intolerably oppressive for everyone else.

Defensive responses and hostile reactions of widening scope and mounting consequence would inevitably follow. If the passive reality of American supremacy, mostly a source of positive reassurance at present, gave way to an active striving for global hegemony, it could only evoke the response that such attempts have always evoked: subterranean resistance by the weak, overt opposition by the less weak. To safeguard their independence, not only China and Russia but also many erstwhile American allies would be forced into a global coalition against a newly "strategic" United States. As of now, the absence of a global anti-American coalition proves that the United States is only potentially the sole global superpower that it could be. For that is the only way that power is ever manifest, in the compliant or adversarial reactions it evokes.

How far or how quickly matters would evolve toward overt forms of confrontation it is impossible to say. But a distinct eagerness to employ at least low-cost, low-risk means to undermine American power and prestige in any available venue would begin to characterize the behavior of former allies, as it already does in the case of France. Even mere diplomatic skirmishing could generate enough ill-will over time to hollow out the Western alliances and the cooperative security arrangements inherited from the Cold War. They might still persist institutionally if only for bureaucratic reasons, but they would cease to function substantively. As for the Western-sponsored institutions that have long since become international regulatory or developmental bodies, such as the World Trade Organization and the World Bank with its affiliates, they could not remain unaffected. As in the case of the UN General Assembly, their usefulness to the United States as to everyone else would drastically decline, once a standing coalition emerged to oppose any and every American proposal merely because it was American.

In other words, the entire superstructure of Western and world institutions that the United States largely designed in its own image, and that it sustained at great cost for half a century, would serve American purposes less and less. That penalty alone might outweigh whatever enhancements of power could be achieved in the first instance (pre-reaction) by a coherent strategy and consistent policies. Coalition building against the United States need never acquire a military dimension at all to be painfully effective. Anti-American diplomatic compacts of variable membership for varied purposes, measures of commercial denial selective or otherwise, intensified technoindustrial efforts on the lines of the Airbus-Boeing "zero-sum" competition, and whatever forms of cultural exclusion still remain technically feasible could all seriously and cumulatively damage American interests without any suggestion of a military threat, let alone any use of force.

In the past, of course, all such instruments of power would have been regarded as feeble, even inconsequential, as compared to the diplomacy of armed suasion and war itself. But we now live in a postheroic era, in which the advanced countries of the world—notably including the United States—are most reluctant to accept the casualties of war and hence to employ it as an instrument of policy. Concurrently, on the "demand side," as it were, territory and therefore the military power useful to seize and hold it count for much less than before.

Only those great novelties, along with the sense that the United States has no purposeful global strategy, can explain the rather relaxed acceptance of its unprecedented military superiority by most governments around the world. But even if the diminished importance of military power persists in coming years, the appearance on the scene of a coherently purposeful United States would soon evoke reactions. Coalition building against the United States could then acquire a military dimension after all, even if still masked in ambiguity and still defensive in intent.

With or without a military dimension, the advent of effective coalition measures to resist, absorb, and deflect the power of the United States would mark the completion of the sequence. Whatever added leverage could have been obtained by purposeful coherence in the first stage, thereby evoking coalition building in the second, would be lost in the third and final stage, in which some sort of global equilibrium would be restored once the original enhancement of American power was negated. Even if incidental disasters were avoided along the way, the United States would lose not merely what it would have previously and briefly gained but much more than that, because of the damage inflicted by intra-Western quarrels on multilateral institutions and long-established cooperative practices. The far from fortuitous congruence of these institutions with all manner of American interests, their role in helping to shape a favorable international environment, is a most valuable possession, which owes as much to American restraint as to American power.

All this simply means that in the wake of the Soviet collapse there is such a thing as a culminating point of success in maximizing the leverage of the United States on the world scene. To overshoot that point, to exceed the limit of what others can accept with sufficient equanimity, must result in diminished rather than increased power and influence.

All the complications, frictions, and political objections that impede practical use of the general theory do not diminish its explanatory and predictive value, nor prohibit its application. These obstacles simply mean that the application of the logic of strategy is burdened with difficulties, just as war and diplomacy are themselves. In many cases all difficulties could and should be overcome to implement the logic and thus obtain better outcomes at any given level, from the formulation of theater strategies and operational methods to the development of specific weapons, from tactical choices to the conduct of foreign policy. Even if the aim is much more ambitious, to devise and implement a grand strategy that will harmonize policy on all levels, the impediments can be overcome by great intellectual effort, sheer tenacity, and much political ingenuity.

There is, however, a permanent danger. Huge uncertainties of fact must be accepted in devising any substantive scheme of grand strategy. Success in both formulation and implementation therefore entails the possibility that error will be systematized. The shortsighted pragmatic decisions and uncoordinated improvisations that frequently mark the daily conduct of governments result in numerous errors, but most of them will be small and with luck many of them will cancel each other out. But while the successful application of a grand strategy should reduce the prevalence of small errors of disharmony, it will do so at the risk of focusing energies to perpetrate much larger errors. That is why the warlike ventures of dictatorships that can impose the tightest policy coordination, exploit the paradoxical logic to the full, and routinely achieve surprise whenever they attack begin well, only to end in utter disaster.

APPENDIX A

Definitions of Strategy

It is my purpose to demonstrate the existence of strategy* as a body of recurring objective phenomena that arise from human conflict, and not to prescribe courses of action. Most current definitions are by contrast exclusively normative, as if it were assumed that no such objective phenomena exist or else that they are too obvious to be worth defining. This of course raises the question of what basis there can be for generic prescriptions, as opposed to specific advice on how to deal with a particular question in a given context.

Carl von Clausewitz, the greatest student of strategy who ever lived, was simply uninterested in defining anything in generic, abstract terms; he regarded all such attempts as futile and pedantic. His own characteristi-

* As with many scientific terms, the word "strategy" (French *strategie*, Italian *strategia*) is a Greek word that no ancient Greek ever used; it is derived indirectly from the classic and Byzantine *strategos* (general), which does not however carry the connotation of the modern word. The Greek equivalent for our "strategy" would have been *strategike episteme* (generals' knowledge) or *strategon sophia* (generals' wisdom). Cognates such as *strategicos*, as in the title of Onosander's work, or the much later *strategikon* (of Mauricius) have a didactic connotation. By contrast, *strategemata*, the Greek title of the well-known Latin work by Frontinus, describes a compilation of *strategema*, precisely "stratagems" or tricks of war *(ruses de guerre)*. Much more commonly used by the Greeks, from Aeneas in the fourth century B.C. to Leo after the seventh century A.D. and beyond, was *taktike techne*, which described an entire body of knowledge on the conduct of warfare, from supply to exhortatory rhetoric, including both techniques and tactics proper as well as petty diplomacy. *Taktike techne*, or rather its Latin translation *ars bellica*, in common use in Roman times, resurfaced by 1518 in Machiavelli's use of *arte della guerra* in the *Discorsi* on Livy (who in fact uses that term) and later in the title of his *Dell' arte della guerra*, and it spread quite widely in other European languages: *Kriegskunst, art de la guerre*, art of war. (See Virgilio Ilari, "Politica e strategia globale," in Jean, ed., *Il pensiero strategico* (1985), pp. 57–59.)

267

cally offhand definition of strategy occurs by distinction from tactics and is presented as no more than common usage:

> Everyone knows fairly well where each particular factor belongs . . . Whenever such categories are blindly used, there must be a deep-seated reason for it . . . We reject, on the other hand, the artificial distinctions of certain writers, since they find no reflection in general usage. According to our classification, then, tactics teaches the use of armed forces in the engagement; strategy, the use of engagements for the object of the war. (*On War,* book 2, chap. 1, p. 128, Princeton edition)

For Clausewitz, therefore, "strategy" was normative, and so it remains in the following contemporary American definition:

> A science, an art, or a plan (subject to revision) governing the raising, arming, and utilization of the military forces of a nation (or coalition) to the end that its interests will be effectively promoted or secured against enemies, actual, potential, or merely presumed. (James E. King, ed., *Lexicon of Military Terms*, 1960, p. 14)

Characteristically, another American definition of official military origin is much more inclusive:

> The art and science of developing and using political, economic, psychological and military forces as necessary during peace and war, to afford the maximum support to policies, in order to increase the probabilities and favorable consequences of victory and to lessen the chances of defeat. (U.S. Joint Chiefs of Staff, *Dictionary of United States Military Terms for Joint Usage*, 1964, p. 135)

Even broader, yet equally prescriptive, is the standard definition of strategy from *Webster's Third New International Dictionary:*

> The science and art of employing the political, economic, psychological, and military forces of a nation or group of nations to afford the maximum support to adopted policies in peace or war.

The definition found in the collective and exceedingly official *Soviet Military Strategy*, attributed to the authorship of Marshal V. D. Sokolovsky, which reveals both Marxist and bureaucratic preoccupations, differentiates between the descriptive and prescriptive meanings:

> Military strategy is a system of scientific knowledge dealing with the laws of war as an armed conflict in the name of definite class interests.

Strategy—on the basis of military experience, military and political conditions, economic and moral potential of the country, new means of combat, and the views and potential of the probable enemy—studies the conditions and the nature of future war, the methods for its preparation and conduct, the services of the armed forces and the foundations for their strategic utilization, as well as foundations for the material and technical support and leadership of the war and the armed forces. At the same time, this is the area of the practical activity of the higher military and political leadership, of the supreme command, and of the higher headquarters, that pertains to the art of preparing a country and the armed forces for war and conducting the war. (Harriet Fast Scott, ed., *Soviet Military Strategy*, 1975, p. 11)

General André Beaufre's succinct definition, normative but based on the descriptive, is congruent with my own purpose in this book: "l'art de la dialectique des volontes employant la force pour resoudre leur conflict" (the art of the dialectics of wills that use force to resolve their conflict; *Introduction à la stratégie*, 1963, p. 16).

The Gulf War Air Campaign

Table 1 Sorties flown

Type of mission	Allies	USAF	Other U.S.	Total coalition
AI[a]	4,600	24,000	11,900	40,500
OCA[b]	1,400	4,500	600	6,500
CAS[c]	0	1,500	1,500	3,000
Total "strike sorties"	6,000	30,000	14,000	50,000
Aerial refueling	1,500	10,000	1,500	13,000
DCA[d]	4,100	3,200	2,700	10,000
SEAD[e]	0	2,800	1,200	4,000
Tactical airlift	4,300	14,000	0	18,000
Other[f]	1,100	6,000	7,900	15,000
Total "nonstrike"	12,000	36,000	12,000	60,000
Approximate total of all sorties				110,000

Sources: USAF, "Air Force Performance in Desert Storm," and author's collation of published data.

a. AI = "Air Interdiction," in this case a conflation of both strategic (against Iraqi installations) and operational (against Iraqi air, ground, and naval forces) bombing, including "battlefield interdiction" (against Iraqi forces behind the front).

b. OCA = "Offensive Counter Air," i.e., attacks against Iraqi air force bases and related facilities.

c. CAS = "Close Air Support," i.e., attacks against Iraqi ground forces at the front.

d. DCA = "Defensive Counter Air," i.e., air-defense patrols and intercepts.

e. SEAD = "Suppression of Enemy Air Defenses," i.e., attacks against Iraqi antiaircraft missiles, guns, and related radar and other facilities.

f. Other = airborne early warning, airborne electronic surveillance, electronic warfare, and other.

Table 2 Aerial ordnance delivered

Part I. U.S. Forces (Air Force, Navy, and Marine Corps)

Air-to-ground missiles

AGM-65 Maverick variants:	
65B (TV guidance)	1,703
65D (imaging infrared)	3,536
65G (imaging infrared)	187
65E (laser)	41 Marine Corps aircraft only
AGM-84E/SLAM (harpoon)	7 (500 lb.) Navy aircraft only
AGM-62 (WALLEYE)	131 (2,000 lb.) Navy aircraft only
Total air-to-ground missiles	5,605
Total estimated warhead weight	495 tons

Guided bombs

GBU-10 (2,000 lb.)	2,263
GBU-15 (2,000 lb.) (electro-optical; all others laser-homing)	71
GBU-24 (2,000 lb.)	284 i.e., F-117s and F-15Es
GBU-10/I-2000	403
GBU-24/I-2000	877
GBU-12 (500 lb.)	4,542 i.e., F-111Fs against tanks
GBU-16 (1,000 lb.)	208
GBU-27 (2,000 lb.)	718 F-117s against hard targets
GBU-28 (4,000 lb.)	2 F-111Fs against superhard targets
Total guided bombs	9,368
Total estimated warhead weight	5,852 tons

Radiation-homing missiles (for SEAD, see Table 1, note e)

AGM-45 (Shrike)	31
AGM-88 (HARM)	1,804
Total ARMs	1,835
Total estimated warhead weight	133 tons
Total number of all air-launched guided weapons	16,808
Total estimated warhead/bomb weight	6,480 tons

Tomahawk sea-launched cruise missiles

RGM-109C	264 1,000-lb. warhead
RGM-109D	27 bomblets
RGM-109B	10
Total number launched	301
Total warhead weight, at 1,000 lb. each	151 tons
Total number of all aerial guided weapons	17,109
Total estimated warhead/guided-bomb weight	6,631 tons

Unguided bombs

Mk.82 500 lb.	64,698
Mk.83 1,000 lb.	10,125
Mk.84 2,000 lb.	11,179
Mk.117 750 lb.	34,808
UK 1,000 lb.	288
Mk.20 500 lb.	27,735 Rockeye, multiple
CBU-78 1,000 lb.	215 "cluster" type
CBU-89 710 lb.	1,107 "cluster" type
CBU-52/58/71(800 lb.)	17,029 "cluster" type
CBU-87 950 lb.	10,815 "cluster" type
Total Mk.20 and "cluster" types	56,901
Total number of unguided bombs	177,999
Total weight of unguided bombs	64,996 tons
Of which delivered in bulk by B-52s:	
Number	72,000+
Weight	25,700 tons

Summary totals

Total aerial warhead tonnage delivered by U.S. forces	71,627 tons
Of which, guided weapons of all types	6,631 tons, or 9.26%
Total number of aerial weapons used by U.S. forces	195,108
Of which, total number of guided weapons	17,109, or 8.8%

Part II. Estimate of Aerial Tonnage Delivered by Non-U.S. Forces

In the absence of comprehensive data (but see Table 3 notes), the calculation that follows generously assumes that the average non-U.S. "strike" sortie tonnage was the same as the U.S. average minus the B-52s.

Total air-ground ordnance delivered by U.S. aircraft (excluding Tomahawk cruise missiles, 151 tons)	71,476 tons
Less 25,700 tons delivered by B-52s	45,776 tons
46,376 ordnance delivered per (non–B-52) "strike"/SEAD sortie	0.987 tons
Total number of non-U.S. "strike" sorties	6,000
Estimated aerial ordnance delivered by non-U.S. forces	5,922 tons

Estimated Grand Total of Aerial Ordnance Delivered

U.S. total (incl. cruise missiles)	71,627 tons
Estimated non-U.S. total	5,922 tons
Grand total	77,549 tons

Sources: USAF, "Air Force Performance in Desert Storm," and author's collation of published data.

Table 3 "Strike" sorties by aircraft type

U.S. Air Force

A-10 attack	7,454 (≫"almost 8,100")
AC-130 turbo-prop, gunship	96
B-52 strategic bomber*	1,812 (≫1,624)
F-111 heavy attack*	2,995 (≫"over 4,000")
F-117 "stealth," attack*	1,466 (≫"almost 1,300")
F-15 heavy fighter[†]	156
F-15E heavy fighter bomber*	2,190 (≫"over 2,200")
F-16 light fighter bomber	12,884 (≫"almost 13,500")
F-4G W/W, specialized for SEAD[†]	2,359 (≫"over 2,500")
RF-4 specialized for reconnaissance[†]	24
BQM-74 reconnaissance drone[‡]	18

U.S. Navy and Marine Corps

A-6 medium attack*	3,331
A-7 medium attack*	722
E-2C airborne radar[‡]	2
EA-6 electronic warfare[‡]	61
F-14 heavy fighter[†]	456
F/A-18 fighter bomber*	7,868
KA-6 tanker[‡]	11
S-3B specialized for ASW/ELINT[‡]	3
TLAM Tomahawk cruise missile	175 (284 reported)
TLAM-C Tomahawk CM submarine-launched	10
AV-8B, light attack	4,292
KC-130 tanker aircraft[‡]	1
MH-53 helicopter[‡]	3

U.S. Army

AH-64 attack helicopter*	9
UH-60 utility helicopter	21

Aircraft Operated by Non-U.S. Forces

A-4 Kuwait, light attack	775
Alpha Jet, Qatar, light attack	10[a]
Buccaneer, U.K., attack	228[b]
CF-18, Canadian, fighter[†]	56
CSS-2 Saudi ballistic missile	3
F-1 fighter	268[c]
F-1CR fighter	44[d]
F-5, Saudi Arabia	1,712
GR-1 Tornado, U.K., attack version	1,607

IDS, Tornado, U.K., interceptor-fighter[†]	802
Jaguar, France, attack	1,249[e]
Mirage 2000, France, fighter	80[f]
Tornado, Italy, attack	199[g]

Definition: "Strike" as here defined (cf. Table 1) includes all aircraft that penetrated hostile air space in the course of ground-attack missions, with or without ground-attack ordnance of their own. See Table 5 for escort/(true) striker ratios.

Symbols: * = Aircraft fully equipped for delivery of guided weapons.

[†] = Aircraft not primarily equipped for ground attack.

[‡] = Aircraft type with no significant ground-attack capability.

Note: USAF EF-111s not included in Table 3 flew 900 sorties, many over Iraq or Kuwait; USAF, "Air Force Performance in Desert Storm," reports a total of 830 sorties flown by AC/EC/MC/HC-130s and other "special operations" aircraft.

a. Qatar reported only 6 sorties.

b. The British government reported a total of "more than 4,000" combat sorties, and 3,000 tons of weapons expended, including 100 JP233 runway-breaking munitions and more than 1,000 laser-guided bombs.

c. F-1 identifies various versions of the Mirage F-1; Kuwait reported 107 F-1CK sorties and Qatar reported 44 F-1EDA sorties for a total of only 151 sorties.

d. Only the French air force operated the Mirage F-1CR reconnaissance variant. It reported a total of 117 sorties. (Table 3 data for F-1CR confuses F-1CR with Qatar F-1EDA sorties.)

e. Only the French air force operated Jaguars. It reported a total of only 656 sorties.

f. The French air force reported a total of 555 Mirage 2000 sorties; in addition, the United Arab Emirates air force reported a total of 53 bombing and 4 reconnaissance sorties.

g. The Italian air force reported 226 sorties in 32 missions including 2 aborted sorties; it reported delivery of 565 Mk.83 1,000-lb. bombs (282 tons in all).

Table 4 Guided/unguided ordnance delivered by selected aircraft

	% of guided weapons
F-117 "almost 2,000 tons"	100.0%
B-52 "over 27,500 tons"	0.0%
Tomahawk cruise missiles, 142 tons	100.0%
All U.S. Navy aircraft, by number	4.8%[a]
All U.S. Air Force aircraft, by number	9.9%[b]
As above, excluding B-52 deliveries	19.2%[c]

a. Air-to-ground ordnance delivered by NAVCENT aircraft:

Unguided	*Guided weapons*
Mk.84: 955	AGM-45: 17
Mk.83: 10,125	AGM-84E: 7
Mk.82: 10,941	AGM-88: 662
Mk.20: 6,543	AGM-62: 131
CBU-78: 148	GBU-10: 202
	GBU-12: 216
	GBU-16: 205
Total: 28,712	Total: 1,440
Combined NAVCENT total: 30,158	

b. Air-to-ground ordnance delivered by CENTAF aircraft:

Unguided	*Guided weapons*
Mk.84: 11,024	AGM-45: 7
Mk.82: 53,757	AGM-65B: 1,703
Mk.117: 34,808	AGM-65D: 3,536
Mk.20: 5,364	AGM-65G: 187
CBU-89: 1,107	AGM-88: 909
CBU-52/58/71: 17,029	GBU-10: 2,007
CBU-87: 10,815	GBU-10/I-2000: 403
UK-1000: 288	GBU-12: 4,124
	GBU-15: 71
	GBU-24: 284
	GBU-24/I-2000: 877
	GBU-27: 718
	GBU-28: 2
Total: 134,192	Total: 14,828
Combined CENTAF total: 149,020	

c. Combined CENTAF total @ 149,020 less bombs delivered in bulk by B-52s @ 72,000 (see Table 2, Pt. I) = 77,020.

Guided total @ 14,828/77,020 = 19.25%.

Table 5 Protective support requirements of non-stealth aircraft

Representative task forces: Days 9–10 of the Gulf war (support ratios declined as the campaign progressed)

F-16: 24 F-16s with 2 Mk.84 bombs each ("strikers")
    4 F-15s, fighter escorts
    4 F-4Gs with ARM missiles, for defense suppression
    2 EF-111 electronic warfare, for defense suppression
   11 KC-135 tankers
Totals: 24 "strikers," 21 support; 45 aircraft for 48 bombs.

F/A-18: 8 F/A-18 with 2 (?) bombs each ("strikers")
    2 F/A-18 as fighter escorts
    4 F/A-18 with ARM missiles, for defense suppression
    2 EA-6B electronic warfare, for defense suppression
    3 KC-135 tankers
    2 KA-6 tankers
    1 E-2C airborne radar/C3I aircraft
Totals: 8 "strikers," 14 support; 22 aircraft for 16 (?) bombs.

F-111: 20 F-111 with 8 CBU-87s each ("strikers")
    8 F-15s fighter escorts
    2 F-4Gs with ARM missiles, for defense suppression
    2 EF-111, electronic warfare, for defense suppression
   11 KC-135 tankers
Totals: 20 "strikers," 23 support; 43 aircraft for 160 bombs.

A-6E: 6 A-6E with 4 (?) bombs each ("strikers")
    4 F-14 as fighter escorts
    4 F/A-18 with ARM missiles for defense suppression
    2 EA-6B electronic warfare, for defense suppression
    3 KC-135 tankers
    1 E-2C airborne radar/C3I aircraft
Totals: 6 "strikers," 14 support; 20 aircraft for 24 (?) bombs.

F-117: 1   F-117 with 2 (guided) bombs
   0.33 KC-135 tanker (one shared by 3 F-117s)
Totals: 1 "striker," 0.33 support; 1.33 aircraft, 2 bombs.

APPENDIX C

Instant Thunder

In broad outline, the initial plan presented by Colonel John R. Warden USAF to the commander in chief of the U.S. Central Command and to the Chairman of the Joint Chiefs of Staff in August 1990 envisaged a self-sufficient air offensive in three distinct phases.

The first and shortest phase, intended to establish air superiority over the whole of Iraq and Kuwait, was to be mainly a standard "defense-suppression" operation, with the systematic attack of warning and tracking radars as well as primary and sector air-defense command centers; the cutting of all runways in civil airports and military bases where Iraqi military aircraft were based; and the attack of the major surface-to-air missile (SAM) batteries, especially those emplaced around intended targets.

In addition to these typical defense-suppression targets, the first phase also contained a "strategic" element, with the bombing of: (a) Iraq's central command-and-control facilities and regime headquarter facilities, mostly in Baghdad; and (b) Iraqi ballistic-missile sites and some chemical-weapon storage depots, in order to diminish the then feared threat of chemical-missile attacks against Israeli and Saudi cities as well as U.S. ports of entry.

The second phase would focus on the incapacitation (not wholesale destruction) of Iraq's military and civil infrastructure. Escorted as required, to deal with residual Iraqi fighter and air-defense units, U.S. and any available allied aircraft would first attack the "military support" targets: ammunition dumps, refineries and refined petroleum product tank farms, and weapon "base" depots. That would effectively limit Iraqi military units to the fuel and ammunition already tactically deployed in forward areas (perhaps enough for only seventy-two hours of intense operations). The main effort of the second phase, however, was to be the bombing of weapon assembly lines, factories, and repair workshops, as well as the laboratories and plants associated with the development and production of chemical, biological, and nuclear weapons. The final element was the attack of Iraq's civil infrastructure: electrical power plants, the major telephone exchanges, water-treatment plants, and so on.

The third phase, which was to start on the second week of the air offensive, would focus on Iraq's deployed military strength with (a) interdiction strikes on the railway facilities and road bridges between Baghdad and Kuwait; (b) the area bombing of Republican Guard and other selected Iraqi ground forces; and (c) attacks on naval and other military targets, including Iraqi aircraft (kept grounded till then by runway-cutting attacks). It was thought that given the virtual absence of indigenous food and water sources, the cutting of the supply lines to the Iraqi troops in Kuwait would soon leave them with the choice of withdrawal, desertion, or starvation and thirst in place. It was believed that "battlefield interdiction" and close air support operations would be required only if the Iraqi leadership chose to respond to the air campaign by launching a counterattack against U.S. and allied ground forces. The initial plan did not envisage the systematic attack of Iraqi ground forces because of both strategic reasons (the postconflict Iranian threat) and tactical ones (the difficulty of destroying dispersed, camouflaged, and partially entrenched ground forces).

Even so, Instant Thunder could enable the United States to achieve its declared objectives in the crisis as defined in both policy statements and UN resolutions: the withdrawal of all Iraqi forces from Kuwait and the reinstatement of the legitimate government. Moreover, the United States could also achieve the undeclared objective of destroying Iraq's capacity for strategic attack, and for self-sufficient military action in general, by eliminating its logistic and industrial prerequisites.

While air operations requiring thousands of sorties would necessarily involve some losses, it was thought that they would be contained by the technical, tactical, and numerical superiority of U.S. and allied air forces and the relatively unsophisticated state of Iraqi air defenses. It was estimated that total aircraft losses might number in the dozens at most. Iraqi casualties would also be contained by air operations aimed at targets mostly well separated from major population centers. In the event, by the time the plan was implemented on January 17, 1991, much larger air forces were present than had been envisaged in August. Hence the three phases of Instant Thunder were compressed.

NOTES

1. The Conscious Use of Paradox in War

1. Carl von Clausewitz, *On War*, book 1, chap. 7; p. 119, in the Princeton edition.
2. Ibid., book 2, chap. 3 ("War Is an Act of Human Intercourse"), p. 149.
3. The Chouf road runs from Jazzin to the Beirut-Damascus highway, which in turn leads eastward to Shtawra, the Israeli objective at the time, where the Syrian military headquarters for Lebanon were located. The Israeli advance was blocked at Ayn Zhalta, a few miles from the highway. See Zeev Schiff and Ehud Yaari, *Israel's Lebanon War* (1984), pp. 160–161.
4. The offensive of Ben-Gal's Corps 446, which began in the early morning of June 10, 1982. Ibid., pp. 117, 171–173.

2. The Logic in Action

1. The campaign only ended officially on June 25, 1940, when Italy also accepted the French armistice offer; but the last week of fighting was half-hearted on both sides, except in the Maginot Line sectors where French Army Group 2 resisted tenaciously until June 22.
2. At the outbreak of war in September 1939, out of 103 German divisions only 16 (Panzer, Motorized, and Light) were fully motorized. Each of the 87 infantry divisions was supposed to have 942 scout cars, staff cars, artillery tractors, and trucks (sufficient to put one man in six on wheels), but most divisional supplies were carried on 1,200 horsecarts. By May 1940, however, because of truck losses on bad Polish roads, the number of trucks had been halved and more carts had been added. From railhead to divisional depots, supplies were to be delivered by special truck regiments; but there were only 3 of these for the entire German army on all fronts, with a total of only 6,600 trucks. See Martin van Creveld, *Supplying War* (1977), pp. 144–147.
3. Burkhart Mueller-Hillebrand, *Das Heer, 1933–1945* (1956), vol. 2, table 29, as cited in van Creveld, *Supplying War*, n. 28, p. 151.
4. On the morning of October 18, 1941, the Tenth Panzer and SS Das Reich

divisions entered Mozhaisk, on the main highway to Moscow. At that point, the Germans were completing the destruction of eight Soviet armies in the Vyazma-Bryansk sectors, in what was to be their last great and unqualified victory on Russian soil (they claimed 665,000 prisoners); see John Erickson, *The Road to Stalingrad* (1975), pp. 216–220. By then, the leading Second and Third Panzer groups (Guderian and Hoth) of Army Group Center had advanced more than five hundred miles on a straight line basis since June 22, 1941, and Guderian's forces had just been redirected toward Moscow, after their southward maneuver to close off the huge Kiev-Romny encirclement.

5. Only two corps could attack at all, out of the two armies on the sector. See Albert Seaton, *The Battle for Moscow* (1983), p. 165.

6. Army Group South's counteroffensive of February 25–March 18, 1943, to the Donets River and Kharkov, added the name of Fritz Erich von Manstein to the celebrity list of military history. Six Soviet tank corps of the army-level "Popov group," which had ventured too far south, were encircled and shattered, and two more Soviet armies were battered in the German reconquest of the Kharkov region. See Earl F. Ziemke, *Stalingrad to Berlin* (1968), pp. 90–105. Also Erich von Manstein, *Lost Victories* (1958), pp. 367–442.

7. Ziemke, *Stalingrad to Berlin*, p. 501.

8. See Raymond L. Garthoff, *Soviet Military Doctrine* (1953) pp. 18–19, for an elaboration of the doctrine.

9. With no railway across Libya and with horsecarts unusable in the waterless and fodderless desert, only the circulation of truck columns from the port of Tripoli to the front could sustain Rommel's forces. The 6,000 tons of truck capacity available to them in April 1941, at the start of the German intervention, could supply the original two divisions of the Afrika Korps out to some three hundred miles at most, and Rommel was therefore explicitly forbidden to attack. When he launched his first offensive nevertheless, outmaneuvering the British forces (also overextended after their previous victory against the Italians), which promptly collapsed, his spectacular and historically unique thousand-mile advance reconquered all of Libya, penetrated into Egypt, and left his leading forces stranded in the desert, barely subsisting on captured supplies and set for their own coming retreat. Van Creveld, *Supplying War*, p. 186.

10. That is, for combat with other fighters as well as ground attack, both in daylight. See Williamson Murray, *Strategy for Defeat* (1983), pp. 1–25.

11. The first bombing of German inland targets, in the Ruhr, occurred on May 15, 1940; the first raid on Berlin was flown on the night of August 25, 1940. From the outbreak of war, in September 1939, through March 1940, Bomber Command dropped only 64 tons of bombs, and none deliberately on German cities, on which only leaflets were dropped. Goering's famous

boast therefore seemed vindicated, but with the Phony War over, France invaded, and Churchill in command, 1,668 tons were dropped on Germany in May 1940, rising to 2,300 tons in June, declining to 1,257 in July (the forward airfields had been lost), and 1,365 in August, before increasing to 2,339 tons in September 1940. See Charles Webster and Noble Frankland, *The Strategic Air Offensive against Germany* (1961), I, 144, 152, and IV, 455; hereafter cited as *SAO*.

12. During May 1942, the British Bomber Command sent out 2,702 sorties, lost 114 aircraft, and had 256 aircraft seriously damaged; in June, there were 4,801 sorties, 199 losses, and 442 damaged aircraft; in July, sorties declined to 3,914, but losses declined less than proportionately to 171, and 315 aircraft were damaged; only 2,454 sorties were flown in August (as opposed to 4,242 in August 1941), with 142 aircraft lost and 233 damaged. See *SAO*, IV, appendix 40, p. 432; and Alfred Price, *Instruments of Darkness* (1977), pp. 55ff.

13. The monthly total of bombs dropped by Bomber Command had declined to 2,714 tons by December 1942, after reaching a peak level of 6,845 tons the previous June; in 1943, by contrast, January's 4,345 tons were followed by 10,959 in February and steadily more thereafter, with the year's peak in August at 20,149 tons; during the same month, the U.S. Eighth Air Force total was 3,999 tons. See *SAO*, IV, appendix 44, p. 456.

14. "Window" was the British code name for metalized strips that reflect radar beams; the American term, now universally employed, is "chaff."

15. The "firestorm effect" is first described in the famous report of the Hamburg Police President dated December 1, 1943. See the extract in *SAO*, IV, appendix 30, pp. 310–315; and Martin Middlebrook, *The Battle of Hamburg* (1981) pp. 214–240.

16. Bomber Command lost 314 aircraft (416 were damaged) in January 1944, 199 (264 damaged) in February, and 283 (402 damaged) in March—rates plainly unsustainable: in March the average aircraft availability was 974. See *SAO*, IV, appendix 40, p. 433, and appendix 39, p. 428.

17. When Window was being tested, it emerged that an older British night-fighter radar (Mark IV) could cope with the countermeasure, while the latest and best (Mark VII) could not. Price, *Instruments*, p. 117.

18. When a German Ju-88 landed by mistake on a British airfield in July 1944, it was found to contain a device code-named Flensburg, which could detect, classify, and locate the signals of "Monica," the British tail-mounted warning radar. Ibid., pp. 214–215.

3. Efficiency and the Culminating Point of Success

1. The Whitehead self-propelled torpedo was demonstrated in Fiume (Austria-Hungary) in January 1867; the Royal Navy commissioned tests in

1869, purchased torpedoes in 1870, and obtained rights of manufacture one year later. Bernard Fitzsimons, ed., *Encyclopedia of Twentieth Century Weapons and Warfare*, XXIII, 2508; hereafter cited as *WW*.

2. Philippe Masson, *Histoire de la marine* (1983), vol. 2, passim.

3. *WW*, XXIII, 2515.

4. See Avraham Adan, *On the Banks of the Suez* (1980), pp. 117–164.

5. The mortar, the first of all firearms, in use since the fourteenth century, continued to perform especially well against the latest weapon of land warfare. Unlike machine guns, not much good beyond a thousand yards or so and largely limited to direct fire, mortars could outrange the Sagger antitank missiles of the Egyptians, and descending from a high trajectory, their bombs could reach into the trenches and firing pits of the antitank missile and rocket crews.

6. They were effective not tactically but at the operational level of strategy, on which see Part II. The old-style unguided hollow-charge weapons, incidentally, proved to be relatively successful if used in the same conditions that had ensured their success in the Second World War: in street fighting with ample cover as well as in densely wooded areas.

7. "Administration" therefore includes everything done in the military realm that does not reflect enemy-specific goals of warfare or any purpose of dissuasion or intimidation. This does not correspond to Clausewitz's distinction: "the activities characteristic of war may be split into two main categories: those that are merely preparations for war and war proper," with the implication that what I call "linear logic" ("science" in his terminology) applies to the former but not to the latter; *On War*, book 2, chap. 1, p. 131. Yet surely "preparations for war" (peacetime military policy) are also shaped by enemy-specific tactical and operational purposes as well as by aims of suasion that reflect particular perceptions of the policies and military structures of specific others; such preparations are not exclusively shaped by enemy-autonomous priorities, including the desire to optimize decisions on the basis of "scientific" criteria. Clausewitz was the first to recognize the fundamental distinction but apparently misplaced the dividing line, circumscribing excessively the boundaries of strategy. Thus in differentiating between "the craft of the swordsmith" and the "art of fencing," he is conflating the design of swords, which is apt to reflect specific expectations of the adversary swords and swordsmanship to be countered, with the metallurgical technique of their manufacture, which should autonomously seek to maximize some generic effectiveness. *On War*, book 2, chap. 2 ("Originally the Term 'Art of War' Only Designated the Preparation of the Forces"), p. 133.

8. There are constant complaints in the U.S. Congress against "duplication," a term applied with pardonable imprecision to the concurrent acquisition of several different types of fighter aircraft, antitank weapons, and so on.

Equally, the asymmetry between Warsaw Pact forces homogeneously equipped with Soviet weapons and Western forces variously equipped with their own national equipment was perpetually deplored during the Cold War as an unredeemed evil.

9. Large-deck aircraft carriers can accommodate a variety of aircraft types in useful numbers as their lesser counterparts cannot, but there is no justification for 50,000-ton supply ships that can only be acquired in small numbers (aircraft carriers soon become useless without the jet fuel and weapons they bring).

10. On August 25, 1943, a German Hs-293 glider bomb missed HMS *Bideford,* but two days later the same weapon damaged the *Athabaskan* and sunk the *Egret,* all in the Bay of Biscay. On September 8, 1943, the Italian battleship *Roma* (on its way to join the Allies) was sunk by German FX (a.k.a. SD-100X) guided, rocket-propelled missiles; see F. H. Hinsley et al., *British Intelligence in the Second World War* (1984), III, 220, 339–340; and *WW,* XVI, 1754. The first ship-launched Soviet antiship missile (Styx) appeared in the 1950s and was fully operational by 1959, and the first Soviet air-launched antiship missile (Kangaroo) was in service by 1960; *WW,* XX, 2419, and XIV, 1558. And if all those warnings were ignored, on October 21, 1967, the Israeli destroyer *Elat* was sunk by Egyptian Styx missiles off Port Said, stimulating worldwide interest in antiship missiles and countermeasures against them. See Edward N. Luttwak and Dan Horowitz, *The Israeli Army* (1975), p. 316.

11. Such was the procedure in the 1970s and 1980s. See e.g. *Report of the Secretary of Defense to the Congress on the FY 1987 Budget,* February 5, 1986. p. 197.

12. Long-range aircraft based on land can now span the oceans to control sea lanes from above, and such aerial "cruisers" have been proposed. As for the conveyance of landing forces, large, nonnuclear transport submarines have been seriously considered even for commercial cargoes.

13. Alistair Horne, *The Price of Glory* (1962), pp. 327–328. The Verdun ossuary, in which the bones of the dead are concentrated, is still much visited but only inspires disbelief in modern Europeans.

14. Pierre Sergent, *Je ne regrette rien* (1972), pp. 149–150.

4. The Coming Together of Opposites

1. SAO, I, 152. (See note 11, p. 282.)
2. Ibid., I, 182.
3. Martin Gilbert, *Finest Hour* (1983), pp. 1103, 1105.
4. SAO, I, 182, 184–185.
5. Ibid., IV, appendix 39, p. 428.
6. Ibid., I, 347.

7. Harris, head of the Bomber Command during the important years, and possibly the most underrated of the Allied war leaders, included a fine analysis of the question in his memoirs: *Bomber Offensive* (1947), pp. 220–234.

8. Wesley F. Craven and James L. Cate, *The Army Air Forces in World War II* (1949), II, 682–684, 702–704.

9. The architect of German war production at the time, Albert Speer, has argued that the attack could have been decisive if it had persisted. But he is wrong, for then decentralization would have ensued. Speer, *Inside the Third Reich* (1970), pp. 284–287.

10. For a brief overview, in historiographical retrospect, see David MacIsaac, *Strategic Bombing in World War Two* (1976).

11. Tim Weiner, "US Cancels Plans for Raid on Bosnia to Capture 2 Serbs," *New York Times*, July 26, 1998, pp. 1, 6.

12. Dana Priest, "Risk and Restraint: Why the Apaches Never Flew in Kosovo," *Washington Post*, December 29, 1999, pp. A1, A22.

5. The Technical Level

1. Firearms first reached Japan in 1542 aboard a Portuguese ship. By 1575 Oda Nobunaga's 3,000 select harquebusiers (he already had some 10,000 in all) destroyed Takeda Katsuyori's cavalry army, the pride of the Takeda clan, and with it a whole way of warfare at the battle of Nagashino in Mikawa. See George Sansom, *A History of Japan* (1961), pp. 263–264, 281. There is a detailed but unreferenced account of Nagashino in S. R. Turnbull, *The Samurai* (1977), pp. 158–160. Swift as they were in equipping commoners with the new weapons, the samurai themselves continued to wear swords, not pistols, until that mark of privilege was abolished along with the entire social class after the Meiji restoration of 1868.

2. A. M. Low, *Musket to Machine-Gun* (1942), pp. 66–67; Michael Howard, *The Franco-Prussian War* (1968), p. 36.

3. See the interesting discussion in William McElwee, *The Art of War* (1974), pp. 141–146.

4. Robert Jungk, *Brighter than a Thousand Suns* (1964), pp. 106–107.

5. This was certainly true of the Strategic Defense Initiative announced by President Reagan in March 1983, following a decision that did not reflect government-wide, authoritative, scientific advice. It seems that science alone escapes all attempts at "scientific" decision making.

7. The Operational Level

1. "The Operational Level of War." *International Security*, 5 (Winter 1980–81), reprinted in Edward N. Luttwak, *Strategy and History: Collected Essays*, vol. 2 (New Brunswick: Transaction Books, 1985). The next edition of the basic

U.S. Army Field Manual 100-5, to which I contributed as a consultant to the U.S. Army Training and Doctrine Command, incorporated and indeed greatly emphasized the operational level, and eventually so did the manuals of the other U.S. services. Major General J. J. G. Mackenzie and Brian Holden Reid, *The British Army and the Operational Level of War* (London: Triservice Press, 1989), explicitly acknowledges the origin of the concept.

2. The German term is *Operativ Kriegskunst,* and the Russian *operativnoye iskusstvo* is clearly derivative. The "operations" that occurs in American military-administrative usage, as in "European Theater of Operations," merely means combat activities in general. Basil Liddell Hart attempted to introduce the term "grand tactics," of identical meaning; but it did not gain official acceptance or wide circulation.

3. Not all officers in Fighter Command were satisfied with that; some advocated an operational-level response. Specifically, Squadron Leader Douglas Bader and Group Commander Trafford Leigh-Mallory advocated the concerted engagement of German bomber formations after they had dropped their bombs, by complete groups (which could not assemble in time for pre-bombing interception) instead of prior interception by individual squadrons. The method was designed to exploit a German limitation, the short endurance of the best fighter of the Luftwaffe, the single-engine Bf-109. It was their calculation that results per fighter would be better, for by then most Bf-109s could no longer maneuver freely for lack of fuel, if they were still around to escort the bombers at all. See John Terraine, *The Right of the Line* (1985), pp. 198–205.

4. The Israelis had crossed the Suez Canal to begin their encirclement maneuver. The initial crossing, on the night of October 15, was duly reported but dismissed as a mere raid that would soon be followed by an evacuation; and indeed less than 3,000 men were initially involved, with few tanks and even those sent across on rafts. It was not until the seventeenth that it was appreciated in Cairo that the Israelis were continuing to reinforce their bridgehead; by then, however, a pontoon bridge had been built and a full division had crossed over. The Israelis were sending out armored teams in all directions to attack antiaircraft missile sites (so their presence was reported in a wide arc) but mainly to advance north toward Ismailia, to widen the bridgehead and thereby cut off the forces of the Egyptian Second Army on the Sinai side of the Canal from their rear services on the Egyptian side. In spite of the great quantity of misleading reports it was receiving (generated by Israeli combat teams moving in the soft rear to attack missile sites), by October 18 the Egyptian high command nevertheless interpreted the Israeli intention of two days earlier quite correctly and duly moved to secure the Ismailia sector. But a day earlier, with another Israeli armored division across the canal, the Israelis had decided to call off the northward thrust and were instead advancing in the opposite direction, to cut off the Third Army in the

southern sector around the city of Suez. By the time the Egyptian high command caught up with the change, on October 19, its expectations had been overturned twice, and nothing seemed certain: imagining that Cairo itself was in imminent danger, it sent the available reserves to shield the city, instead of attacking the Israelis converging on the city of Suez. See the documented account in Hanoch Bartov, *Dado* (1981), pp. 482ff.

5. As noted earlier in another context, the Soviet Union had the necessary depth in facing the German blitzkrieg, whereas Poland and France did not. Actually, Stalin's war plan did not even try to exploit the Soviet Union's advantage in sheer size during the 1941 campaign, in which the Germans were stubbornly resisted all the way east as they advanced toward Leningrad and Moscow; by the summer of 1942 the lesson had been learned, and when the Germans advanced again, this time in a southwestern direction toward Stalingrad and the Caucasian oil fields, they were outraced by the retreating Soviet forces, whose strength was thus preserved to rebuild a solid new front.

6. The effect was far more psychological than physical for the Wehrmacht in the blitzkrieg years 1939–1942, because its deep-penetration columns mostly consisted of motorcycles, armored cars, very light tanks, half-tracked carriers, artillery tractors, a great many trucks, and not many battle tanks (one regiment of 100–150 tanks per Panzer division). The Soviet army's columns, by contrast would have contained a solid phalanx of armor, with as many as 322 tanks in first-line tank divisions.

7. A contemporary example is the American M-1 tank, which among other things has an innovative gas turbine engine that offers excellent acceleration at the expense of range. By the time the new tank came into service, the operational doctrine of the U.S. Army had changed considerably, and while tactical mobility—the ability to dash around the battlefield and climb steep grades—remained desirable, it was operational mobility (autonomous range) that had become essential. For this, a plain diesel engine would have been superior. Similarly, the new tank also has excellent protection in a new kind of composite armor, but in accordance with old tactical priorities, much of the armor is distributed in the frontal aspect, at the expense of all-around protection, which the new operational doctrine makes more important.

8. Theater Strategy I

1. During the 1970s and 1980s, a total of 30 Soviet tank and motor-rifle divisions were distributed between East Germany (19 divisions), Czechoslovakia (5), Hungary (4), and Poland (2) including 10,500 tanks; the number of infantry combat carriers was larger. IISS, *Military Balance, 1985–86,* p. 26.

2. It is assumed throughout that East German and other Warsaw Pact forces, along with minor Soviet units simulating complete formations, would have

been employed to present a threat by demonstrations and feints in those segments of the front where no major Soviet offensive thrust was intended. In due course, the deception would be unmasked, but by then the fight should have been over. That, incidentally, would be the safer use of troops of doubtful loyalty. By contrast, the number of antitank guided weapon launchers assigned to NATO's central front upon mobilization was some 2,100, including forces in Norway and Denmark as well (ibid., p. 186).

3. They were exemplified by General Maurice G. Gamelin, chief of the French general staff at the outbreak of World War II. His memoirs, *Servir,* amply demonstrate the man's intellectual powers—and tortuous character. See the comments in Robert J. Young, *In Command of France* (1978), pp. 48–51.

4. Many intercontinental warheads and bombs are in the range of one million tons of TNT equivalence ("megaton"), while most battlefield devices are in the range of one thousand tons of TNT ("kiloton"), or one-fourteenth of the energy yield of the Hiroshima bomb and one-nineteenth that of the Nagasaki bomb. Blast, heat, and immediate radiation effects are commensurate, and except in the case of enhanced-radiation ("neutron" bomb) devices, it is usually the blast effects that set effectiveness limits against ground-force targets.

5. As it happens, the inertia caused by contradictory inhibitions kept in Greek and Turkish service until the late 1980s one of the earliest nuclear weapons, the forty-kilometer-range Honest John rocket first deployed in 1953. That would have been reckless, had the warheads been provided as NATO war plans required. But there was no chance of that in practice. See IISS, *Military Balance, 1985–86,* pp. 85–86.

6. The so-called Massive Retaliation policy that demanded a quick escalation to nuclear war was repudiated by the United States at the outset of the Kennedy Administration but was retained as NATO policy at the insistence of West Germany and other member states until 1967. Only then did the Military Committee of NATO member states finally agree to the new policy of "flexible response" (officially promulgated in 1968, as NATO Document MC 14/3) and promise to provide the additional forces required for a "stalwart" nonnuclear defense. In a large literature, see e.g. Raymond E. Burrel, *Strategic Nuclear Parity and NATO Defense Doctrine* (1978), p. 13.

9. Theater Strategy II

1. Jochen Löser, *Weder rot noch tot* (1982).
2. Franz Uhle-Wettler, *Leichte Infanterie im Atomzeitalter* (1966). A prescription for a spongelike "amorphous" defense is contained in Guy Brossollet, *Essai sur la nonbataille* (1975), a seminal work.
3. Steven L. Canby, "Territorial Defense in Central Europe" (1980), and many other works by Canby.
4. William Scotter, "A Role for the Non-Mechanized Infantry" (1980).

5. The proponents of these schemes did not always remember that decentralized supply arrangements would also have been required. Larger stocks would have been needed to allow their distribution in small depots and caches throughout the zone of combat.

6. Perceptions of automaton-like rigidity may reflect nothing more than the process of dehumanization of the enemy that attends all conflict. Thus during the Second World War the knowledge that the German army's greatest strength was its exceptional flexibility coexisted with images of German officers and men as martinets and robots. In reality, of course, the German army allowed great latitude to its junior officers and noncommissioned officers; in its command and control, hierarchic authority smoothly gave way to operational necessity in a way that not even the American, let alone the British, army could emulate. It does seem, however, that the Soviet army was afflicted by rigidity at the lower levels of command at least. This reflected neither innate cultural limitations nor official doctrine (which supposedly called for initiative at all levels) but rather the de facto balance of institutional incentives: even if successful initiative was duly rewarded, penalties for errors that followed from unauthorized actions were systematically greater than penalties for counterproductive obedience. Combat in Afghanistan predictably resulted in official demands for "more initiative." For a comparative analysis of the institutional framework, see Richard A. Gabriel, *The Antagonists* (1984).

7. Walter Laqueur's *Guerrilla* (1976) remains the most useful compendium. The classic anatomy of revolutionary war is contained in Roger Trinquier's *La guerre moderne* (1961).

8. Laqueur, *Guerrilla*, pp. 202–238. For a detailed assessment of the effectiveness of the French resistance in accomplishing a specific task of exceptional urgency, in the favorable post-Overlord conditions of June 1944, see Max Hastings, *Das Reich* (1981).

9. For a participant's revealing account, see Stefan Korbonski, *Fighting Warsaw* (1968).

10. But an occupier can receive local assistance. The Germans did during the Second World War, even within the Soviet Union. In fact in some places, pro-German militias were sufficiently effective to replace the reprisal policy, as for example in the "Autonomous Administrative District" of Lokot, in the Orel-Kursk region south of Bryansk, which contained some 1.7 million inhabitants and was defended by a purely Russian militia some 10,000 strong during 1942–43. Here the basis of collaboration was political (anticommunism), and the Lokot militia, jointly created by General Rudolf Schmidt of the Second Panzer Army and a Russian engineer (later replaced by the notorious Bronislav Kaminsky), was known as the Russkaya Osvoboditelnaya Narodnaya Armiya (Russian Liberation Popular Army). It was a crucial element of the bargain that the SS was forbidden to operate in

the area, where the Germans agreed to refrain from any reprisals for such guerrilla attacks as still took place. See M. Cooper, *The Phantom War* (1979), pp. 112–113. Such arrangements, though usually less formal, became common in German-occupied areas and were vehemently advocated by many Wehrmacht officers; see H. K. Guenther, "Der Kampf Gegen Die Partisanen" (1968). They were opposed just as vehemently by the SS, who denied the need to arm "subhumans"—until the worsening war situation and manpower shortage induced the SS to reverse its attitude. It still opposed militias, but only because it wanted to recruit all available men for its many ethnic units.

11. Personal observation, Morazan departemento, El Salvador, 1982–83.

10. Theater Strategy III

1. These included Follow-on Forces Attack, strictly nonnuclear, which envisaged attacks across a wide spectrum of ranges to attack advancing Soviet units in depth; AirLand Battle 2000 and AirLand 2000, U.S. Army concepts that emphasized attacks in depth coordinated at corps level; Deep Strike, primarily nuclear but with a nonnuclear variant that stressed the employment of ballistic missiles to deliver submunitions on fixed targets; and Counter Air 90, which prescribed attacks on Soviet airfields.

2. The most economical missiles for the attack of large fixed targets with submunitions (airbases, supply dumps, railway yards), as well as strongly fortified targets (command centers), would be high-trajectory ballistic missiles, identical to the weapons employed for nuclear delivery. Indeed, the most economical of remedies would have been to redeploy to Europe U.S. intercontinental ballistic missiles no longer kept in service for nuclear missions, duly converted for shorter ranges with much larger, nonnuclear payloads. But the peacetime stationing of such weapons in Europe would have wrecked U.S.-Soviet arms-control negotiations. When launched from any location, moreover, their trajectories could easily be misinterpreted as presaging nuclear attacks. Finally, large ballistic missiles, whether conversions or newly produced, could be economical only if stationed in fixed housings, and then they would be vulnerable to varied forms of attack, nonnuclear as well as nuclear, even if fortified. Aerodynamic cruise missiles with large nonnuclear warheads are efficient against small and hard targets, such as bridges and viaducts. Cargo cruise missiles with submunitions would be as effective as ballistic missiles against larger and softer targets such as supply dumps, railway yards, and airbases. One issue still in contention is the cost of one-sortie cruise missiles as opposed to manned aircraft capable of an unknown number of sorties but requiring costly pilot training and elaborate, even more costly, protection when actually used in combat. Another open issue is the vulnerability of cruise missiles to air defenses (including balloon

barrages around high-value targets); while presenting very small radar and visual targets (even smaller in "stealth" models), pilotless aircraft are incapable of evasive maneuvers. See Fred N. Wikner, "Interdicting Fixed Targets with Conventional Weapons" (1983); Richard K. Betts, ed., *Cruise Missiles* (1981), pp. 184–211; Steven L. Canby, "New Conventional Force Technology and the NATO–Warsaw Pact Balance, I" (1985), pp. 7–24; and Donald R. Cotter, "New Conventional Force Technology and the Nato–Warsaw Pact Balance, II" (1985), pp. 25–39.

3. Some 220,200 of the total of 399,600 sorties flown by the U.S. Air Force during the entire Korean war were classified as interdiction strikes—a huge effort, which sometimes contained Chinese offensives but which mostly meant that the Chinese had to employ more porters. Interdiction claimed an even larger proportion of a much greater number of sorties during the Vietnam war, with results that were impressive but not decisive. For the Korean war statistics and the Vietnam estimate, see William D. White, *U.S. Tactical Air Power* (1974), p. 68.

4. As early as the 1960s, before much additional road construction, it was estimated that even if the "flow capacity" of the road and rail nets from the western Soviet Union to West Germany were 90 percent destroyed, the remaining 10 percent would still sustain a full-strength Soviet offensive. Alain C. Enthoven and K. Wayne Smith, *How Much Is Enough?* (1971), p. 222.

5. Cotter, "New Conventional Force Technology, I," pp. 25–38. For a pessimistic view, see Canby, "New Conventional Force Technology, II," pp. 7–24.

6. Clausewitz *On War*, book 7, chap. 18, pp. 555–556.

11. Nonstrategies

1. Alfred Thayer Mahan, *Naval Strategy* (1911), p. 6, as cited by Philip A. Crowl, "Alfred Thayer Mahan," in Peter Paret, ed., *Makers of Modern Strategy* (1986), p. 458. Crowl shows (pp. 456–457) that Mahan derived the concept from Henri Jomini (1779–1869). One great simplificator borrowed from another.

2. The absolute priority accorded to this concept in the post-Mahan submarine era was duly criticized after the First World War. See John H. Maurer, "American Naval Concentration and the German Battle Fleet, 1900–1918" (1983), pp. 169–177.

3. Many institutional writings fall into this category. See, for example, *The Maritime Strategy*, published by the U.S. Naval Institute (1986), containing articles by the secretary of the navy, the chief of naval operations, and the commandant of the Marine Corps. Most scholarly works avoid the misleading usage—thus Herbert Rosinski's *The Development of Naval Thought* (1977) and L. W. Martin's classic *The Sea in Modern Strategy* (1967). Hervé Couteau-Bégarie's important study, *La puissance maritime: Castex et la strate-*

gic navale (1985), includes the offending term, but his content is actually equivalent to Rosinski's (*La pensée strategique navale*). One famous exception is Bernard Brodie's *A Layman's Guide to Naval Strategy* (1942), later republished in revised form as *A Guide to Naval Strategy* (1965), whose contents, however, are largely technical, tactical, and operational.

4. For the prophet of autonomous air power, Giulio Douhet, targeting actually constituted the substance of "aerial strategy"; see Barry D. Watts, *The Foundations of U.S. Air Doctrine* (1984), p. 6. There is an interesting analysis of Douhet's thought in Ferrucci Botti and Virgilio Ilari, *Il pensiero militare italiano* (1985), pp. 89–139.

5. Mahan, *The Influence of Sea Power upon History, 1660–1783*, and *The Influence of Sea Power upon the French Revolution and Empire, 1793–1812*, and many ephemera. For intellectual sources, see Robert Seager, *Alfred Thayer Mahan* (1977), and more recently, Crowl's review, "Alfred Thayer Mahan," pp. 449–462.

6. Mahan was actually quite inconsistent in using the term "sea power," which he claimed as his own original contribution to strategic thought; see Couteau-Bégarie, *La puissance maritime*, p. 45; and Crowl, "Alfred Thayer Mahan," p. 451.

7. Gerald S. Graham, *The Politics of Naval Supremacy* (1965).

8. For the sequence, see Mahan, *The Influence, 1660–1783*, pp. 222–223, as cited in Crowl, "Alfred Thayer Mahan," pp. 451–452.

9. A Second World War bestseller, Alexander P. De Seversky's *Victory through Air Power* (1942), actually a collection of articles, encapsulates the Douhet-Mitchell-Trenchard prediction in some of its chapter titles: "The Twilight of Sea Power," "The Emancipation of Air Power," "Organization for Air Supremacy."

10. For this divergence in brief, see Barry D. Watts, *The Foundations of U.S. Air Doctrine* (1984), pp. 5–10.

11. Mitchell did not share this view: "a Bombardment formation . . . is certain to suffer heavy casualties if subjected to incessant attack by a greatly superior pursuit [fighter] force." See Watts, *Foundations*, p. 7, citing a pre-1923 text.

12. While persuasively refuting the misconception that the Luftwaffe leaders in their chronic disunity actually rejected the thesis and were content to serve as the army's ancillaries, Williamson Murray, *Strategy for Defeat* (1983), pp. 8–9, 19–21, overstates his case: strategic bombing *was* seen as important but was not the highest priority. Murray cites the four-engine He-177 as unambiguous evidence of strategic intent (p. 9), but it received a low production priority; also, its extreme design complications were imposed by the dive-bombing requirement, quite unnecessary for strategic bombing.

13. The postwar U.S. Strategic Bombing Survey reached this conclusion; the re-

sults that bombing did achieve remain a subject of great controversy. See e.g. David MacIsaac, *Strategic Bombing in World War Two* (1976).

14. This point was noted e.g. by Bernard Brodie, *Strategy in the Missile Age* (1959), p. 73; Watts, *Foundations*, p. 39, n. l, cites Brodie's 1952 memorandum entitled "The Heritage of Douhet."

15. Bernard Brodie, *The Absolute Weapon* (1946) p. 76, typically included a reservation that others then overlooked: in publicizing the notion of deterrence, already in the air, he described it as the chief purpose of the military establishment, adding, "It can have almost no other purpose."

16. Positive suasion (compellence) is admittedly more difficult to apply than negative suasion (deterrence)—one of the many elucidations found in Thomas C. Schelling, *The Strategy of Conflict* (1960, 1980), pp. 195–199.

17. See Edward N. Luttwak, "Perceptions of Military Force and U.S. Defense Policy" (1977).

18. These assessments are explored in many configurations by Thomas C. Schelling, *Arms and Influence* (1966).

19. These were the crucial words in the "massive retaliation" speech of Secretary of State John Foster Dulles (Department of State Bulletin, January 25, 1954).

12. The Renaissance of Strategic Air Power

1. USAF F-111Fs hit more than 1,500 armored vehicles with GBU-12 laser-guided 500-pound bombs. U.S. Air Force White Paper, "Air Force performance in Desert Storm," April 1991, p. 4.

2. "Airpower in Desert Storm: Iraq's POWs Speak," Pentagon draft document, undated, p. 3.

3. One armored brigade reported the loss of 62 out of 80 tanks. Of three infantry divisions, one had lost almost half its armored complement, another lost 75 percent, and a third lost all of it. In two transportation companies with 80 trucks only 10 were left. Ibid., p. 7.

4. See Appendix B, Table 1. For the (high) escort-to-striker ratios, see Table 5.

5. "Air Force Performance in Desert Storm," p. 5. The modified "Big Belly" B-52Ds employed in Vietnam (and no longer in service) could still carry 24 bombs externally (500- or 750-pound) like other B-52s, but they could also carry 84 (instead of 27) 500-pound bombs, or 42 (instead of 27) 750-pound bombs internally.

6. The maximum was 5,400 kilograms, according to IISS, *Military Balance 1990–1991*, table 2, p. 220; two Mk.84s at 2,000 pounds (equalling 908 kilograms each) amount to 1,816 kilograms, or 33 percent of 5,400 kilograms.

7. Their loads totaled 2,000 tons; "Air Force Performance in Desert Storm," p. 3.

8. See Table 2, Part II.

9. See Table 2, Part II.

10. "Air Force Performance in Desert Storm," p. 5.

11. See Table 4.

12. See Table 2, Part I.

13. The commonly used "area target" (and "area bombing") connote the bombardment of urban-industrial zones, not practiced in the Gulf war.

14. One notable exception was the bombing of the exceptionally concentrated German forces in the Falaise Gap in July 1944.

15. I.e., when the bombing is for "close air support" (CAS), in direct conjunction with action on the ground. But CAS accounted for only 3,000 of the 50,000 "strike" sorties of the Gulf war. See Table 1.

16. These tales appear to have emanated from British intelligence sources (cf. Graham Greene, *Our Man in Havana*).

17. This was 33.65 percent: 27,735 Mk.20s and 29,116 CBUs were dropped by U.S. forces. See Table 2, Part I.

18. The Mk.20s alone dispersed 6,850,545 bomblets—and that is an antiarmor weapon, not optimized to attack humans.

19. In that case, ground forces are meant to attack while the enemy is still shocked or, defensively, the bombardment is meant to break the momentum of an enemy attack.

20. "Airpower in Desert Storm: Iraq's POWs Speak" p. 3. The initial numbers, however, refer to "ration" strengths, not the (unknown) initial totals actually present.

21. "Airpower in Desert Storm: Iraq's POWs Speak," p. 4.

22. Ibid., p. 4.

23. Ibid., p. 6.

24. "Airpower in Desert Storm: Iraq's POWs Speak," p. 4.

25. The latest navigation-attack systems allow level bombing and shallow dive median errors of as little as 15 feet in *optimum* circumstances, which include release altitudes of 2,000–3,000 feet—an extraordinarily dangerous regime, within which almost all classes of antiaircraft weapons are effective.

26. When the two diverge, the military goal is inherently subordinate. In the 1991 Gulf war, for example, it is quite clear in retrospect that Saddam Hussein's (dominant) political goal was to conserve enough strength to survive in the aftermath, while the military goal of holding Kuwait was secondary. In the context of his strategy, the passivity of Saddam Hussein's forces was therefore perfectly rational.

27. The campaign, called Instant Thunder, is outlined in Appendix C.

28. Noted in "Air Force Performance in Desert Storm," p. 14.

29. See Table 5.

30. See Table 2.

13. The Scope of Grand Strategy

1. The quality of empires is in their tenacity, the fear of empires is their appointed end. For one view of Soviet apprehensions of decline, see Edward N. Luttwak, *The Grand Strategy of the Soviet Union* (1983).

14. Armed Suasion

1. One more reason for the failure to anticipate the attack on the fleet was that U.S. Navy estimates of its power was rather pessimistic: "I thought it would be utterly stupid for the Japanese to attack the United States at Pearl Harbor. We could not have materially affected their control of the waters they wanted to control whether or not the battleships were sunk at Pearl Harbor." Testimony of Captain Vincent R. Murphy before Congress, *Pearl Harbor Hearings*, part 26, p. 207, as cited in Ronald H. Spector, *Eagle against the Sun* (1985), p. 3.

2. Its counterpart, "first strike," is a contraction of "would-be disarming first strike" (aimed at enemy nuclear forces), as opposed to the "first use" of nuclear weapons, not against nuclear forces but in reaction to a nonnuclear attack that cannot be resisted otherwise. These distinctions were first elucidated in the celebrated RAND study by Wohlstetter, Hoffman, Lutz, and Rowen, *Selection and Use of Strategic Air Bases* (1954), and first publicized in Albert Wohlstetter, "The Delicate Balance of Terror," *Foreign Affairs* (1959). Not coincidentally, Roberta Wohlstetter, Albert's wife, had conducted a careful analysis of the Pearl Harbor episode, later published as *Pearl Harbor* (1962).

3. There was an attempt to assassinate President Chun Doo Hwan of South Korea and his most important civil and military officials in Rangoon on October 9, 1983, in which three Korean ministers and fifteen other officials were killed and more wounded.

4. For example, in American "strategic" force planning, second-strike-capability requirements were calculated on the assumption of an all-out Soviet first strike, launched against American forces at a normal state of alert and therefore only partially available, with many missile submarines in port and few bombers on runway alert. Similarly, all Soviet missiles were assumed to be operational, whereas U.S. forces were assumed to be further diminished, after attack losses, by predicted malfunctions. For ballistic missiles, cumulative "degradation factors" for the launch, boost, flight, warhead separation, terminal trajectory, and detonation phases could exceed 40 percent. Thus the same inventory of weapons that seemed grossly excessive to others was viewed as barely adequate in the skewed net assessments of prudent force planners, who calculated very conservatively both postattack survival and

subsequent malfunctions. The oft-cited overkill calculation simply ignored the cumulative effects of prior attack, availability limits, and malfunctions, and further assumed that only cities were to be attacked, thus comparing full weapon inventories with the much smaller number of targeted cities.

5. At the height of the Cold War in mid-1985, the IISS estimated 10,174 warheads for the United States and 9,987 for the Soviet Union. *Military Balance, 1985–86*, p. 180.

6. The technically inclined reader will recognize the purely technical error: even if U.S. intercontinental delivery platforms had been reduced to a dozen missile submarines, one hundred bombers, and as many land-based missiles (but presumably mobile), a counterforce offensive against them could still have employed as many Soviet warheads as desired, for area-wide "barrage" attacks against mobile-missile deployment zones, the air space around airfields (to catch bombers after takeoff), and even the open ocean around suspected missile-submarine locations.

15. Harmony and Disharmony in War

1. A. Hillgruber, *Hitlers Strategie* (1965), pp. 190–192.

2. The British Intelligence estimate of February 17, 1941, concluded that because of the preparations that would be needed for desert warfare, "a considerable time must elapse before any serious counter-offensive can be launched from Tripoli"; see F. H. Hinsley et al., *British Intelligence in the Second World War* (1979), p. 389. This opinion was shared by the German Army High Command.

3. Martin van Creveld, *Supplying War* (1977), p. 139.

4. For the OKH view as recorded by Chief of Staff Franz Halder, see Larry H. Addington, *The Blitzkrieg Era and the German General Staff* (1971), pp. 162–163.

5. Van Creveld, *Supplying War*, pp. 184–185.

6. What follows is based on Ronald Lewin, *Life and Death of the Afrika Korps* (1967), and David Irving, *The Trail of the Fox* (1977), pp. 67ff. (highly colored but accurate).

7. Addington, *Blitzkrieg Era*, p. 165.

8. Hinsley, *British Intelligence*, pp. 389–393.

9. Rommel's willful disorganization of his own formations did not extend down to the tactical level, over which he had little influence: while the British fought by separate infantry, artillery, and tank units, the Germans fought by mixed task forces of all three. By elegant teamwork, when the task forces were attacked by British tanks, they engaged them with anti-tank guns well shielded in the terrain. The German tanks themselves were reserved for flanking moves and mainly for attacks against "soft" motor

columns and infantry, in which their technical superiority would be decisive. The classic description is in F. W. von Mellenthin, *Panzer Battles* (1971), pp. 71ff.

10. Otherwise he would have recognized that the forces that could be supplied across the fifteen hundred miles from Tripoli to the Suez Canal were too small to defeat the British, while forces large enough for the task could not be supplied. See van Creveld, *Supplying War,* pp. 181–201.

11. Many historians have criticized Hitler's refusal to send reinforcements to Rommel in the summer of 1942, pointing out that large German forces were sent *after* Rommel's defeat at El Alamein. But then the German purpose was no longer to conquer Egypt but rather to keep Italy as an ally in the war, by preventing the fall of Tunisia, the last North African territory in Axis hands opposite Sicily. Unlike a conquest of Egypt, this was a goal of importance at the level of grand strategy.

12. The only documents ever published on the subject are contained in Hanoch Bartov, *Dado* (1981); for the divisional counts, see the October 8 graphics.

13. Most of the strongholds of the so-called Bar-Lev line were unmanned. On October 6, 1973, there were some 450 soldiers scattered in the 14 manned strongholds from one end of the Suez Canal to the other, a density of some 4 soldiers per kilometer. The Israeli defense plan (called Dovecot) relied instead on the 290 tanks and 14 artillery batteries of the Sinai standing division. Bartov, *Dado,* October 6 graphics.

14. See Barton Whaley, *Codeword Barbarossa* (1973).

15. See e.g. Bartov, *Dado,* pp. 188–217.

16. For a detailed account, see Avraham Adan, *On the Banks of the Suez* (1980), pp. 91–164. See also the excellent analysis in Martin van Creveld, *Command in War* (1985), pp. 218–231.

WORKS CITED

Adan, Avraham. *On the Banks of the Suez.* Novato, Calif.: Presidio Press, 1980.

Addington, Larry H. *The Blitzkrieg Era and the German General Staff, 1865–1941.* New Brunswick: Rutgers University Press, 1971.

Bartov, Hanoch. *Dado, 48 Years and 20 Days.* Tel Aviv: Ma'ariv Book Guild, 1981.

Beaufre, André [General]. *Introduction à la stratégie* (Introduction to strategy). Paris: Librairie Armand Colin, 1963.

Betts, Richard K., ed. *Cruise Missiles: Technology, Strategy, Politics.* Washington: Brookings Institution, 1981.

Bond, Brian. *Liddell Hart: A Study of His Military Thought.* London: Cassell, 1977.

Botti, Ferrucci, and Virgilio Ilari. *Il pensiero militare italiano dal primo al secondo dopoguerra, 1919–1949* (Italian military thought from the aftermath of the First World War to the aftermath of the Second). Rome: Stato Maggiore dell'Esercito, Ufficio Storico, 1985.

Brodie, Bernard, ed. *The Absolute Weapon.* New York: Harcourt Brace, 1946.

——— *Strategy in the Missile Age.* Princeton: Princeton University Press, 1959.

——— *A Guide to Naval Strategy.* New York: Praeger, 1965.

Brossollet, Guy. *Essai sur la nonbataille* (Essay on the nonbattle). Paris: Belin, 1975.

Burrel, Raymond E. *Strategic Nuclear Parity and NATO Defense Doctrine.* Washington: National Defense University, 1978.

Canby, Steven L. "Territorial Defense in Central Europe." *Armed Forces and Society,* 7 (Fall 1980).

——— "New Conventional Force Technology and the NATO–Warsaw Pact Balance, I." *New Technology and Western Security Policy.* IISS Annual Conference Papers, Adelphi Papers 198. London: IISS, 1985.

Churchill, Winston S. *The Second World War: Triumph and Tragedy.* Boston: Houghton Mifflin, 1953.

Clausewitz, Carl von. *On War* (1833, 3 vols.). Ed. and trans. Michael Howard and Peter Paret. Princeton: Princeton University Press, 1976.

Cooper, M. *The Phantom War.* London: Macdonald and Jane's, 1979.

Cotter, Donald R. "New Conventional Force Technology and the NATO–Warsaw Pact Balance, II." *New Technology and Western Security Policy.* IISS Annual Conference Papers, Adelphi Papers 198. London: IISS, 1985.

Couteau-Bégarie, Hervé. *La puissance maritime: Castex et la stratégie navale* (Naval power: Castex and naval strategy). Paris: Fayard, 1985.

Craven, Wesley F., and James L. Cate. *The Army Air Forces in World War II.* 6 vols. Chicago: University of Chicago Press, 1948–1955.

Crowl, Philip A. "Alfred Thayer Mahan: The Naval Historian." In Peter Paret et al., eds., *Makers of Modern Strategy: From Machiavelli to the Nuclear Age.* Princeton: Princeton University Press, 1986.

De Seversky, Alexander P. [Major]. *Victory through Air Power.* New York: Simon and Schuster, 1942.

Douhet, Giulio. *Il dominio dell'aria.* Rome, 1921. English translation: *The Command of the Air,* trans. Dino Ferrari. New York: Coward McCann, 1942.

Enthoven, Alain C., and K. Wayne Smith. *How Much Is Enough? Shaping the Defense Program, 1961–1969.* New York: Harper and Row, 1971.

Erickson, John. *The Road to Stalingrad.* London: Weidenfeld and Nicholson, 1975.

Fitzsimons, Bernard, ed. *Encyclopedia of Twentieth Century Weapons and Warfare.* New York: Columbia House, 1971–1977.

Gabriel, Richard A. *The Antagonists: A Comparative Combat Assessment of the Soviet and American Soldier.* Westport, Conn.: Greenwood, 1984.

Garthoff, Raymond L. *Soviet Military Doctrine.* Glencoe: Illinois University Press, 1953.

Gilbert, Martin. *Finest Hour: Winston S. Churchill, 1939–1941.* London: Heinemann, 1983.

Graham, Gerald S. *The Politics of Naval Supremacy: Studies in British Maritime Ascendancy.* Cambridge, Eng.: Cambridge University Press, 1965.

Guenther, H. K. "Der Kampf gegen die Partisanen" (The war against the partisans). *Wehrwissenschaftliche Rundschau,* 1968.

Harris, Arthur. *Bomber Offensive.* London: Collins, 1947.

Hastings, Max. *Das Reich: The March of the Second SS Panzer Division through France.* New York: Holt, Rinehart, and Winston, 1981.

——— *Bomber Command.* London: Pan Books, 1981.

Hillgruber, A. *Hitlers Strategie.* Frankfurt am Main: Wehrwesen, Bernard, und Graefe, 1965.

Hinsley, F. H., et al. *British Intelligence in the Second World War: Its Influence on Strategy and Operations.* New York: Cambridge University Press, 1979 (vol. 1), 1984 (vol. 3, pt. 1).

Horelick, A. L., and M. Rush. *Strategic Power and Soviet Foreign Policy.* Chicago: University of Chicago Press, 1966.

Horne, Alistair. *The Price of Glory, Verdun 1916.* London: Penguin, 1961.

Howard, Michael. *The Franco-Prussian War.* London: Rupert Hart-Davis, 1968.

Ikle, Fred C. *Every War Must End.* New York: Columbia University Press, 1971.

Ilari, Virgilio. "Politica e strategia globale" (Global politics and strategy). In Carlo Jean, ed., *Il pensiero strategico.* Milan: Franco Angeli, 1985.

International Institute of Strategic Studies (IISS). *The Military Balance*. London: IISS, 1985 (for volume 1985–86), 1986 (1986–87), and 1990 (1990–91).

Irving, David. *The Trail of the Fox*. New York: Dutton, 1977.

Isby, David C. "Air Assault and Airmobile Brigades of the Soviet Army." *Amphibious Warfare Review*, 3 (August 1985).

Jean, Carlo, ed. *Il pensiero strategico* (Strategic thought). Milan: Franco Angeli, 1985.

Joint Chiefs of Staff. *See* United States.

Jungk, Robert. *Brighter Than a Thousand Suns: A Personal History of the Atomic Scientists*. London: Penguin Books, 1964.

King, James E., Jr., ed. *Lexicon of Military Terms Relevant to National Security Affairs on Arms and Arms Control*. Washington: Institute for Defense Analyses, 1960.

Korbonski, Stefan. *Fighting Warsaw*. N.p.: Minerva Press, 1968.

Laqueur, Walter. *Guerrilla: A Historical and Critical Study*. Boston: Little, Brown, 1976.

Lewin, Ronald. *Life and Death of the Afrika Korps*. London: Corgi Books, 1967.

Löser, Jochen. *Weder rot noch tot: Überleben ohne Atomkrieg, eine sicherheitspolitische Alternative* (Neither red nor dead: Survival without nuclear war, an alternative security policy). *Geschichte und Staat*, vol. 257–258. Munich: Olzog, 1982.

Low, A. M. *Musket to Machine-Gun*. London: Hutchinsons, 1942.

Luttwak, Edward N. *The Grand Strategy of the Roman Empire: From the First Century* A.D. *to the Third*. Baltimore: Johns Hopkins University Press, 1976.

——— "Perceptions of Military Force and US Defence Policy." *Survival* (London, IISS), 19 (January–February 1977). Reprinted in Edward N. Luttwak, *Strategy and Politics: Collected Essays*. New Brunswick: Transaction Books, 1980.

——— *The Grand Strategy of the Soviet Union*. New York: St. Martin's Press, 1983.

——— "The Operational Level of War." *International Security*, 5 (Winter 1980–81). Reprinted in Edward N. Luttwak, *Strategy and History: Collected Essays*, 2. New Brunswick: Transaction Books, 1985.

Luttwak, Edward N., and Dan Horowitz. *The Israeli Army*. New York: Harper and Row, 1975; Cambridge: Abt Books, 1983.

MacIsaac, David. *Strategic Bombing in World War Two: The Story of the United States Bombing Survey*. New York: Garland, 1976.

Mahan, Alfred Thayer. *The Influence of Sea Power upon the French Revolution and Empire, 1793–1812*. Boston: Little, Brown, 1905–1912.

——— *The Influence of Sea Power upon History, 1660–1783*. Boston: Little, Brown, 1911.

——— *Naval Strategy: Compared and Contrasted with the Principles and Practice of Military Operations on Land*. Boston: Little, Brown, 1911.

Manstein, Erich von. *Lost Victories*. Chicago: Regnery, 1958.

Martin, L. W. *The Sea in Modern Strategy*. Studies in International Security, 11. New York: Praeger, 1967.

Masson, Philippe. *Histoire de la marine* (History of the [French] navy). 2 vols. Paris: Lavauzelle, 1982, 1983.

Maurer, John H. "American Naval Concentration and the German Battle Fleet, 1900–1918." *Journal of Strategic Studies,* 6 (June 1983).

McElwee, William. *The Art of War: Waterloo to Mons.* London: Weidenfeld and Nicholson, 1974.

Mellenthin, F. W. von. *Panzer Battles: A Study in the Employment of Armor in the Second World War.* New York: Ballantine Books, 1971.

Middlebrook, Martin. *The Battle of Hamburg: Allied Bomber Forces against a German City in 1943.* New York: Scribner's, 1981.

Mitchell, William. *Winged Defense: The Development and Possibilities of Modern Air Power—Economic and Military.* New York: G. P. Putnam's, 1925.

Mueller-Hillebrand, Burkhart. *Das Heer, 1933–1945.* 3 vols. Frankfurt am Main: Mittler, 1956–1969.

Murray, Williamson. *Strategy for Defeat: The Luftwaffe, 1933–1945.* Maxwell, Ala.: Air University Press, 1983.

Osgood, Robert E., and Robert W. Tucker. *Force, Order, and Justice.* Baltimore: Johns Hopkins University Press, 1967.

Paret, Peter, ed., with Gordon A. Craig and Felix Gilbert. *Makers of Modern Strategy: From Machiavelli to the Nuclear Age.* Princeton: Princeton University Press, 1986.

Polmar, Norman. "Soviet Naval Infantry." *Amphibious Warfare Review,* 3 (August 1985).

Price, Alfred. *Instruments of Darkness: The History of Electronic Warfare.* New York: Scribner's, 1977.

Rietzler, R. S. "Erfahrungen aus Kleinkrieg und Jagdkampf" (Experiences of guerrilla and light-infantry combat style). *Truppendiest,* 2 (1979).

Rosinski, Herbert. *The Development of Naval Thought.* Ed. B. Mitchell Simpson III. Newport, R.I.: Naval War College Press, 1977.

Sansom, George. *A History of Japan, 1334–1615.* Stanford: Stanford University Press, 1961.

Schelling, Thomas C. *The Strategy of Conflict.* Cambridge: Harvard University Press, 1960, 1980.

——— *Arms and Influence.* New Haven: Yale University Press, 1966.

Schiff, Zeev, and Ehud Yaari. *Israel's Lebanon War.* New York: Simon and Schuster, 1984.

Scott, Harriet Fast, ed. *Soviet Military Strategy.* Written by V. D. Sokolovsky, Marshal of the Soviet Union. 3d ed. New York: Crane Russak, 1975.

Scotter, William [General]. "A Role for the Non-Mechanized Infantry." *RUSI Journal,* 125 (December 1980), 59–62.

Seager, Robert, II. *Alfred Thayer Mahan: The Man and His Letters.* Annapolis: U.S. Naval Institute, 1977.

Seaton, Albert. *The Battle for Moscow.* New York: Jove, 1983.

Sergent, Pierre. *Je ne regrette rien*. Paris: Fayard, 1972.

Sokolovsky. *See* Scott.

Spector, Ronald H. *Eagle against the Sun*. New York: Vintage Books, 1985.

Speer, Albert. *Inside the Third Reich*. New York: Macmillan, 1970.

Terraine, John. *The Right of the Line: The Royal Air Force in the European War, 1939–1945*. London: Hodder and Stoughton, 1985.

Trinquier, Roger [Colonel]. *La guerre moderne* (Modern war). Paris: La Table Ronde, 1961.

Turnbull, S. R. *The Samurai: A Military History*. New York: Macmillan, 1977.

Uhle-Wettler, Franz. *Leichte Infanterie im Atomzeitalter* (Light infantry in the atomic age). Munich: J. F. Lehmann, Bernard und Graefe, 1966.

United States Air Force (USAF). "Air Force Performance in Desert Storm." White Paper. Washington, April 1991.

United States Department of Defense. *Report of the Secretary of Defense to the Congress on the FY 1987 Budget (February 5, 1986)*. Washington, 1986.

United States Joint Chiefs of Staff. *Dictionary of United States Military Terms for Joint Usage*. Washington, 1964.

United States Naval Institute, James Watkins, et al. *The Maritime Strategy*. Annapolis, January 1986.

Van Creveld, Martin. *Supplying War: Logistics from Wallenstein to Patton*. Cambridge, Eng.: Cambridge University Press, 1977.

——— *Command in War*. Cambridge: Harvard University Press, 1985.

Watts, Barry D. *The Foundations of U.S. Air Doctrine: The Problem of Friction in War*. Maxwell, Ala: Air University Press, 1984.

Webster, Charles, and Noble Frankland. *The Strategic Air Offensive against Germany, 1939–1945*. 4 vols. London: HMSO, 1961.

Whaley, Barton. *Codeword Barbarossa*. Cambridge: MIT Press, 1973.

White, William D. *U.S. Tactical Air Power: Missions, Forces, and Costs*. Washington: Brookings Institution, 1974.

Wikner, Fred N. "Interdicting Fixed Targets with Conventional Weapons." *Armed Forces Journal*, March 1983.

Wohlstetter, A. J., F. S. Hoffman, R. J. Lutz, and H. S. Rowen. *Selection and Use of Strategic Air Bases*. RAND R-266, April 1, 1954. Santa Monica: RAND Corporation, 1954.

Wohlstetter, Albert. "The Delicate Balance of Terror." *Foreign Affairs*, January 1959.

Wohlstetter, Roberta. *Pearl Harbor: Warning and Decision*. Stanford: Stanford University Press, 1962.

Young, Robert J. *In Command of France: French Foreign Policy and Military Planning, 1933–1940*. Cambridge: Harvard University Press, 1978.

Ziemke, Earl F. *Stalingrad to Berlin: The German Defeat in the East*. Army Historical Series. Washington: Office of the Chief of Military History of the U.S. Army, 1968.

INDEX

DATE DUE

DEMCO 38-296

Edward N. Luttwak

STRATEGY

The Logic of War and Peace

REVISED
AND
ENLARGED
EDITION

The Belknap Press of Harvard University Press
Cambridge, Massachusetts
London, England
2001

Library of Congress Cataloging-in-Publication Data

Luttwak, Edward.
Strategy : the logic of war and peace / Edward N. Luttwak.—Rev. and enl. ed.
p. cm.
Includes bibliographical references and index.
ISBN 0-674-00508-2 (cloth : alk. paper)—ISBN 0-674-00703-4 (paper : alk. paper)
1. Strategy. 2. Paradox.   I. Title.

U162.L874 2002
355.4—dc21   2001037407